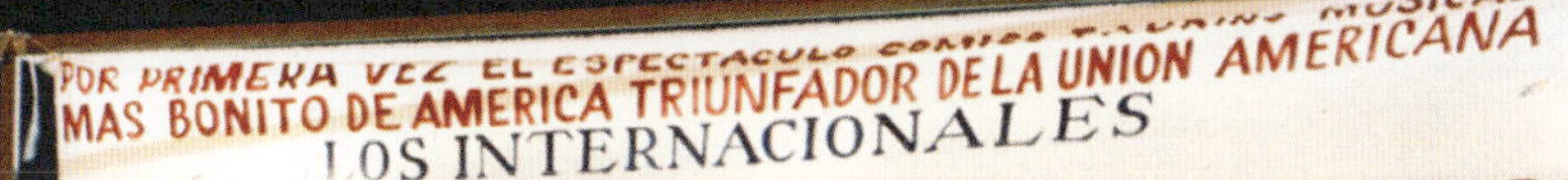
POR PRIMERA VEZ EL ESPECTACULO COMICO TAURINO MUSICAL
MAS BONITO DE AMERICA TRIUNFADOR DE LA UNION AMERICANA
LOS INTERNACIONALES

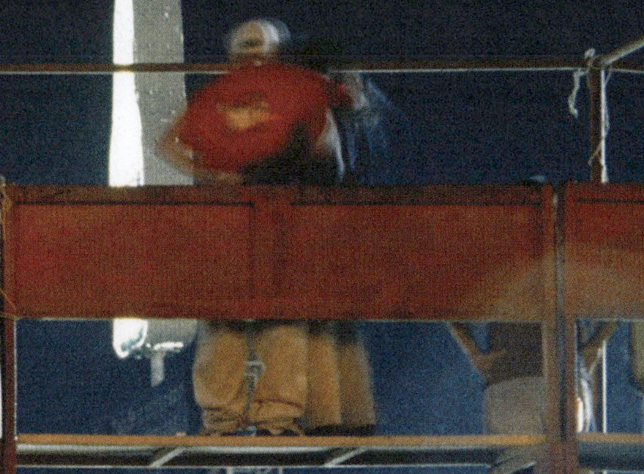

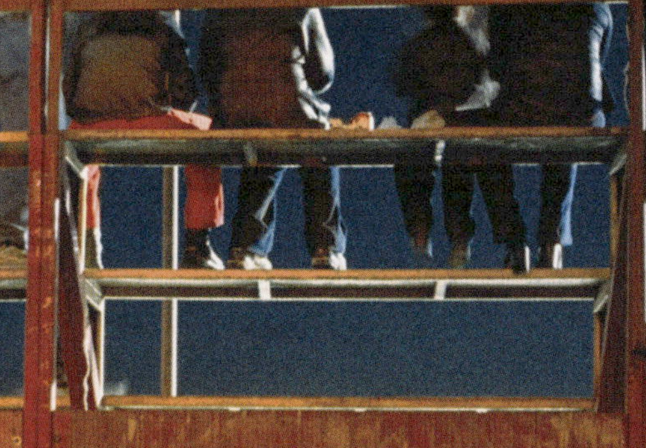
ENANITOS TOREROS

TECATE TE
INVITAN
DOM. 24 FEB.
PLAZA DE TOROS
NUEVO LIENZO CHARRO
CABO SAN LUCAS
LA SAN LUQUENA
a Las
3:30

ENANITOS TOREROS

PHOTOGRAPHS AND INTERVIEWS BY **LIVIA CORONA**

pH powerHouse Books BROOKLYN, NY

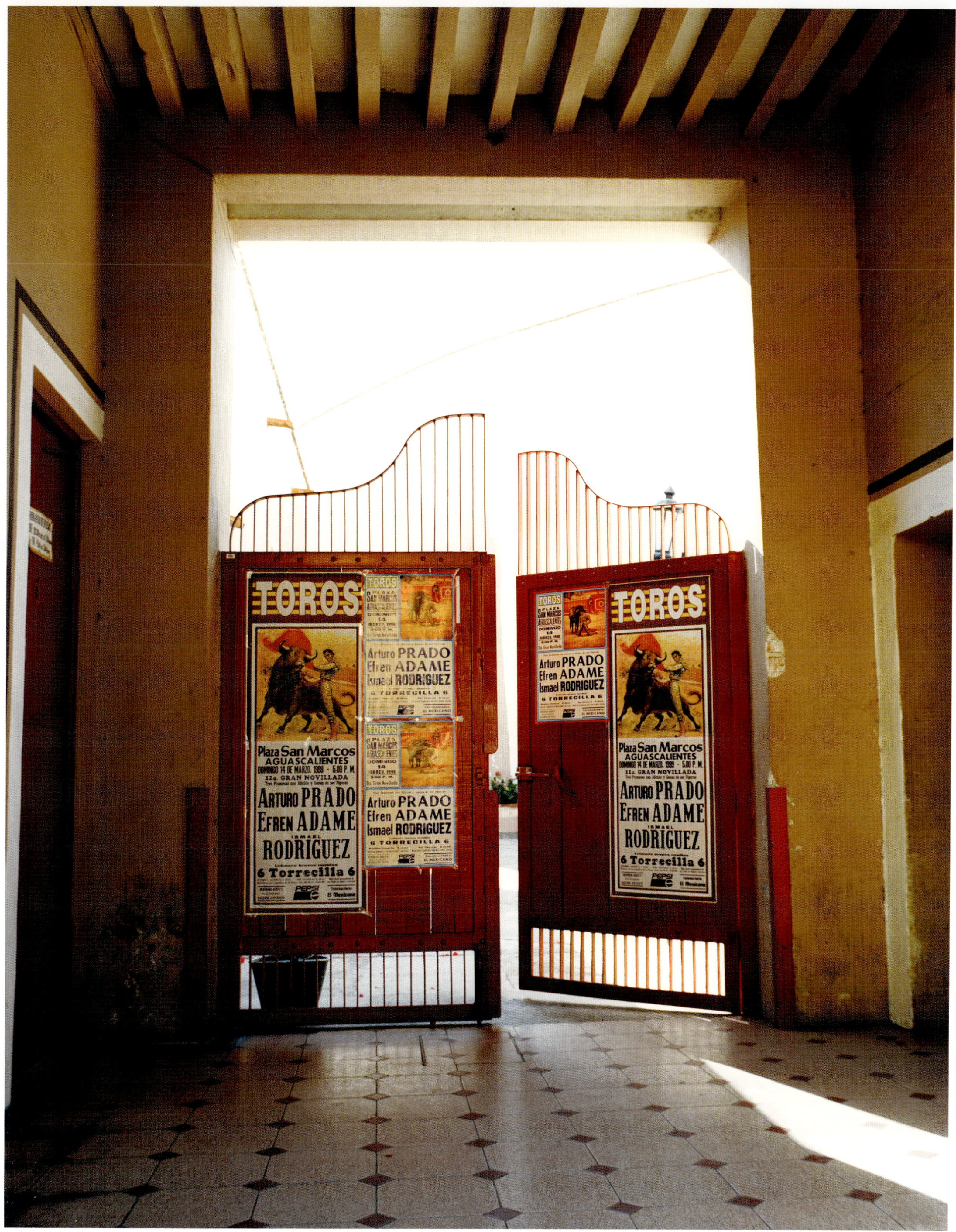

TOROS
Plaza San Marcos
AGUASCALIENTES
DOMINGO 14 DE MARZO, 1999 - 5:00 P. M.
11a. GRAN NOVILLADA
Arturo PRADO
Efren ADAME
Ismael RODRIGUEZ
6 Torrecilla 6
PEPSI
El Mexicano

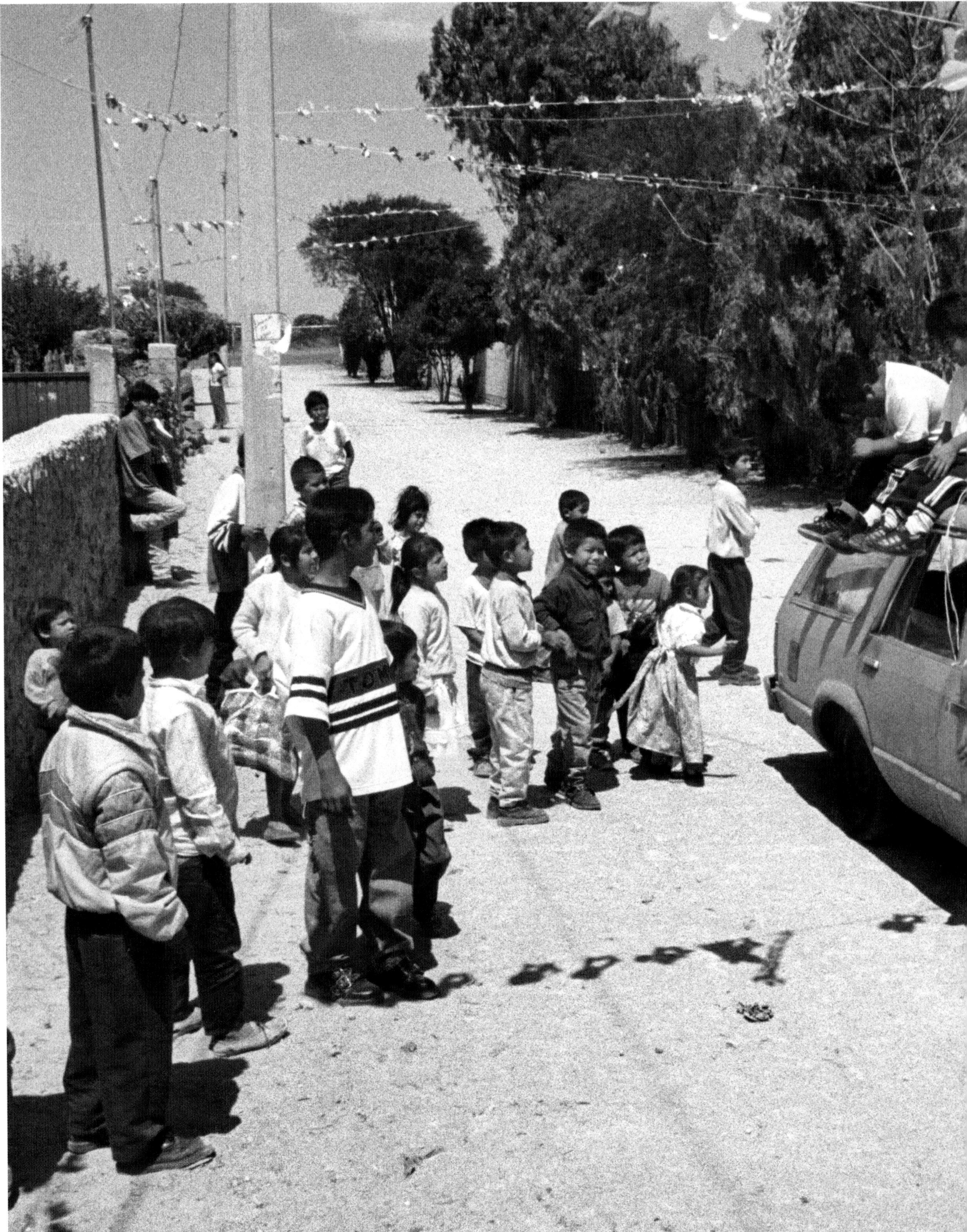

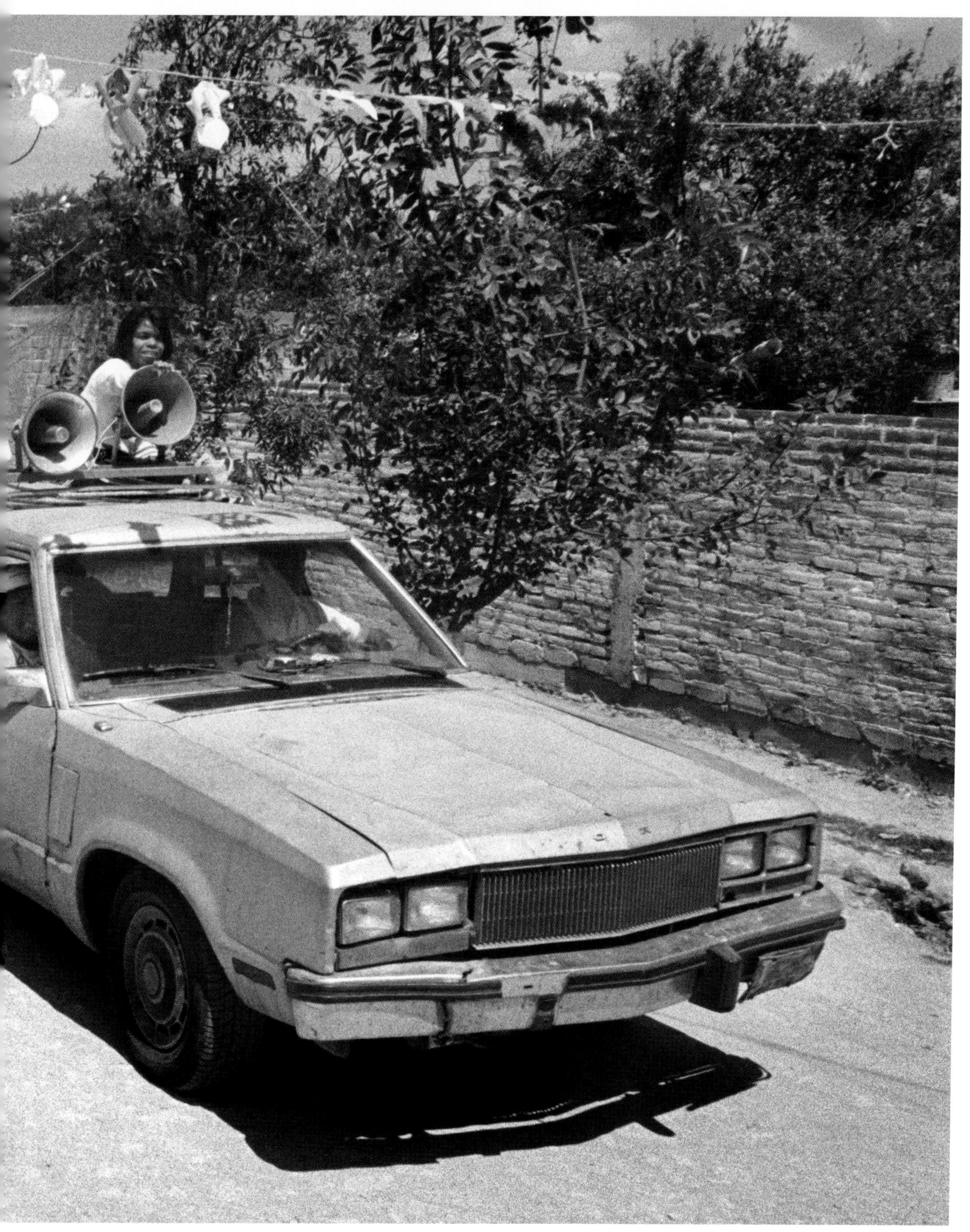

ENANITOS TOREROS

During the summer of 1998, I was on a photo shoot in Guanajuato, Mexico, and a poster taped to a storefront window caught my attention: "*Directo de Taurilandia——Los Enanitos Toreros* [Direct from the Land of Bulls——The Dwarf Bullfighters]." Like most people, I did not know anything about dwarfism. The issue had rarely come up in my life, and when it did, it was usually presented in film and radio shows, with the purpose of comic effect. The poster I saw displayed a different perspective. In it, there was a man (a dwarf) in control of himself, standing his ground against a fearsome animal.

The show was scheduled for that evening at the bullring located next to the place where I was staying, and I went to see it. Several performers, all dwarfs, appeared in front of a small audience, while their average-height promoter introduced their sketches over a loudspeaker in a tone less formal than the poster had implied. When the show ended one of the performers saw me leaving with my camera in hand and asked me if I would photograph her. She introduced herself as Isabel Cortez——she was from Mexico City, and at the time she needed a publicity headshot. Her husband, Gustavo, asked for the same, and so did a few other people employed by the same promoter.

While I was photographing her backstage, Isabel invited me to join her *cuadrilla* [team of bullfighters] for its upcoming shows in the state of Queretaro. We traveled in a small station wagon driven by their promoter, who had once been a famous bullfighter and now made his living promoting his Enanitos Toreros show. While traveling, Isabel, Gustavo, and I became friends. Through this and some coincidences that followed, I got to know and befriend many other people employed as Enanitos Toreros in the eight or more cuadrillas that currently perform throughout Mexico and parts of the United States.

When Isabel first invited me, I accepted, as I related the opportunity to the familiar story of "photographer traveling with band." But in time it became clear to me that the Enanitos Toreros performances were not the usual exchange between audience and entertainer. I realized that the shows are built on centuries of cultural construction about what and who a dwarf is.

As we spent more time together, I realized that although some performers have a genuine interest in the performing arts, the majority participate in the Enanitos Toreros because of a lack of viable employment options. Even so, many described to me the satisfaction they take in making dwarfs more visible and in defying stereotypes about their ability and skill through these shows.

In the absence of support organizations in Mexico created by and for little people, the Enanitos Toreros shows have, as an accidental side-effect, served as an itinerant meeting ground for individuals and families of children with dwarfism. Many people told me that these shows were their first-ever opportunity to engage with others who share their physical characteristics.

This book, with photographs and interviews made over the course of almost a decade, documents some of the experiences, relationships, and family ties that have formed throughout the years. By presenting these images and conversations, made in their homes and at their workplaces, on their tours, and in some cases at their specific request, I hope to share a perspective on the relativity of scale and physical appearance.

Livia Corona

Durante el verano de 1998, estaba tomando fotos en Guanajuato, México, cuando un póster pegado en la ventana de una tienda llamó mi atención: "Directo de Taurilandia— Los Enanitos Toreros". Como la mayoría de la gente, yo no sabía nada sobre el enanismo. El tema casi nunca había surgido en mi vida, y si acaso se aparecía, usualmente era presentado en películas o programas de radio con el propósito de lograr un efecto cómico. Aquel póster prometía un punto de vista diferente. En este había un hombre (un hombre enano) seguro de sí mismo, parado firmemente ante un animal imponente.

El evento estaba programado para esa tarde en una plaza de toros que estaba cerca del lugar en donde me hospedaba, así es que fui a verlo. Varios intérpretes, enanos todos, actuaban frente a una pequeña audiencia. Mientras su promotor, un hombre de estatura normal, narraba cada número a través de un altavoz en un tono mucho menos formal de lo que el póster había sugerido. Cuando el evento terminó, una de las intérpretes me vio salir con mi cámara en la mano y me preguntó que si podía tomarle una foto. Se llamaba Isabel Cortés, era de la Ciudad de México y aquel día necesitaba que alguien le tomara un headshot. Su esposo Gustavo y otros intérpretes que trabajaban para el mismo promotor, me pidieron lo mismo.

Mientras tomaba las fotos Isabel me invitó a acompañar a su cuadrilla en sus próximas presentaciones en el estado de Querétaro. Viajamos en una pequeña camioneta que manejaba su promotor, quien había sido un matador celebre y ahora se ganaba la vida promoviendo su show de Enanitos Toreros. Durante el viaje, Isabel, Gustavo y yo nos hicimos amigos. A través de esto y de algunas coincidencias que sucedieron, llegué a conocer y hacer amistad con muchas otras personas que trabajan como Enanitos Toreros en las ocho o más cuadrillas, que actualmente se presentan en México y parte de Estados Unidos.

Cuando Isabel me invitó a acompañarlos en su gira acepté, al relacionar la idea de esta experiencia con el contexto ya familiar de "fotógrafo viajando con la banda." Pero pronto me quedó claro que sus representaciones no eran el típico intercambio entre público y artista. Me di cuenta de que estos espectáculos se fundamentan en siglos de construcción cultural sobre qué significa ser enano.

Platicando con varios de los artistas que forman parte de estos espectáculos descubrí que aunque algunos tienen interés genuino por actuar, la mayoría participa en los enanitos toreros debido a la escasez de trabajo digno. Aun así, los intérpretes describen la satisfacción que conlleva presentarse como gente pequeña, al tiempo que desafían los estereotipos sobre sus habilidades y destrezas, por medio de estos espectáculos.

Debido a la falta de organizaciones de apoyo en México creadas por y para gente pequeña, los espectáculos de los Enanitos Toreros han funcionado, de manera accidental, como un punto de encuentro itinerante para individuos y familias con niños con enanismo. Mucha gente me dijo que estos espectáculos fueron su primera oportunidad para entablar relaciones con otras personas que comparten sus características físicas.

Este libro con fotografías y entrevistas realizadas a través de casi una década, documenta algunas de las experiencias, relaciones y lazos familiares que se han formado a través de los años. Al presentar estas imágenes y conversaciones hechas en sus hogares, en sus lugares de trabajo, en sus giras y en algunos casos bajo su propia indicación, espero ofrecer una perspectiva sobre la relatividad del tamaño y la apariencia física.

Livia Corona

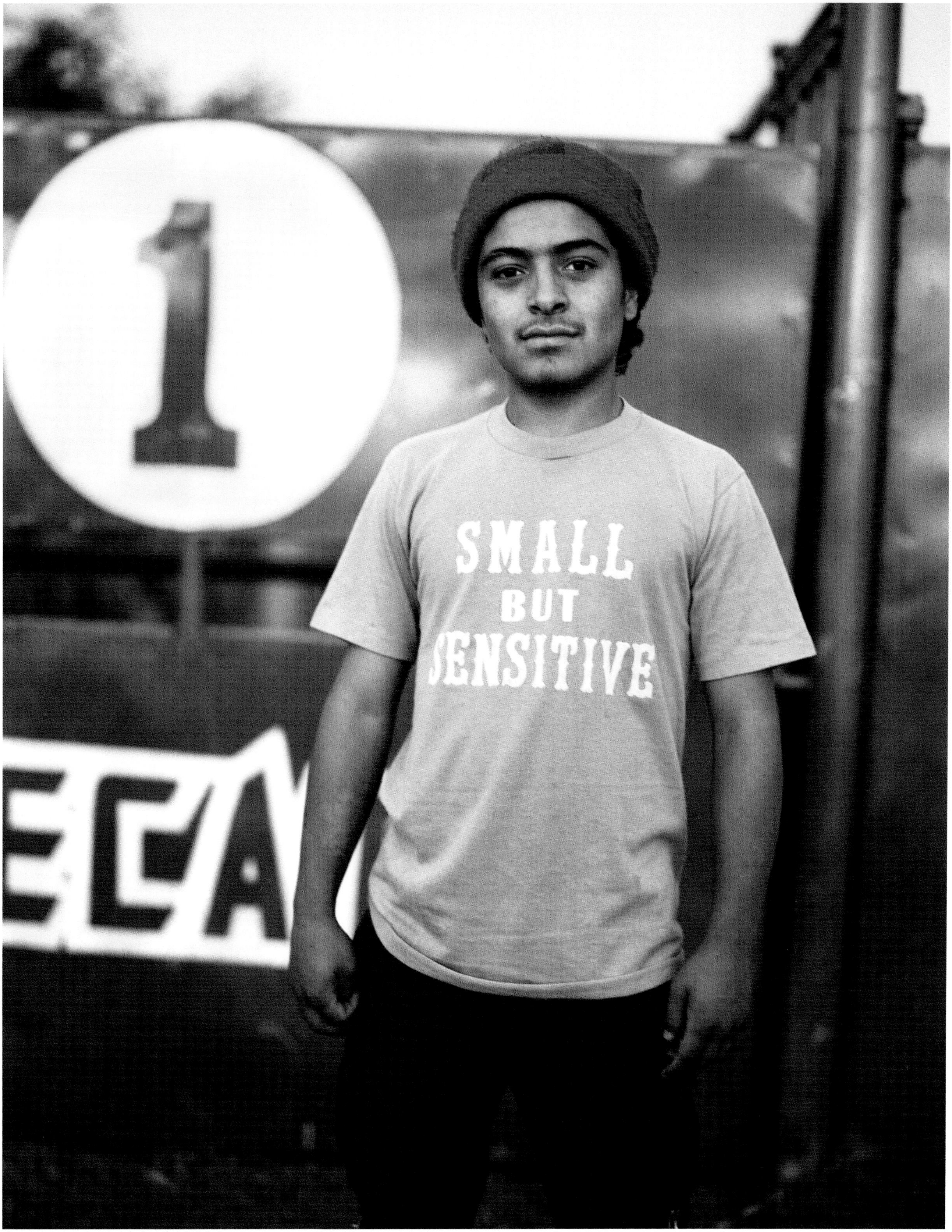

1
SMALL
BUT
SENSITIVE
ECA

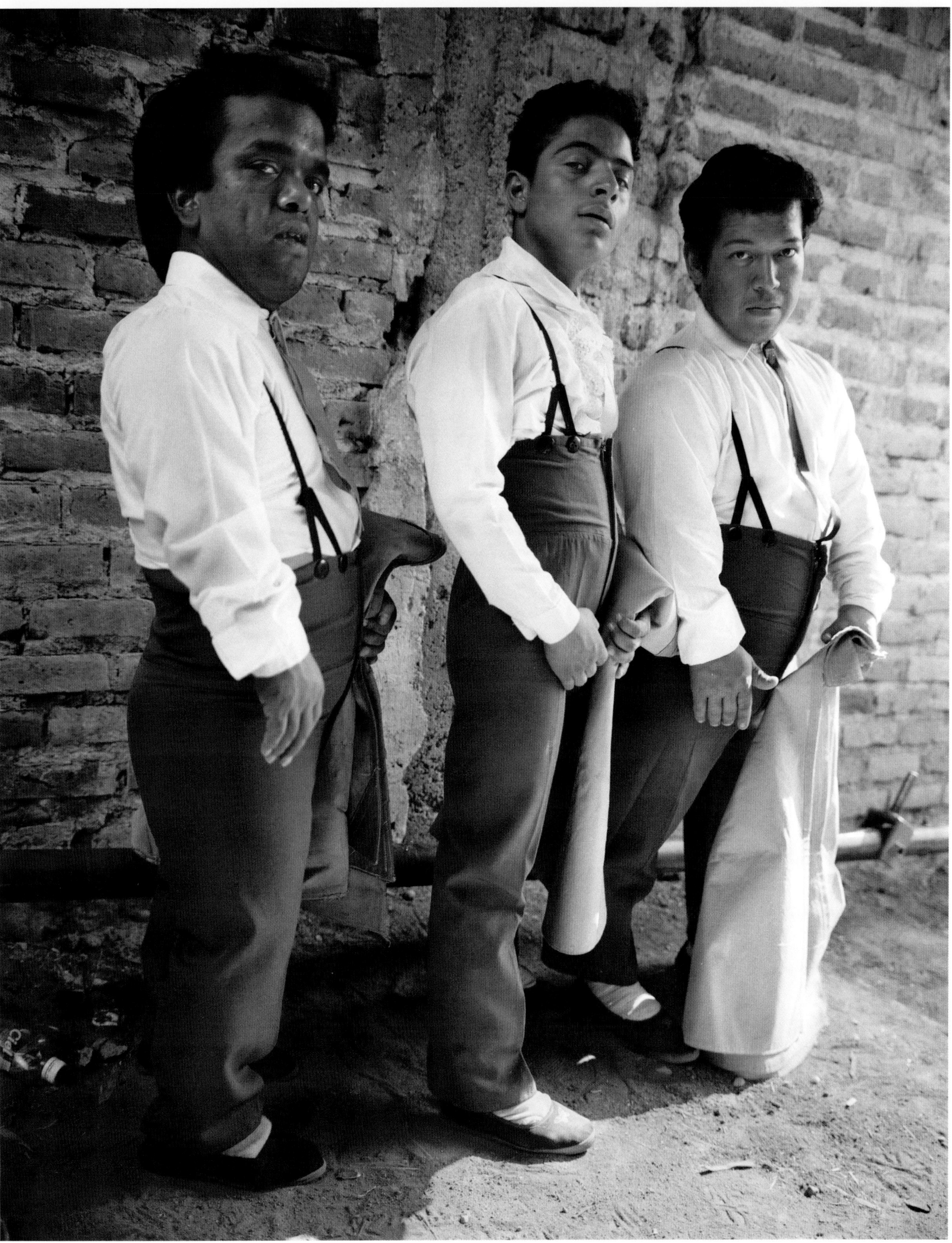

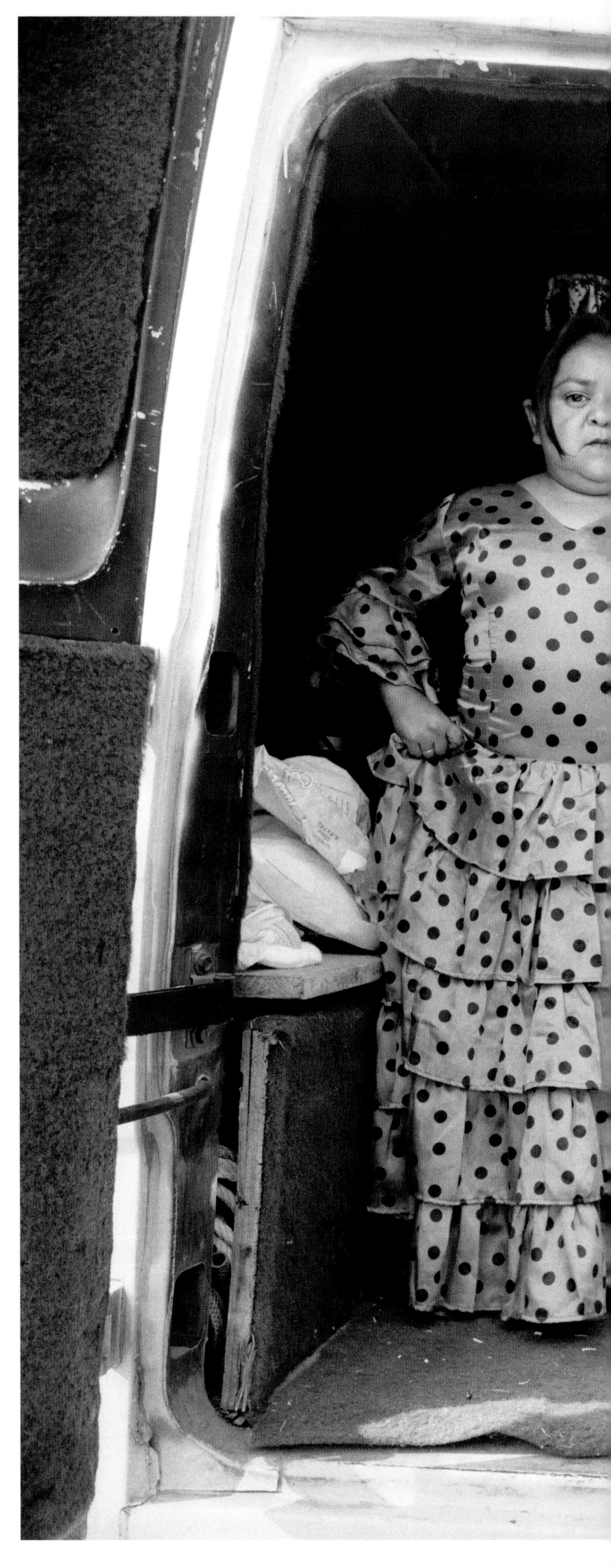

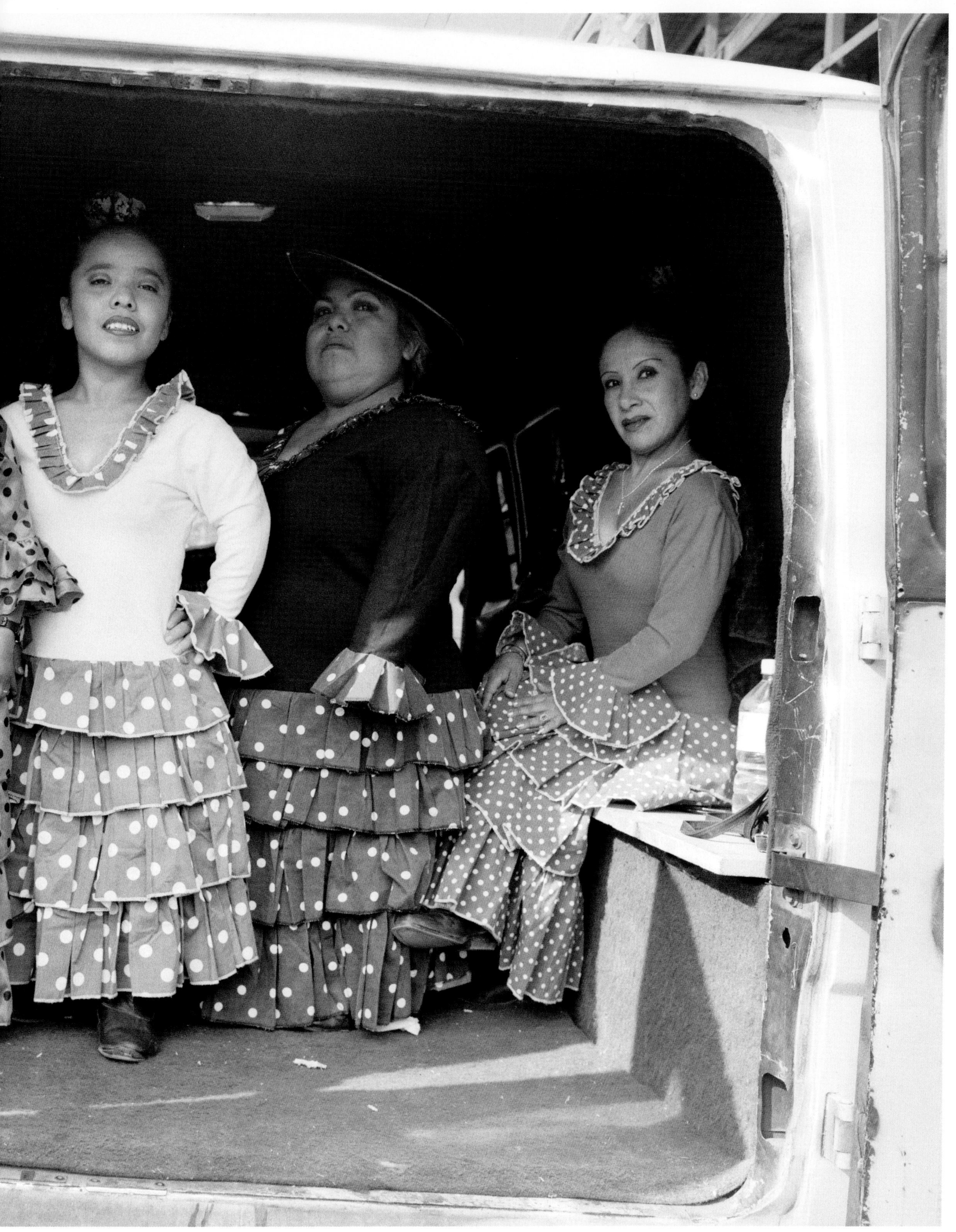

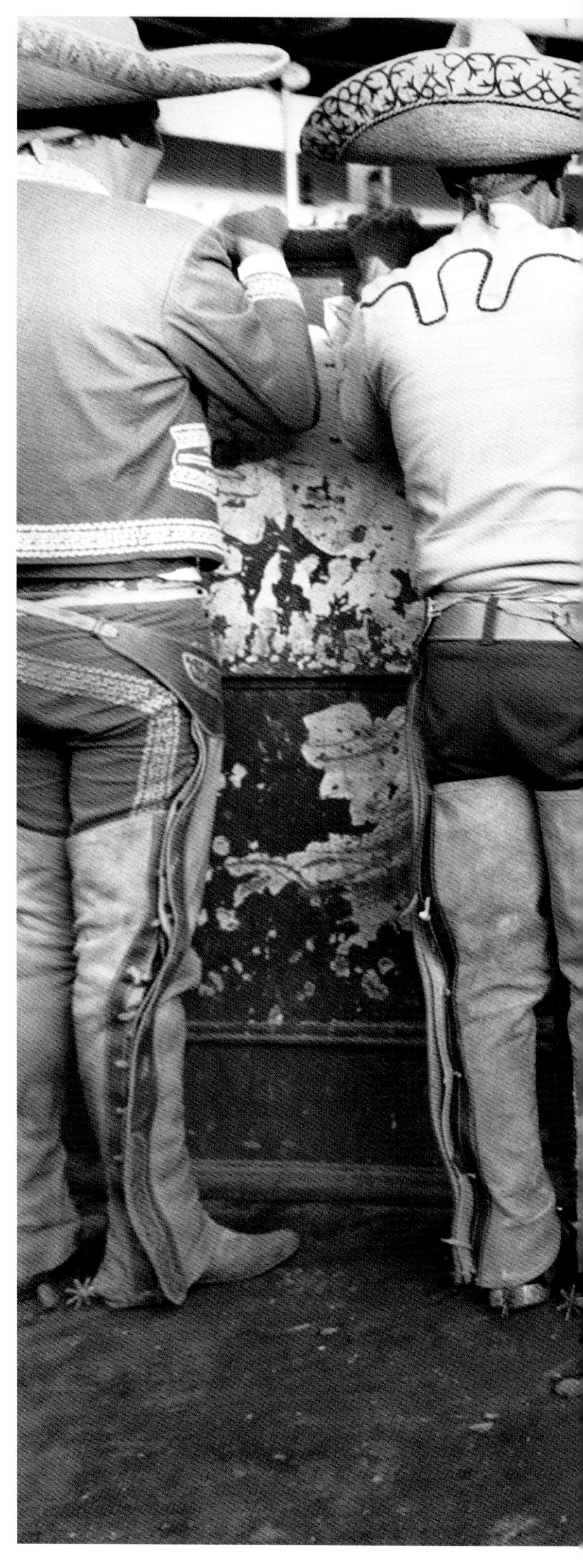

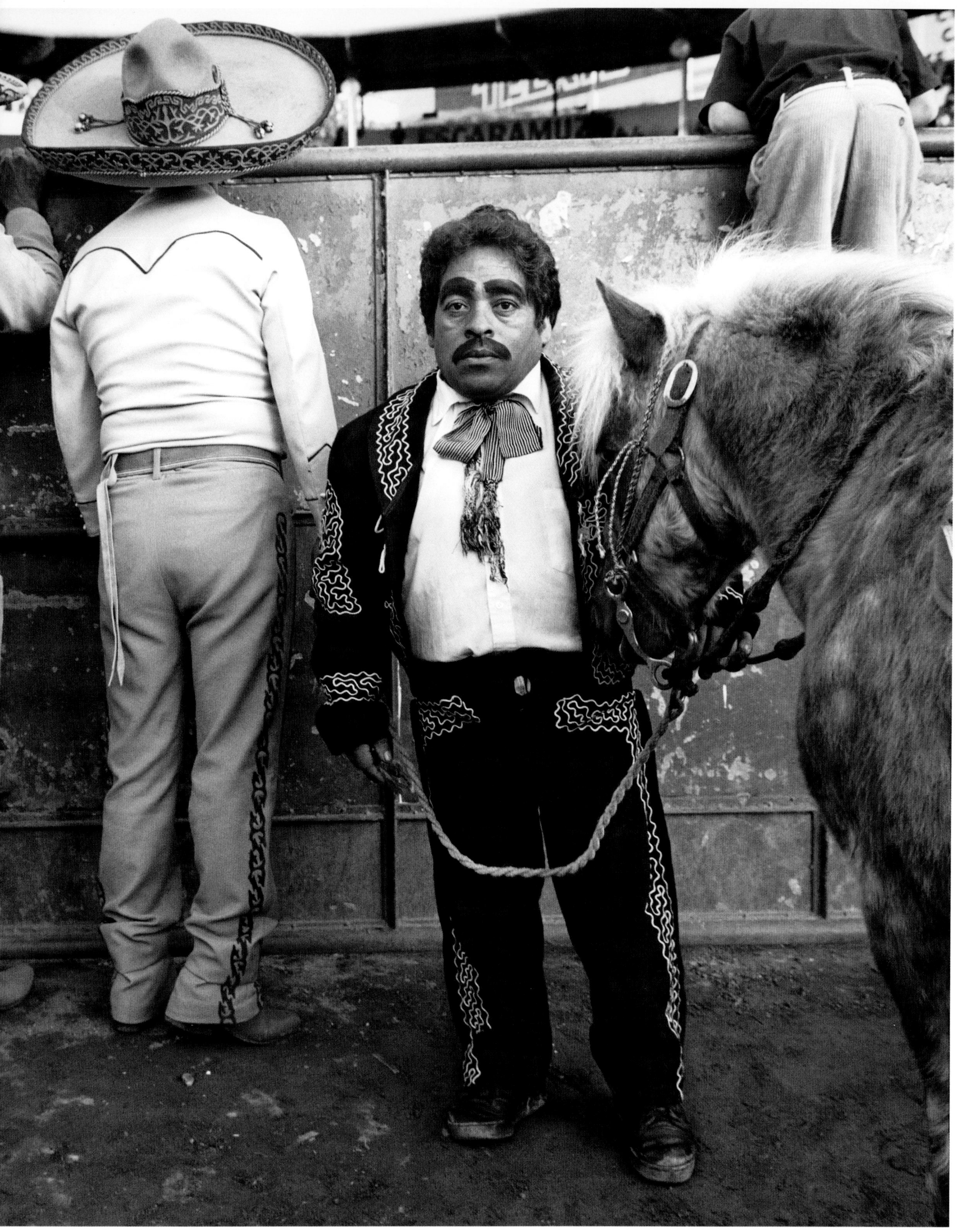

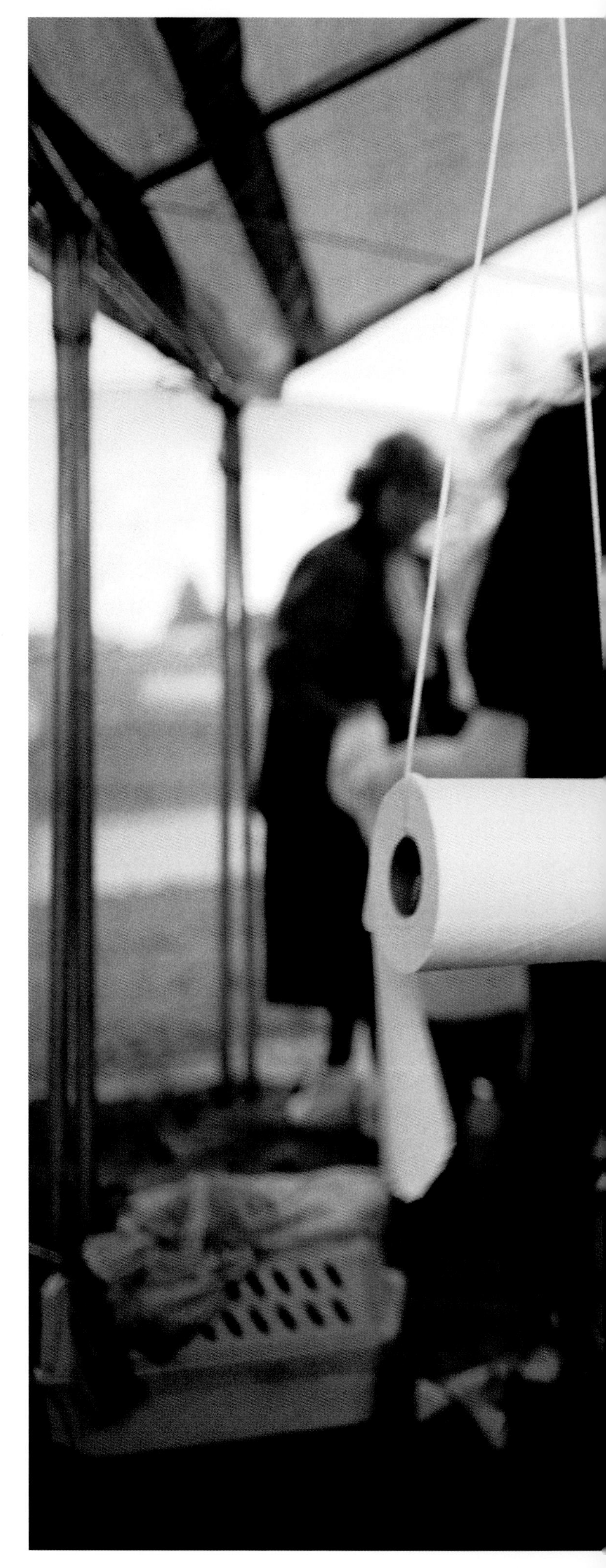

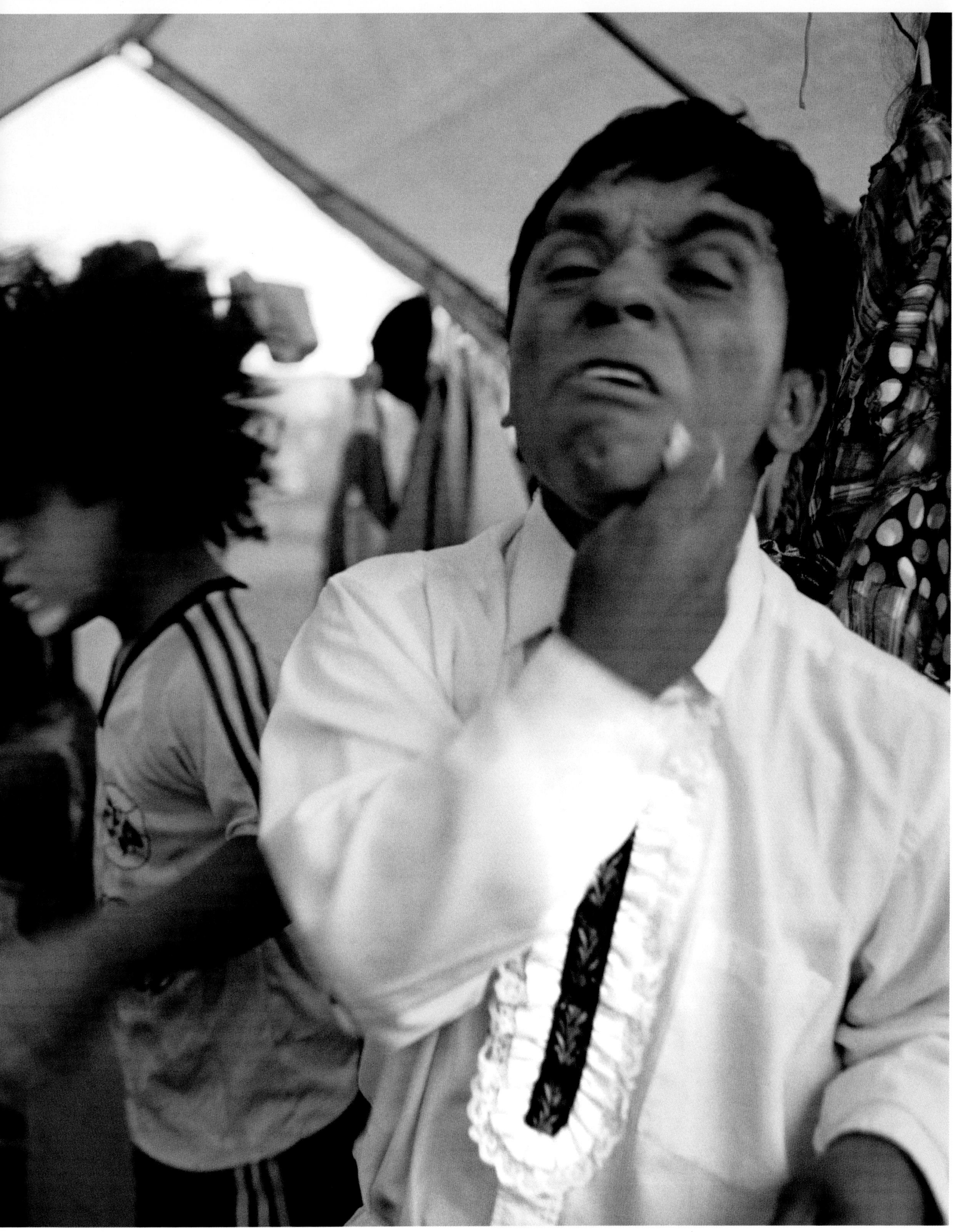

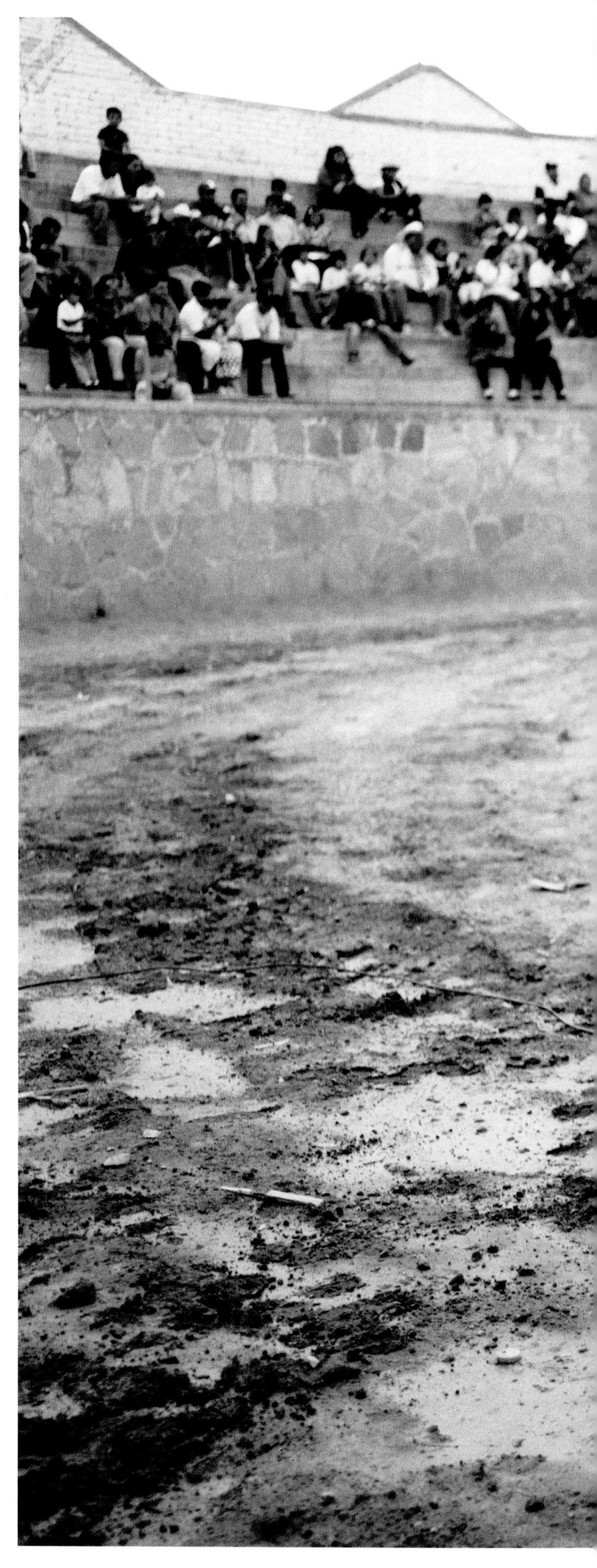

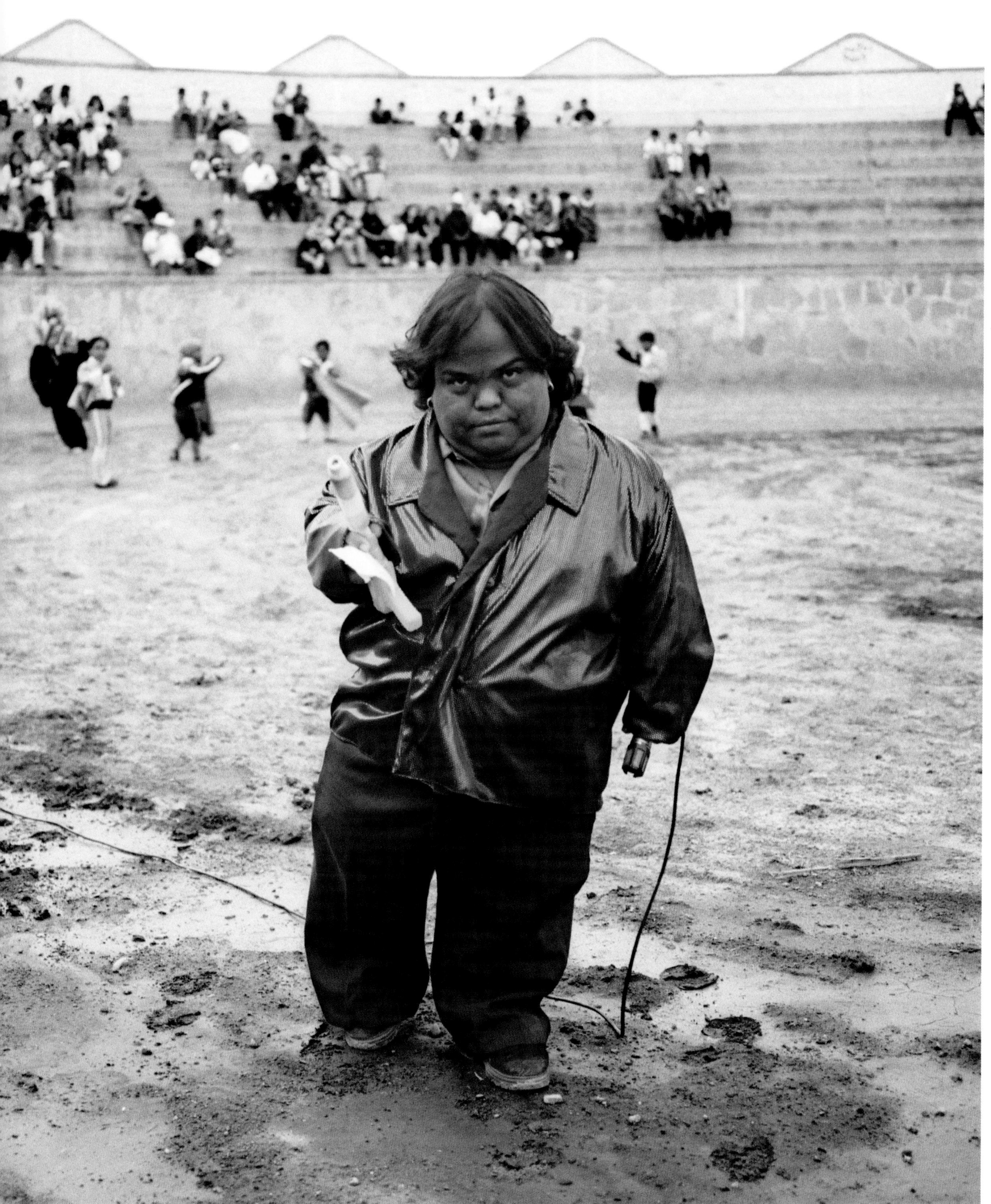

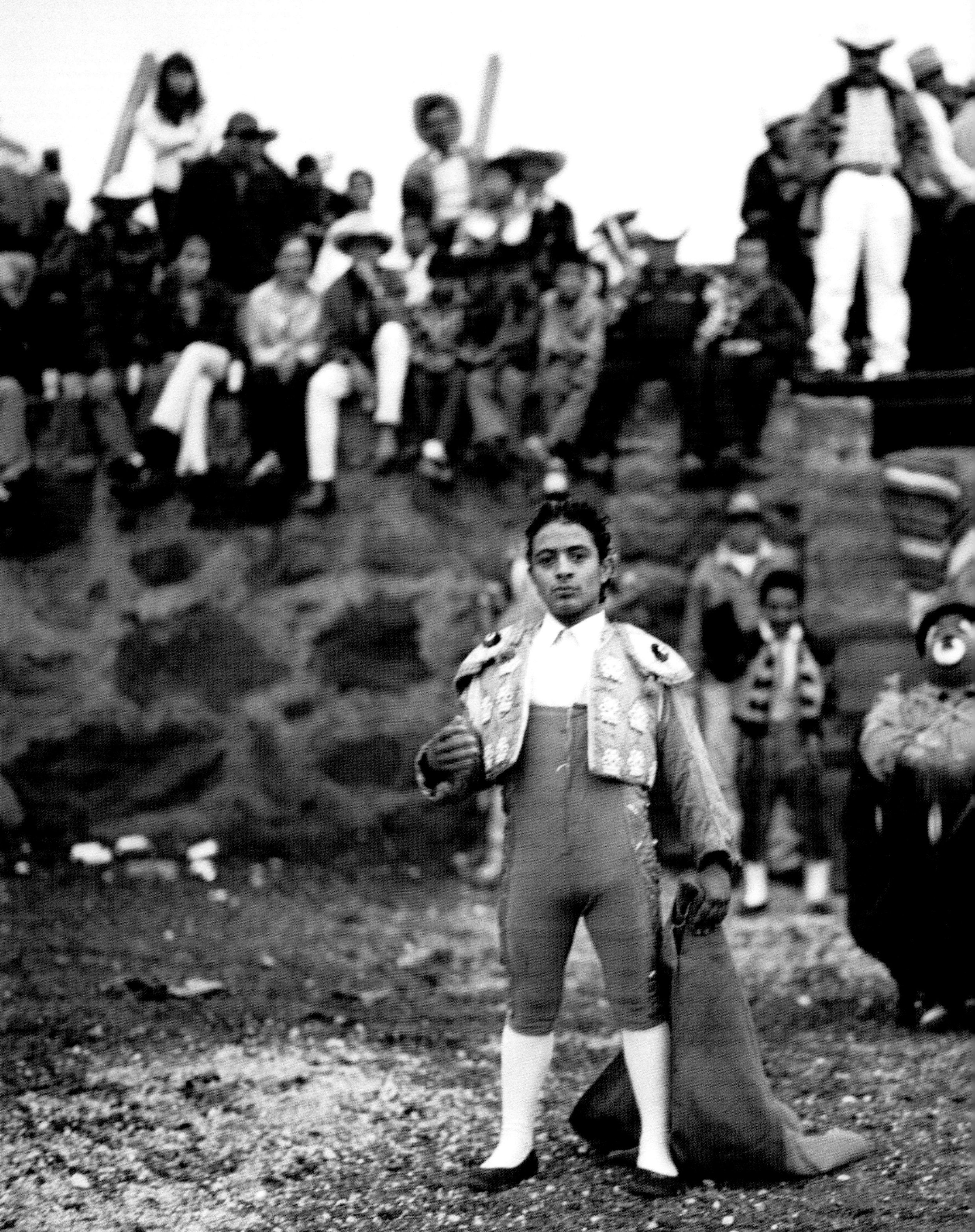

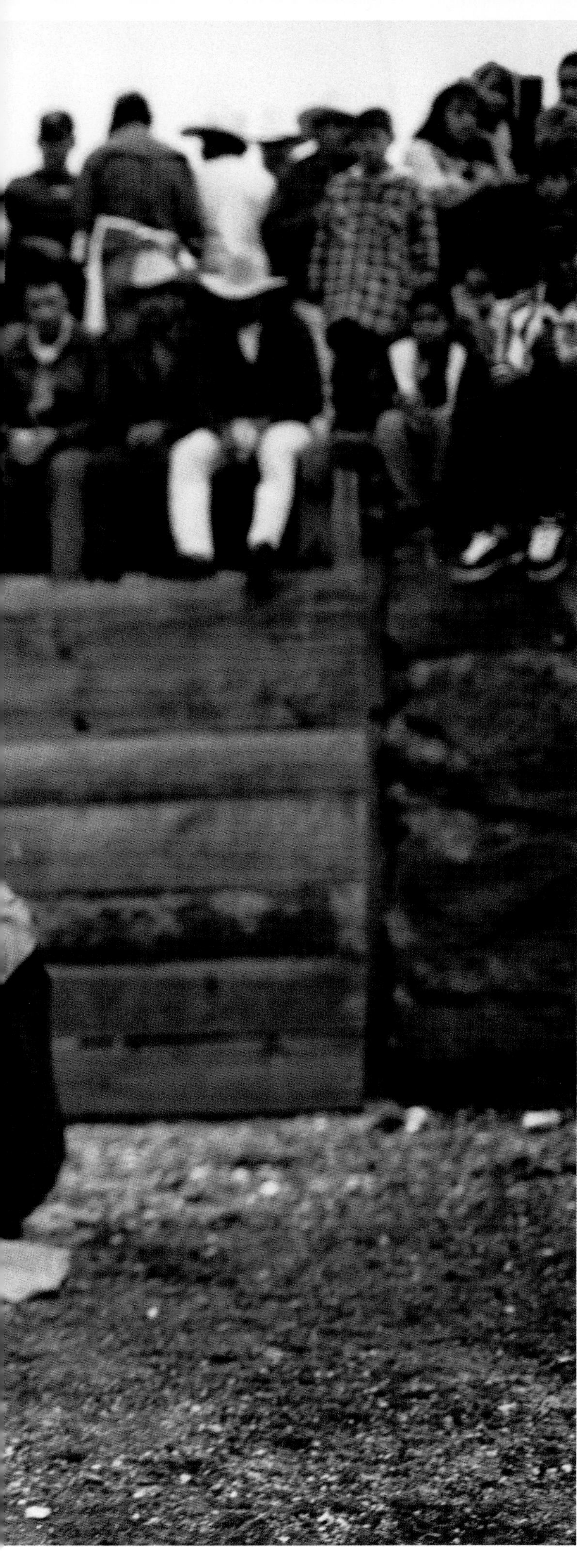

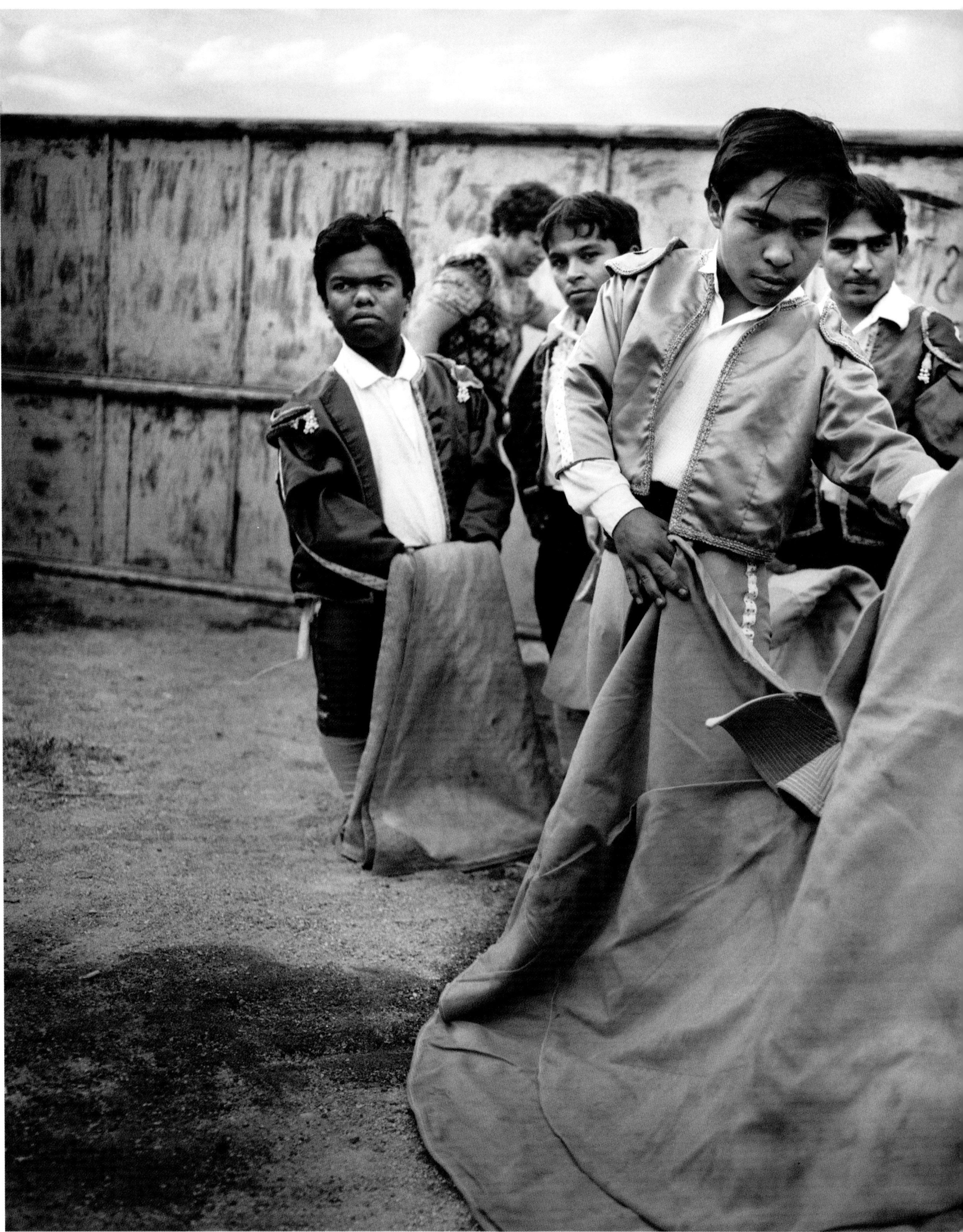

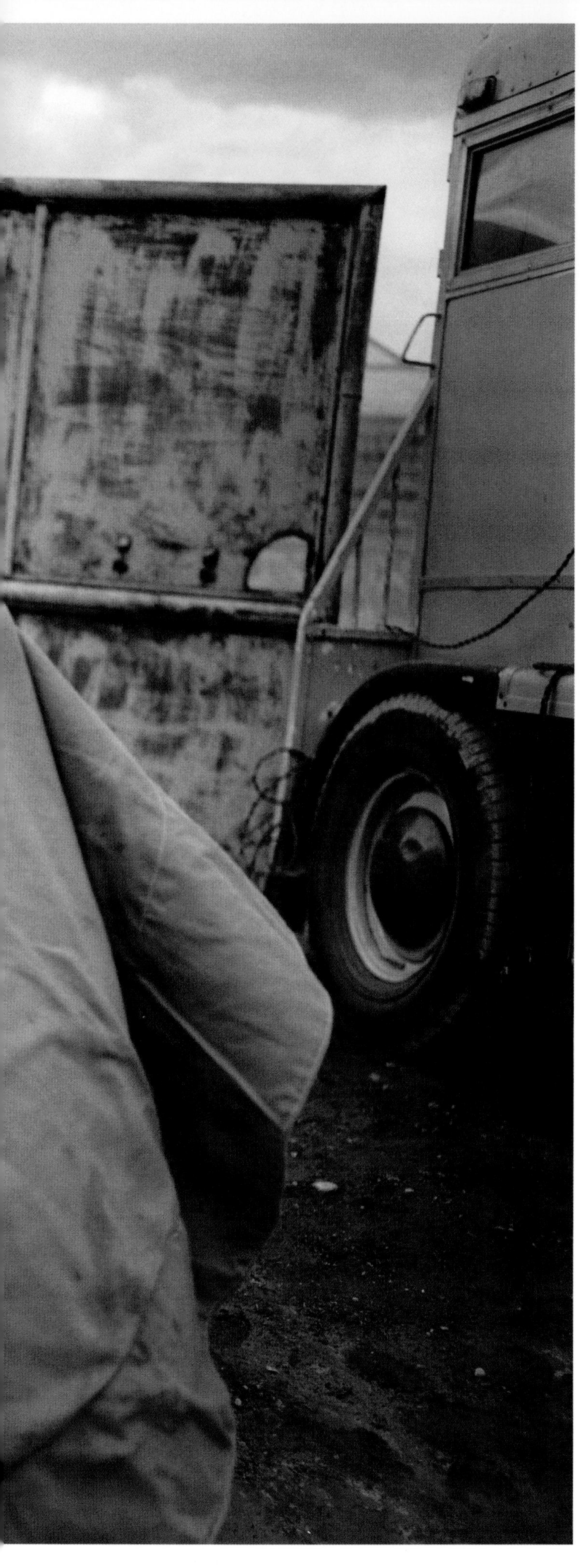

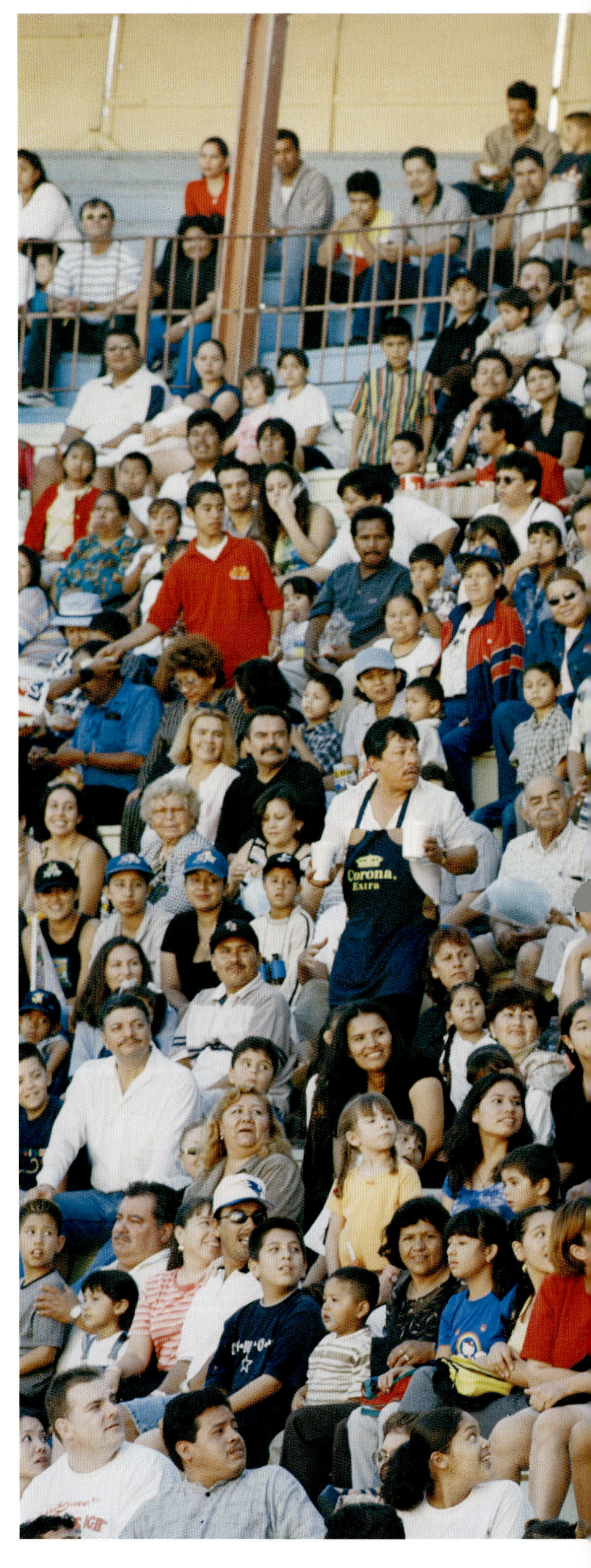

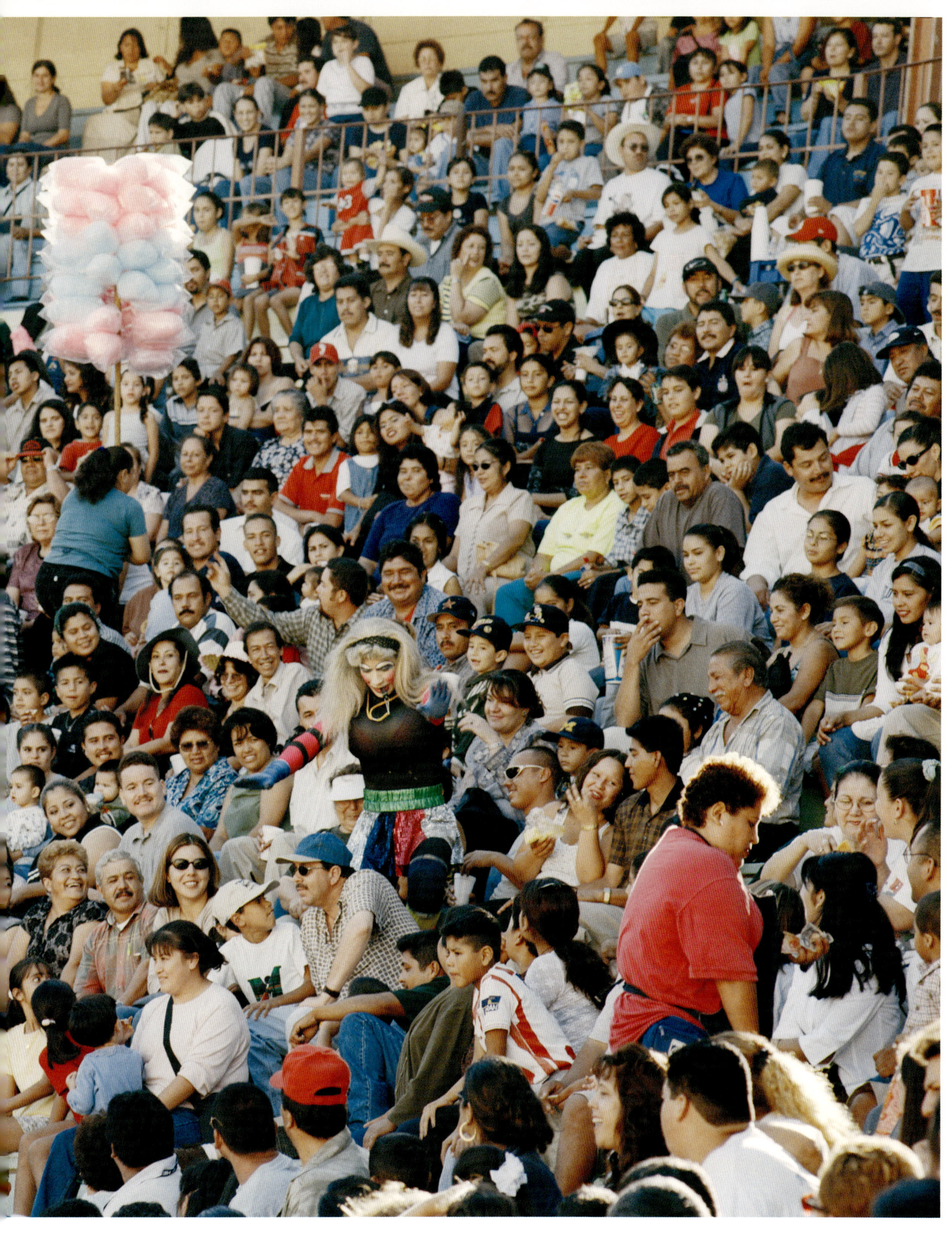

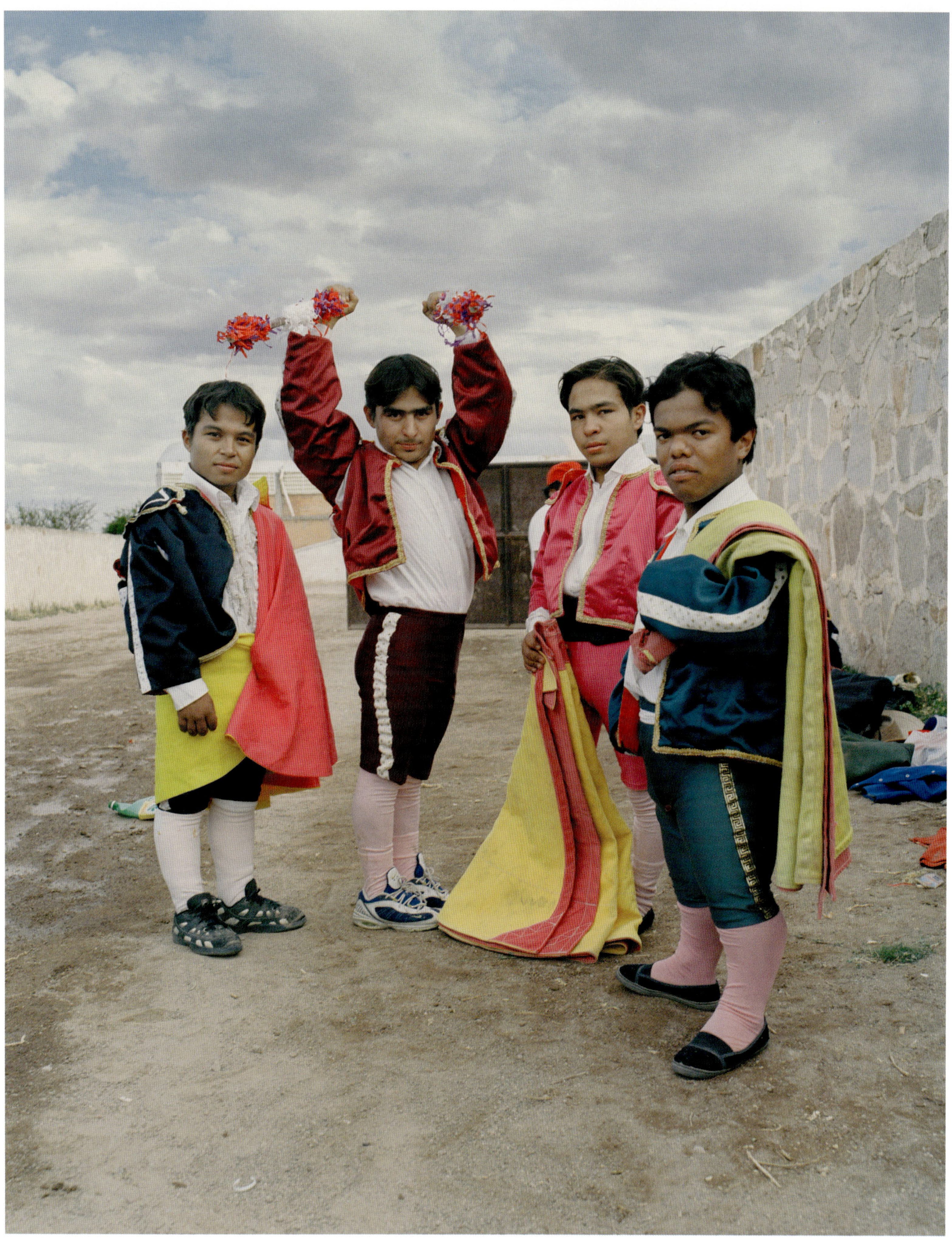

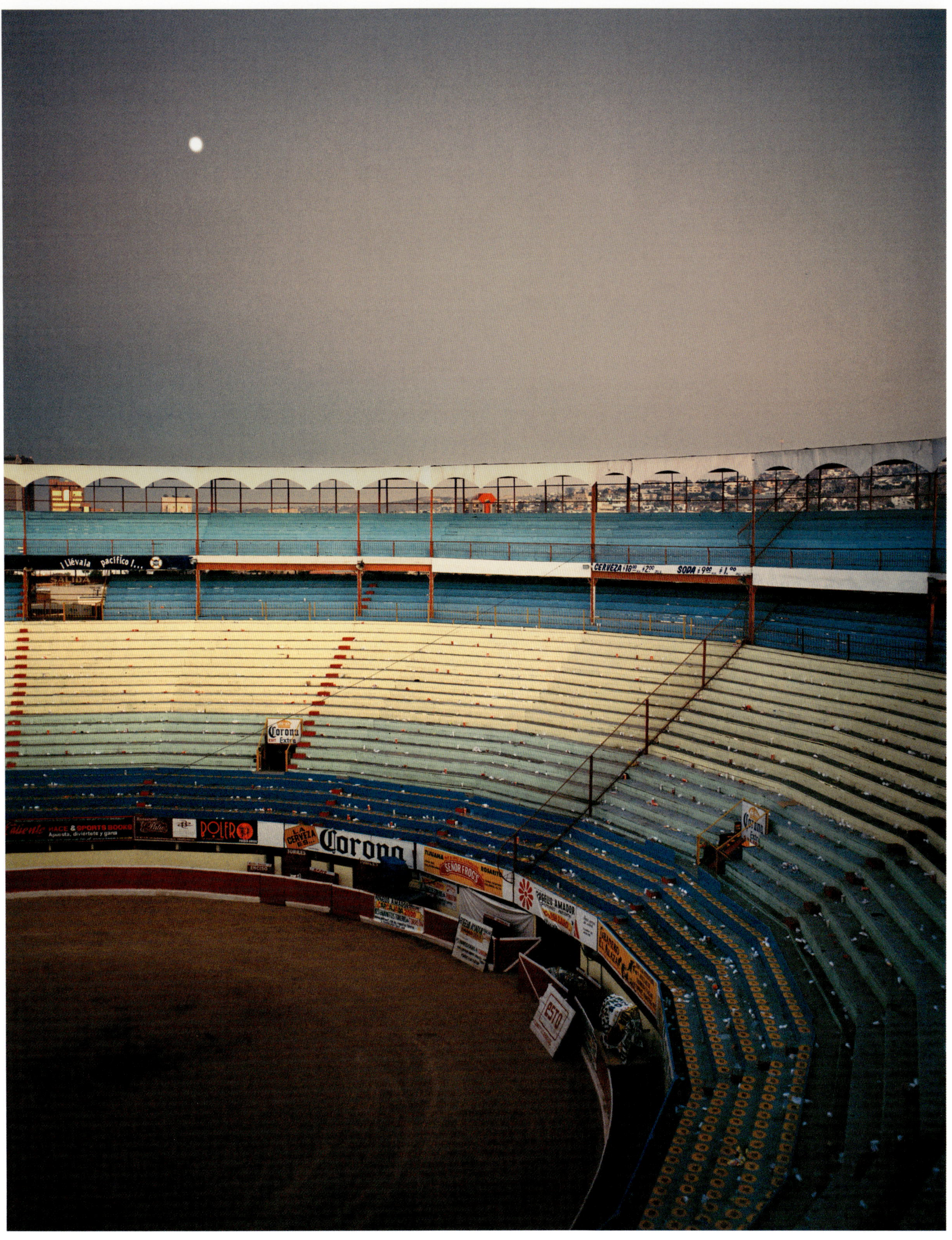
¡ Llévala pacífico !...
SALIDA
CERVEZA 18⁰⁰ 2⁰⁰   SODA 9⁰⁰ 1⁰⁰
Corona
Extra
Corona
POLER
Corona
SEÑOR FROG'S
AMADOR
ESTO

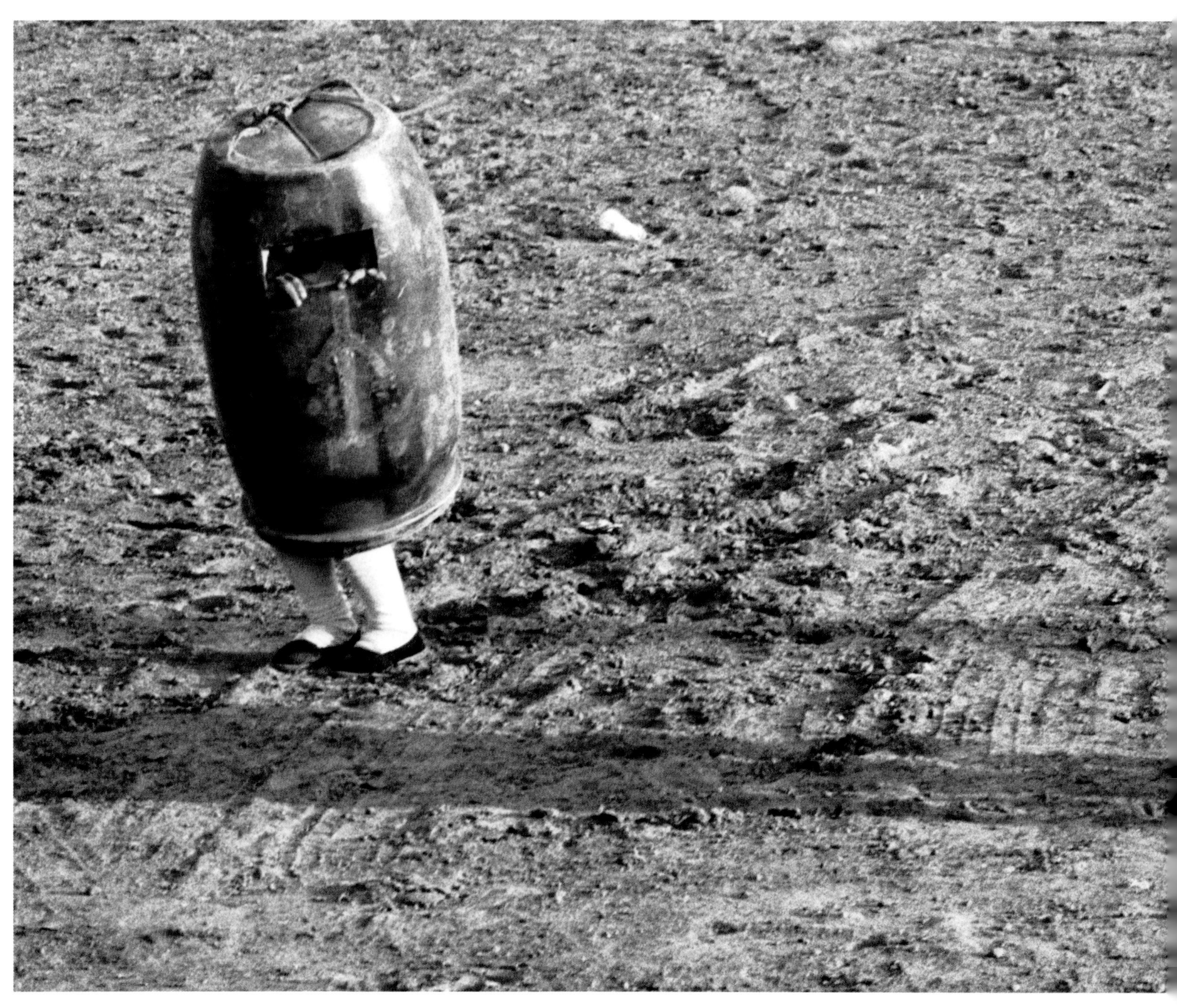

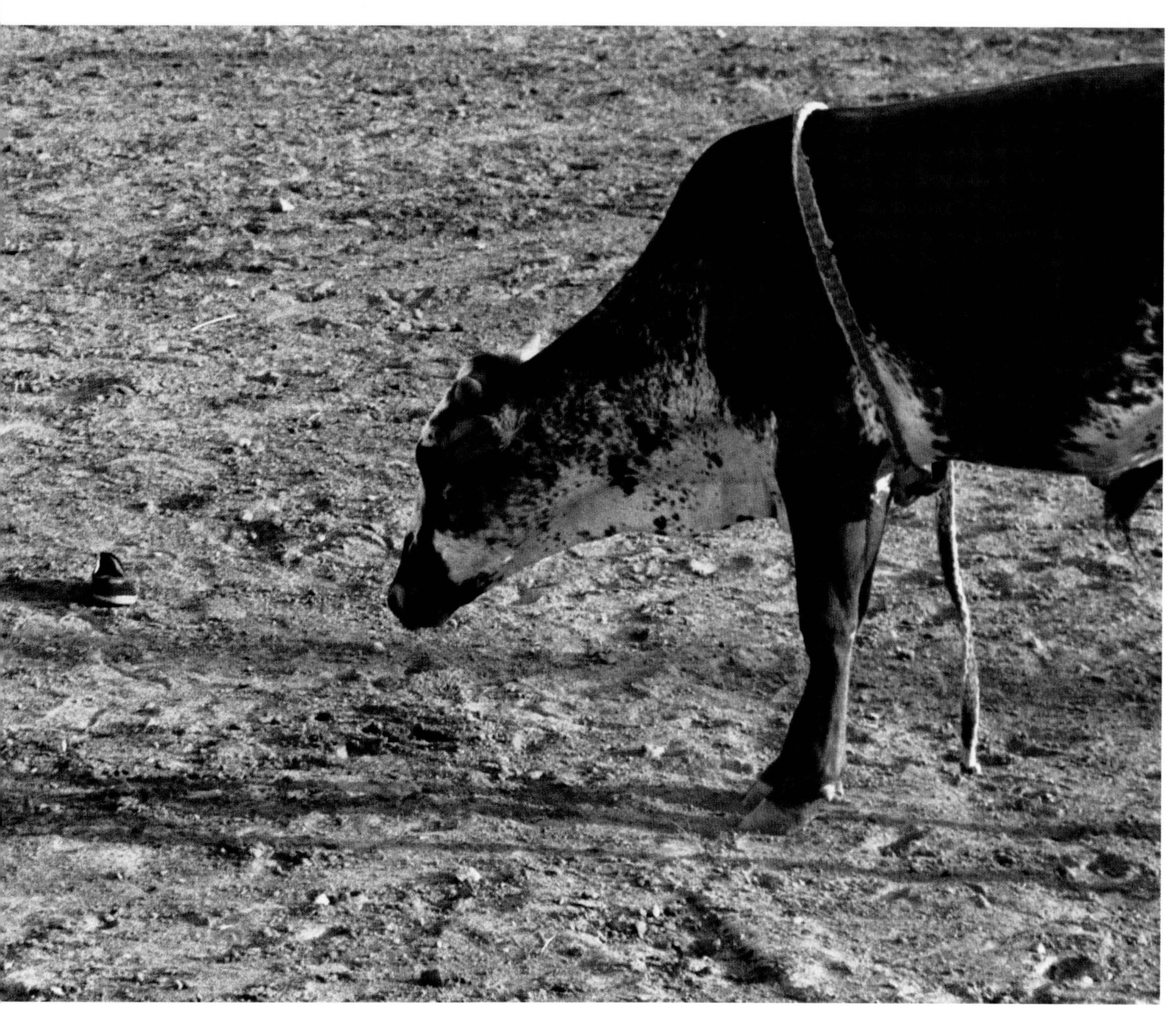

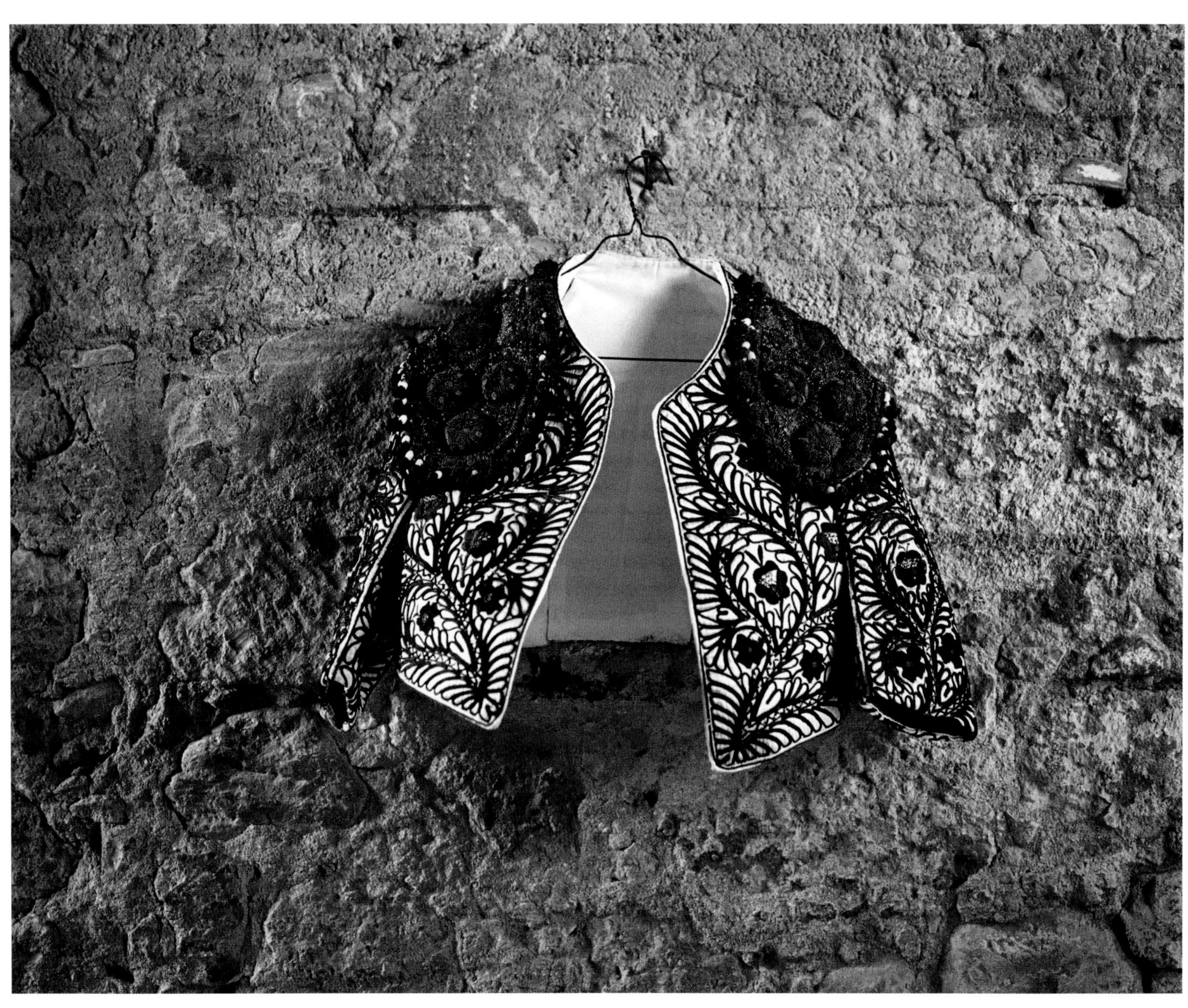

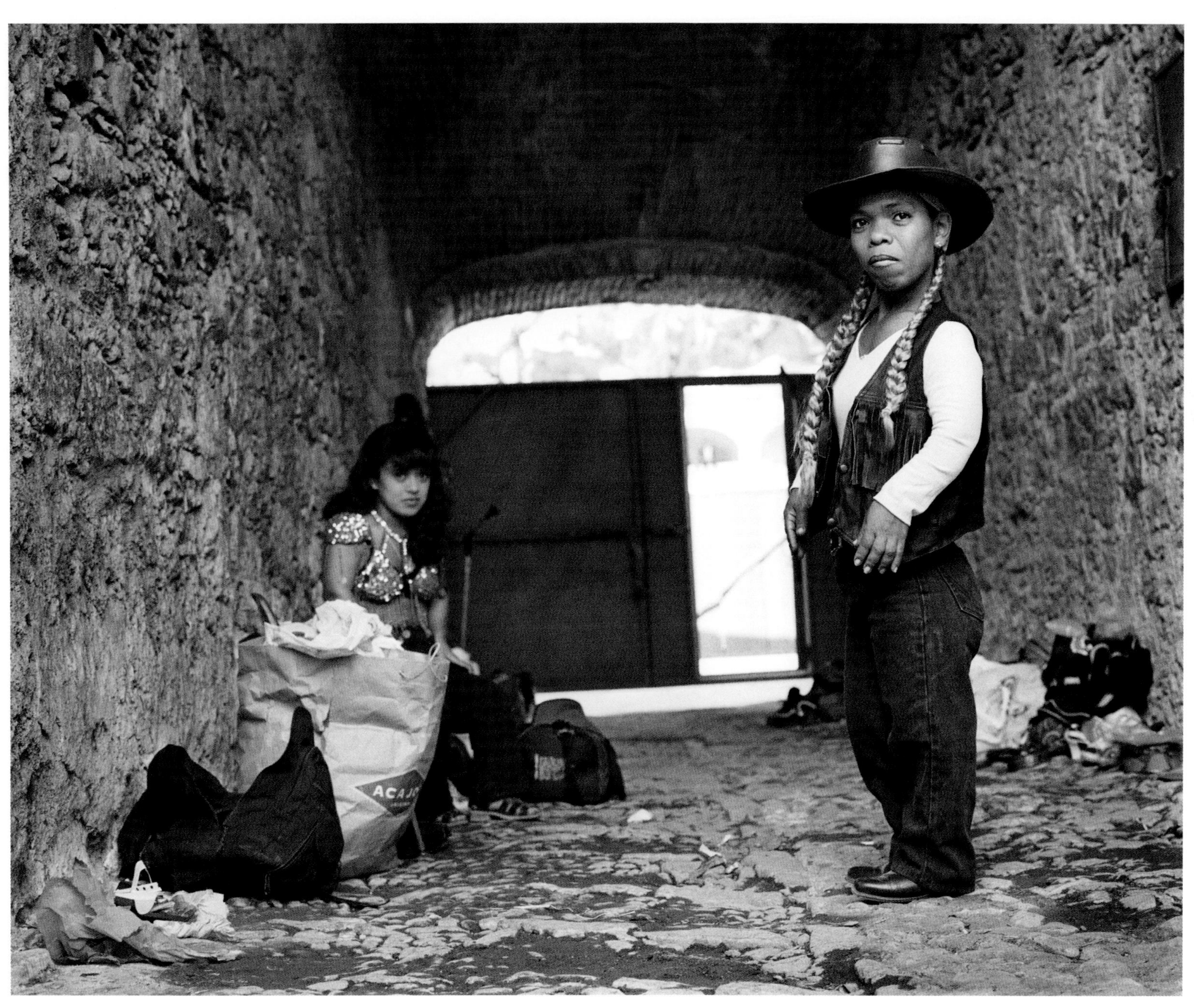

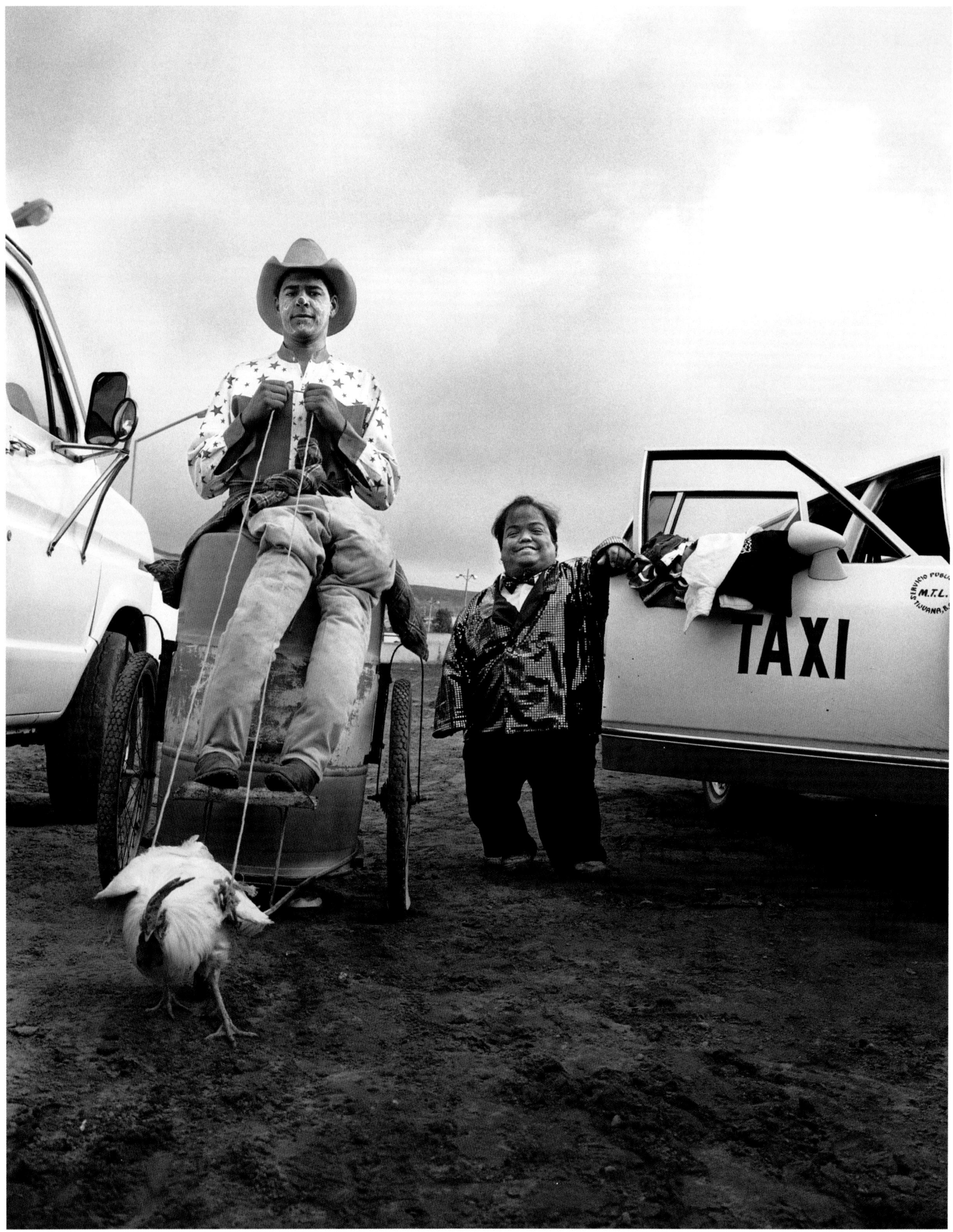

TAXI
SERVICIO PUBLICO
M.T.L.
TIJUANA, B.C.

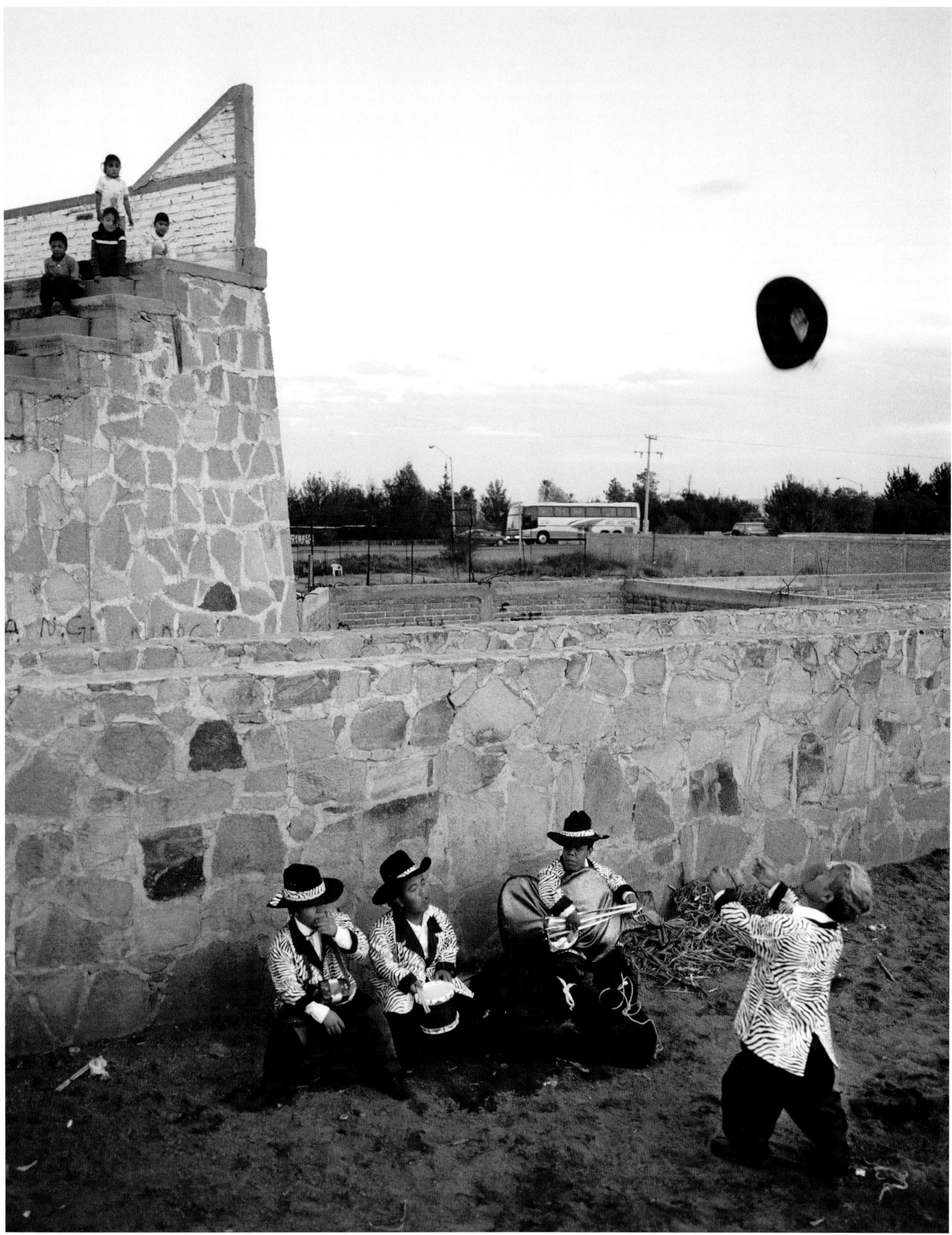

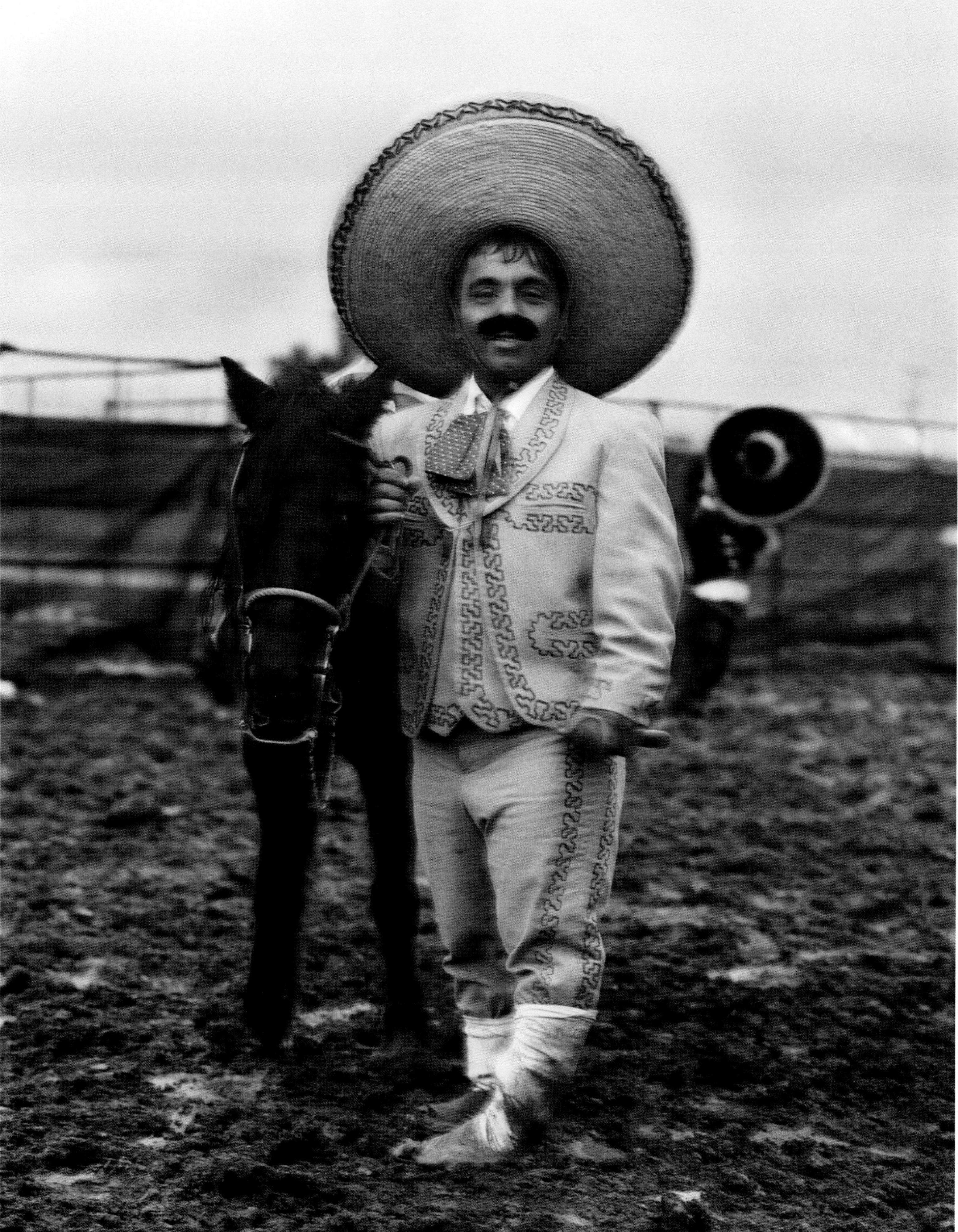

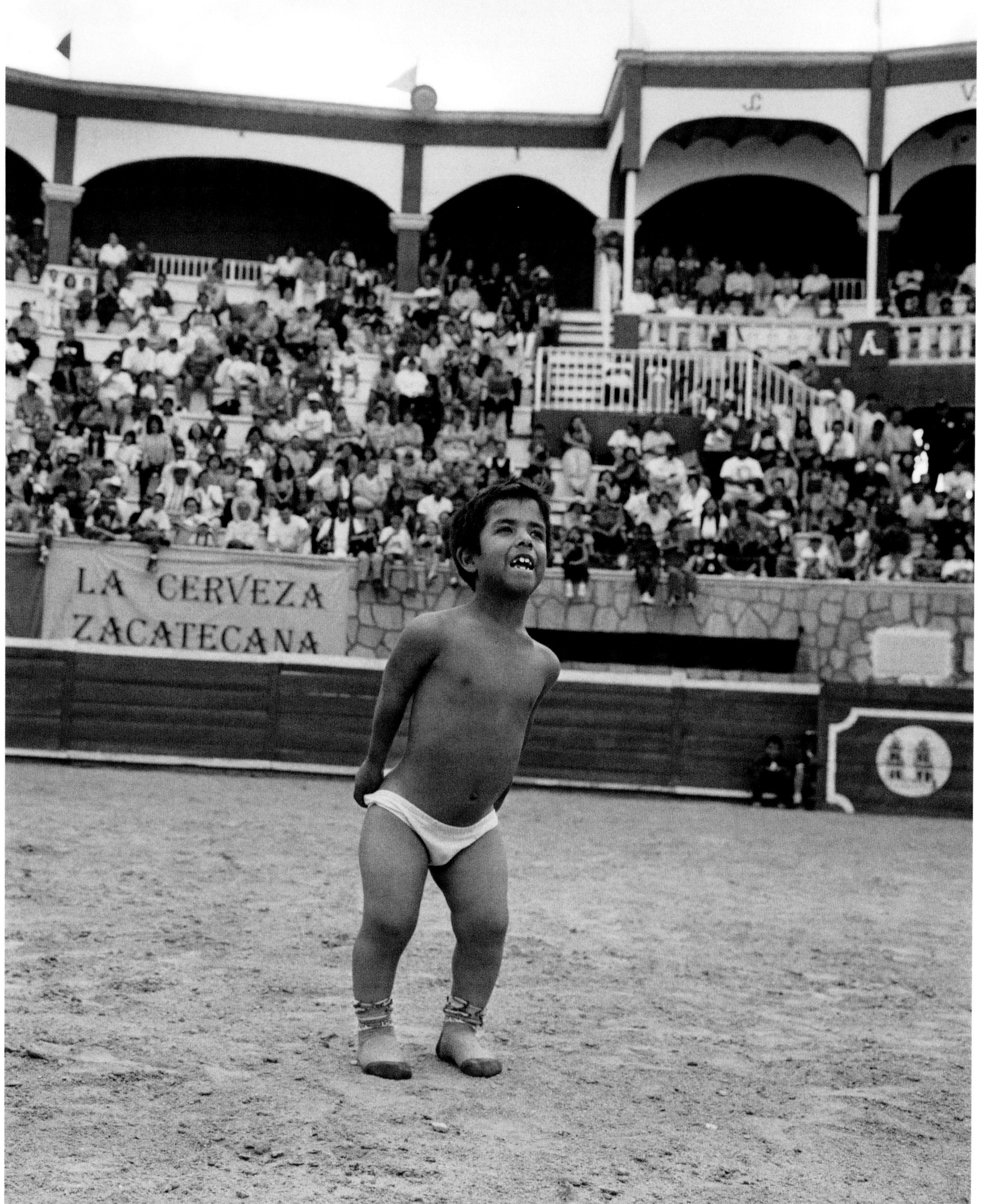
LA CERVEZA
ZACATECANA

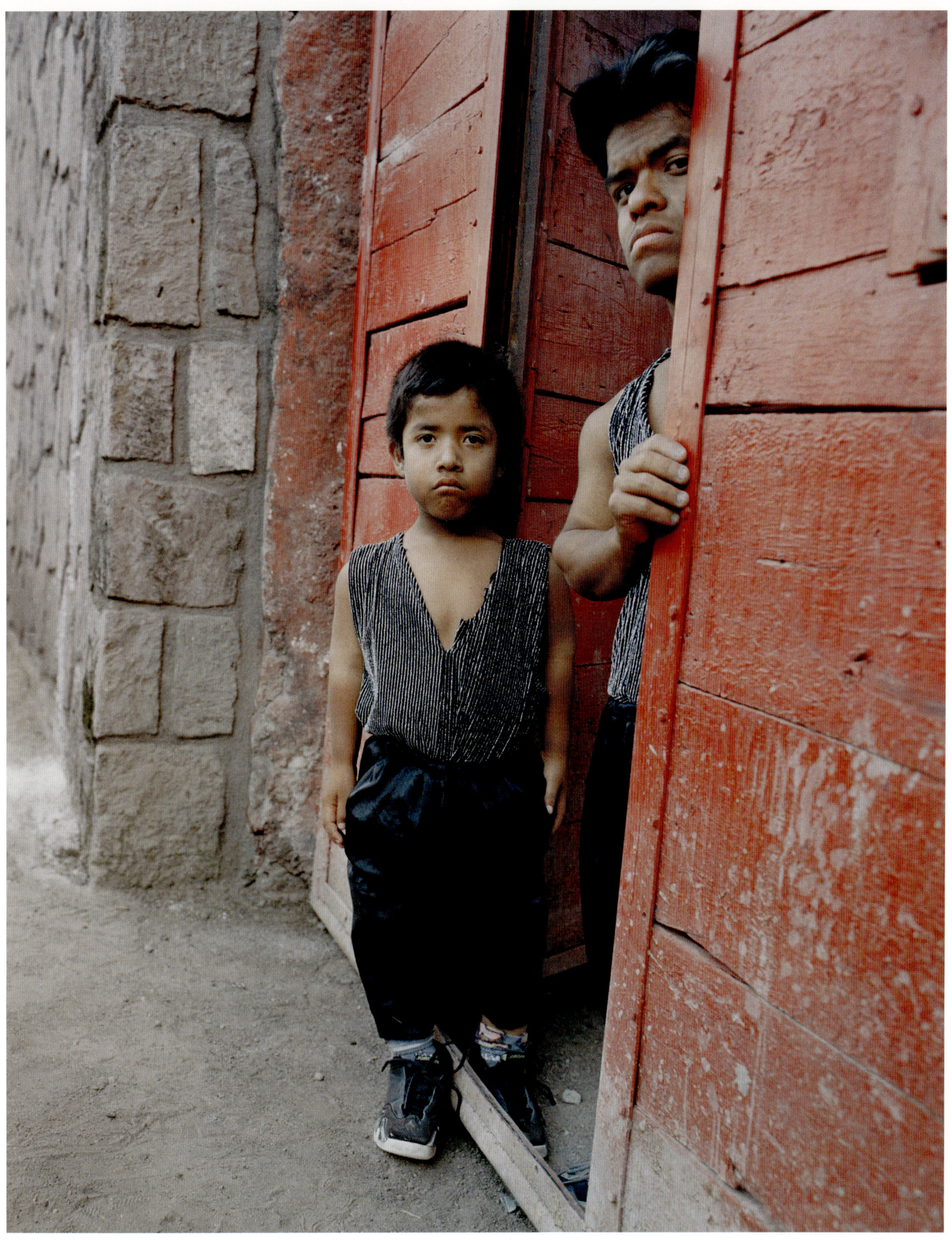

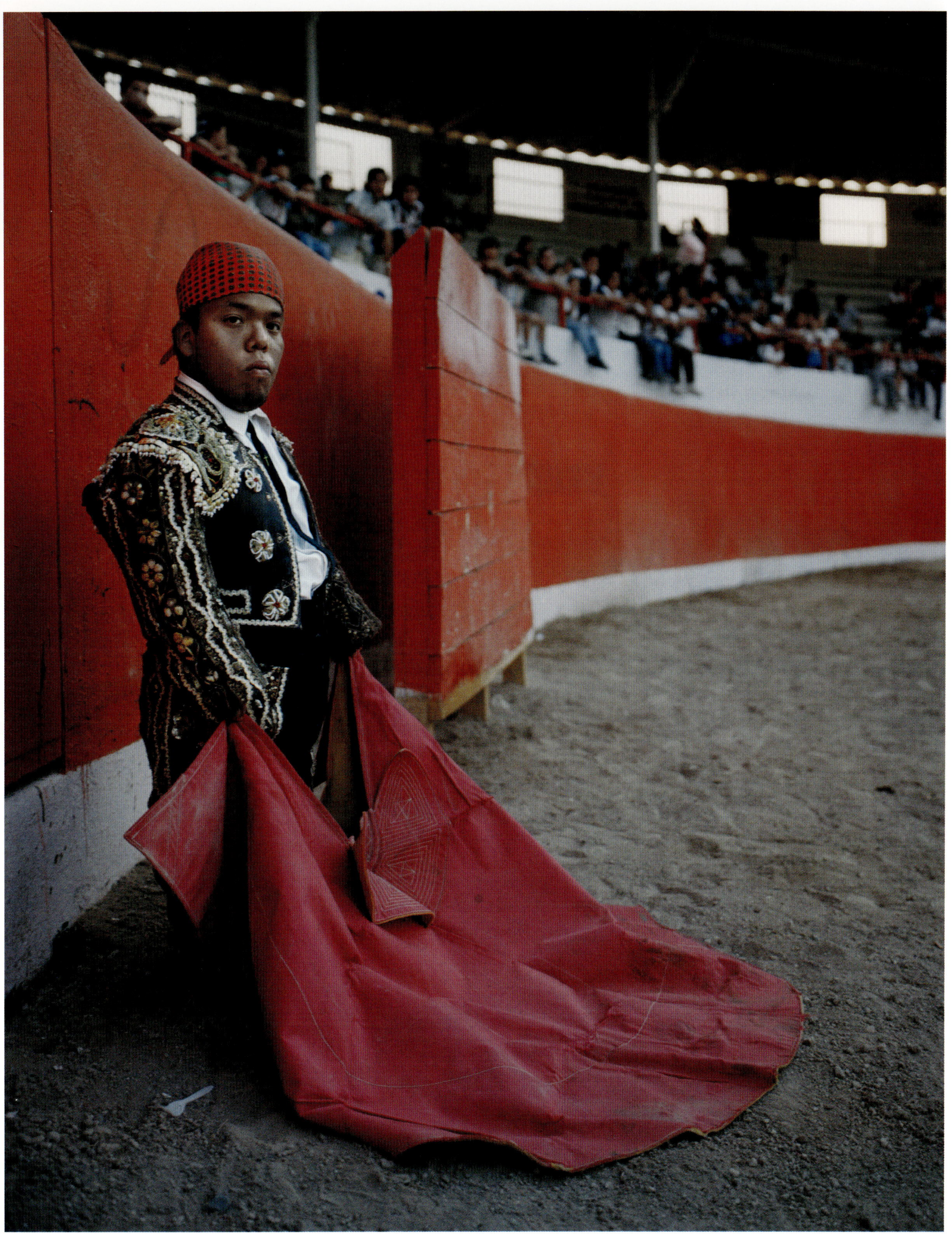

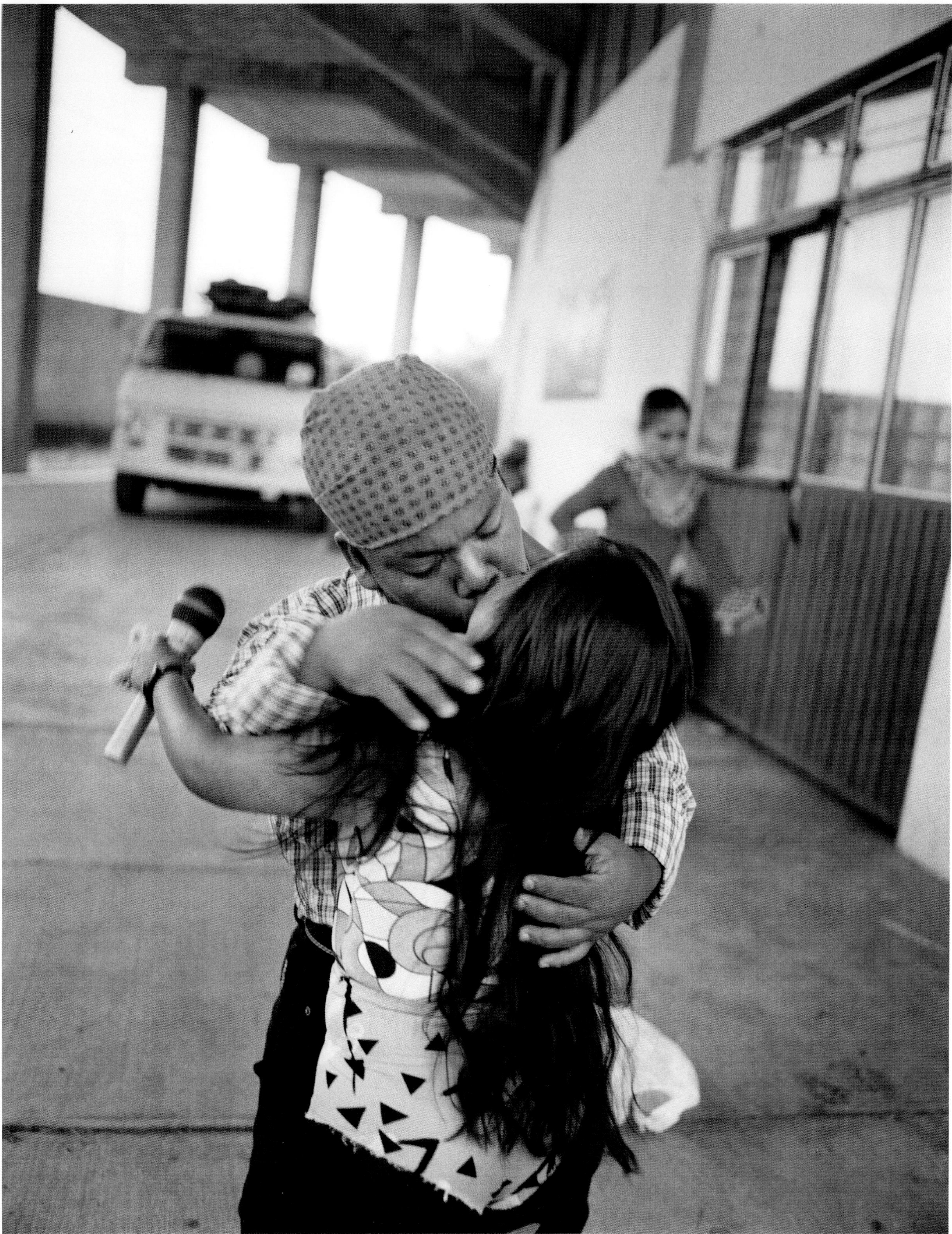

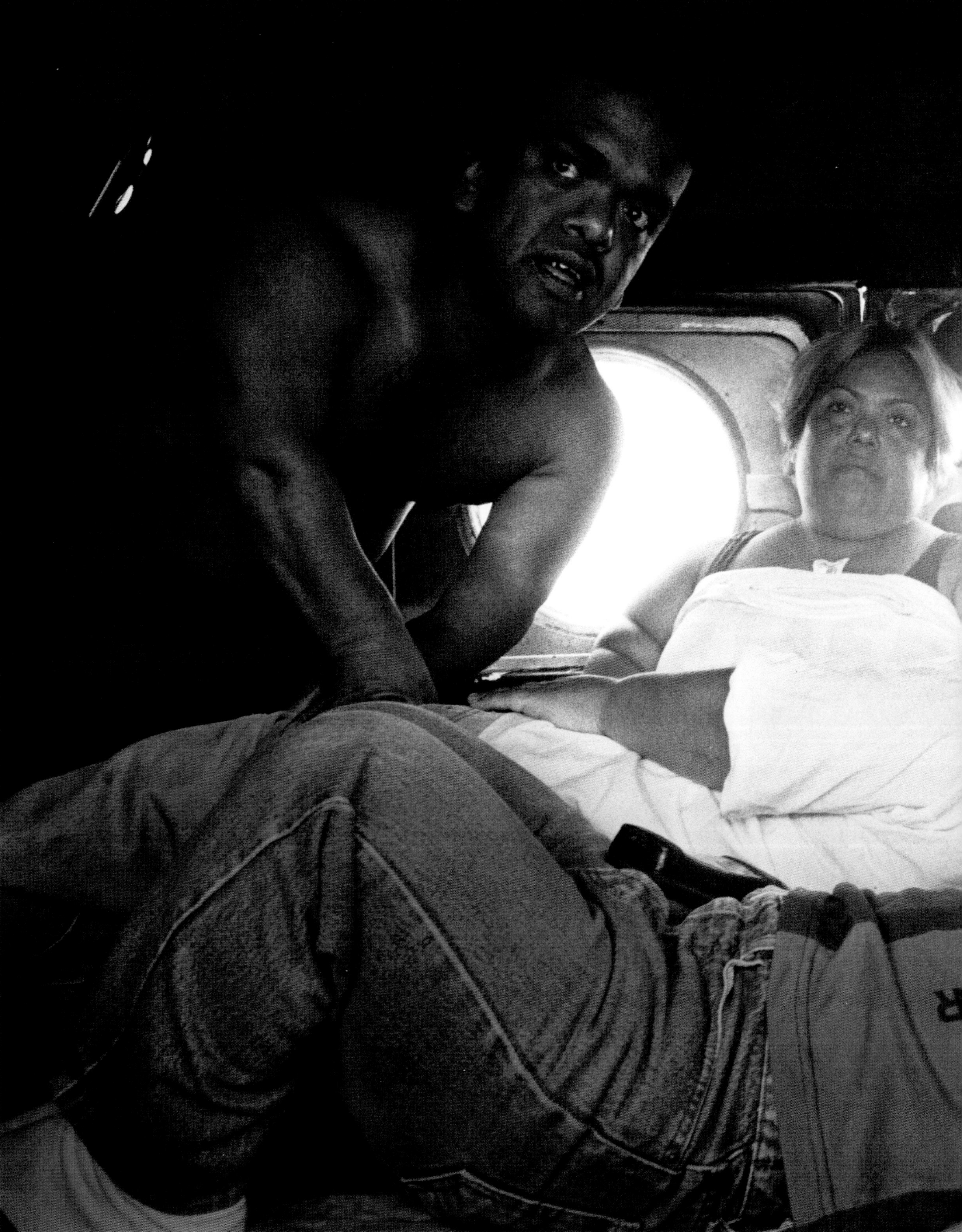

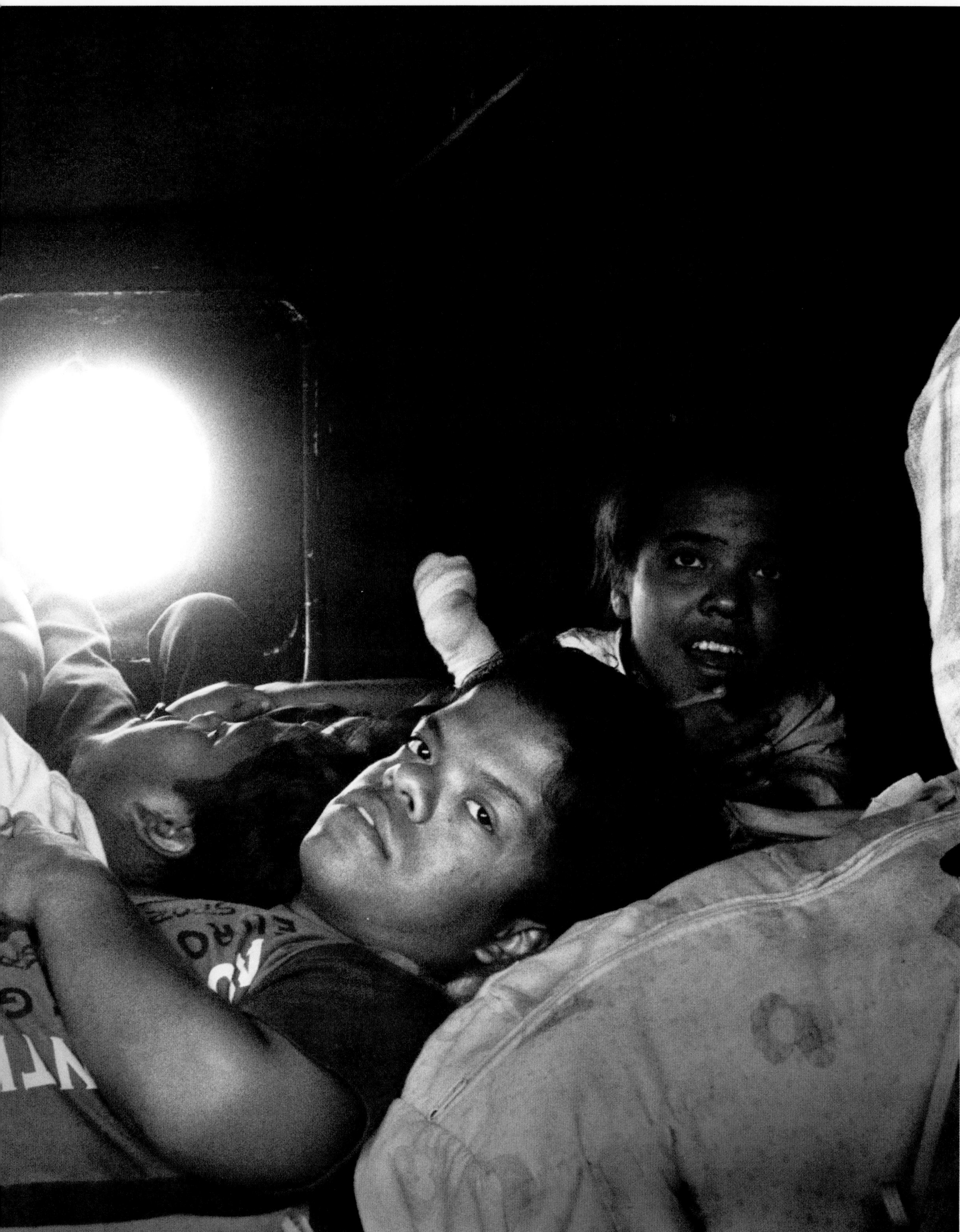

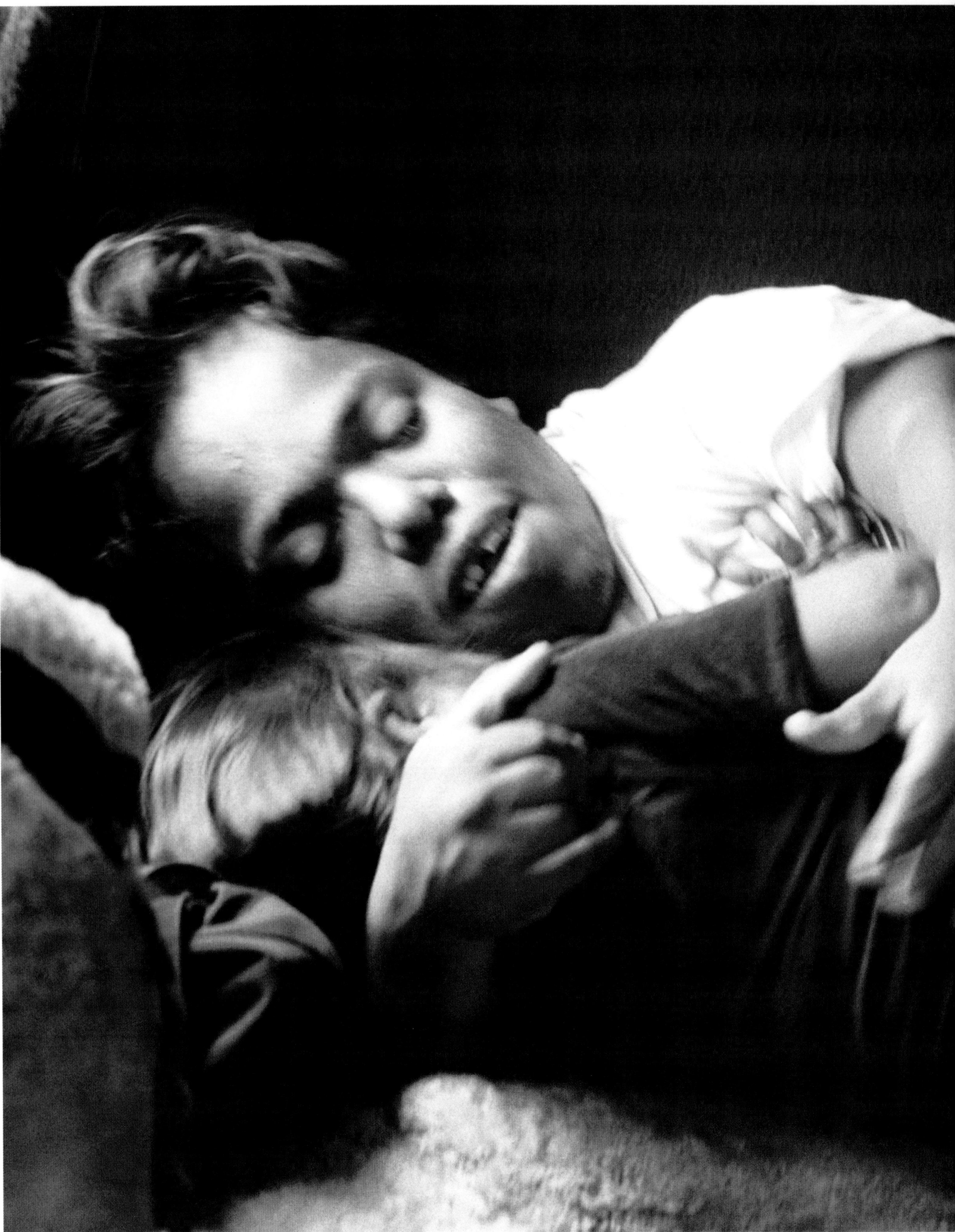

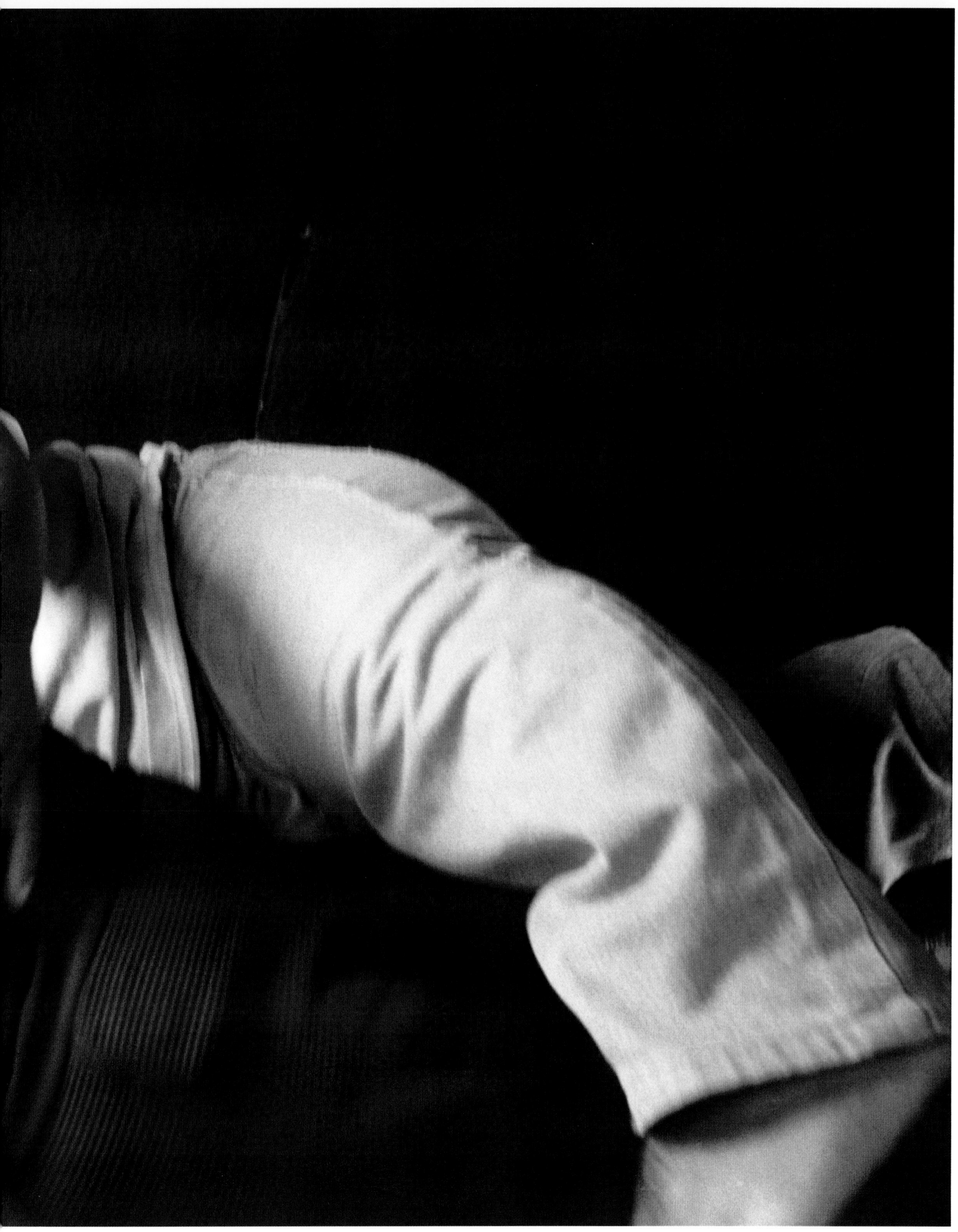

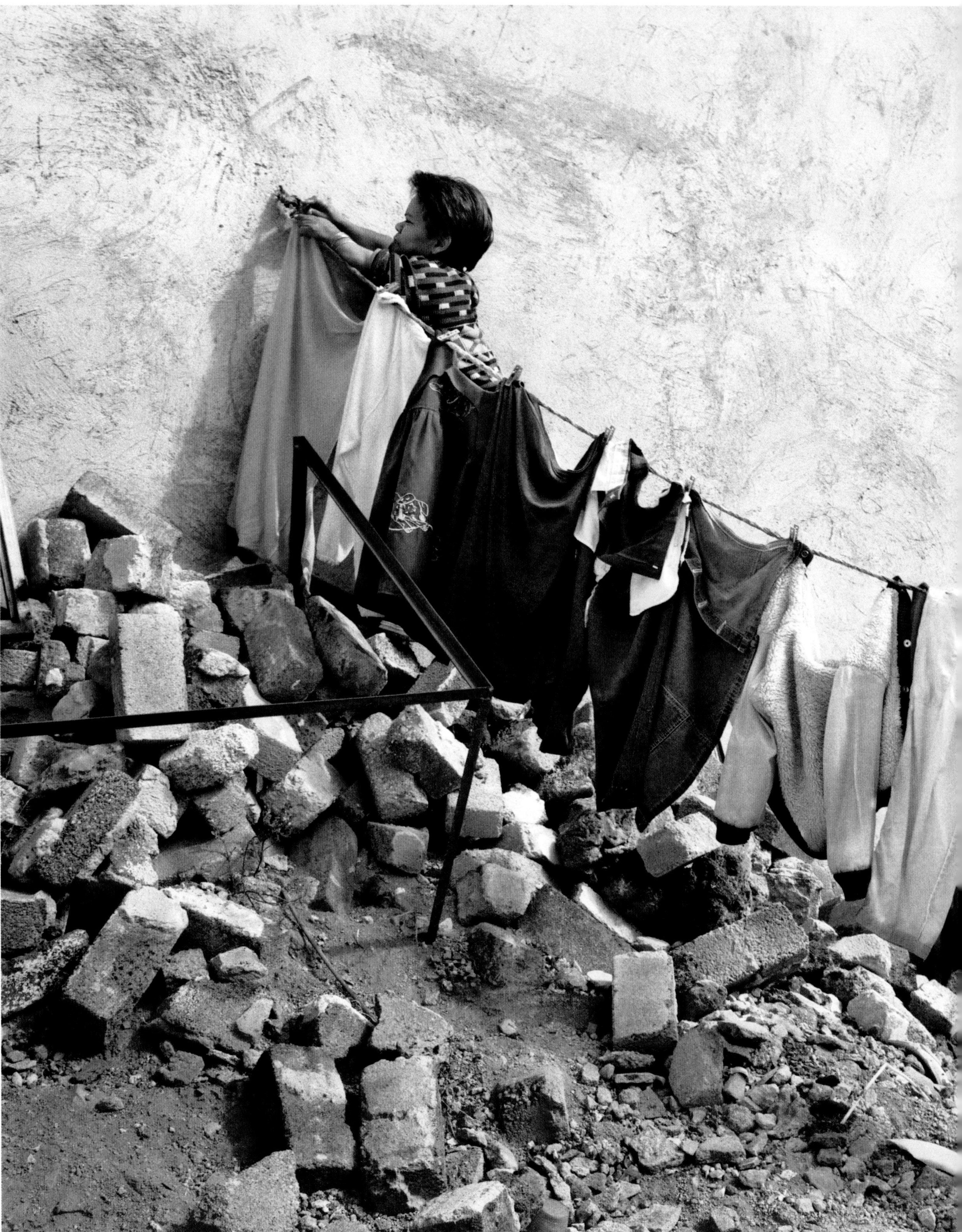

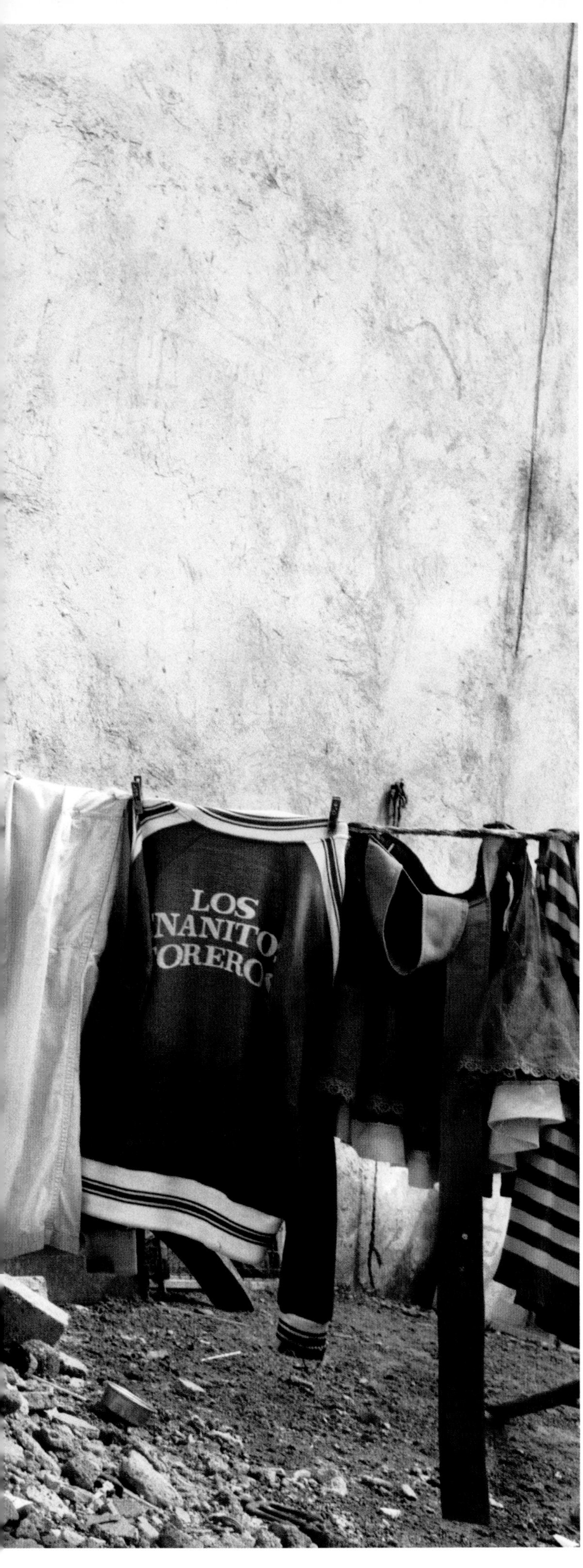
LOS
ENANITO
TORERO

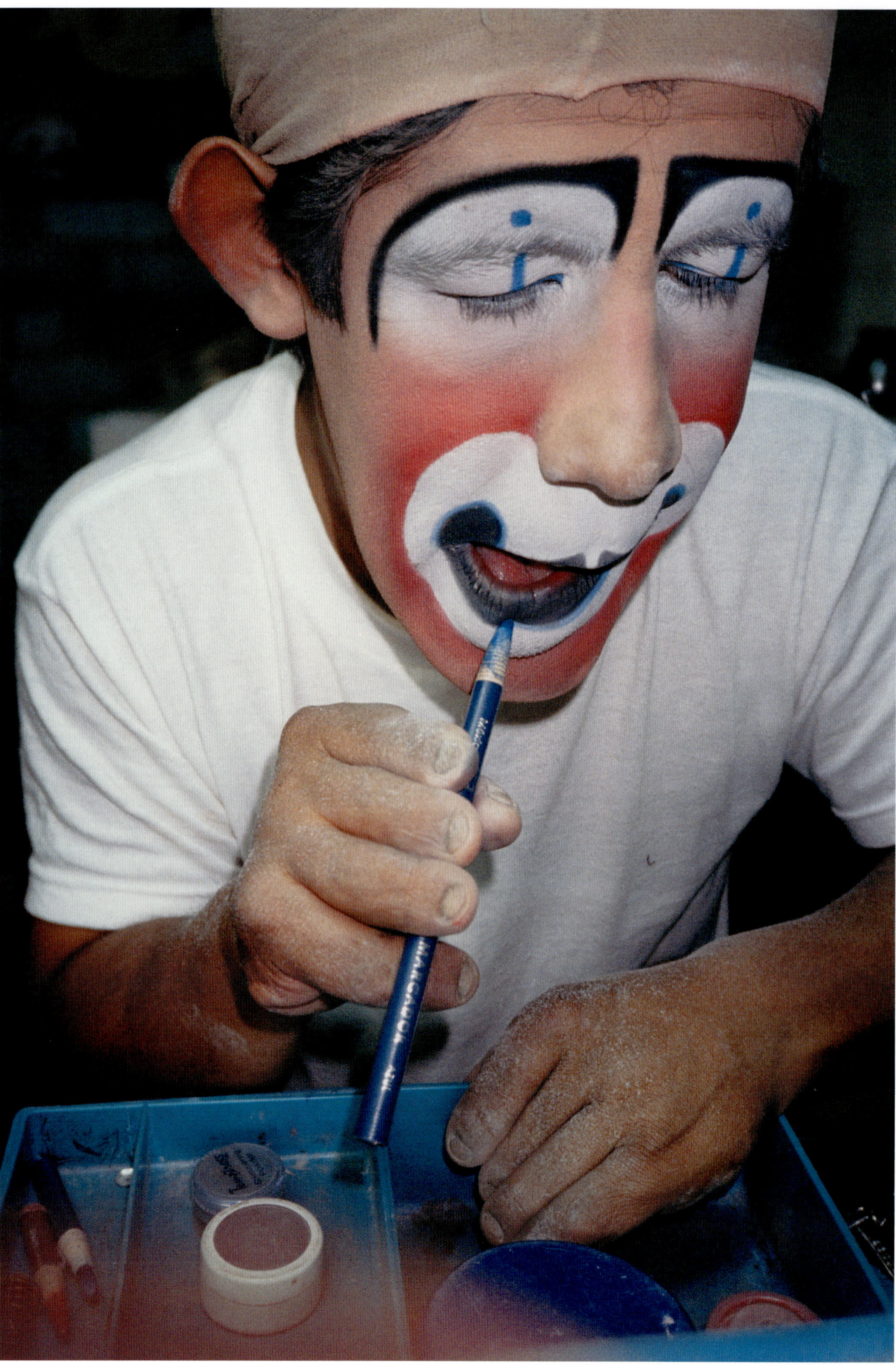

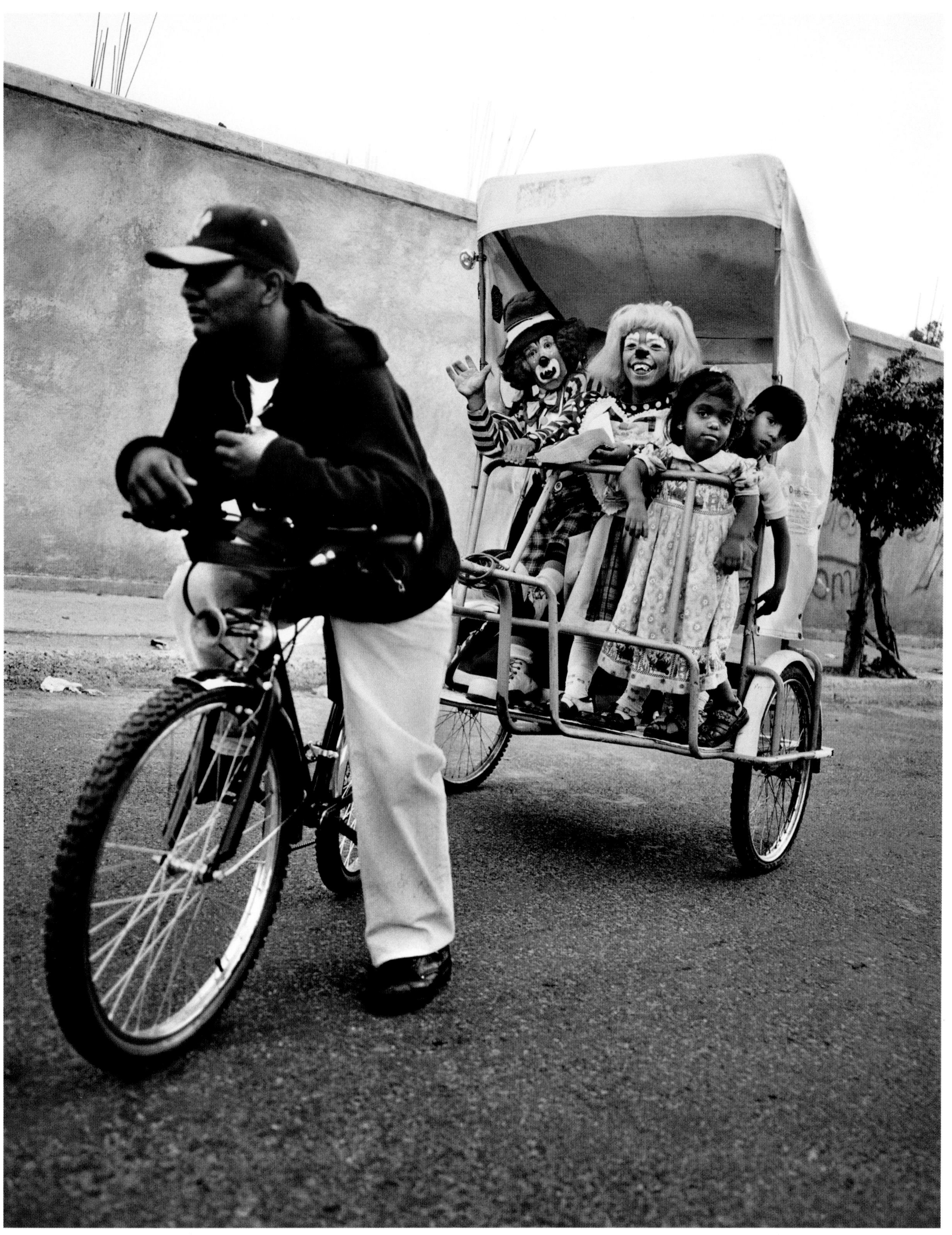

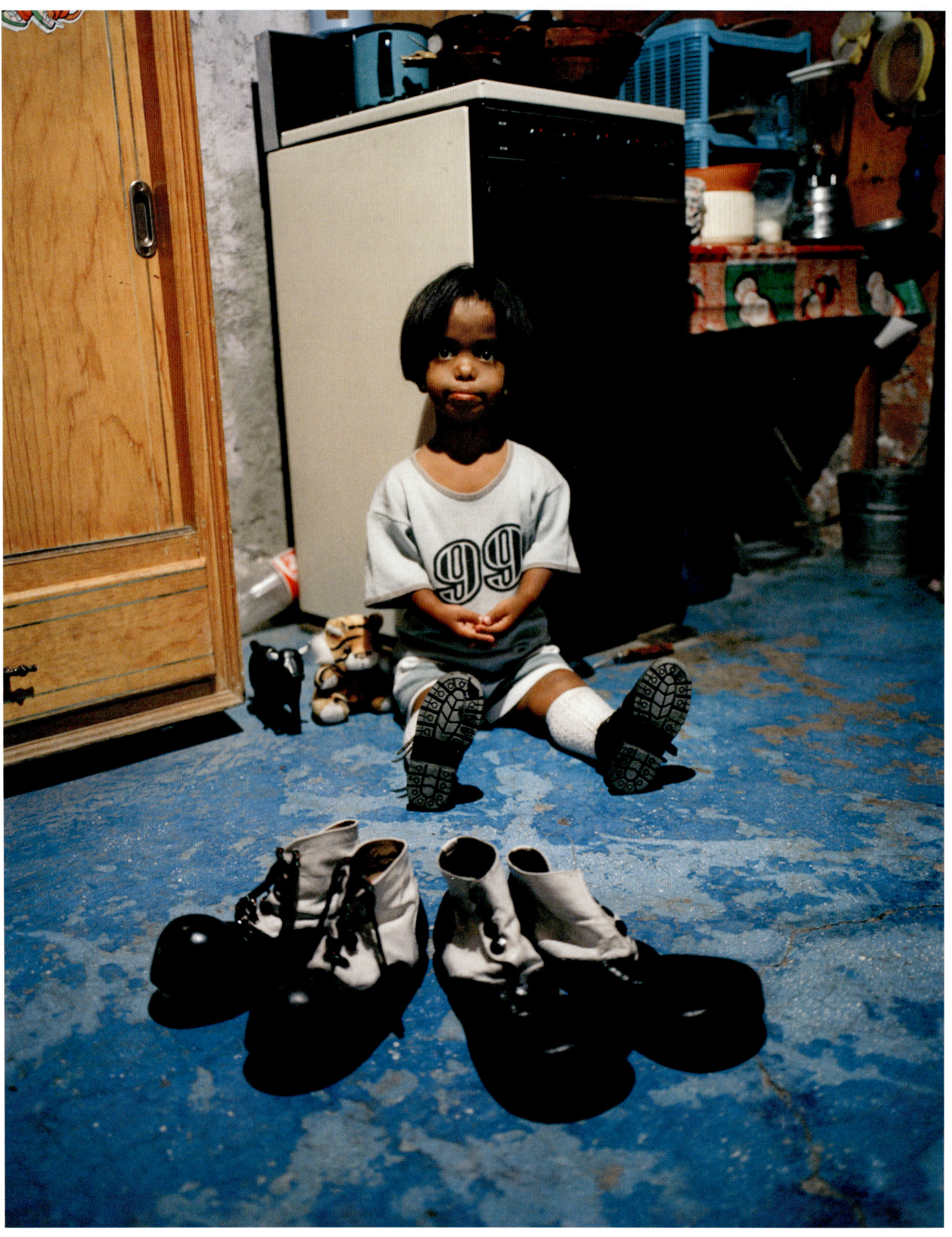

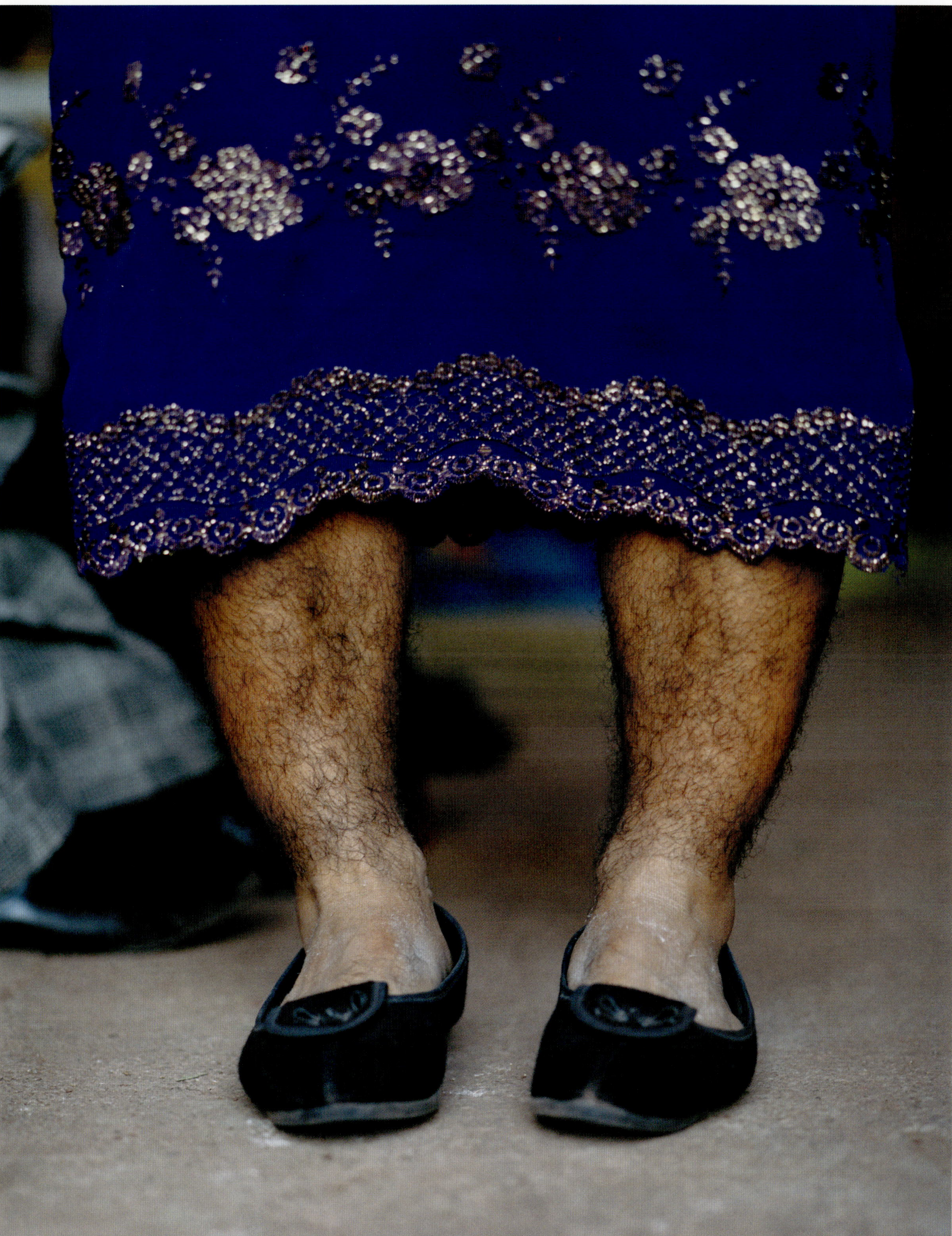

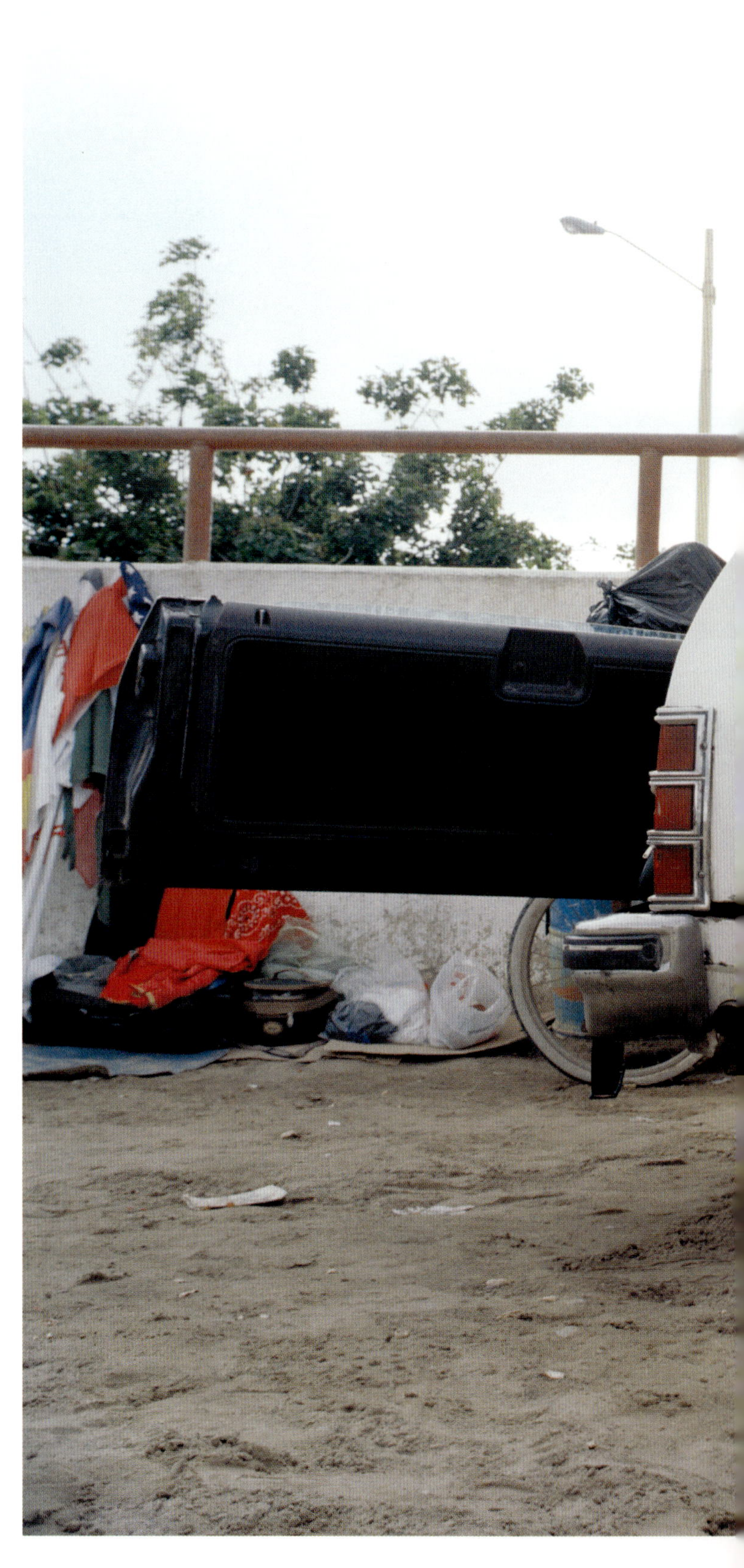

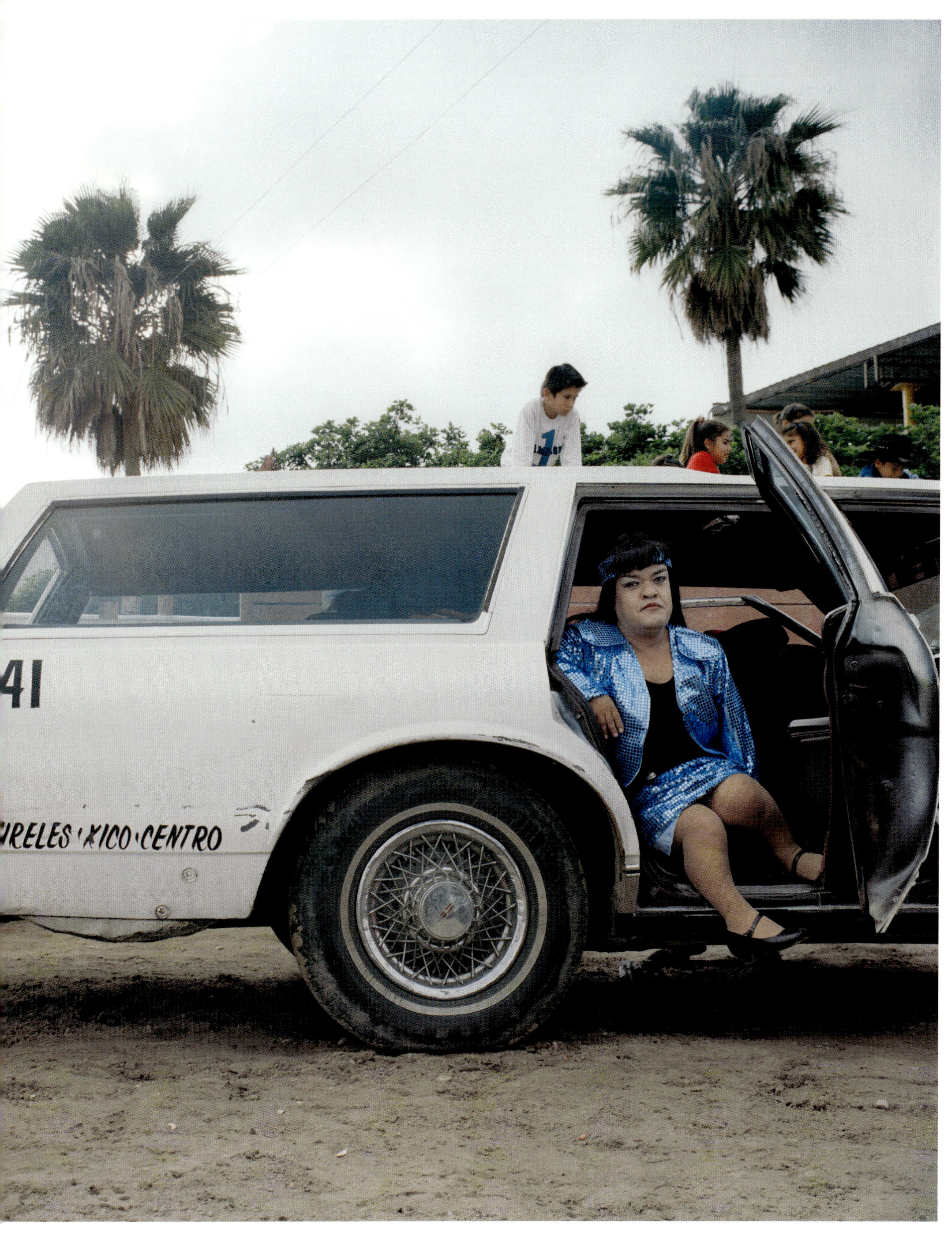
41
RELES·XICO·CENTRO

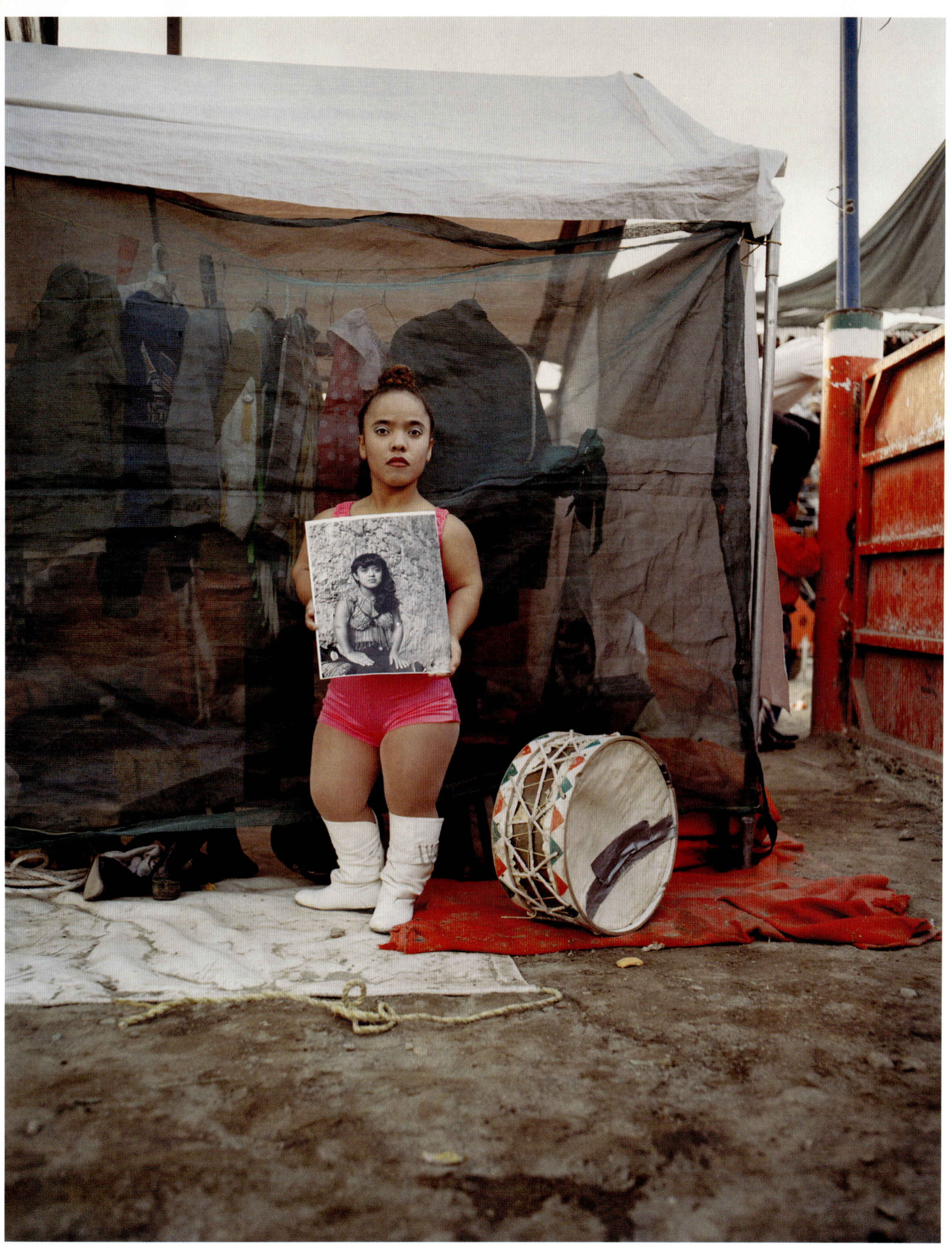

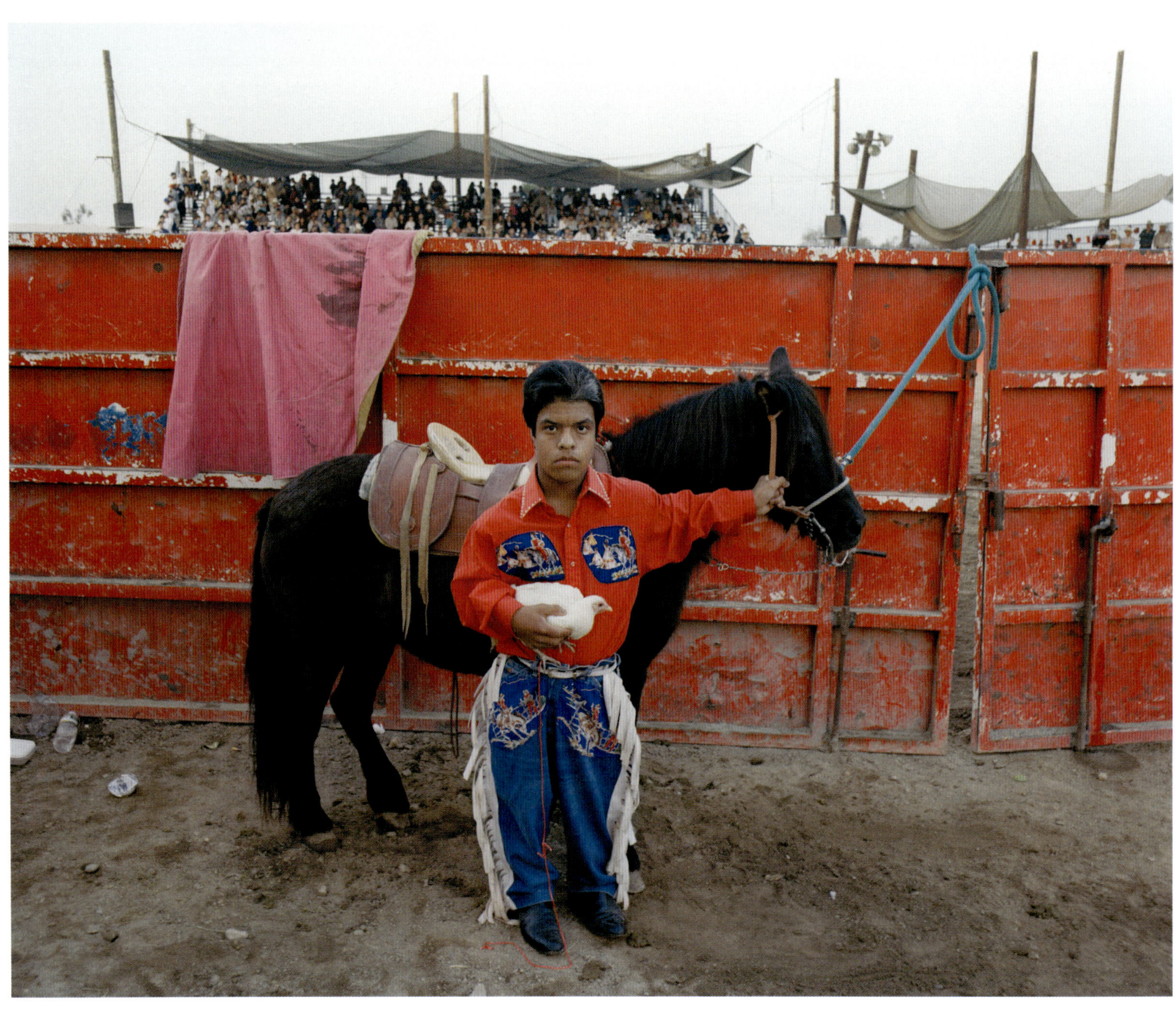

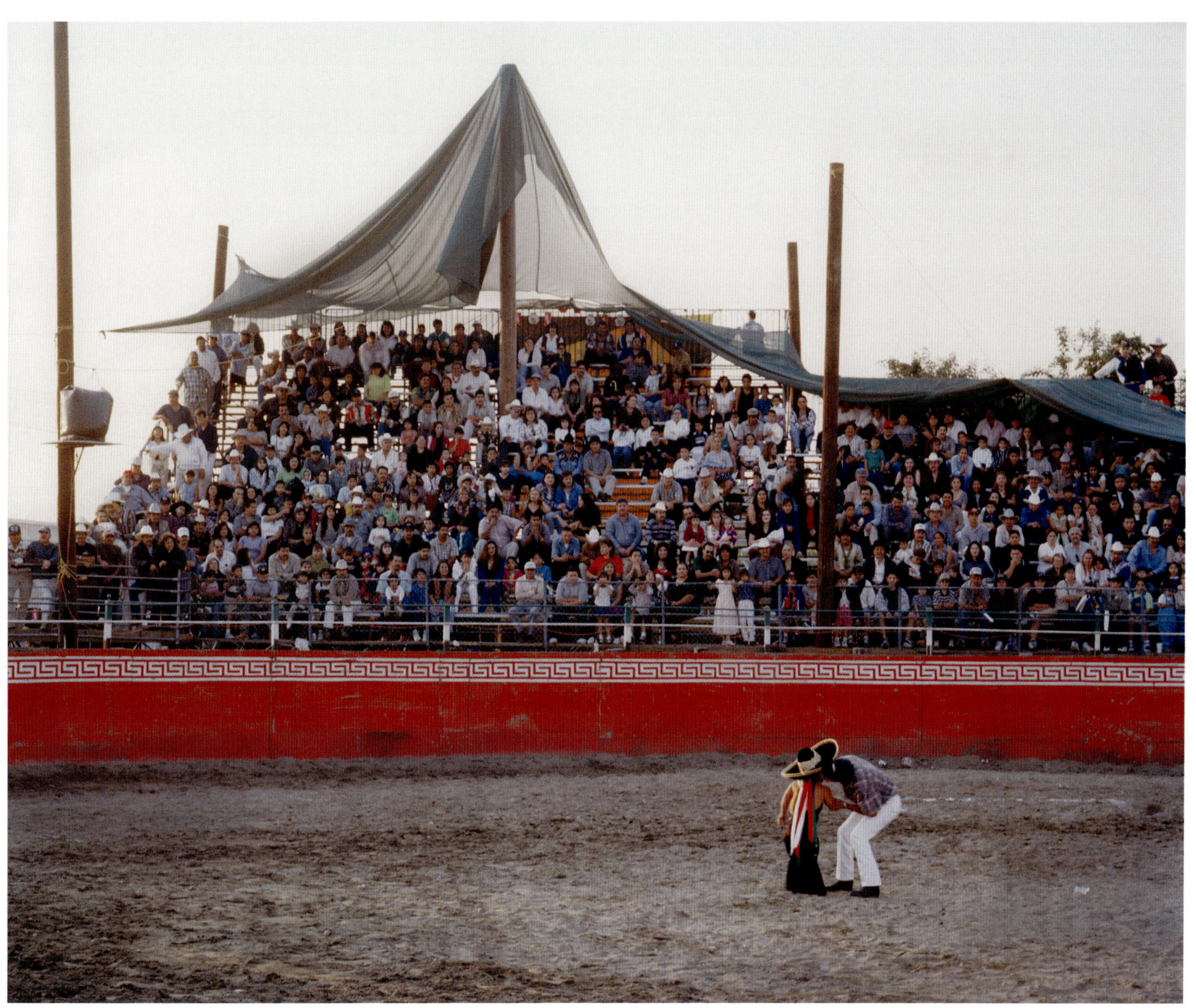

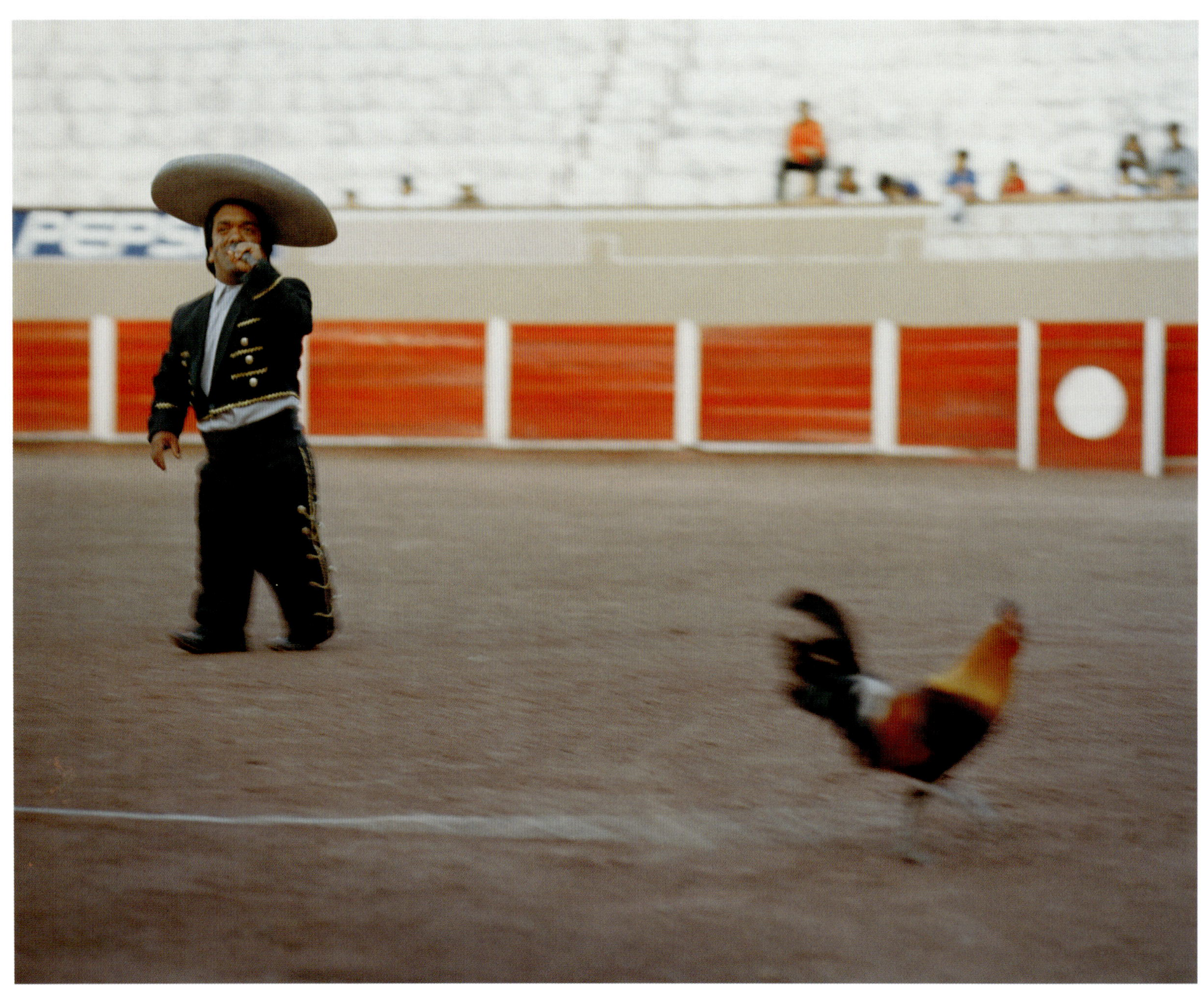
PEPSI

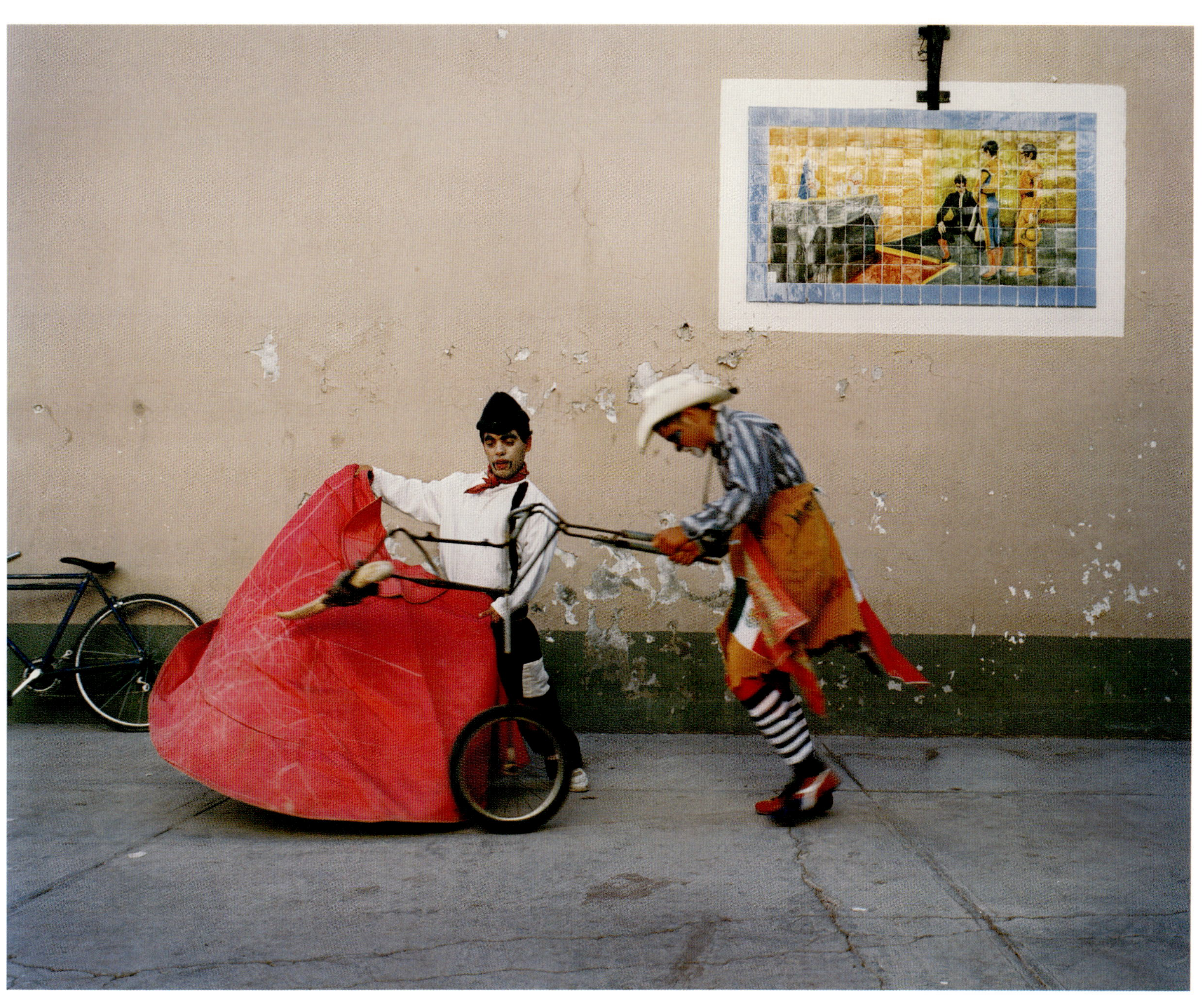

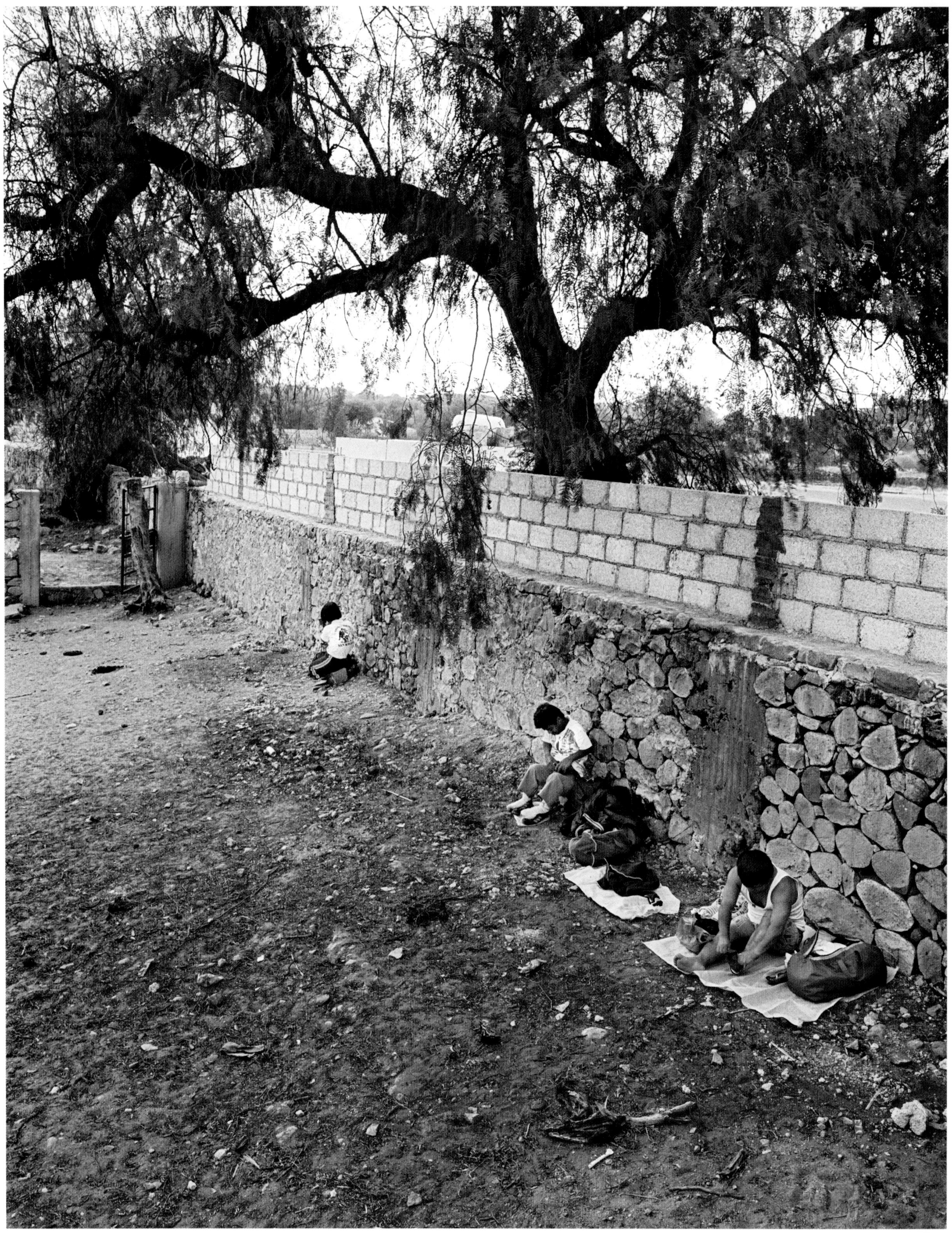

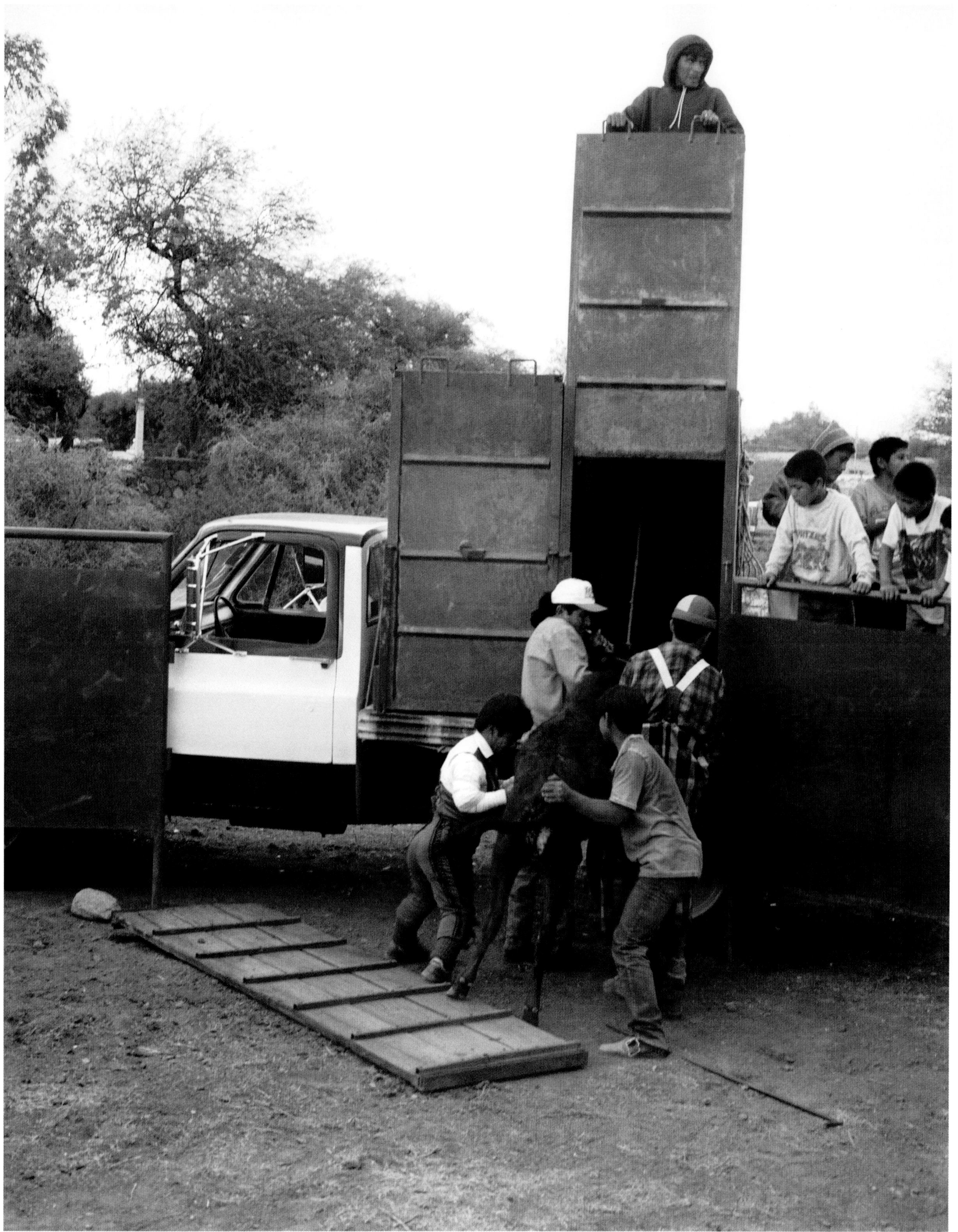

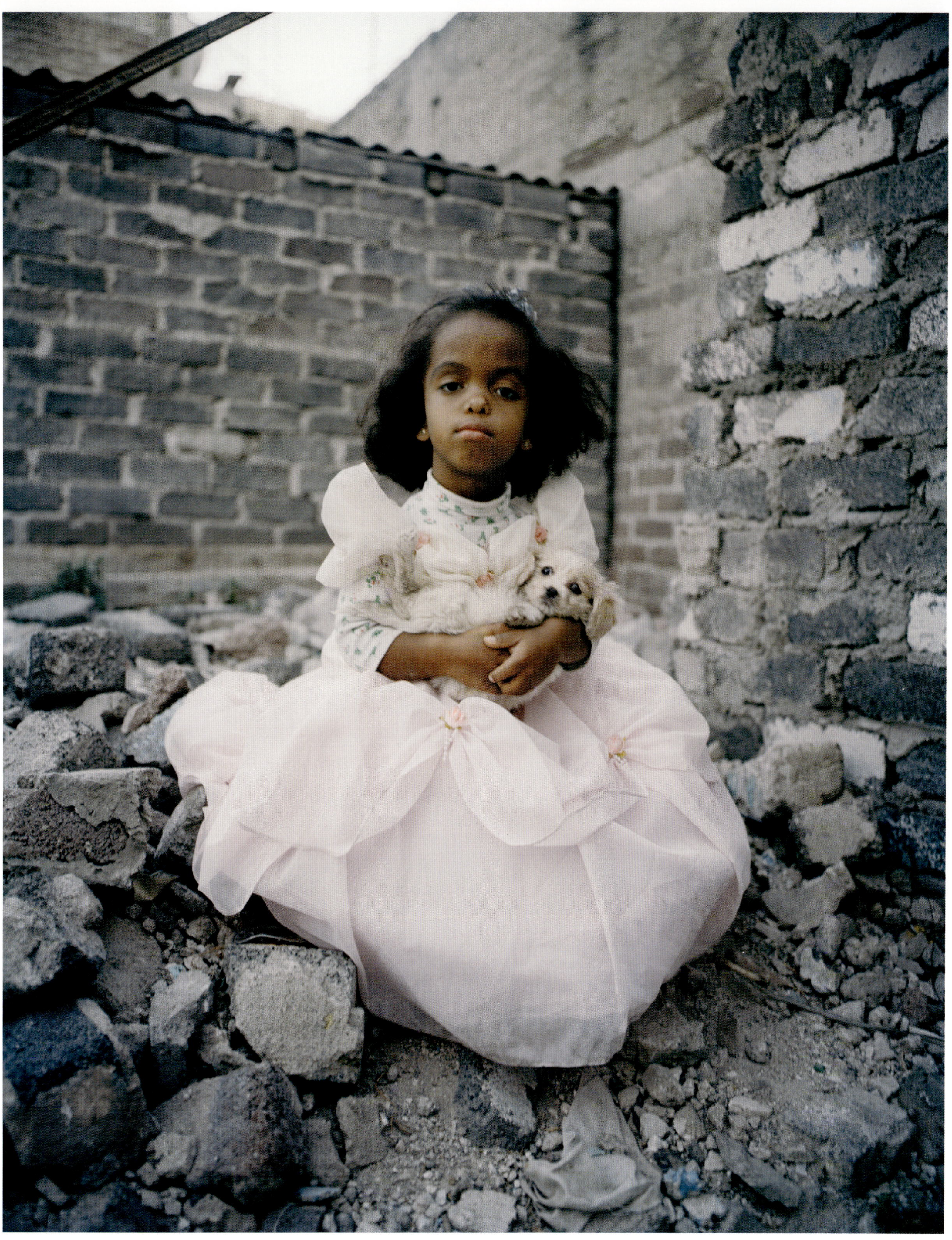

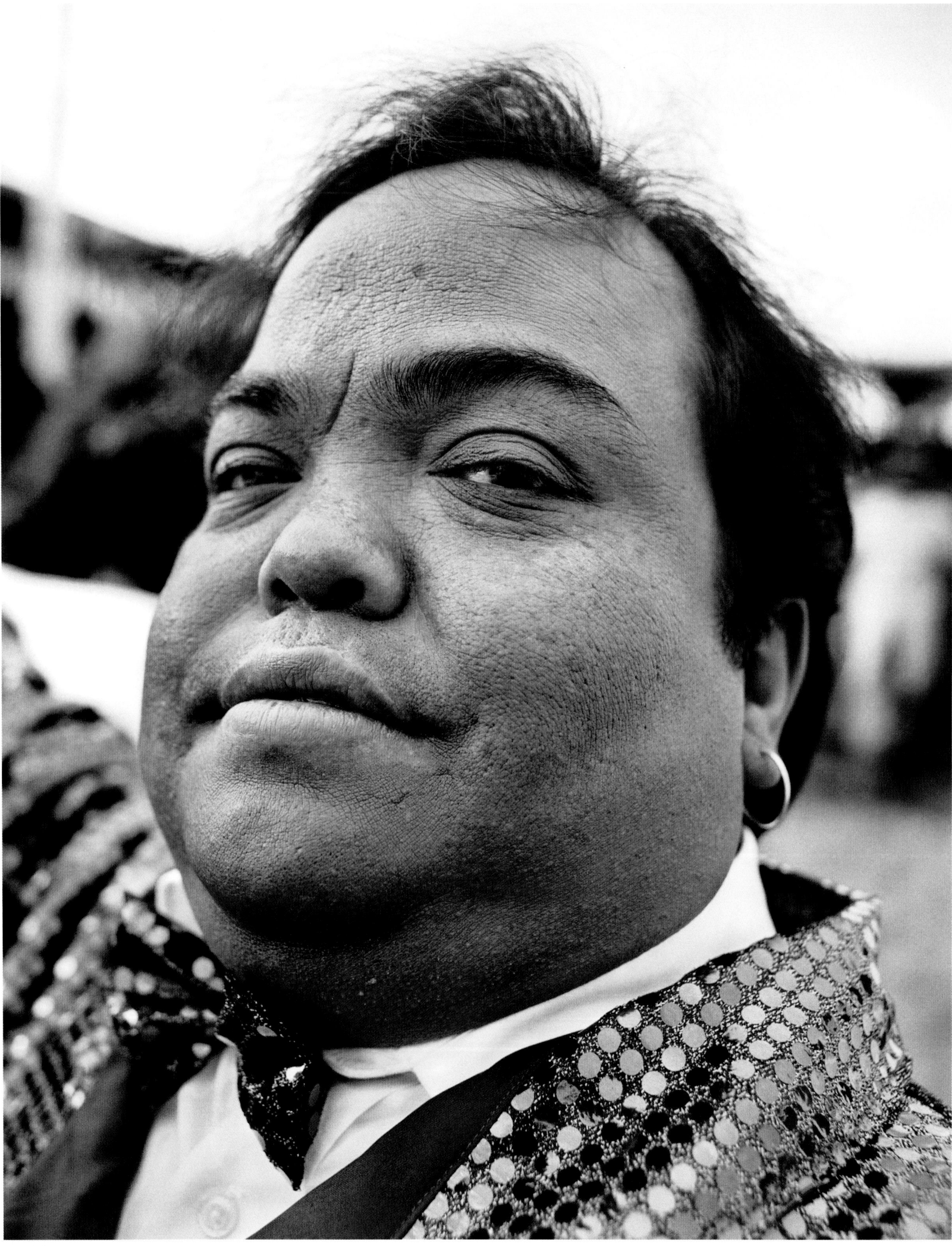

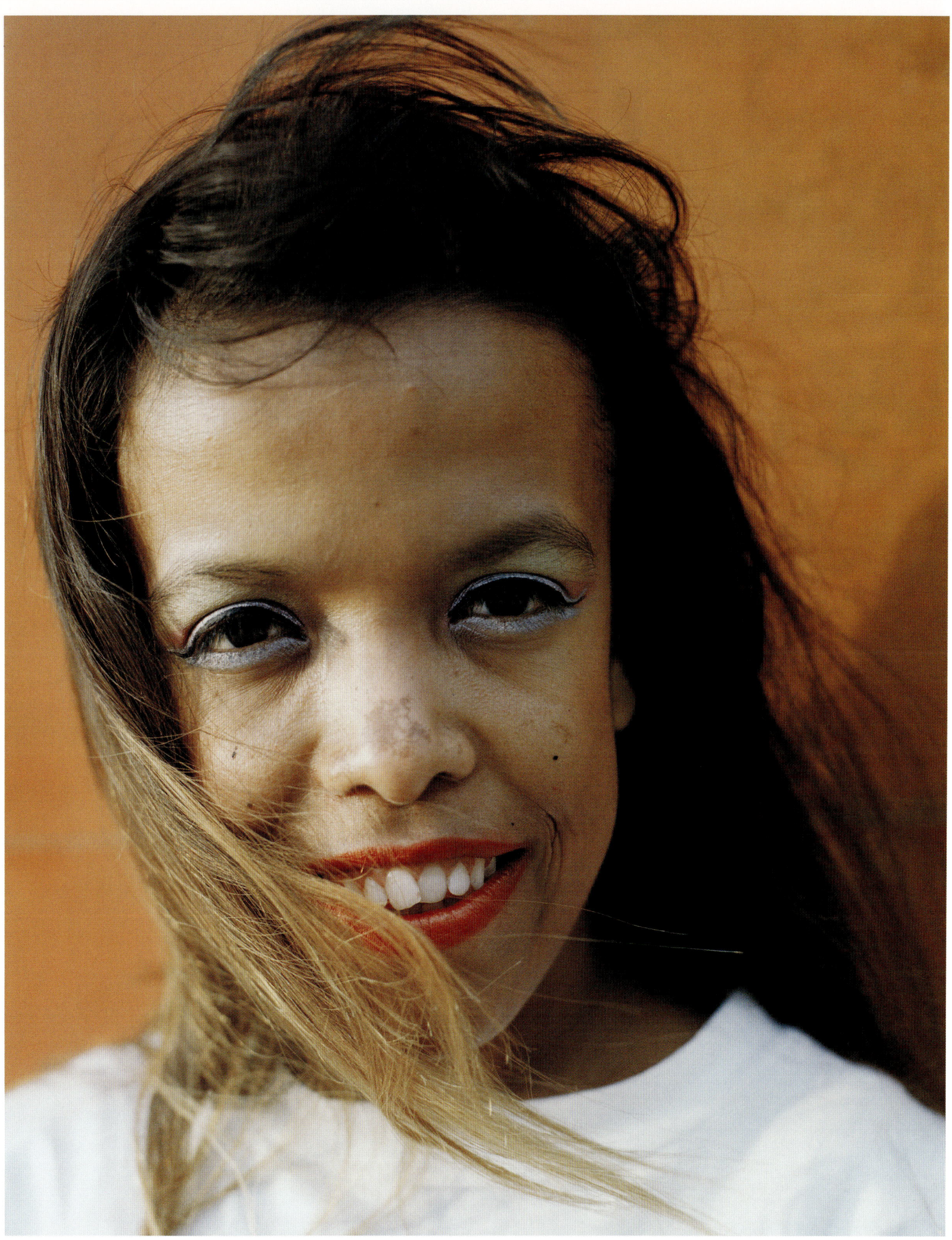

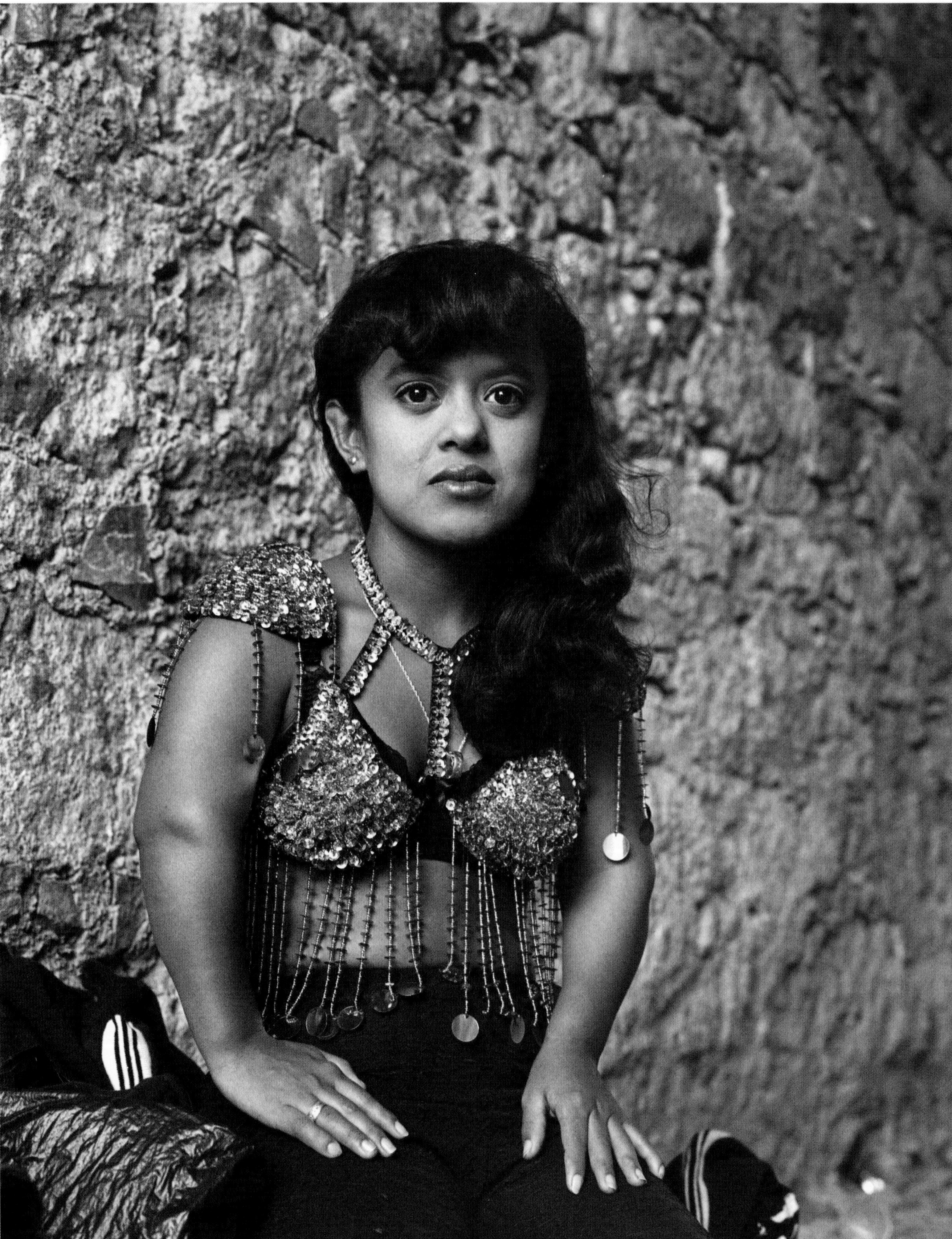

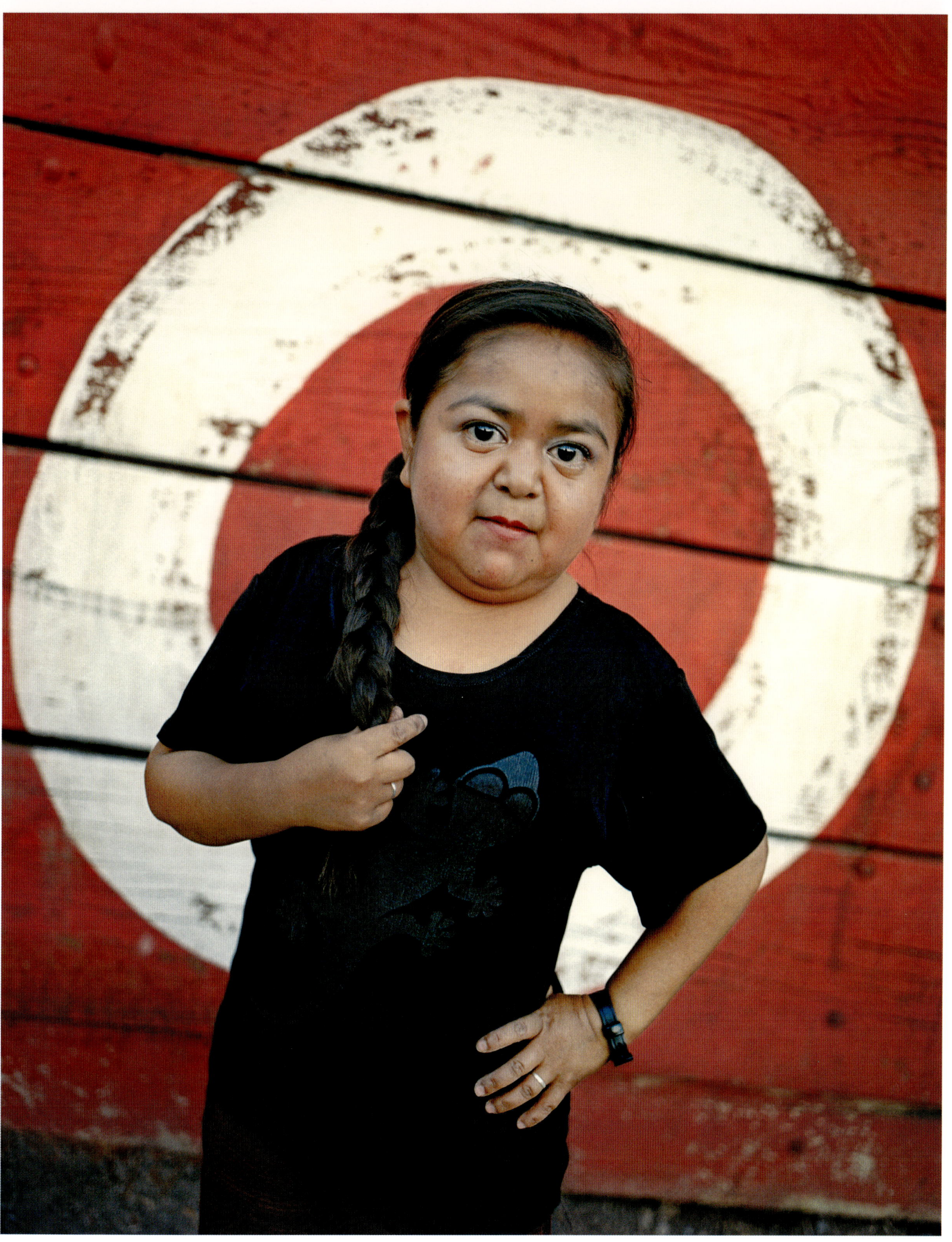

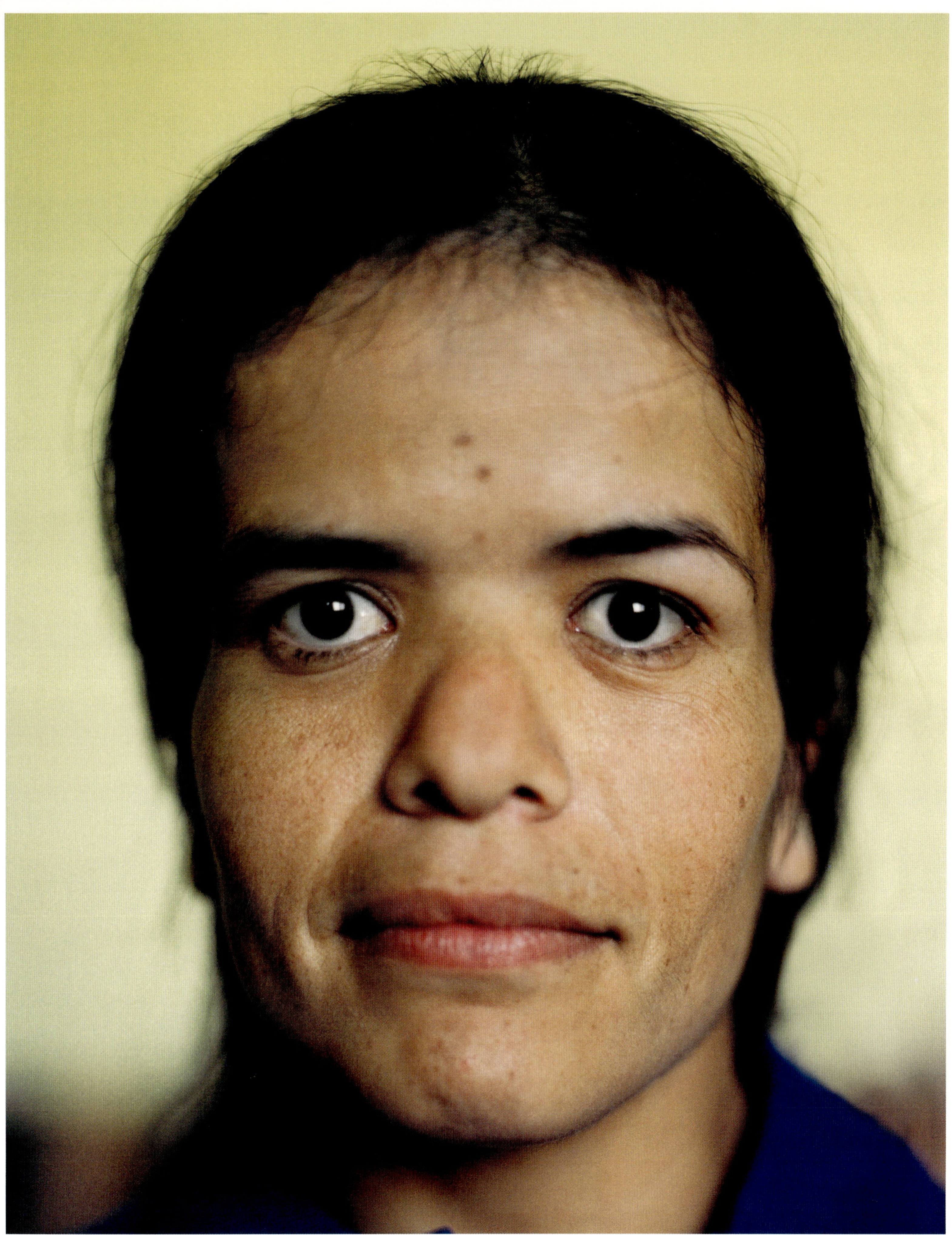

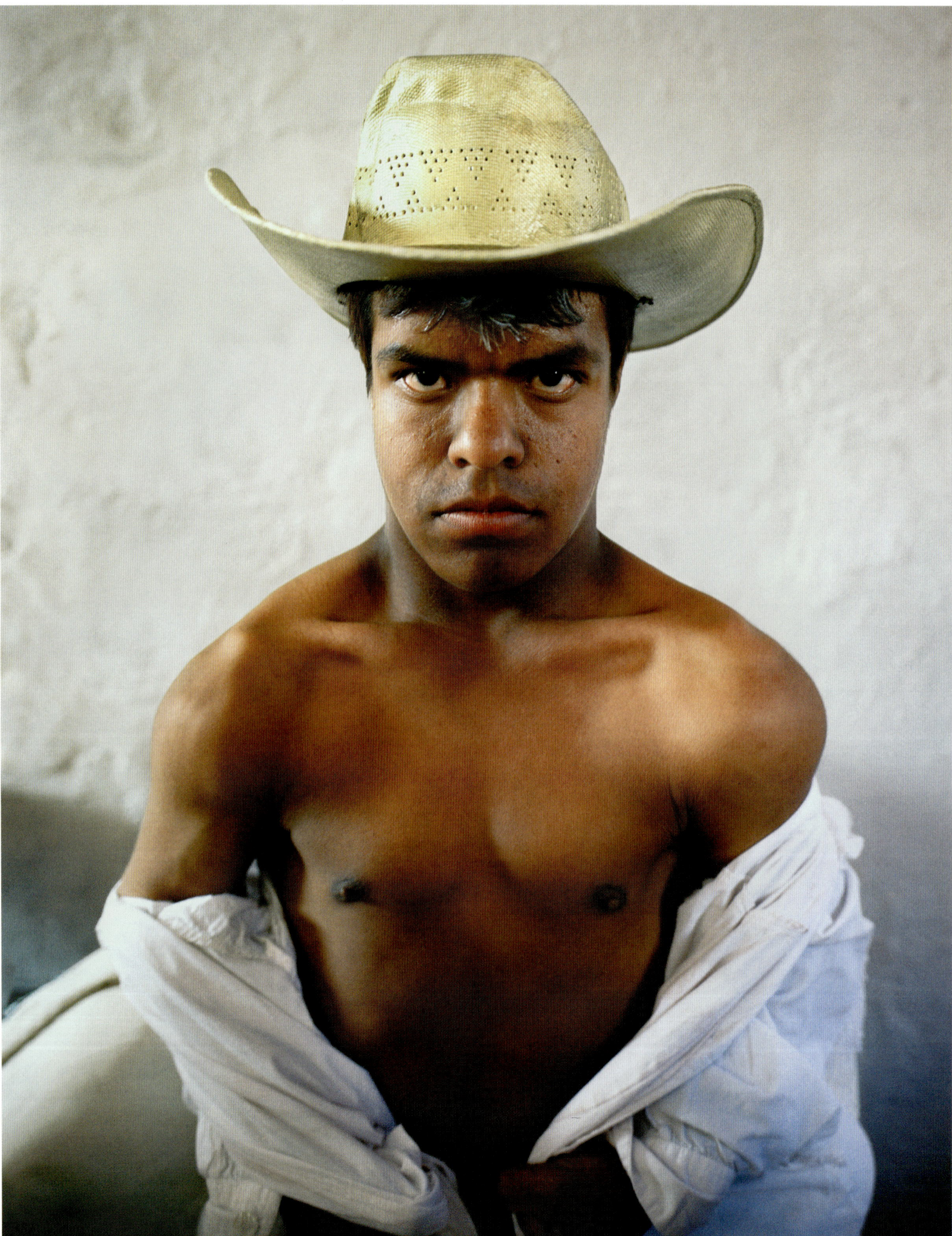

INTERVIEWS

Bullfighting started in Spain centuries ago; it goes back to the Roman circus. The first shows of Enanitos Toreros [Dwarf Bullfighters] were also started in Spain, by El Bombero Torero around the 1950s. Then the matador Ernesto San Román, El Queretano, invited El Chino y sus Enanitos Toreros to perform in Mexico. That's where San Román got the idea of doing something similar with dwarfs here in Mexico. Many people worked with him and copied his ideas. Now there are *cuadrillas* [teams of bullfighters] all around Mexico, and also in Colombia and Portugal.

El Chino Torero met me in 1979, when he saw me walking in a subway station here in Mexico City. That's how I met the Spaniards—on the street. I was very ignorant then. They found me in the subway, and they changed my life. A man called me over and offered me a job on the show. To test whether I was physically capable, he asked me for a favor: "Would you go get me a soda?" And so I ran fast. He asked me to become a bullfighter on his cuadrilla and he introduced me to other little people. He was very protective of me—when he introduced me, he said, "I don't want you guys to give him a hard time." Víctor, a Colombian, offered to teach me how to bullfight. They were all very nice. We fought bulls together, with two bullfighters holding one cape from each side as the calf passed through it. We opened the show with a live brass band from Fresnillo, Zacatecas. They'd play a *pasodoble*, and we'd enter the bullring marching and waving. I would pretend to conduct the band with a baton and then I'd circle around the bullring to greet the audience. That was my first job. I've been working in this for many years.

Now I'm on Ernesto San Román's cuadrilla. He was a matador. He is all about the fine art of bullfighting. Our wardrobe is better than other cuadrillas; we wear *trajes de luces* custom-made by tailors of formal bullfighting wear. For San Román, the actual bullfighting is more important than the musical impersonations. We perform *forcados* [facing the bull barehanded], *cruzadas,* back-to-back—all of it done by little people. The other cuadrillas just botch the Enanitos Toreros show with bad costumes and too many impersonations which have nothing to do with the art of the bullfight. They have no real affinity for bullfighting. Other cuadrillas have a charlot, which is more like a clown bullfighter, like La Güera Mitotes, a guy dressed as a transvestite who just works up the audience.

In the past, the Enanitos Toreros promoters would pay us better, and there was more work because there weren't so many cuadrillas. Now we don't get paid much—it's the same in all the other cuadrillas, only the dwarfs are different. These days, for one show we only get paid what you earn in a week working minimum wage. But in reality we're actually lucky. Thanks to being a dwarf I've traveled to a lot of places and earned a little cash, at least enough to spend on wine and women, as they say. It's each little person's business to decide how he or she wants to live their everyday life, because bullfighting isn't everything.

A lot of people come up to me and talk me up to find out whether I'm like an average-sized person, and after getting to know me they've said to me, "My respects, you're better than a lot of taller people." I'm going to tell you the truth: in sex—and I'm grateful for this—tall women have more curiosity towards dwarf men than tall men do toward little women. Women are always one step ahead of men. I think there are two kinds of curiosity: one is natural and the other one is morbid, unhealthy. For instance, when I posed for *Playboy*, I posed with naked women, and when you see so much of that, it doesn't really turn you on anymore. Here in Mexico it's rare, but in the United States and in Spain dwarfs are presented in this way more often. I've always said height means nothing if you're not smart and clever. I've done all sorts of jobs. I've done everything; I can do anything. I want to write a book about what I've done and how I've gotten where I have, because I've had a lot of obstacles and I've overcome every single one.

SAMUEL LÓPEZ "EL PATORRO" promoter

In the early years of the Enanitos Toreros the bulls were stabbed with *banderillas* and killed during the bullfights. This is no longer common practice, not by choice but for economic reasons, because they'd have to buy a new bull. The more you play a bull, the more it learns, and instead of charging toward the cape or area of movement, it aims for the bullfighter. Fight after fight, the bull becomes more and more dangerous, but it would be very expensive to replace it every time. I think that formal bullfighting developed from comic bullfighting moves, like a game of comic spectacle that later became formal. Comic bullfighting has a very rich tradition, but it has not been well-documented. It started with the *mojigangas* [a parade of giant papier-mâché puppets] with tall people, who would march through the streets of town, inviting everyone to follow them into the bullring. This practice went on for more than four centuries, until it lost popularity and disappeared. But that is where this whole idea of Enanitos Toreros comes from. Comic bullfighters and other people in the bullfighting business started incorporating dwarfs into these comedy acts, making use of their physical characteristics to make a bigger impact. Little people had never been seen that way before——even seeing them on the street was not very common. I'm talking about the 1970s. The dwarf bullfighters came here from Spain, and I think that for the first time mothers brought out their dwarf children, so they could meet other little people without the fear that they would be made fun of or stolen by the circus.

So a lot of us started looking for dwarfs. Little by little they've come out and you realize that there are little people in this country who need jobs. They had to be taught how to fight bulls and all the rituals and formalities that govern serious bullfighting. There are a lot of similarities between comic and serious, formal bullfighting. Things started to go very well for us. We got a lot of recognition from small towns, and tours through Guatemala and the United States. But in 1996, there was a big problem within people in the bullfighting business. [Promoters] started offering members of my cuadrilla more money than I was paying them, and so the group disbanded. At that point, I realized that I was still the promoter for Patorro y sus Enanitos Toreros [Patorro and His Dwarf Bullfighters], so all I had to do was recruit new little people, train them, and continue with my show. So that's what I've been doing and how things have gone for me.

I read a book that I think helped me understand and get along with little people. It's written by Og Mandino, and it's called *The Ten Commandments of Success*. The book talks about Zacchaeus, a character from the Bible who was the chief tax collector of Jericho. He was very wealthy, and he was a dwarf. Most people hated him because he worked for the Roman government. There's a passage from the bible which I think made me realize the greatness that little people can attain——something that I otherwise would not have

thought possible. It's when Jesus went to Jericho and the crowds gathered to see him. Because Zacchaeus was so short, he couldn't see Jesus through the crowd. So, he had to climb up a tree. When Jesus saw him up there, he said, "Zacchaeus, come down from that tree, because tonight I'm staying at your house." When people say that Jesus slept in the home of pagans, they're talking about the time he slept at Zacchaeus's. Christ stayed at the home of this much-hated small man, eighty centimeters tall. I think the fact that I knew this story was very helpful when I started working with little people.

GERSON VIRGEN enanito torero

We should all get a raise. Period. Rogelio [a promoter] says it's thanks to him that people come see us, thanks to him that the bullrings sell out, that everything is thanks to him. But we are all a team. Here in Mexico people won't hire you for other jobs; they just tell you, "We're not hiring, there are no jobs available," and with that they get their point across. They think that because you're short, you can't do a lot of things. That is why little people have to work in entertainment, because here in Mexico they don't get any support. It seems that in the United States, if I ask for a job and don't get it because I'm a little person, I can sue and win because it's discrimination. That's why the Enanitos Toreros have served a purpose for little people, because it has opened up a job opportunity for us, but they should raise our pay. Rogelio makes very good money——he sells the show well. But considering what we get paid, dwarfs don't have a future here in Mexico. Promoters get in this business because it's profitable. Most promoters are tall retired bullfighters or people in the entertainment business. They don't earn as much as they do with actors and singers, but the investment is less, it's less work, and they earn some profit, because this is a popular show that everybody knows of. Most promoters of Enanitos Toreros shows are despots, but since there aren't other jobs for us, we have to put up with it. My current boss is a cool guy. He's very serious. He never laughs when he is ripping us off.

People pointing at us and saying, "Look, there goes a dwarf. Look at how good he looks"——that has always happened, and will continue to happen, because as humans we are always drawn to what is different. Using the word "*enanito*" [dwarf] or "*gente pequeña*" [little person] makes no difference. Everybody knows us as Enanitos Toreros, it attracts more attention that way. But it is one thing for them to say, "There goes an enanito, look at how good he looks," and another to say, "Look at that *pinche enano* [worthless dwarf]."

CECILIA DÍAZ de MÉNDEZ impersonator

Whenever I'd go see other Enanitos' performances, I would see the women performers show off——I think it's because they knew I was watching them. Many other dwarf women didn't like me. Sometimes they wouldn't even talk to me. My friend Isabel says it might be because of my bad temper. I used to be very short-fused, or was it that I was just stuck-up? I always felt like I was the one and only. It could be because I got a lot of encouragement from my parents. My mother, who is tall, never had a complex about me being a dwarf; on the contrary, she always took me everywhere, all dressed up. I was her princess. My dad, who is short, used to tell me I was his one and only, and always he would say to me: "You are the shit!"

My father was the founder of dwarf wrestling; he worked in it for twenty-five years. Since he was a wrestler, I always felt pretty confident, and well protected. I felt that if anybody did anything to me, my dad could come out and defend me. He punched my husband, José Luis, once when we'd just started dating, and also some neighbors who got smart-mouthed.

José Luis is the only little person in his family. The odds of being born with dwarfism are like one in twenty thousand and something—it can happen to anyone. When I gave birth to Juanito, people in the hospital thought he was going to be too tiny—that he would fit inside a shoebox, and we think that's why people got curious and they would come and look at him. The doctor told us, "Everything's fine, but the baby has achondroplasia," and my husband was shocked. He'd never heard that word before, and he assumed it was a deformity, until the doctor finally explained, "The baby will be just like his mother." The doctor said it with a sad tone, like he thought we wouldn't accept it, because that's what happens with many couples, even when they are little people themselves. But I said, "Well then, he's normal." From the beginning I'd been told I was likely to give birth to a baby with dwarfism. Besides, it's as if he was born into an inheritance. My father is a dwarf, so my baby is the third generation to be born like one of us.

I feel that a lot of people approach us just out of morbid curiosity, not because they are really attracted to us as a person. You might notice little women have big curvy butts—when I was single, guys would often tell me, "I like your butt." They would say it just to hit on me, to experience what it's like to be with a small woman. They think that because we are little we have something different in other areas, and I think this is because for a long time the media has spread the image of dwarfs as horny. There are dwarfs who are willing to humiliate themselves because they need to make a dime. If they demanded more respect, people would have more admiration toward us. But even so, people still make fun of us a lot. Supposedly, if we perform in this show it is so that people will have esteem for us, so that they see that at times we can do even more than a tall person can. We don't put ourselves out there to be made fun of.

TERESA MONTIEL   impersonator

I grew up in Acapulco. My mother was tall and for a very long time the only other little person I knew was my father. Later I had David and Claudia, my two children, who are also little. My father knew nothing about the Enanitos Toreros. He has never worked in this business. When he was young, he worked as a pirate. He would dress up like a real pirate and pretend to raid a tourist yacht in Acapulco. I didn't know anything about this type of work until one day the promoter Félix Corona came to Acapulco with the Enanitos Toreros de América. I saw the advertisements and felt curious about seeing what they were like. I went to see them with Claudia, and we liked the show. When they saw us they reimbursed our money and gave us free chips and soda, and we were invited backstage to meet the performers. That's when Félix Corona and his wife asked us to come work for them. That was in November of 1995. Claudia was twelve years old and I was thirty. The next day Félix showed up at our house. He invited us to go to the beach with the Enanitos and that's where he convinced me. Two days later Claudia and I left with them to give a show in Guadalajara. David stayed in Acapulco to finish junior high school but joined us

afterwards. We all traveled together in one small van, stuffed like canned sardines. But since everything was a new experience for us, Claudia and I were mesmerized. Félix paid choreographers to teach us how to dance and walk nicely, like models do. He also got us one of those physical education coaches. He'd take us to the *Nuevo Progreso* bullring in Guadalajara every day for workouts at seven in the morning.

Before working in this environment, I worked nights for nine years as a cashier at the same place my father worked at—one of those dance bars, with loose women. My kids would see me go to that place, but it didn't make me feel embarrassed. I've never done anything to be ashamed of. I also worked ironing clothes, but I never worked as a clothes washer, because I couldn't reach the sink. There's no little people's association in Mexico City, there used to be one but they would always change presidents and make promises they couldn't keep. On one occasion they said they were going to build a restaurant and a Laundromat to scale, so we'd have a place to work, but that never happened.

I impersonate Paquita la del Barrio, a very "colorful" Mexican singer. I really like the emotion she puts into her songs—she sings with a lot of heartache and anger. All the songs are about men, about machismo. She sings to the men but in a tone that's very crass sometimes, with lyrics that make people laugh hard. She tells the poor guys a thing or two—"You're a good for nothing, worthless!"—and she even tells them what they're going to die from. My impersonation of Paquita la del Barrio is comical; given my small stature, as a dwarf, everything has to be done with humor. I come out with a lot of excitement, I dance and shake, and I have a good time. But Claudia says to me, "Mom, it doesn't even show whether you're wiggling around or not. Come on now, dance like Laura León for real!" I tell her, "I do dance, I shake it all over the place!" But she says, "Yeah, but you've gotten so chubby, it doesn't even show, no one can see it." The most important thing is the applause from the audience, and how they respond to your performance. That's where you can truly feel which number people like, by how they stand up and cheer you. When the Paquita act is introduced over the speakers, the audience stands up and applauds. They think the real Paquita will show up, but when I come out, with my pudgy cheeks, they think it's hilarious and begin to laugh. But I like that—it feels really great to be inside the ring. I give it everything I've got. I like the world of bullfighting and haven't been able to leave it. My only hope is that my granddaughter and other dwarf children don't get sucked into it because in this scene dwarfs get exploited a lot.

DAVID RODRÍGUEZ MONTIEL   enanito torero, promoter

I'm in this thing with the Enanitos Toreros, and I know pretty well how things work around here. In the ring, toward the public, it's one thing, but behind the scenes, backstage, things get handled very differently. Every dwarf has his or her story. Some are here by choice, others by necessity, to avoid feeling alone, to make friends, because they feel ignored by their own families. Some seek out company, and so we become friends. Whenever other dwarfs come to see our show we make it a point to meet them and talk to them. Sometimes, there are families with dwarf children that come see us perform. They come over to ask us if we know where they can take their children for treatment, or if we know of any social support organizations. They ask us if we are involved in one. We're not. We tell them to go ask for help from the DIF [Desarrollo Integral de la Familia, or Integral Family Development] but even there, the subject of dwarfism is largely unknown. In this scene we support each other, but it's very difficult for a family who has a baby with dwarfism. Sometimes they see us as an option. I think that by accident, we have become a gathering place for other little people. People always congratulate us and tell us that they like what we do. They think we make a good living. We don't tell them about the bad stuff, we don't spoil the fantasy. That's something we have to keep up: their illusions.

Some promoters are liars because they lead people to think that their cuadrillas are like a small foundation that protects and benefits little people. If people knew the truth——the promoters are like tyrants, they treat the Enanitos like subordinates, frightening them, almost as if they were their slaves. There are certain seasons when the promoters are only able to book one show in the entire month. They don't pay well yet they don't allow the enanitos to work for other cuadrillas, and if they do, they get fined. The pay is around three to four hundred pesos [thirty or forty dollars] per show, and then, if they don't hand out enough flyers, they get fined fifty or one hundred pesos. They make you hand out flyers, and when you're done, they put you on a van for, like, two hours to advertise the show. Not even in the back of a pickup truck——no, they sit you on the roof of a van, and you're fucked if you fall off. They drive you around and around the whole town, under that burning afternoon sun. You end up exhausted and after all that, what energy do you have left for work? None; there's nothing left at all.

One time my friends Cucuy and Lupillo and I went to work for some promoters in El Grullo, a town in Jalisco. The seats sold out for the first show and lot of people couldn't get in. So they offered a second show to follow right after, and the plaza sold out again. They paid us four hundred pesos for the first show, and for the second show they only wanted to pay us two hundred. Lupillo and I protested, we said, "But why? That isn't fair! Pay us another four hundred!" "Actually, fifty percent is the norm." They finally said, "We'll give you another hundred, but not two hundred." So we said, "No, we quit!" "What do you mean, you quit?" "We quit." The promoter's husband got really aggressive. Lupillo and I refused to work, but Cucuy didn't, and when he was mounting a calf, he fell off. The calf ran after him, and Cucuy jumped over the partition wall, fell on his head and bam! He twisted his neck. Somebody called in the ambulance and the first-aid guys carried him off and put a neck brace on him. But since there was no one to replace him, the promoter told him, "Don't worry, son, with an aspirin you'll be just fine." And she took off his neck brace and forced him to work. That's where I realized how shameless the promoters can be. There are a lot of very dark things in this scene. Sometimes I feel like putting up a website with all of this and telling people how things really are. How can they think they are helping dwarfs? Then some promoters form cuadrillas with dwarfs that don't know a thing about bullfighting, and they throw them in the bullring. Some of them get hurt because they don't know what they're doing. We could avoid getting treated this way if we organized an association, but we are not very united.

IMELDA LARA VILLEGAS homemaker

I was in Santiaguito, my hometown, when suddenly the Enanitos Toreros came around to do a show. They ended up at my house because a bunch of nosy kids told them, "There's a dwarf in this town, she's at home, but she doesn't want to come out right now." And my sister said to me, "Take a look outside——what could they possibly do to you?" "Nothing," I said, but I was embarrassed. Before then I'd never spoken with another

dwarf. Once I went to Guadalajara with my whole family, to go shopping at the Wal-Mart there, and that's where I saw another dwarf for the first time. He was sitting on a bench by himself just looking around, and my brother said, "Look, there's someone just like you." I looked him up and down, scrutinized everything about him——and I was thinking, "Let's see, is he handsome, is he good-looking, would he make a good husband for me?" I stared at him and felt like being his friend, but then we went into the store and I didn't get a chance to talk to him. I looked for him when we came out, but he wasn't there anymore. Now I'm thirty years old. When the Wal-Mart thing happened, I must have been about twenty-one.

I'd often get told there was another little person in Amatitlán, a town near Santiaguito. They said they'd get us mixed up, that she looked a lot like me. I was very curious to meet her. Then one day my father said, "If you want to meet her, I'll take you, because her father is a distant relative of mine. Let's go so you can meet her and make a friend." We planned it with her, but when we got there, she wasn't around. We got tired of waiting for her and left. I finally saw her at the fiesta of Santa Cruz in my town, on May 3. I was walking behind her with my brother and sister, because in my town it is a tradition to walk around the square to meet boys. One walks and circles around the square and the boys throw compliments at you, they throw flowers and confetti and say, "*Adiooooos mamacita,*" or, "Can I walk along with you?" If you like the guy, well ,you accept. Then if you talk and want to get to know him better, he'll say "I'll call you on such and such a day," and that's how you end up dating. I was walking behind her and since they said we looked so much alike, I was criticizing her. I would say to my brother, "How can they mix us up when she's so ugly?" She didn't even acknowledge me, I just noticed she would look at me out of the corner of her eye. She disappeared into the crowd and I never saw her again.

Four years passed after that incident in the square, until the Enanitos Toreros showed up at my house. I finally got the nerve to go out and greet them and they invited me to come see their show but I refused. "Why don't you come in and have a seat instead?" I offered them a soda and *pozole,* and they stayed for lunch. And that's when I noticed David, but he was Yolis's boyfriend then. I remember seeing David with all his teeth, though they say that by then he was already missing some. I don't know, he seemed perfect to me, because to be honest with you, I really liked him. My sisters told me that it looked like David was interested in me, because his eyes followed me everywhere. When they left, my sister said, "How could you find any of them handsome when they are all so short and ugly? If you marry a dwarf you'll be embarrassed because you'll have to carry him around. You should marry a tall guy." And I told her, "No, because a big tall guy with a little woman is just not a good match. If you discriminate against someone it's because you yourself have a complex about something; that's why you think that way."

The Enanitos gave us tickets to see their show. We went and it was cool. I thought it was very beautiful. When the show ended they told me to join them and work together: "You can earn some money, travel to the United States, and all over Mexico." But I didn't like traveling——I almost never left the house. In my hometown they grow *mezcal,* sugarcane, *nopal,* guava——those are the things I know about. It's not the same to go to nearby towns like Amatitlán or Tequila, but traveling anywhere farther . . . no, it's not for me. Four years went by, and then one fine day David showed up all by himself. His excuse was that he was there to rent the bullring for an Enanitos Toreros show. But later he told me that he came just to find me, because he'd been told that I'd gotten married, had children, and wasn't living in town anymore. I don't know who told him, but he came to see if it was true. All the men in my town are very possessive and all of the people who live here are related, everyone has the last names López, Sánchez, or Hermosillo. Men kidnap their girlfriends here, and if a girl starts dating a guy from another town, they wait for him in the middle of the highway to beat him up and threaten him so he leaves her. In my family there are twelve of us, and the men in my household are also very possessive of their women.

When he got here, David sat near the bullring because it's right next to my house. Earlier that same day I went to the market in Arenal and on the way back we both boarded the same bus. I was sitting up front, and David went straight to the far back. We didn't say hello, because as soon as he got on, all the passengers started teasing us: "Imelda, here comes your boyfriend." The bus driver kept at it: "Look, it's your boyfriend, you make a nice couple. You better catch him or you'll stay a spinster—you're already thirty!" They also teased him: "Look at her, she's pretty, hardworking, she's perfect for you, she even makes tortillas by hand. She's an excellent homemaker." They went on and on, teasing him, because everyone knows me around here.

After that we each went our own way. Then a little bit later he showed up at my house. "Is Imelda home?" He didn't forget my name, even after four years, he still remembered me. I asked him if he was hungry, and we ate together, by ourselves, because at that time my parents still trusted me. We started seeing each other just as friends and I thought, "Let's see what happens, but I'm not going to pay too much attention to him." But suddenly things happened. I started feeling a little nervous, my heart was beating really fast, like this, I don't know, it gives you goose bumps. A few days later I got sick, and my mother took me to the doctor. David called, and my brother told him that I was in the hospital. And he rushed here all the way from Guadalajara. In the end I didn't have anything serious. When I returned home that afternoon, he was sitting on a tree trunk outside my house waiting for me. He surprised me. I said, "Mom, look who's here!" And she said, "Ooooh, I think he likes you." I told my mom I just couldn't stand him, and my mom said, "That's what all women say, then they marry the guy. Look at your sister: when she was dating, she also said her boyfriend was annoying, that she did not love him, and she was going to leave him. And now look at her—she already has two kids." "But mom, it's true, I really can't stand him." "Don't even say that, because you'll end up marrying him." And yes, what she said turned out to be true.

At first, people in Santiaguito were cool about him. When the workers with the agave truck would see him walking on the side of the highway they would stop and ask him, "Are you going to Imelda's?" And since they knew where I lived, they'd drop him off at my front door. But when they saw things getting serious between us, a lot of people in town stopped talking to him. Some even told him he'd better stop coming around or they were going to do something to him. I was actually worried for him, because they had beaten up the boyfriend of a neighbor. They would lie to him and say that I was moving to the United States. One day we were talking and suddenly he got a little fresh and tried to steal a kiss from me. I warned him, "If you kiss me, I'm going to slap you, I'm going to kick you out, and you will never see me again." He would say, "Just one little kiss." I would say, "No! Why should I? We're not even dating!" "Come on, say yes!" "I already said no!" The truth is that I was just really nervous because I'd never been kissed before.

Two days or so before his birthday, he stole a kiss from me, and this time I just sat there and allowed it. I didn't know how to kiss or anything, and he said, "Well, learn! Look, it's like this, and it's like this." And then he said, "I'm going to talk to your parents and ask them for permission to be your boyfriend," and they gave it to him.

We kept seeing each other for four or five months and as things got more serious we started thinking about getting married. That's when my family changed their mind about him, because they found out that he wasn't a Catholic. Then people in town started spreading rumors about him—that he was a drunk, a scrounger—all lies, but since my parents believe everything, things got difficult. My father started cutting our time together short. Sometimes he'd only let him say hello to me and then make him leave. It would make me sad because he would come from so far, tired, sun-dazed and wanting to see me. Then they told David, "Imelda's no good for you, she's very lazy, she doesn't know how to do anything. She doesn't even know how to cook." They said it so he'd get disappointed and leave me.

One day he arrived in a taxicab from Guadalajara and told me, "Let's talk like we usually do, and when nobody is watching, let's jump in the cab and run away together." But a woman from town noticed something suspicious and warned my mother, "Come look, the guy arrived in that taxicab, and he's probably going to take her with him." So my mother screamed at me: "Get in the house." David kept saying, "Let's go, let's go." But we couldn't because my brother grabbed me and locked me inside the house. My father came home a little later and gave me a serious beating. My legs got all bruised and I couldn't even walk.

Another day, the agave workers' truck came by, and David asked the driver for a lift and he said yes. He didn't tell him we were running away. When he saw the two of us get in together, he said, "Why didn't you tell me what was going on?" and he stepped on the gas so they wouldn't catch us. He took us to Arenal. There we got into a taxi, and the driver said, "I'll take you, but give me a location where you won't be living, because I don't want your parents asking me where I took you to. This way I can't deny telling them I don't know." He left us at the Plaza del Sol shopping center. From there we came to Guadalajara and moved in together. Now we have Emilio. He's six months old. My parents haven't met him because we haven't baptized him.

EZEQUIEL VIRGEN   enanito torero, promoter

I was training to become a wrestler, and my dream was to wrestle in the Triple-A division and be on television, like a brother of mine, who is a wrestler in the mini-wrestling category. In my family four of us are dwarfs, and the other seven are tall. The four short ones are Enanitos Toreros. There didn't used to be any dwarfs in our family—well, maybe before, because it's a gene that takes about five generations to reappear, like being blue-eyed, which shows up all of a sudden.

I used to work washing freight trucks at the wholesale market. I met a guy there who used to tell me, "There's a group of Enanitos Toreros near where I live and they're going on tour. Don't you want to join them?" A week went by and I didn't go, and then another, and this guy kept asking me every day. I would hide from him because it was tiring. I didn't want to go. I didn't like the idea because I wanted to be a wrestler——and I felt that the Enanitos Toreros promoters exploited dwarfs, they would put costumes and wigs on them and dress them up like puppets so people would laugh at them. But still, one day I decided to join the Enanitos Toreros to try my luck and to get out of the poverty I was living in.

It's hard to get used to in the beginning. It takes time to realize that the whole world is a spectacle. This is just one more spectacle, but it's a show by little people meant to entertain tall people. But when the bull comes out into the ring and we manage to overpower it, then people's attitude toward us changes and they see us with respect, they leave with a different mindset about dwarfs. Thanks to this work, people have begun to understand that we're regular people, with a slight disability which is our small stature, but with the same big mindset and a big heart with feelings, ideas, and goals. It's not as if the world is off-limits to you because you're short. When you learn to laugh at yourself, you can entertain people and you can have a good time yourself. You stop having a complex about it. If you don't manage to get over that phase, you can stay in that rut your entire life. That's what I learned with the Enanitos Toreros. In the end, I got into this wholeheartedly——I became a bullfighter and I like it very much. Read my T-shirt. It says, "DWARF BULLFIGHTERS." If you stop bullfighting, you're no longer a dwarf bullfighter, you're simply a dwarf.

We spent three years working for a promoter named Félix Corona. That's where I met Claudia and we started dating. Then we went with other promoters that paid us very little. We began to dream about not working for anyone but ourselves. One day, after many years of working for tall promoters, we decided to form our own independent group. Now we have our own company. You feel like you've taken a step forward. We risk our lives. The calves see you, and they don't care if you're tall, short, fat, or skinny. If you don't know how to bullfight, you're going to get gored, and if you're not careful you can end up an invalid or even get yourself killed. The enanitos are the ones taking all of the risks.

Promoters go to small towns, they find some dwarfs, they train them, teach them to dance, and they enslave them by paying them a pittance. Thank God we finally got tired of that. You know what finally provoked us to form our own company? A promoter who owed us back wages. One day we showed up to work for him at a bullring and saw that the plaza was packed, and he still didn't want to pay his debt to us. We all told him we weren't going to perform until he paid up. We said, "And another thing: you have to give us a raise!" That's when he started crying and saying, "My *gachí* [woman] left me, this money is child support for my three children," and it wasn't true.

On another occasion, we were coming back from Mazatlán to Guadalajara after a show one night, and I asked the promoter, "Hey, aren't you guys going to feed us dinner?" He said, "Yes, we'll stop in the next town." I fell asleep and woke up around ten at night. "What's up? Are we going to eat soon?" He said, "Yes, in the next town." And I fell asleep again. I woke up again around one in the morning and told him, "Felipe, why don't we stop for some food? Claudia and the kids are with me." And he said, "I didn't do so well, so I don't have enough money to pay for dinner." So it turns out that if they don't do well, they don't feed you. That's when I said, "Enough." When all the Enanitos Toreros become independent, they're going to tell all the promoters to go to hell.

The bullfighting tradition is weakening and it's slowly disappearing. It's pushed aside by the two hours of comedy acts, musical impersonations, motorcycle stunts, and everything else they've added. People have gotten used to the comedy acts and they don't even remember the Enanitos Toreros. Many kids don't go to bullfights because they get scared when the bulls are killed, because when a child sees blood he gets frightened. But since the Enanitos Toreros are a family show, there's no blood here. In the United States they treat animals better than they treat us. One day we were bullfighting in Chicago and the calf really messed with us, it knocked us over, flipped us up in the air and everything. When we put a rope around its neck, the gringo security guards said, "Take the rope off the bull." Animals have more rights. It's the total opposite in Chiapas. The promoter let out a cow that had just given birth and she was really fierce. We were bullfighting when the cow suddenly keeled over and didn't get up again. It died that very instant and the audience was laughing hysterically——they thought it was hilarious. Here in Mexico they support two causes: that you beat the animal and that the animal beats you.

There is one very important point about bullfighting: people come to the show to watch you get mauled by the bull, to see it beat the crap out of you. Once I was bullfighting and the calf flipped me over and stomped all over me. I stood up, and it struck me down again. The audience was dying of laughter and clapping like mad. You know what the difference is between country people and city people? City people want to see a clean, purebred animal; they want to see artful *faenas* [traditional bullfighting passes]. Country people come to watch the animal beat the crap out of you.

In the United States, people are more considerate toward their animals. I don't know how they are with their dwarfs. Here in Mexico, even cops say things to you. They say, "*Enano, pinche enano,*" and one gets used to it. Once at a restaurant here in Guadalajara, a friend who is also a dwarf introduced me to a very well-educated woman. Since I met her through him, I assumed she understood the concept of little people. While talking, she said to me, "You know, I don't like it when people make fun of you guys, I don't make fun of you. I've helped children with Down syndrome, children with cancer, and more than anything, I feel sorry for people like you." She said it so seriously, I couldn't believe it. She basically said, "I don't make fun of you, I pity you." She wrecked me.

GUSTAVO VÁZQUEZ BUENDÍA enanito torero, promoter

Many promoters don't treat dwarfs very well at all. That's why my wife Isabel and I formed our own cuadrilla, made up only of dwarfs, so that we can be our own bosses. Some of the enanitos who work for us end up leaving because they think we are getting wealthy at their expense. But even if we barely earn enough to pay all of us the same, we'll take on the driving and the running around, all the tiring stuff. Their only thought is, "They are making money, they are exploiting us." Well, if that were true, I should own a house by now, drive a brand-new car. But our goal is to unite for a common cause, so that we can all have a job. Sometimes there isn't enough money to pay wages but, well, I never give anyone the runaround. I tell them, "Don't ask, just show up tomorrow. I want you here at this hour," and give no further explanations——that's the way cuadrillas are run. But I hire them and then they ask, "Who else is going to be there? Oh no, I can't stand that guy." I just say, "I'm asking you to work for me. I'm not asking who annoys you. If you don't feel like it, too bad." It's hard sometimes, because there is so much conflict between us.

The first time one of the tall promoters found out I had my own cuadrilla, he called me on the phone: "Hey, jerk! What do think you're doing?" And I answered, "Well, what do you want me to be doing? I have my own cuadrilla, what's the problem?" "And who's in it?" "Well, there's this guy, this guy, and this guy." He said, "Well, if I want to, I can take Méndez from you." I said, "What? Okay, look, it's no problem with me. It's his choice." Then other tall promoters started calling me up: "What's up, Gustavo—you have your own cuadrilla? Well, congratulations, keep up the good work." But then the egotism and competition began. The guy called me back again and said, "Hey you bastard, what's going on? Don't invade my venues, or you'll be sorry." And I would say, "I'm just going to work, and I am the one getting called, and besides, people know the Enanitos Toreros from a long way back."

Amongst us we talk about how we have to give it our best so the audience leaves the show happy. And I say this because sometimes, after the show, they go to the dressing rooms and say, "Hey, shorty, that was a great show, we'd never seen you guys before!" Sometimes people see the show two or three times, and I recognize them and they also remember. That makes us very happy. It's very satisfying to know that people have faith in us. We use that affection to keep on going.

The promotion and advertising for these events is really expensive. You have to place ads in radio and television, hand out flyers and rent cars with loudspeakers. Normally, bullrings belong to the municipal government, and they take a percentage of the earnings. You have to pay for the bullring and also invest. The worst is when you work with promoters who aren't financially sound and don't pay enough to cover expenses. They want to keep all of the profits. And now there's even competition coming from smaller cuadrillas run by dwarfs. Well, I wouldn't call it competition . . . it's not as if I discriminate against little people or anything like that. But it's not the same if you, as a tall person, deal with a tall impresario, as if a short person does—even if they know the enano himself is a promoter of Enanitos Toreros. Unfortunately, here in Mexico discrimination against dwarfs is very big. Usually they don't get taken seriously, and a tall person gets more credibility than a little person does. A show involves many things—promotion, publicity, renting the cows—so right now it's not very reliable to do this part of the business with the Enanitos in Mexico.

I thought that Enanitos who had started up their own cuadrillas were doing very well, because I heard they'd gotten bookings at bullrings here and there—it's such a small scene, everyone knows everything about where they've toured. But they don't have money to invest on renting the bullrings or the bulls. So if their show flops in one town, they're finished, because they've lost the little capital they have, and they can't underwrite the next show.

Today we had a box office of nine thousand pesos, and I barely made a profit: the cows cost me fifteen hundred; the sound system, five hundred; and the ring, two thousand. Each Enanito earns four hundred, and the ones who do the actual bullfighting get eight hundred. I paid for that and everything else. I spent about fifteen hundred on gas and flyers and went to the town four days in a row. If you hire dwarfs from out of state, you spend more money on fares, but I feel it's better to do that so you don't have to deal with these local little people, because they're too antagonistic. They always meddle in what you're doing and they can't keep quiet—they're always looking to find something to complain about. They complain and they leave, but three or four months later, they're working for you again. It's a conflict for me because I can't have my competition as part of my own cuadrilla. I'd rather have them work exclusively for me, but they won't. There've been times when I've gone to pick them up for a show we are doing and they are not there. They've stood me up, with the explanation that someone else offered them more pay to work that same day. I'm the type of person who doesn't want to be on bad terms with them, because you never know. I always try to be accommodating, like with Claudia—I allow her to bring her kids along when she performs with us out of town, so that she won't have to leave them alone. The promoters in other cuadrillas are very selfish and they tell her: "Just bring yourself, because you're coming here to work, and not to babysit." But not me, and even so, if the kids travel with us, it benefits everyone, because if the Enanitos know that in my cuadrilla they are allowed to bring their children, they'll be more willing to working for me.

What I would like to capture at a certain point in time, whether through a movie or a novel, is the lack of respect that society has toward a little person. It astounds me that even in the twenty-first century there is still discrimination against little people. If dwarfs were given support instead of being relegated into a subcategory, they could do a million things, but they're not taken into consideration as they should be. I've experienced this in the flesh, and the truth is, I feel very angry at society because the majority doesn't have much trust in little people. Little people get exploited because the majority of them lack a formal education. I'm not a very cultured person, but I do have a better education than many of them. That's why I stopped working in the Enanitos Toreros shows. What promoters pay doesn't correspond to what the Enanitos do; they should earn more.

Promoters are only looking to make a profit, and the dwarfs can't see it because it's their only source of employment. They think this is the only place where they can get work. When we were coming back from our United States tour, a promoter said, "Now all of you guys are going back to your hometowns, but I've already organized our next trip to the States, and you're all coming with me because, why would you stay anyway if you're not wanted anywhere?" She even told me once, "And you? Who would want to hire you? You get rejected everywhere." It made me really angry.

Something else I see with little people is a lack of unity. I don't know if it's out of envy, because they feel inferior. A friend told me that I was conceited, that I thought I was so cultured and that often, with my way of speaking, I make an impression on people. I like to read, and I don't do it to show off—it's just a personal interest. Not long ago, I was telling my psychologist what little people say to me, and she said, "Look, Vero, it's not envy—the thing is that they feel bad because they see you as self-assured, happy, educated. It shows from your appearance that you love yourself, and they don't see themselves that way. You don't know if they've gone through a lot of hard things throughout their lives. Maybe they feel like outcasts, maybe they don't have anyone who cares for them."

What makes me feel bad sometimes is that I didn't finish getting my university degree. Now that I really want to, it's not so easy, with two children to support. They see me coming and going, with a lot of enthusiasm. People tell me they always see me working, and I like that; it makes me feel good. I was doing a BA in social work, but I dropped out to get leg-lengthening surgery when I was seventeen. I decided to do it because I always wanted to be tall. I felt bad after the experience. I got a complex from the trauma of having had steel pins in my legs, from not being able to walk for a long time, from the pain of the procedure, and from having had my skin torn open. It was a very painful experience that, in a way, was also very damaging——the friends I did have, I lost. It made them sad to see me in that way.

As a kid I was very happy, very sociable. I loved it when they called me "doll." But as a teenager in high school, I started getting a complex because I could see that guys flirted with my classmates but treated me differently. They always treated me like a little girl and I liked that, but at the same time it made me feel inferior because I saw the other girls as really gorgeous. People can be very cruel to you. Once when I was in high school they sent us to do social work in a community where there were a lot of children. It really depressed me, and I still don't understand why it happened: they followed me around with a chain, and they were going to hit me with it——and these were, like, nine-year-old children. The same age my son is now. By the time I got home I was soaked in my own tears, I locked myself in a room, I wanted nothing to do with the outside world. But it's because adults misrepresent a lot of things about little people; they picture you as an evil dwarf, a villain, someone who destroys everything.

I used to have a lot of hang-ups, but now I see things very differently. Once I went to a job interview for a secretarial position. A businesswoman, who was sitting at her desk, looking very professional, interviewed me. She looked me up and down and said, "You know what, sweetie? I see here that you have all the requirements, you're very smart. But I'm going to tell you something: employers don't want people like you because they're looking for tall women with attractive bodies who can give a positive impression about their company." I told her, "Okay, that's all right. If I'm not right for this job, I understand. I am not going to feel bad, I am not going to get angry. Thank you for your time." When she got up, I saw she had polio and had to use crutches. I thought, "Oh God, she feels so awful that she wanted me to feel even worse, poor woman."

We're just like anyone else, we're not handicapped——our brains are exactly the same as a "normal" person's. I even think, though this may sound awful, that a little person's brain may be more developed than a "normal" person's. When someone looks you up and down, it makes you feel terribly uncomfortable. It gets to a point where you wish you could turn into dust and disappear.

I wish there was an institution for little people to get support, to help them build a career, and to provide psychological help for the damage they've experienced from so many people who have rejected them. I also have had my wings clipped many times. Teachers at the Catholic school where I studied had the gall to tell my mother, "This is where your daughter's education ends. She can't become a teacher. She'll scare the children because she is a dwarf." The truth is, the way little people are treated is really depressing because we're not animals. We shouldn't be treated like a toy that you dress up and put in the middle of a bullring and move around like a marionette. Little people have feelings——they can feel and get hurt by a lot of things. I hope that some day it'll all be different.

YOLANDA BIVIANO   actress

Ever since I was a child I wanted to be on television. I would tell my mother, and she would say, "Yes, I'll help you." But she couldn't, because she's a shopkeeper, and she was busy all the time with the stores and couldn't leave them. So I had to be patient and wait. When I was fifteen I found out about a little people's association in Mexico City. At the meetings I got to know other little people, because at first you think you're the only one, that there aren't any others. My brother is also a little person, and you think, "Well, maybe it's just the two of us who are like this." That's where I met a friend, David's mother, Teresa, and she told me, "Hey, let's go to Guadalajara and work in the Enanitos Toreros show." My mother didn't want me to, because I was going by myself, with people I didn't know. I went anyway, for five months, dancing, impersonating singers. I lived with Tere in a hotel in Guadalajara. That was all a lot of fun. I went on as a Sevillana and also impersonated Gloria Trevi. I sang "*Pelo Suelto*" and "*Doctor Siquiatra*."

What I don't like is that the promoters don't pay us well. We don't get medical insurance, and if something happens to you they don't take responsibility, but except for that, everything else is all right. When I used to work with the Enanitos Toreros I started dating David, but we weren't getting along. In a way, that's one of the reasons why I came back to Mexico City. We had a lot of arguments, and I came back to live my life in peace. Someone told me that without that job I wasn't going to make it. I was depressed for a while, because I had nothing to do and I had quit doing something that I enjoyed, because of relationship problems.

When I got back I joined the ANDA [the national actors' association] and started working on television. I played the part of a little girl who played pranks on people. They'd get angry, but I'd just tell them, "Come on, don't get mad, smile for the camera, you're on *Te Caché* [Gotcha!]. I have a lot of new friends now, and I tell them, "If I had to go through everything I went through in Guadalajara to have what I have now, I don't regret it." Maybe that had to happen for me to discover new things. I love dancing, impersonating singers, but I think destiny has its ways, and what can you do? I thank life for putting me through a test that way. I didn't give up, I managed to get ahead. I didn't let people walk all over me.

VANESA GARCÍA de VIRGEN   homemaker

I was in Tijuana studying for a bachelor's degree in tourism management. I'd go to shopping malls, and people would start asking me questions as if I was a performer with the Enanitos Toreros. They'd ask me for my autograph and ask when we would be performing next. They told me I looked like one of the girls there. I didn't know what they were talking about, so it made me curious to meet them. I went to the show and met all the performers and their promoter, Rogelio Amador. He told me that if I wanted to work for him I could help him with the interviews and all that——and because of my studies, I was able to do so. He said that if I wanted to perform that would be my choice, but that more than anything I would just deal with the press. He gave me his card, and it stayed at that. I was in school, and I didn't see it as an option. Besides, my mother thought the show was "morbid"——not the show itself, I don't know the right terminology for that, but more than anything my mom thought that some people only go see it out of morbid curiosity. I went to three performances, and at the last one I met Gerson, the cutest guy there, and a well-known figure in bullfighting.

I was going to college, but that also has its limits. Regardless of how much schooling and experience you have in your field, you don't get hired, simply because of your height, because they don't believe you're sufficiently capable of doing things just like anybody else. I was studying for a BA in tourism, but now I'm working for the Coca-Cola Christmas parade. I come out dressed as one of Santa's elves.

JUAN CHÁVEZ   actor

I got out of the Enanitos Toreros because I want to be an actor. I want to be a serious artist, not clown around anymore. The bullring is for clowning around. The promoters make you get beat up, make you pull your pants down——that's what they ask of us. Then they make you travel around very uncomfortably, like fifteen to a van, piled on top of each other. I prefer to work as an actor. In acting you get treated like an artist, and in the Enanitos Toreros you don't. The Enanitos Toreros have nothing to do with the art of acting; it's a very different kind of show. I joined the ANDA a while ago, and when Pavarotti came to Mexico they called me up for the first time and hired me. While he was singing, I had to come out in the nude, dancing, and go like this, hugging my body as if I was a ball. Then a French woman would come out, and pretend to throw spears at a sphere and the spears would stick to it. So there you have me, on stage, in nothing but a loincloth, naked, walking in circles around the French woman. Then she kneels and we sit together while Pavarotti keeps singing. I don't know what the ball represented for Pavarotti, or what it means that he wanted to show a nude dwarf as part of his show. It was a song about a dream of the year 3000 and during the song the woman and I walk towards a kind of galaxy into which we disappear, holding hands. We were dancing and I felt embarrassed, but I wanted to meet Pavarotti. He's so fat! In another movie I played a bad guy who was hitting a dark-skinned woman inside a cave, and then Arnold Schwarzenegger comes and I start cheering, running around all over the cave.

What I want is for people to see us with respect and not think of us as puppets. Before, dwarfs were only seen at the circus, but now people don't get startled when they see us on the street. Before, I used die of embarrassment anytime people stared at me, but not anymore. The world is changing little by little; now you see more dwarfs walking on the streets with their heads up high.

ENTREVISTAS

Esto de la tauromaquia empezó en España hace muchos siglos, viene desde el circo romano. Lo del espectáculo de los Enanitos Toreros también empezó con los españoles, con el Bombero Torero, allá por los años cincuenta. Luego el matador Ernesto San Román, El Queretano, trajo a México a El Chino y sus Enanitos Toreros. De ahí le nació a San Román la idea de hacer algo parecido con enanitos aquí en México. Muchas personas trabajaron con el y le copiaron sus ideas. Ahora hay cuadrillas por todo México, también hay cuadrillas en Colombia y Portugal.

El Chino Torero me conoció en el año de 1979, cuando me vio pasando por el metro Revolución, aquí en la Ciudad de México. Ahí, en las calles, conocí a los españoles. Yo era todo un ignorante. Me encontraron en el metro y cambiaron mi vida. El Chino me sacó platica, y para probar si tenía habilidades me pidió si le podía traer un refresco. Yo corrí muy rápido y fue entonces cuando me pidió trabajar de torero en su cuadrilla y cuando acepté me presentó a otros enanos como yo. Él me cuidaba mucho y, cuando me presentó con los demás enanitos, dijo: "No quiero que le hagan mala cara". Víctor, un colombiano, se ofreció a enseñarme a torear. Todos eran muy lindos. También toreábamos al alimón, cuando entre dos toreros se sostiene un capote y la becerra pasa por en medio de los dos chaparritos. Abríamos con la orquesta de música en vivo de Fresnillo, Zacatecas. Tocaban un pasodoble y todos entrábamos marchando y saludando. Yo hacía como que dirigía la orquesta con una varita, y partía la plaza en cuatro partes para saludar. Ése fue mi primer trabajo. Llevo muchos años trabajando en esto.

Ahora trabajo con la cuadrilla de Ernesto San Román. Él fue matador. Él sí tiene buen gusto y le gusta la calidad, sí, se metió a lo fino del toreo, a la calidad. Está mejor nuestro vestuario que el que llevan otras cuadrillas, llevamos trajes de luces hechos por sastres de torero formal. El matador San Román le da más preferencia al toreo que a las personificaciones musicales. Hacemos los forcados, las cruzadas, espalda con espalda . . . con puros enanitos. Las otras cuadrillas sólo queman el espectáculo de los Enanitos Toreros usando mal vestuario y presentando muchas personificaciones que no tienen nada que ver con el arte del toreo. No tienen afición a la tauromaquia. Ahora algunas de las otras cuadrillas traen charlot, que es el payaso del torero, como la Güera Mitotes, un hombre vestido como travesti que no más alborota al público.

Antes, en los Enanitos Toreros se pagaba más y había más trabajo porque no había tantas cuadrillas. Lo que pasa es que ahora ya no nos pagan bien, en todas las cuadrillas es lo mismo, nada más cambian los enanos. Hoy en día, nos pagan por una función no mas de lo que tú ganas en una semana trabajando por un salario mínimo. Pero en verdad, sí tenemos buena suerte. Gracias a que soy enanito, he conocido muchas partes y he ganado poquito dinero, siquiera para gastar en mis diversiones . . . en la golfería como dicen. Es cuestión de cada pequeño y de cómo se quiere desenvolver en la vida cotidiana porque no todo es el toreo.

Mucha gente se acerca a mí y me habla para saber si soy igual que una gente grande, y después de conocerme me dicen: "Mis respetos para ti, eres mejor que mucha gente alta". Te voy a decir la verdad: en el sexo, y yo he dado las gracias por esto, las mujeres altas tienen más morbo hacia los hombres chaparros que los hombres altos hacia las chaparritas. Cuando nosotros vamos, las mujeres ya vienen de regreso. Creo que hay dos tipos de morbo: uno es curiosidad y el otro ya es morbo malsano. Por ejemplo, cuando posé en la Playboy, una vez lo hice junto a mujeres desnudas y de tanto ver ya no se antoja. Aquí en México casi no se usa, pero en Estados Unidos y en España sí presentan más de esta forma al chaparrito.

Yo siempre he dicho que la estatura de nada te sirve si no tienes mentalidad e inteligencia. He trabajado en todo tipo de trabajos. He hecho de todo y puedo hacer todo. Quiero escribir un libro que hable de lo que he hecho y de como he llegado hasta aquí, porque barrera que me ponen, barrera que brinco.

Al principio, en las primeros corridas de Enanitos Toreros se banderilleaba y se mataba a los toros. Actualmente ya no se hace, no porque no se quiera hacer, sino por cuestiones económicas, porque se tendría que comprar otro toro. El toro, entre más lo toreas más aprende y en vez de irse contra el capote o al área de movimiento se va hacia el torero. A través de las corridas se va convirtiendo en un animal más y más peligroso, pero se gastaría mucho en estarlos remplazando. Yo pienso que el toreo formal se inició como un juego de toreo cómico que luego se convirtió en formal. El toreo cómico tiene una riqueza tremenda pero no ha sido bien documentada. Se inició con las mojigangas con gente alta, quienes, a modo de desfile, pasaban por las calles del pueblo invitando a la gente a que los siguiera a la corrida de toros. Eso lleva más de cuatro siglos, hasta que dejó de tener éxito y desapareció. Pero de ahí viene toda esta idea de los Enanitos Toreros. Los toreros cómicos, y otras gentes en el ambiente taurino, metieron a enanos a estos espectáculos de toreo cómico; aprovechando sus cualidades físicas para causar mayor impacto. Nunca antes se había visto a gente pequeña de esta manera, no los veías ni en la calle. Te estoy hablando de los setenta. Llegaron los espectáculos de los Enanitos Toreros españoles y pienso que por primera vez las mamás sacaron a sus hijos enanitos a que conocieran a gente pequeña sin el temor a la burla, y sin esa idea que tenían de que se los iba a robar el circo.

Así es que muchos empezamos a buscar a enanitos. Poco a poco van saliendo y te das cuenta que también hay gente pequeña en el país que necesita trabajar. Hubo que enseñarlos a torear y que aprendieran todos los ritos que rigen las formalidades del toreo serio. Hay mucha similitud entre el toreo cómico y el toreo serio y formal. Nos empezó a ir muy bien, llegamos a tener mucha proyección, desde poblaciones pequeñas hasta giras por Guatemala y la Unión Americana. Pero en 1996 surge un gran problema con la gente del ambiente taurino. Empezaron a ofrecer le a los enanitos de mi cuadrilla mayores cantidades de dinero que lo que yo les pagaba y así fue que el grupo se desintegró. A partir de eso me di cuenta que yo seguía siendo el promotor "Patorro y sus Enanitos Toreros", así es que lo único que necesitaba simplemente era reclutar a nuevos enanos, entrenarlos y seguir con mi espectáculo. Así lo he estado haciendo. Gracias a Dios me ha ido bien.

Yo leí un libro que creo me ayudó a tratar de comprender y entender a los enanos. Este libro lo escribió Og Mandino. Se llama "Los 10 Mandamientos del Éxito". En ese libro habla de Zaqueo, un personaje bíblico de Jericó quien era el jefe de los recaudadores de impuestos. Era muy, muy rico y era enano. Como trabajaba para el gobierno Romano la mayoría de la gente lo odiaba. Hay un pasaje bíblico donde creo que me di cuenta de la grandeza que pueden tener los enanos, algo que antes me hubiera imaginado imposible. Es cuando llega Jesús a Jericó y la multitud se reúne para verlo. Como Zaqueo era enano pues no podía, entre tanta gente, ver pasar a Jesús. Así es que se tuvo que trepar a la rama de un árbol. Cuando Jesús lo ve ahí encaramado le dice "Zaqueo, baja de ese árbol porque esa noche duermo en tu casa". Cuando te hablan de que Jesucristo durmió en casa de paganos están hablando de cuando durmió en casa de Zaqueo. Jesús se quedó a dormir en la casa de ese hombre odiado y diminuto de 80 centímetros. Creo que cuando empecé a trabajar con la gente pequeña el que yo conociera la historia de este personaje me sirvió mucho.

Nos tienen que subir el sueldo a todos y punto. Rogelio [promotor], dice que es gracias a él que la gente entra a vernos, que gracias a él se llenan las plazas, que por él esto, que por él lo otro. Pero todos somos un equipo. Aquí en México no te dan trabajo en otras cosas, nada más te dicen "No hay trabajo", y con eso te están diciendo todo. Piensan que porque uno es bajito no puede hacer muchos tipos de cosas. Por eso los chaparritos trabajan en espectáculos, porque aquí en México no se les da apoyo. Parece ser que en Estados Unidos, si yo pido trabajo y no me lo dan por chaparrito, los puedo demandar y ganar porque me están discriminando. Por eso los Enanitos Toreros han servido a los chaparritos porque nos ha abierto una oportunidad de trabajar, pero que nos suban el sueldo.

Rogelio gana muy bien, vende muy bien el espectáculo. Pero con lo que un enanito gana . . . ningún futuro tiene el enanito en México. Los promotores se meten a esto porque es negocio. La mayoría de los promotores son altos, toreros retirados o gente de negocios del mundo de la farándula. No ganan lo mismo que con los artistas, pero la inversión es menos, es menos trabajo y se enriquecen algo. Porque este es un espectáculo popular que ya todo el mundo conoce. La mayoría de los patrones son muy déspotas pero como no hay otros trabajos, pues tenemos que conformarnos. Mi patroncito de ahorita es buena onda. Es muy serio, no se ríe cuando nos estafa.

Que la gente nos señale y diga "mira ahí va un enano", "mira que bien se ve", eso siempre ha existido, y existirá porque a los humanos siempre nos atrae lo diferente. Aquí todo el mundo nos conoce como Enanitos Toreros, así llama más la atención. El uso de la palabra "enanito" o "gente pequeña", da lo mismo. Pero una cosa es que digan "ahí va un enanito", y otra es que digan "mira ése pinche enano".

Cuando yo iba a ver los espectáculos de otros enanitos, las enanitas se sentían que tenían que lucirse. Creo que era porque sabían que yo las iba a ver. A muchas enanitas yo no les caía bien, a veces ni me hablaban. Mi amiga Isabel dice que a lo mejor es por mi mal genio. Antes yo era muy mal encarada, muy enojona, ¿sería por que me creía mucho? Yo me sentía que era la única. Será porque tuve mucho apoyo de mis papás. Mi mamá que es alta nunca se acomplejo de mi, al contrario, me traía por todos lados, muy bien arreglada, como una princesa. Mi papá, que también es enano, me decía: "¡Tu eres la única y la más chingona!"

Mi papá fue el iniciador de la lucha libre de enanos, y allí trabajó 25 años. Como fue luchador, yo siempre me sentía bien segura y protegida, sentía que si me hacían algo mi papá iba a salir a defenderme. A José Luis, mi esposo, un día le pegó cuando apenas éramos novios y también a unos vecinos cuando se pasaban de listos.

José Luis es el único chaparrito en su familia. La probabilidad de que le toque a uno nacer con enanismo es como de uno en veinte mil y algo. Cuando yo tuve a Juanito la gente en el hospital se imaginaba que iba a ser demasiado chiquito, que cabría en una caja de zapatos, y pensábamos que por eso les daba curiosidad y venían a verlo. El doctor nos dijo: "Todo está bien, pero el bebé tiene acondroplasia", y mi esposo se quedó en shock, nunca había oído esa palabra y pensó que era una deformidad, hasta que por fin el doctor explicó que el bebé iba a ser igual que su mamá. Lo dijo con un tono triste, como si nosotros no lo fuéramos a aceptar, porque así pasa en algunas parejas, aunque sean chaparritos. Pero yo dije, pues es normal, desde un principio me dijeron que yo estaba expuesta a tener un bebé chaparrito. Además es como si naciera ya con una herencia. Mi papá es enano, mi bebé es la tercera generación que nace como uno de nosotros.

Yo siento que muchas personas se acercan a nosotros simplemente por que les damos morbo, no porque de verdad les atraiga la persona. Si te das cuenta las chaparritas están bien nalgoncitas, a mí me lo decían los chicos cuando yo era soltera, "Me gustan tus pompis", pero lo decían nada más para ligar, para experimentar cómo es andar con una pequeña. Piensan que por ser pequeñas tenemos algo diferente en muchas partes y sé que por mucho tiempo en los medios difundieron nuestra imagen como si los enanitos fuéramos mas cachondos. También hay chaparritos que por ganar un peso se humillan. Si ellos mismos se dieran a respetar la gente nos vería con mas admiración. Pero aún así, la gente se burla mucho de nosotros. Se supone que si nosotros presentamos un espectáculo es para que nos admiren, para que vean que podemos hacer a veces hasta más que un alto., No estamos ahí para que se burlen de nosotros.

TERESA MONTIEL   *imitadora*

Yo crecí en Acapulco. Mi mamá era alta y al único otro enanito que conocí durante mucho tiempo fue a mi papá. Después tuve a David y Claudia, mis dos hijos, que también son chaparritos. Mi papá no sabía nada de los Enanitos Toreros. Él nunca ha trabajado en esto, cuando era joven trabajó de pirata. Se vestía de pirata de verdad y hacía como que invadía un yate de turistas, en Acapulco. Yo tampoco conocía este ambiente hasta que una vez el promotor Félix Corona fue a Acapulco con los Enanitos Toreros de América. Vi los anuncios y sentí curiosidad, quería saber cómo eran. Fui con Claudia a verlos y nos gustó su show. Cuando ellos nos vieron nos devolvieron el dinero, nos regalaron papitas y refresco, y nos invitaron a conocerlos. Fue ahí, donde el promotor de estos Enanitos, el señor Félix Corona, y su esposa nos ofrecieron trabajar para ellos. Esto fue en 1995. Claudia tenía doce años, y yo tenía treinta. Al día siguiente Don Félix llego a buscarnos a la casa. Nos invitó a la playa con los demás Enanitos y ahí me convenció. A los dos días nos fuimos Claudia y yo a Guadalajara a trabajar con ellos, David se quedó en Acapulco estudiando la secundaria pero se unió después. Viajábamos todos apretadísimos en una camionetita, como sardinas enlatadas. Pero como todo era nuevo para nosotras, pues Claudia y yo íbamos encantadas. Don Félix pagó a coreógrafos para enseñarnos a bailar, a caminar bien, como las modelos.

También nos pusieron uno de esos entrenadores de educación física. Nos llevaban a hacer ejercicio a la plaza de toros Nuevo Progreso, en Guadalajara, todos los días a las siete de la mañana.

Antes de trabajar con los Enanitos Toreros, trabajé nueve años durante la noche de cajera en un negocio, en el que también trabajaba mi papá, en uno de esos bares de baile, de chicas malas. Mis hijos me veían ir a ese lugar pero yo no me sentía mal. Jamás he hecho nada de lo que me pueda avergonzar. También trabajé planchando ropa. Nunca fui lavandera porque no alcanzaba el lavabo. En la Ciudad de México no hay asociación de gente pequeña, antes había una pero siempre cambiaban de presidente y prometían cosas que luego no cumplían. En una ocasión dijeron que iban a hacer una cocina pública y una lavandería, para que tuviéramos donde poder trabajar, pero luego se olvidaron de eso.

Yo interpreto a Paquita la del Barrio, una artista mexicana muy folklórica. Me gusta mucho el sentimiento que le pone a sus canciones, las canta con mucho dolor y con mucho coraje. Todas las canciones tratan de los hombres, del machismo. Le canta a los señores pero en un tono algunas veces muy vulgar, con letras que hacen reír mucho a la gente. De todo les dice a los pobres: "No sirves para nada, inútil", y les dice hasta de lo que se van a morir. La caracterización que hago de ella es cómica, debido a mi estatura. Como chaparrita, tengo que hacer todo cómico.. Salgo con muchas ganas, le muevo y le bailo y me la paso bien. Aunque Claudia me dice: "Mamá, ya ni se ve si te meneas o no. Báilale como Laura León, de veras". Y yo le digo: "¡Sí le bailo, me muevo para todos lados!", y me dice: "Sí, nada más que tan gordita que estás ya ni se ve, ya no se nota". Lo mas importante son los aplausos de la gente, y cómo te recibe el publico cuando estás bailando. Ahí se siente en verdad qué número le gusta a la gente, en el ánimo cuando se paran y te aplauden. Cuando empiezan a anunciar el show de Paquita, la gente se levanta de sus asientos y aplaude. Piensan que va a salir Paquita en grandote y cuando salgo de Paquita, bien cachetona, pues se botanean más y empiezan a reír. Pero a mí me gusta esto, se siente bien padre estar en el ruedo. Me entrego toda. Me gusta el ambiente taurino y ya no me he podido desterrar. Yo lo único que espero es que mi nieta y los demás niños chaparritos no se claven en este ambiente taurino porque aquí explotan muchísimo a los enanos.

DAVID RODRÍGUEZ MONTIEL   *enanito torero, promotor*

Yo trabajo en este ambiente de los Enanitos Toreros y conozco bien cómo se mueve todo. Del ruedo al público es una cosa, pero atrás del ruedo, en los vestidores, las cosas se manejan muy diferente. Cada enanito tiene su historia. Algunos están por gusto, otros por necesidad, por no sentirse solos, por tener amigos, porque se sienten ignorados por sus propias familias. Algunos buscan compañía y por eso nos hacemos amigos. Cuando vienen otros chaparritos a ver el show nosotros siempre tomamos la iniciativa de conocerlos y platicar con ellos. De repente nos vienen a ver familias que tienen algún hijo enanito. Se acercan para preguntarnos si sabemos donde lo pueden llevar a tratar, y que si sabemos de alguna asociación de apoyo social. Nos preguntan que si estamos asociados o integrados a una. No lo estamos. Les decimos que vayan a pedir ayuda al DIF pero desafortunadamente, hasta incluso ahí este tema del enanismo es muy desconocido. Nosotros nos entendemos dentro de este medio pero a una persona que tiene un bebé pequeño le cuesta mucho trabajo, y a veces cuando nos ve a nosotros es una alternativa. Creo que accidentalmente acabamos siendo como portadores sociales para otros enanos.

La gente siempre nos felicita y nos dicen que les gusta lo que hacemos. Piensan que nos va muy bien. Lo malo no lo platicamos con ellos, los dejamos en la fantasía, eso es lo que debe mantener uno, las ilusiones.

Algunos promotores son muy farsantes porque dan a entender a la gente que sus cuadrillas son como una fundación que ayuda y protege a los chaparritos. Si la gente supiera la verdad . . . los promotores son como verdugos, tienen a los enanitos muy subordinados, con miedo, casi son sus esclavos. Hay temporadas en que los promotores sólo nos consiguen un show en todo el mes. No pagan bien pero tampoco dejan a los enanos trabajar para otras cuadrillas y si lo hacen, los multan. Pagan entre trescientos o cuatrocientos pesos por función y, además, si no reparten tantos volantes los multan con cincuenta o cien pesos. Te ponen a repartir volantes y cuando acabas te suben a una camioneta a hacer publicidad, como dos horas. Nada de que un camión con cajón atrás, no, arriba, en el techo de una camioneta, jodido que se caiga uno. Te traen dando vuelta y mas vueltas por todo el pueblo, bajo ese sol quemador de las dos y tres de la tarde. Acabamos agotados, y después de eso ¿qué ganas y que fuerzas le quedan a uno para trabajar? Ninguna, no te queda nada.

Una vez, mi amigo Cucuy, Lupillo y yo fuimos a trabajar para unos promotores a El Grullo, un pueblo en Jalisco. Se llenó la plaza en la primera función y se quedó mucha gente afuera. Entonces programaron una segunda función y también llenaron la plaza. Nos pagaron cuatrocientos pesos por la primera función y por la segunda nos querían pagar solo doscientos. Lupillo y yo protestamos, decíamos "Pero ¿por qué? ¡No es justo! ¡Páguenos otros cuatrocientos!". "Ah, es que sólo se da la mitad". Por fin dijeron: "Ahí les van cien pesos más, pero doscientos pesos, no". Entonces dijimos: "¡No vamos a trabajar!". "¿Cómo que no van a trabajar?". "No. No vamos a trabajar". El esposo de la señora promotora se puso muy agresivo. Lupe y yo renunciamos pero Cucuy sí trabajó, y al montarse sobre el becerro se cayó. Luego el becerro lo empezó a corretear y Cucuy se cayó de cabeza sobre el burladero y ¡pum!, que se tuerce el cuello. Alguien del publico llamo a una ambulancia y los de primeros auxilios le pusieron un collarín. Pero como no había ningún otro chaparrito dispuesto a trabajar, los promotores le dijeron: "No te preocupes, mijo, que con una aspirina se te quita el torcijón". Y la señora le quito el collarín y así, todo torcido, lo obligaron a trabajar.

Fue ahí cuando me di cuenta de lo sinvergüenzas que los promotores pueden llegar a ser. Me dan ganas de poner una página en Internet y decir realmente lo que son. ¿Cómo piensan que ayudan a los enanitos? Luego los promotores arman unas cuadrillas de enanitos que no saben nada del toro y los meten así, a la brava. Algunos de ellos se lastiman pues los agarran inocentes. Nosotros podríamos evitar que se nos trate de esta forma si nos juntáramos y nos pusiéramos de acuerdo. Pero estamos muy desorganizados.

IMELDA LARA VILLEGAS   ama de casa

Yo estaba en mi pueblo, Santiaguito, y de repente llegaron los Enanitos Toreros a hacer una función. Llegaron a la puerta de mi casa porque se les arrimaron muchos niños curiosos a decirles: "En este pueblo hay una enanita, está dentro de su casa, nomás que no quiere salir". Y me decía mi hermana: "Asómate, ¿qué van a hacer?". Yo le dije que nada, pero me daba vergüenza. Antes de eso nunca había hablado con un enanito. Una vez fui con mi familia a Guadalajara para comprar en la Wal-Mart y ahí fue que vi a un enano por primera vez. Estaba sentado en una banca ahí solito "pispiriteando" para todos lados y me dijo mi hermano "Mira ahí esta uno como tú". Lo miré de los pies a la cabeza, lo critiqué todititito. Pensé: "A ver . . . está guapo, bien parecido, ¿me convendrá para esposo?". Lo miré y me daban ganas de amistar pero nos metimos a la tienda y ya no pude hablar con él . Lo busqué cuando salimos pero ya no estaba. Ahorita tengo 30 años. Cuando pasó esto del Wal-Mart estaba de cotorrona, tendría unos 21 años.

A mí me decían que había otra pequeña en Amatitlán, un pueblo cerca de Santiaguito. Me decían que la confundían conmigo, que se parecía mucho a mí. Y a mí me daba mucha tentación conocerla. Hasta que un día mi papá me dice: "Si la quieres conocer yo te llevo porque su papá es tío lejano mío. Vamos para que la veas y se hagan amigas". Quedamos con ella pero cuando llegamos no estaba. Nos enfadamos por esperarla tanto y nos fuimos. Cuando por fin la vi fue en una fiesta de mi pueblo, la Santa Cruz, el 3 de mayo. Yo iba caminando con mis hermanos, detrás de ella, porque en mi pueblo se acostumbra ir a dar vueltas a la plaza para agarrar chavo. Uno va dando vueltas y vueltas y los chavos te avientan flores, confeti y te dicen "Adióooooos mamacita" o "Invítame a dar una vuelta". Y si te gusta el chavo, pues aceptas. Después, si platicas y te quiere conocer más, te dice nos vemos tal día y ya de ahí nace el noviazgo. Yo iba atrás de ella y como decían que se parecía mucho a mí, la venía criticando. Yo le decía a mi hermano: "¿Cómo la comparan conmigo si está refea?". Ella nunca me saludó, sólo vi que me miraba de reojo. Se me perdió entre la multitud, y no la volví a ver.

Pasaron cuatro años después del incidente de la placita, hasta que llegaron los Enanitos Toreros a buscarme a mi casa. Al final me animé a saludarlos y me invitaron a que fuera con ellos a ver su show. Pero les dije que no. "Mejor pásense para que se sienten". Les ofrecí un refresco y pozole, y se quedaron a comer. Y ahí fue donde le eché el ojo a David, pero él estaba de novio de Yolis. Yo me acuerdo de haber visto a David con todos sus dientes, aunque dicen que para ese entonces ya estaba chimuelo. No sé, a mí se me hizo perfecto y es que me gustó mucho, para serte sincera. Me dijeron mis hermanas que parecía que a David le gustaba yo, pues me seguía con los ojos para todos lados. Cuando se fueron, mi hermana dijo: "¿Cómo te van a gustar si están chaparros y feos? Si te casas con un chaparro al rato te va a dar vergüenza porque lo vas a tener que andar cargando. Tú cásate con uno alto". Y yo dije: "No, pues no combina un altote con una chaparrita. Si discriminas es que tú misma estás acomplejada de alguna cosa, y por eso piensas así".

Los enanitos nos regalaron boletos para su show. Fuimos y estuvo chido, se me hizo muy bonito. Al terminar el show me dijeron que me uniera a trabajar con ellos: "Se gana dinero, viajamos a Estados Unidos, y por todo México". Pero a mí viajar no me gustaba, casi nunca salgo de mi casa. En este pueblo se hace el mezcal, se cultiva la caña, el nopal, la guayaba, los guajes, son cosas que conozco. No es lo mismo andar en pueblos cercanos como Amatitlán o Tequila, pero salir a lugares más lejanos, no, no es para mí.

Pasaron cuatro años y un buen día regresó David solito. Fue con el pretexto de buscar plaza para dar show. Pero después me dijo que me fue a buscar a mí porque le habían contado que ya estaba casada, tenía hijos, que no vivía ya en mi pueblo. No sé quién se lo dijo, pero vino a ver si era cierto. Todos los hombres en mi pueblo son muy celosos y es que casi todos los que viven aquí son puros familiares, todos se apellidan López,

Sánchez o Hermosillo. Aquí sí se roban a las chavas y si alguna mujer se hace novia de algún hombre de fuera, los del pueblo lo esperan a media carretera para agarrarlo a trancazos y lo amenazan para que la deje. En mi casa somos doce. Y los hombres de mi casa también son muy celosos de sus mujeres.

Cuando llegó David se sentó cerca de la plaza de toros que esta ahí al lado de mi casa. La mañana de ese mismo día, fui al mercado de Arenal, y de regreso los dos nos subimos al mismo autobús. Yo venía adelante en el camión y David se sentó lejos. No nos saludamos porque en cuanto subió todos los pasajeros nos estaban echando carrilla: "Imelda, ahí viene tu novio". Y el chofer del camión: "Mira tu novio, hacen bonita pareja, conquístalo para que no te quedes de solterona, ¡ya tienes treinta!". Y a él le decían: "Mírala, está guapa, bonita, te conviene, hace tortillas a mano, es mujer de su casa". Y ahí se lo agarraron de carrilla y es que por aquí todo el mundo me conoce.

Después de eso cada quien agarró su rumbo. Poco tiempo después, vino a mi casa. "¿Se encuentra Imelda?". No se le olvidó mi nombre, después de cuatro años todavía se acordaba de mí. Le ofrecí de comer y comimos solos, pues en ese tiempo mis papás todavía no desconfiaban de mí. Empezamos viéndonos como amigos y yo pensé: "A ver qué pasa, pero yo no le voy a hacer mucho caso". Pero de repente se dieron las cosas. Empecé a sentir miedito, que el corazón me latía así, un friego, no sé, ñañarucas . . . A los pocos días me enfermé y mi mamá me llevó al médico. A esa hora David llamó a la casa y mi hermano le dijo que yo estaba en el hospital. Y él se vino en joda desde Guadalajara. Al final resultó que yo no tenía nada grave. Cuando regresé a casa esa tarde, él estaba ahí, sentado en un tronquito esperándome. Me sorprendió y dije: "¡Amá, vino éste!". Y ella dijo: "Uy, pa mí que ya te quiere". Yo le dije a mi mamá que me caía regordo y mi mamá: "Así dicen todas y luego se casan con ellos. Fíjate en tu hermana, cuando andaba noviando ella también dijo que le caía bien gordo, que no lo quería y que lo iba a dejar. Y ahora mírala, ya tiene dos chilpayates". "Ay, amá pero a mí sí me cae gordo". "Ni digas porque al ratito vas a casarte con él". Y sí, salió cierto lo que dijo.

Al principio la gente en Santiaguito lo vió bien. Los trabajadores con el camión del agave lo veían por la carretera y paraban y le decían: "¿Vas a ver a Imelda?", y pues como ya sabían dónde vivía yo, lo bajaban en la puerta de mi casa. Pero cuando vieron que la cosa ya iba más seria, muchos del pueblo le dejaron de hablar. Hasta le dijeron que mejor ya ni fuera porque le iban a hacer algo. Yo estaba preocupada por él, porque ya habían golpeado al novio de una vecina. Le mentían diciéndole que yo me iba a ir a vivir a Estados Unidos. Un día estábamos platicando y de repente se alocó y me intentó robar un beso. Y lo amenacé, "Si me besas, te voy a dar una bofetada, te voy a correr y no me vas a volver a ver". Él decía: "Nomás un besito". Yo decía "¡No! ¿Por qué, si no somos nada?". "¡Ándale, sí!". "Ya te dije que no". La verdad es que estaba bien nerviosa porque nunca había besado a nadie. Después, como dos días antes de su cumpleaños me besó, y esta vez sí lo dejé. Yo no sabía ni besar ni nada y me dice él: "Pues aprende! Mira, así y asá". Y ya ahí me dijo: "Voy a hablar con tus papás pa decirles si me dan permiso de ser tu novio". Y sí se lo dieron.

Duramos así como cinco meses y como la cosa se puso más seria empezamos a pensar en casamiento. Ahí mi familia ya no estuvo de acuerdo porque se enteraron de que no era católico. Luego la gente del pueblo inventó chismes acerca de él — que era un borracho, un vividor - puras mentiras, pero como mis papás se creen todo, se puso difícil la cosa. Mi papá empezó a cortarme las horas de plática. A veces nomás lo dejaba que me dijera buenos días y lo corría. A mí me daba tristeza con él porque venía de cómo a dos horas de lejos, cansado, asoleado y a quererme ver. Luego a él le dijeron: "Imelda no te conviene, es bien güevona, no sabe hacer nada, no sabe hacer de comer". Le decían para que se desilusionara y me dejara.

Un día llegó David en un taxi de Guadalajara y me dijo: "Vamos a platicar como lo normal, ya cuando nadie nos vea, nos fugamos en el taxi". Pero una señora del pueblo lo vió sospechoso y avisó a mi mamá: "Mira, ven, el muchacho llegó en ese taxi y de seguro se la va a llevar". Y mi mamá me gritó: "Métete". Él me decía: "Vámonos, vámonos". Pero no se pudo porque un hermano me detuvo con fuerza, y me encerró en la casa. Al poco ratito llegó mi papá y me puso una chinga bien buena, me dejó moreteadas las piernas, casi no podía ni caminar.

Otro día pasó el camión que traía a los trabajadores de agaveros y David le preguntó al chofer que si le daba un raite y aceptó. No le dijo que nos fugaríamos. Cuando vió que nos subimos los dos, nos dijo: "¿Cómo no me dijeron bien esto?". Y le dió vuelo al carro para que no nos alcanzaran. Nos llevó a Arenal. Ahí agarramos un taxi y el taxista nos dijo: "Los voy a llevar, pero díganme un lugar donde ustedes no vivirán porque no quiero que sus papás me pregunten dónde los dejé. Así no puedo negarme a decirles que no sé". Nos trajo hasta Guadalajara y nos dejó en el centro comercial Plaza del Sol, de ahí nosotros llegamos a Guadalajara a hacer casita. Ahora tenemos a Emilio, ya cumple sus seis meses. Mis papás todavía no lo conocen porque no lo hemos bautizado.

Yo estaba entrenando para la lucha libre y mi sueño era luchar en la Triple A, salir en la televisión, como un hermano mío, que es luchador en la categoría mini. En mi casa cuatro somos chaparritos y los otros siete son altos. Los cuatro chiquitos somos toreros. En mi familia no había enanos, a lo mejor antes, porque es un gen que tarda como cinco generaciones en reaparecer, como tener el ojo azul, que de repente te sale.

Yo trabajaba lavando camiones en el Mercado de Abastos. Ahí conocí a una persona que me decía: "Por donde yo vivo hay unos Enanitos Toreros y se van a ir de gira, ¿no quieres ir con ellos?". Pasó una semana y no fui, y otra y tampoco, y este cuate me iba a buscar a diario. Yo me escondía porque no quería ir, no me gustaba la idea porque yo quería ser luchador y porque sentía que los empresarios taurinos usaban a los chaparritos, los disfrazaban, les ponían pelucas y los vestían como títeres para que la gente se riera de ellos. Sin embargo, un día decidí unirme a los Enanitos Toreros para probar suerte y para tratar de salir de la economía en la que vivía.

Primero no te acostumbras. Toma tiempo darse cuenta que todo en el mundo es un espectáculo. Esto es un espectáculo más, pero un espectáculo de gente pequeña para divertir a la gente alta. Pero cuando sale el toro a la plaza y lo logramos torear, entonces la actitud de la gente cambia y nos miran con respeto, se van con una impresión diferente sobre los enanos. Gracias a este medio la gente ha comprendido que somos gente normal, con una pequeña discapacidad que es el tamaño, pero con la misma mentalidad grande, un corazón grande con sentimientos, con ideas, con metas. No por ser pequeño se te cierra el mundo. Cuando aprendes a reírte de ti mismo, puedes divertir a la gente y tú mismo te puedes divertir . . . dejas de ser un acomplejado. Si no alcanzas a salir de esta etapa, ahí te puedes quedar atorado toda tu vida. Eso fue lo que yo aprendí con los Enanitos Toreros. Al final me metí del todo en esto, me hice torero y me gusta mucho. Lee mi camiseta, dice "Enanitos Toreros". Si dejas de torear ya no eres enanito torero, eres simplemente un enanito.

Duramos tres años con el promotor Félix Corona. Ahí conocí a Claudia y nos hicimos novios. Después nos fuimos con otros empresarios que nos pagaban muy poco. Empezamos a soñar con ya no trabajar para un patrón, sino para nosotros mismos. Un día, después de tantos años de trabajar para los empresarios altos, decidimos nosotros hacer nuestro grupo independiente. Ahora nosotros somos la empresa. Se siente que hemos ido para adelante. Nosotros nos arriesgamos la vida. Los becerros lo ven a uno y no se fijan si tú eres alto, chaparro, flaco o gordo. Y si no sabes torear, te van a meter una cornada, y si te descuidas te pueden dejar inválido o incluso hasta matar. El que arriesga todo es el chaparrito. Los promotores van a los pueblos, encuentran enanos, los entrenan, les enseñan a bailar, y los esclavizan pagándoles una miseria. Gracias a Dios nosotros por fin nos hartamos de eso ¿Sabes qué fue lo que nos provocó a hacer nuestra propia empresa? Un promotor nos debía varios pagos. Un día llegamos a trabajar con él a una plaza y vimos que la había llenado y no nos quería pagar la deuda. Nos pusimos de acuerdo y dijimos que no toreábamos hasta que no nos pagara. Dijimos "es más, nos tiene que subir el sueldo". Ahí fue cuando empezó a llorar y decía: "Es que mi gachí [mujer] me dejó, es para ayudar a mis tres hijos", y no era cierto.

En otra ocasión, una noche íbamos regresando de Mazatlán a Guadalajara y yo le digo al promotor: "Oye, ¿no nos van a dar de cenar?". "Sí, ahora paramos en el otro pueblo". Yo me quedé dormido y me desperté como a las diez de la noche: "¿Qué, vamos a cenar?". Y me dijo: "Ahora, en el otro pueblo". Y ya me quedé dormido otro rato. Me levanté como a la una de la mañana y le digo: "¡Felipe, por qué no nos paramos a cenar? Traigo a Claudia y a los niños". Y me dijo: "Me fue mal y no tengo para pagar la cena". Resulta que si les fue mal, no te dan de comer. Ahí fue cuando dije: "No más". Cuando todos los Enanitos Toreros se independicen van a mandar a volar a todos los empresarios.

Cada vez es menos la tradición de los toros y se está perdiendo. Se deja de lado porque meten dos horas de payasadas, de imitaciones de artistas, motos y todo lo demás. La gente se acostumbró a las payasadas y ni se acuerda de los Enanitos Toreros. Muchos niños no van a las corridas porque se asustan cuando matan a los toros, porque cuando un niño ve sangre le da miedo. Pero como los Enanitos Toreros es un show familiar aquí no hay sangre. En Estados Unidos cuidan más a los toros que a uno. Un día estábamos toreando en Chicago y luego el becerro nos metió una friega, nos metió revolquizas, volteretas y todo. Cuando le pusimos una soga en el cuello, nos dicen los gringos de seguridad: "Quítenle la soga al toro". Los animales tienen más derechos. Todo lo contrario que en Chiapas. El promotor nos soltó una vaca que se acababa de parir y era bravísima. Estábamos toreando cuando de pronto azotó la vaca y ya no se levantó. Se murió al instante y el público atacado de la risa, pensando que era payasada. Aquí en México apoyan las dos cosas: que tú pegues al animal y que el animal te pegue a ti.

Ahora quiero hablar de un punto muy importante de la fiesta de los toros. La gente va a la plaza a que te golpee el toro, a que te parta la madre. Una vez toreando el becerro me dió una buena revolcada, me pasó por encima y le pegué otro desplante, y me pegó otra revolquiza. La gente estaba muerta de risa y empezó a aplaudir como loca. ¿Sabes cuál es la diferencia entre la gente del pueblo y la gente de ciudad? La gente de la ciudad quiere que el animal sea limpio, quiere ver unas faenas de arte. La gente de pueblo quiere que el animal te parta la madre.

En Estados Unidos la gente es más considerada con sus animales, no se cómo serán con sus enanos. Aquí en México no, hasta los policías te dicen: "Enano, pinche enano" y uno se acostumbra. Una vez en un restaurante aquí en Guadalajara conocí a una muchacha muy estudiada por medio de un amigo también chaparrito, y yo pensé que ella entendía el concepto de la gente pequeña. Al platicar con ella me dice: "Fíjate que a mí no me gusta que la gente se burle de ustedes, yo no me burlo de ustedes. Yo he ayudado a niños con Síndrome de Down, con cáncer, y más que nada, la gente como ustedes me da lástima". Me lo dijo tan sería que yo no lo podía creer. Básicamente dijo: "Yo no me burlo de ustedes, me dan lástima". Me dejó destrozado.

GUSTAVO VÁZQUEZ BUENDÍA   enanito torero, promotor

Muchos empresarios no tratan nada bien a los enanitos. Por eso mi esposa Isabel y yo montamos nuestra propia empresa, de puros enanos, para ser nosotros nuestros propios jefes. Algunos enanitos que trabajan para nosotros se acaban yendo, porque piensan que nos estábamos enriqueciendo a costa suya. Pero nosotros, aunque salga nada más los sueldos parejos de todos, nos aventamos a manejar, el cansancio, el andar ahí para arriba y para abajo. Ellos lo único que piensan es: "Ellos ganan, me están explotando". Pero si así fuera yo ya debería de tener casa propia, un carro último modelo. Pero nuestra meta es solidarizarnos para que todos tengamos trabajo. Hay veces que no hay con qué pagar pero pos yo nunca les doy malos motivos. Yo les digo: "Tú no preguntes, vienes mañana, te quiero a tal hora", sin dar explicaciones. Así se manejan las empresas. Los invito a trabajar y me preguntan quién va a estar. "Ay no", dicen "porque fulanito me cae mal". Yo sólo digo: "Yo te estoy invitando a trabajar, no te estoy preguntando quién te cae mal, si no quieres, ni modo". Es difícil a veces por que hay mucho chisme entre nosotros

Cuando por primera vez se enteró un promotor alto que yo ya tenía mi propia cuadrilla me habló por teléfono: "¡Oye cabrón! ¿Qué estás haciendo?". Y yo contesto "Pues, ¿qué quieres que haga? Tengo mi cuadrilla, ¿cuál es el problema?". "¿Y a quiénes tienes?". "Pues está éste, éste y éste". Me dice: "Si yo quiero, te quito al Méndez". Yo digo: "¿Qué? Pues mira, por mí no hay problema, el que decide es él". Después me empezaron a llamar otros empresarios altos: "¿Qué onda, Gustavo, ya tienes tu cuadrilla? Pues te felicito, échale ganas". Pero luego empezó la competencia y el egoísmo. Me volvió a llamar y dice: "¡Oye, oye cabrón! ¿Qué pasó? No me andes invadiendo mis lugares o te va a ir mal".

Entre nosotros platicamos que hay que echarle ganas para que el público salga contento. Y esto lo digo porque cuando termina el espectáculo, a veces van a los camerinos y dicen: "Oye chaparrito "¡Muy buen espectáculo!" A nosotros nos da mucha felicidad. Es una satisfacción muy grande que la gente nos tenga fe, y ese afecto lo sabemos aprovechar.

FELIPE MORALES   promotor

La promoción y la publicidad de estos eventos son muy caras. Hay que meter publicidad en la radio y televisión, dar volantes y rentar carros de sonido. Normalmente, la mayoría de las plazas son de las presidencias municipales y reciben un porcentaje de las ganancias. Hay que pagar las plazas e invertir. Lo malo es cuando uno trata con empresas que no están financieramente bien y no te pagan ni para los gastos. Se quieren quedar con todas las ganancias. Ahora hay competencia hasta con empresas más chicas, de enanitos. Bueno, no es que sea competencia, lo que pasa es que, no es porque yo, que soy alto, discrimine a la gente pequeña o alguna otra cosa, pero no es lo mismo que tú, como alto, vayas con un empresario alto, a que vaya un chaparrito. Aún cuando saben que el enanito es el que trae a los enanitos. Desgraciadamente, en México la discriminación hacia los enanos es grande. Casi no se les toma en serio, y se suele dar mas credibilidad a las personas altas que a los chaparritos. Un espectáculo incluye muchas cosas, promociones, entregar publicidad, contratar las vaquillas y entonces no es muy fiable hacer todo esto con ellos [Los Enanitos] ahorita en México.

Yo pensé que a los enanitos que empezaron sus empresas les estaba yendo muy bien, porque han trabajado en una que otra placita de toros. Uno se entera de donde andan, porque en este ambiente tan chiquito todo se sabe. Pero ellos no tienen para invertir en rentar las plazas de toros ni para rentar las vaquillas. Así es que si no venden bien un solo evento ya están acabados, pues se quedan sin dinero para hacer otro.

Hoy vendimos como nueve mil pesos de entrada, y así apenas gano algo: las vacas me costaron mil quinientos pesos, quinientos de sonido y la plaza costó dos mil. Cada chaparrito gana cuatrocientos pesos y los que torean ochocientos. Pagué eso y todo la demás. Me gasté unos mil quinientos en gasolina, volantes y fui cuatro días al pueblo. Si traes a enanitos de fuera te gastas más dinero en pasajes, aun así se me hace mejor traer gente de fuera para no tener problemas con estos mismos chaparritos porque son muy conflictivos. Se meten siempre en lo que uno anda y no se pueden quedar callados, están viendo qué hace y no hace uno para estar quejándose. Se quejan y se van, pero como a los tres o cuatro meses ya están trabajando aquí otra vez. Para mí es un conflicto porque yo no puedo traer a la competencia dentro de mi propio espectáculo. Prefiero que los chaparritos trabajen exclusivamente para mí, pero ellos no lo hacen. A veces me ha tocado que yo voy por ellos para ir a dar una función y ya no están, y me dejan plantado, con la explicación de que otra gente les ofreció más que yo. Pero yo soy de las personas que no quiere tener con ellos ninguna enemistad, porque el mundo da muchas vueltas. Siempre trato de que ellos estén a gusto, como hago con Claudia, yo le permito que se traiga a sus tres niños cuando da espectáculo con nosotros, para que no se queden solos. En otros espectáculos los promotores son muy egoístas y le dicen: "Ven tú nada más, porque aquí vienes a trabajar y no a cuidar niños". Pero yo no, y es más, algunos chaparritos saben que en mi cuadrilla se pueden traer a sus niños, pues les da más interés trabajar conmigo.

VERÓNICA ÁLVAREZ CASTRO   imitadora

Yo lo que quisiera plasmar en un momento dado, ya sea en una película o en una novela, es la falta de respeto que tiene la sociedad ante un pequeño. Me extraña que en pleno siglo XXI todavía se discrimine al pequeño. Si a los pequeños se les apoyara,

en vez de relegarlos a un inframundo, podrían hacer una y mil cosas, pero no se les toma en cuenta como debería de ser. Yo lo he vivido en carne propia y la verdad me siento molesta con la sociedad porque no tienen confianza en un pequeño. Al pequeño se le explota, porque la mayoría no tienen la suficiente preparación académica. Yo no soy una persona muy culta pero sí tengo más preparación que muchos de ellos. Por eso dejé de trabajar en los espectáculos de Enanitos Toreros. Lo que los promotores pagan no va de acuerdo con los enanitos hacen, deberían de ganar más.

Los promotores sólo buscan lucrarse y los enanitos no lo ven porque es su única fuente de trabajo y creen que es el único lugar donde pueden trabajar. Cuando veníamos de la gira en Estados Unidos, una promotora, nos dijo a todos: "Ahora cada quien va a regresar a su lugar de origen, pero ya tengo preparada la próxima salida a Estados Unidos y van a ir todos conmigo porque, de todos modos, ¿a qué se quedan si nadie los quiere en ningún lugar?". A mí me llegó a decir: "A ti, ¿quién te va a querer en algún trabajo? Dondequiera te rechazan". Me dió mucho coraje.

Otra cosa que veo con los chaparritos es que hay mucha desunión, no sé si sea por envidia, porque se sienten inferiores. Un amigo me dijo que yo me creía mucho, que me creía muy culta, y que muchas veces, por cómo platico, la gente se queda impresionada. Me gusta leer y no lo hago por presumir, sino por interés propio. Hace poco le comenté a mi psicóloga lo que me dicen los chaparritos y ella me comentó: "Mira Vero, no es envidia, lo que pasa es que ellos se sienten mal porque te ven segura, te ven contenta, te ven preparada. Se ve en tu exterior que te quieres mucho y ellos no se ven así. ¿Cómo sabes tú si ellos por dentro han pasado muchas cosas muy duras en sus vidas? A lo mejor son rechazados, tal vez no tienen quien los quiera de verdad".

Lo que a veces me hace sentir mal es el no haber terminado una carrera profesional. Ahora que tengo muchas ganas ya no es tan fácil con dos hijos que mantener. Ellos me ven que ando de aquí para allá, con mucho entusiasmo. La gente me dice que siempre me ven trabajando y eso me gusta y me hace sentir bien. Yo estaba estudiando licenciatura en Trabajo Social, pero no terminé porque me operé las piernas para crecer más cuando tenía diecisiete años. Lo decidí porque siempre quise ser alta. Yo me sentía mal después de la experiencia, acomplejada por el trauma de haber tenido clavos en las piernas, por no caminar por mucho tiempo, por el dolor del tratamiento y por haber desgarrado mi piel. Fue una experiencia muy dolorosa que en cierta forma me dañó mucho porque los amigos que tenía se retiraron por la tristeza de verme así.

De chiquita era muy alegre, muy social, me encantaba que me dijeran muñeca. Pero en la adolescencia y preparatoria me empecé a acomplejar mucho porque yo veía a las compañeras que eran cortejadas por los muchachos y conmigo eran diferentes. Me trataron siempre como una niña chiquita y me gustaba, pero al mismo tiempo me hacían sentir menos porque las veía a ellas muy guapas. La gente es muy cruel con uno. Una vez en la preparatoria nos mandaron a hacer trabajo social a una comunidad donde había muchos niños. Se me hizo muy triste y aún no entiendo qué pasó: me siguieron con una cadena, con la que me iban a golpear y eran niños como de nueve años, la misma edad que tiene ahora mi hijo. Llegué a mi casa hecha un mar de lágrimas, me encerré en un cuarto, no quería saber nada del mundo exterior. Pero es que la gente adulta distorsiona mucho lo que es un chaparrito, lo ponen como un duende malo, un villano, el que destruye todo.

Antes estaba muy acomplejada, pero ahora soy muy diferente en mi forma de pensar. Una vez fui a pedir trabajo para secretaria. Llegué a la entrevista con una licenciada, estaba sentada en su escritorio, muy estudiada. Ya que me ve de arriba a abajo y me dice me dice: "¿Sabes qué mija? Ya vi que pasaste todos los exámenes, eres muy inteligente. Pero te voy a decir una cosa, los empresarios no quieren a gente como tú porque ellos buscan mujeres altas de cuerpos bonitos que les proyecten algo bueno a su empresa". Le dije: "Bueno, está bien, si yo no soy apta para ese trabajo lo entiendo, no me voy a sentir mal, no me voy a enojar, muchas gracias por atenderme". Cuando ella se paró, vi que tenía polio y no podía caminar, traía bastones. Pensé: "Híjole, pobrecita, tan mal se siente que quiso hacerme sentir peor que ella, pobre mujer".

Somos totalmente iguales que toda la gente, no tenemos ninguna discapacidad, nuestro cerebro es totalmente igual al de una gente "normal". Incluso pienso, y tal vez se escuche mal, que el cerebro de un pequeño tiene más capacidad que el de una persona "normal". Cuando la gente te mira de arriba abajo, uno se siente demasiado incómodo. Llega el momento en que uno quisiera hacerse polvo y desparecer.

Me gustaría que hubiese una institución en la que se apoyara a los pequeños para que se formaran en una carrera, con apoyo psicológico por lo dañados que están, por tanta gente que los ha excluido. A mí también me cortaron las alas muchas veces. Maestras del colegio religioso donde estudié con todo el descaro le dijeron a mí mamá: "Aquí terminan los estudios de su hija, ella no va poder ser maestra pues va a asustar a los niños por ser enana". La verdad es realmente deprimente el trato que se le da al pequeño. Porque no es un animal, no es una persona a la que hay tratar como un juguetito, al que hay que vestir y poner en medio de una plaza de toros a que se mueva como un marioneta. El pequeño tiene sentimientos, siente y le duelen muchas cosas. Yo tengo la esperanza de que algún día todo sea diferente.

YOLANDA BIVIANO actriz

Desde que era chiquita quería salir en la televisión. Le decía a mi mamá y ella me contestaba: "Sí, te vamos a echar una mano". Pero no podía porque como es comerciante, estaba cien por cien ocupada con los puestos del mercado y no los podía dejar. Así que yo me tenía que aguantar. Cuando tenía quince años había una asociación de gente pequeña en México. En las juntas fui conociendo más chaparritos, porque al principio piensas que eres la única, que no hay más. Mi hermano también es chiquito y dices: "Bueno, a lo mejor nada más somos así de chiquitos nosotros dos". Ahí conocí a una amiga, Tere, la mamá de David y Claudia, y ella me dijo: "Oye, vamos a Guadalajara a trabajar en el show de Los Enanitos Toreros". Mi mamá no quería porque me iba sola, con gente que no conocía. De todos modos me fui por cinco meses, bailando, imitando artistas. Vivía con Tere en un hotel en Guadalajara. Es muy padre todo eso. Salía de sevillana y también imitaba a Gloria Trevi. Cantaba la de "Pelo Suelto" y "Doctor Psiquiatra".

Lo que no me gusta es que los promotores no nos pagan bien, no nos dan seguro médico y si te pasa algo ellos no responden por ti, pero todo lo demás está bien. Cuando trabajaba con los Enanitos Toreros, me hice novia de David, pero no nos llevábamos muy bien. En cierta manera ésa fue una de las razones por las que me regresé al Distrito Federal. Teníamos muchas discusiones. Entonces, para llevar la vida en paz me regresé.

Una persona me dijo que yo sin ese trabajo no iba conseguir hacer nada. Estuve triste por un rato porque no tenía nada que hacer y me había salido de algo que me gustaba, que es bailar. Siempre me ha gustado ese ambiente. Dejé algo que me gusta por discusiones de pareja.

Ya cuando regresé me inscribí en la ANDA [Asociación Nacional De Actores] y empecé a trabajar en la tele. Yo hacía el personaje de una niñita y le hacía bromas a la gente. La gente sí se enojaba, pero yo nada más les decía "Ay, no te enojes, regálanos una sonrisa para la cámara de *Te Caché*". Tengo muchos amigos nuevos y les digo: "Si tuve que pasar por todo lo que pasé en Guadalajara para tener lo que tengo ahorita, no me arrepiento". A lo mejor eso me tenía que pasar para conocer otras cosas. Me encanta bailar, imitar, pero creo que el destino es así y ¿qué le vamos a hacer? Le doy gracias a la vida por ponerme esas pruebas, supe salir adelante, no me di por vencida. No dejé que me hiciera como se le diera la gana.

VANESA GARCÍA de VIRGEN ama de casa

Yo estaba estudiando licenciatura en turismo en Tijuana. Iba a centros comerciales y la gente me hacía preguntas, como si yo formara parte de los Enanitos Toreros. Me preguntaban cuándo íbamos a torear y me pedían mi autógrafo. Decían que me parecía a una de ellas. Yo no sabía de qué estaban hablando y entonces me entró la curiosidad por conocerlos.

Fui a la función y así conocí a todos los que toreaban y conocí al promotor Rogelio Amador. Me dijo que si quería trabajar con él. que lo podía ayudar en lo que son las entrevistas y todo eso, porque estaba preparada. Que si yo quería torear era ya mi decisión, pero más que nada sólo iría con la prensa. Me dió su tarjeta y así quedó. Yo estaba estudiando y no lo vi como una opción. Aparte, a mi mamá se le hizo un espectáculo morboso——no el espectáculo en sí, no sé qué terminología darle, pero más que nada mi mamá pensó que algunas personas solo van a verlo por morbo. Fui a tres funciones y en la última conocí a Gerson el más galán de ahí, la figura del toreo.

Estaba estudiando, pero eso también se limita. Por más preparación y experiencia que tengas al respecto de la materia, no te contratan simplemente por la estatura, porque no creen que seas lo suficientemente capaz de hacer algo como cualquier persona. Yo estaba estudiando licenciatura en turismo pero ahorita estoy trabajando en la caravana navideña de Coca-Cola. Salgo vestida de duende de Santa Clos.

JUAN CHÁVEZ actor

Yo me salí de los Enanitos Toreros porque quiero ser actor. Quiero ser artista serio, no payasear. En el ruedo todo es pura payasada. Los promotores hacen que te pegues, que te bajes los pantalones, eso nos piden los promotores. Luego nos traen viajando todos incómodos, como a quince en una camioneta todos apretados. Yo prefiero trabajar como actor. En la actuación te toman como artista y en los Enanitos Toreros no. Lo de los Enanitos Toreros no tiene que ver con lo que es el arte de la actuación, es un espectáculo muy diferente. Hace tiempo me inscribí en la ANDA y cuando llegó Pavarotti a cantar a México por fin me hablaron y me contrataron. Mientras él cantaba, yo tenía que salir desnudo bailando, haciendo así, abrazando mi cuerpo como si fuera un pequeño bulto. Luego salía una francesa y hacía el gesto de que está tirando lanzas a una bola y se quedan pegadas. Pero ahí me ves en el escenario con un taparrabos nomás, desnudo, caminando, dándole vueltas a la mujer francesa. Luego ella se hinca y nos sentamos los dos y él, Pavarotti, sigue cantando. No sé qué representaba la bola para Pavarotti y qué representa que haya querido tener un enano desnudo en su espectáculo. Era una canción de un sueño sobre el año 3000 y durante la canción, la mujer y yo nos vamos caminando hacia una especie de galaxia en donde desaparecemos, de la mano. Estábamos bailando y yo sentía pena, pero quería conocer al tal Luciano Pavarotti.

¡Está reeegoooordo! En otra película me tocó hacer el papel de un malo que le está pegando a una mujer morena dentro de una cueva. Luego llega Arnold Schwarzenegger y yo empiezo a echar porras corriendo por toda la cueva.

Lo que quiero es que la gente nos vea con un respeto grande y que no nos imaginen como si fuéramos unos títeres. Antes, los enanitos solo se veían en el circo; pero ahora la gente ya no se espanta al vernos por la calle. Yo antes, me moría de vergüenza cada vez que la gente se me quedaba mirando, pero ya no. El mundo va cambiando poco a poco, y ahora se ven mas enanitos caminando por las calles con la cabeza en alto.

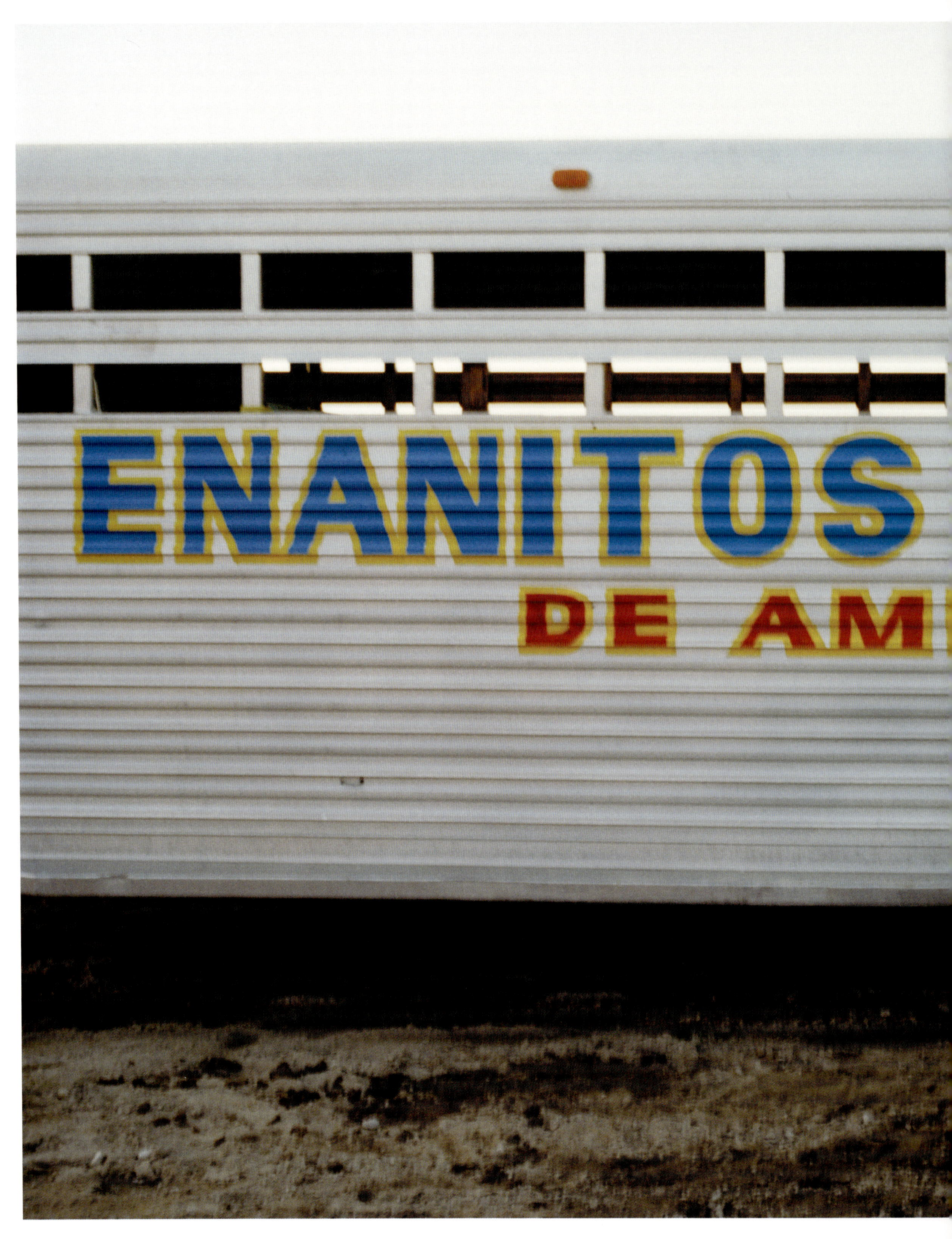
ENANITOS
DE AM

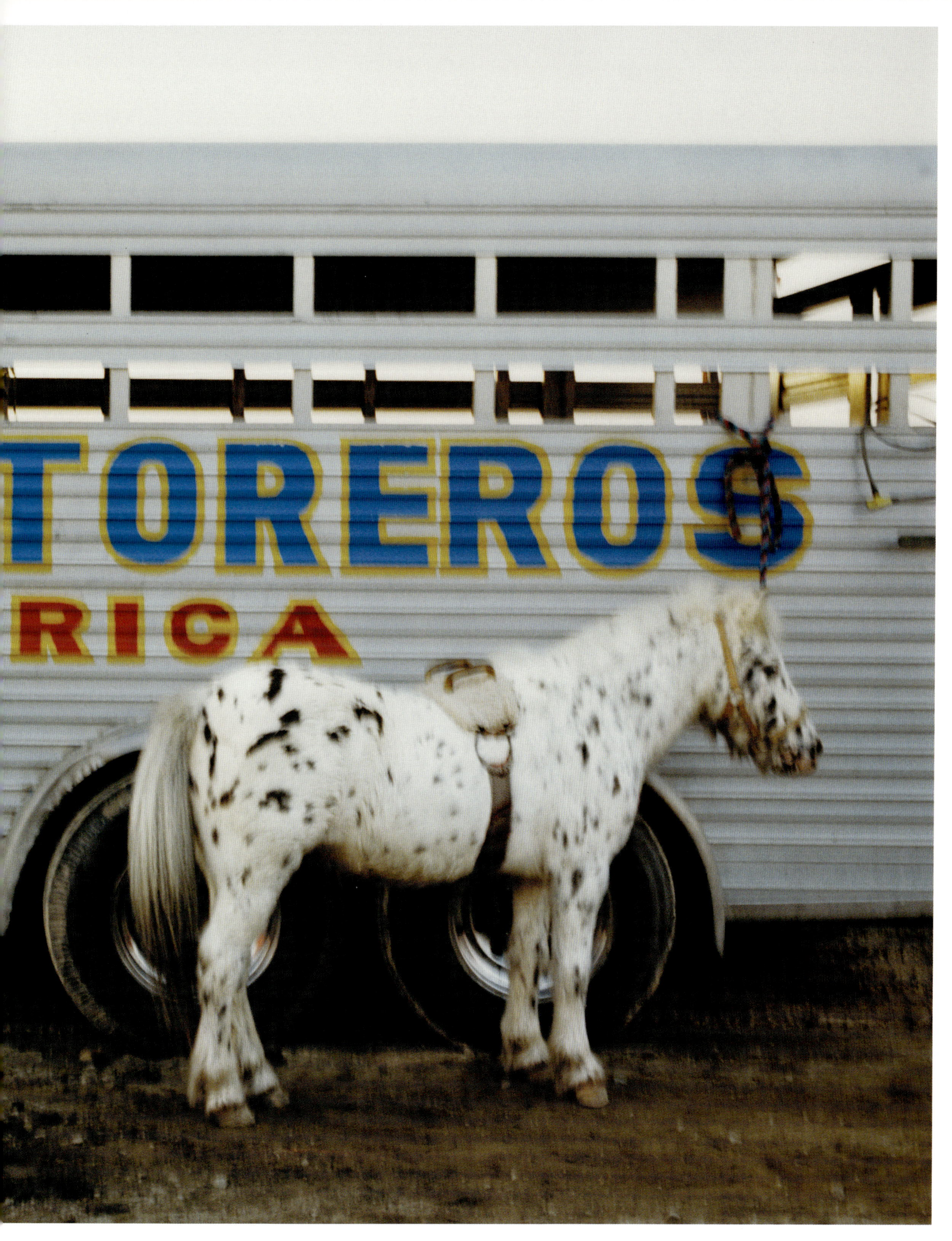
TOREROS
RICA

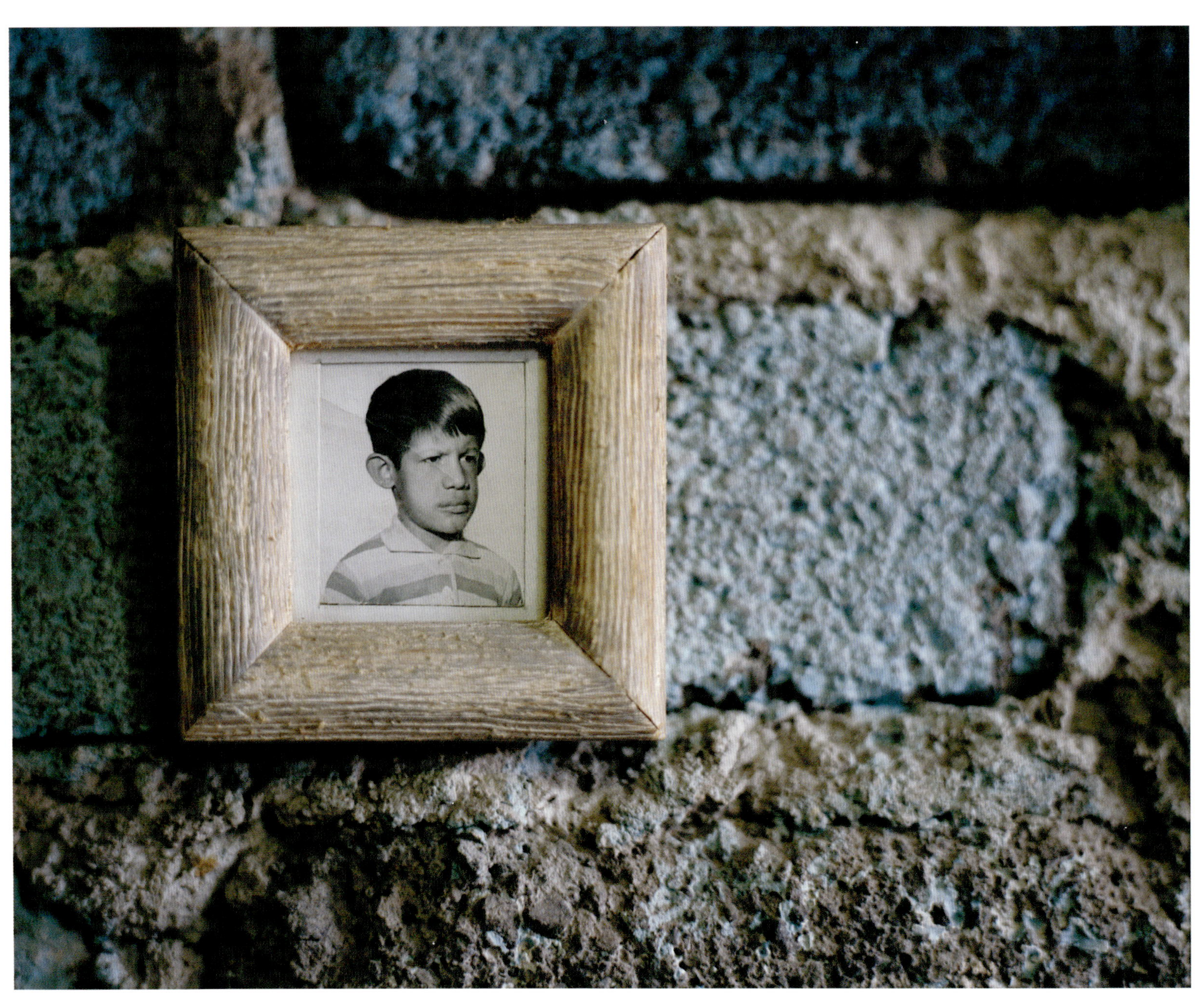

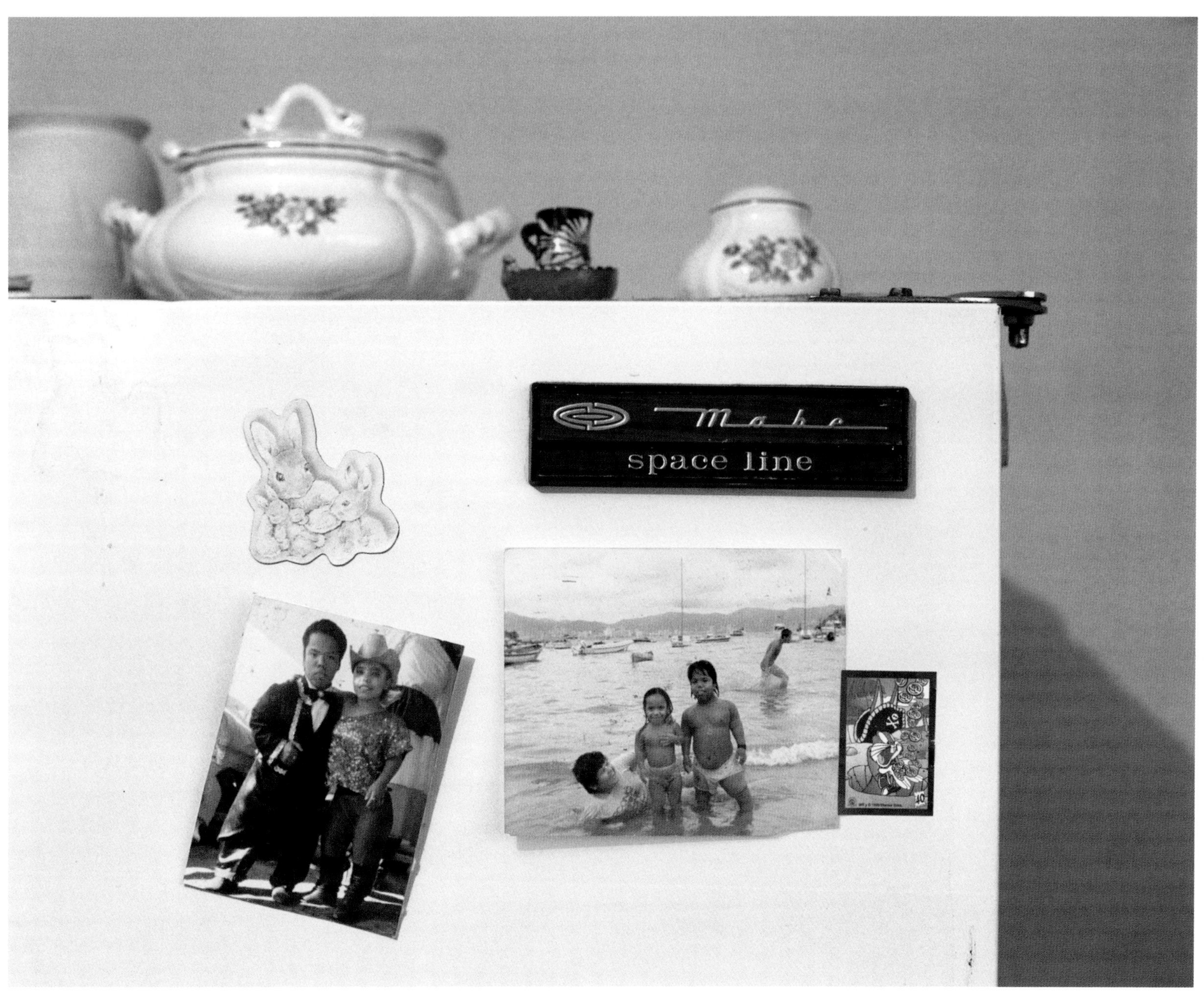
Make
space line

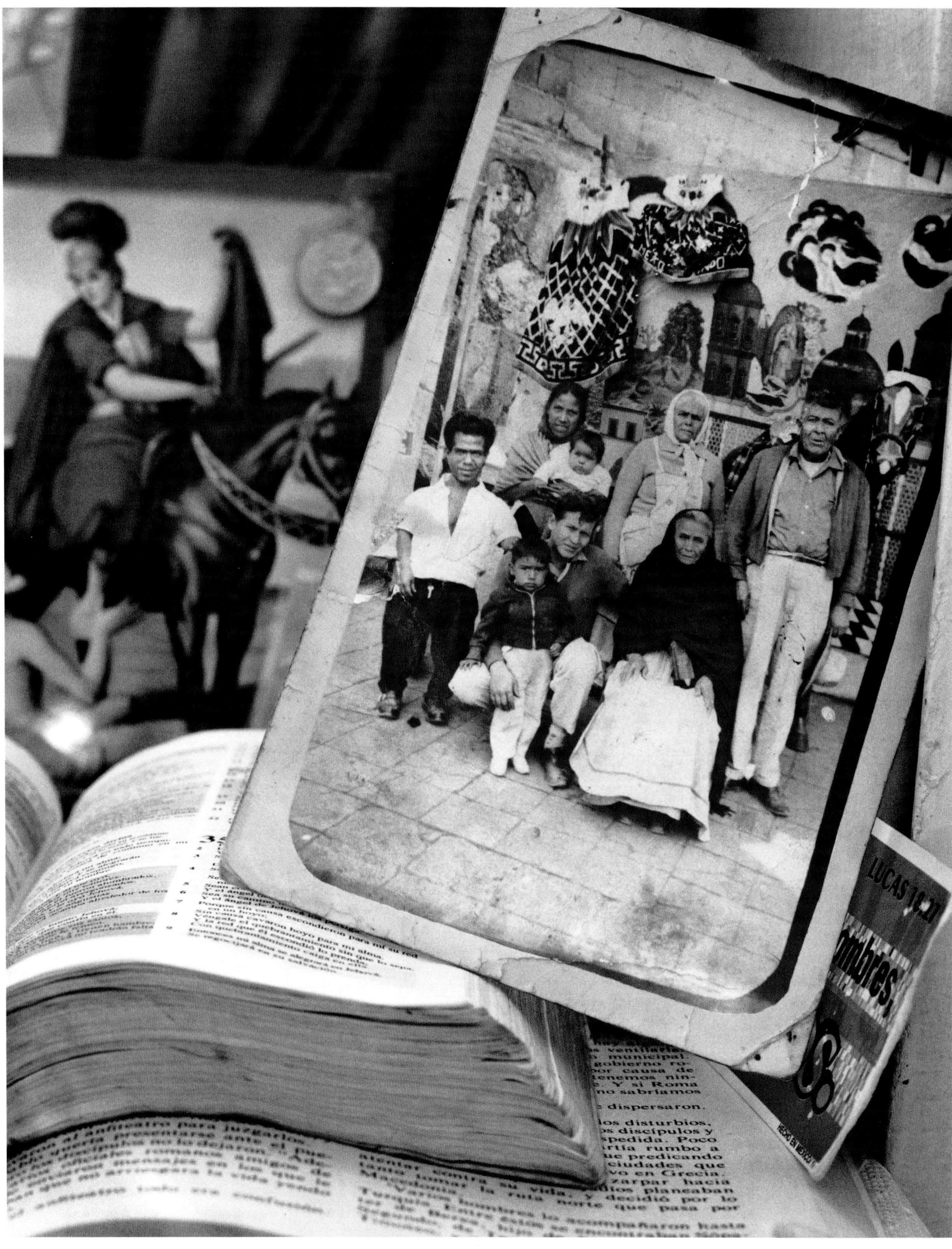

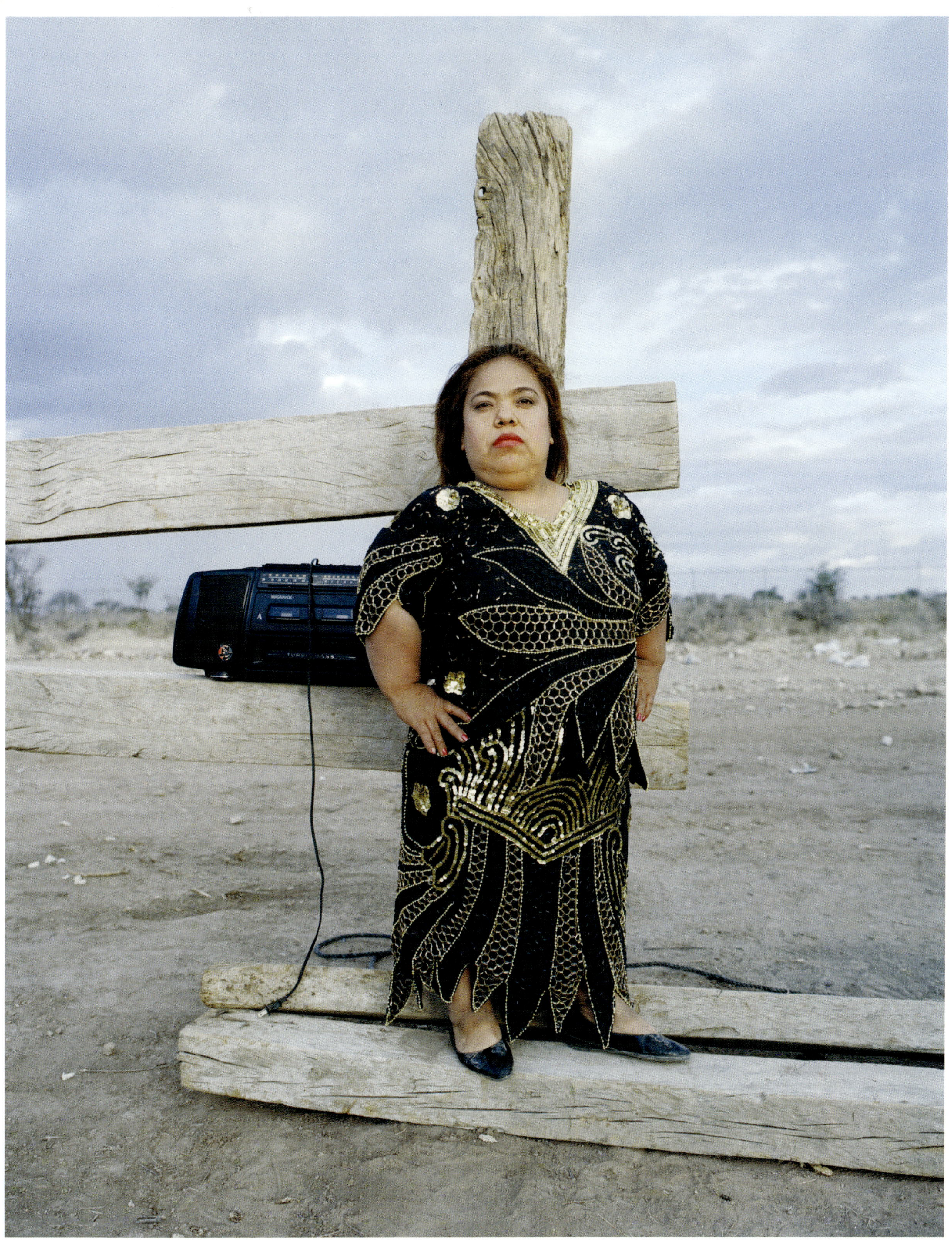

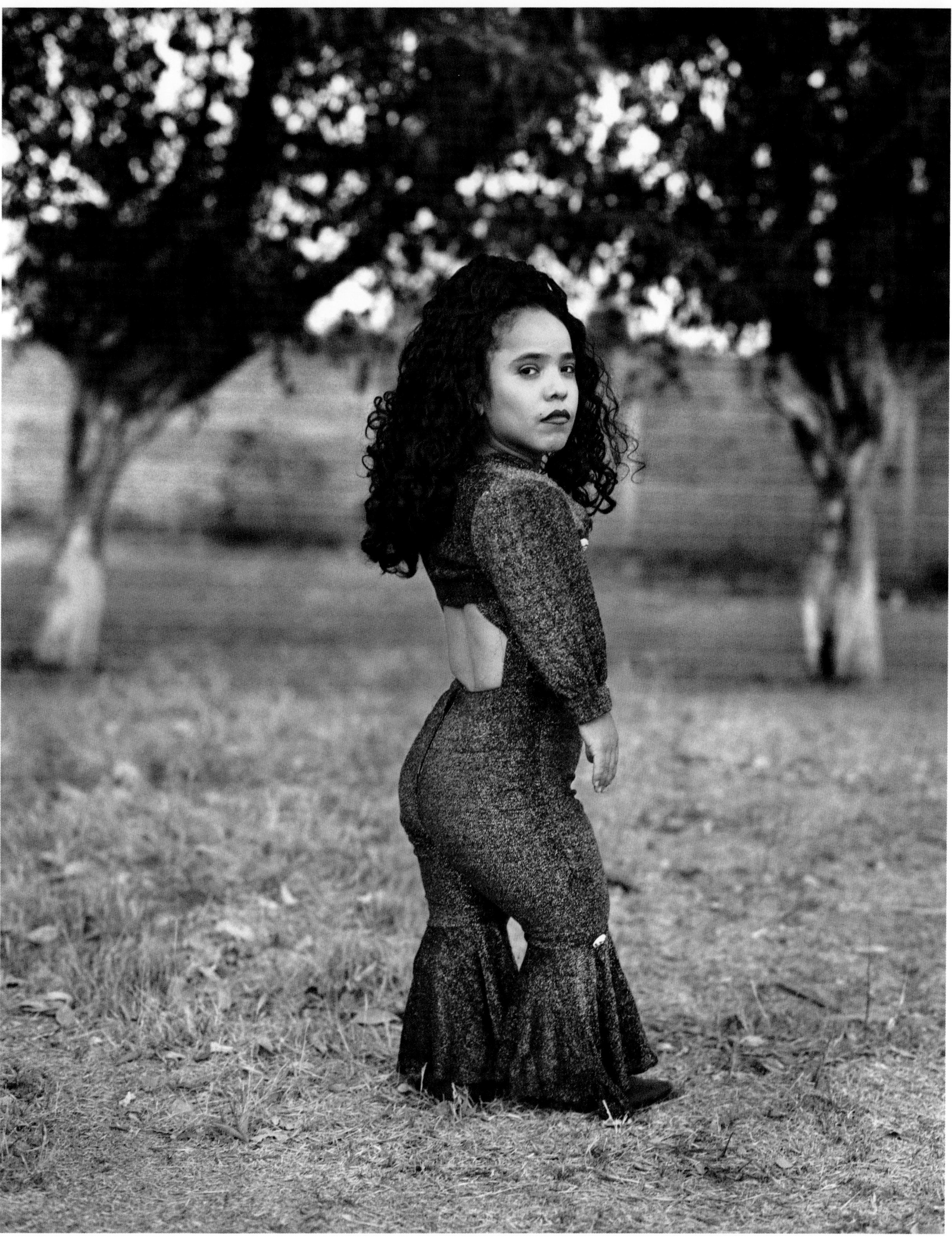

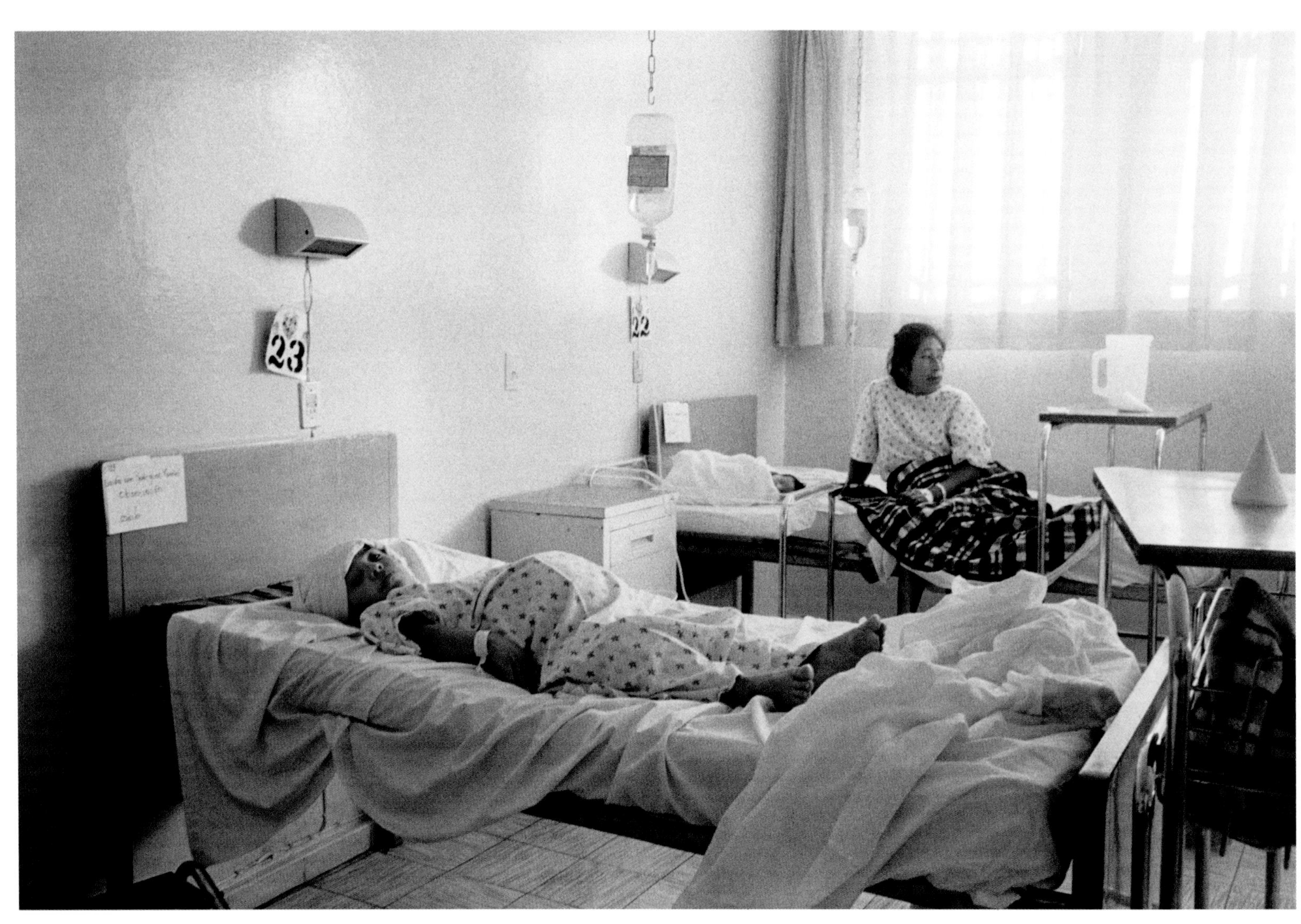

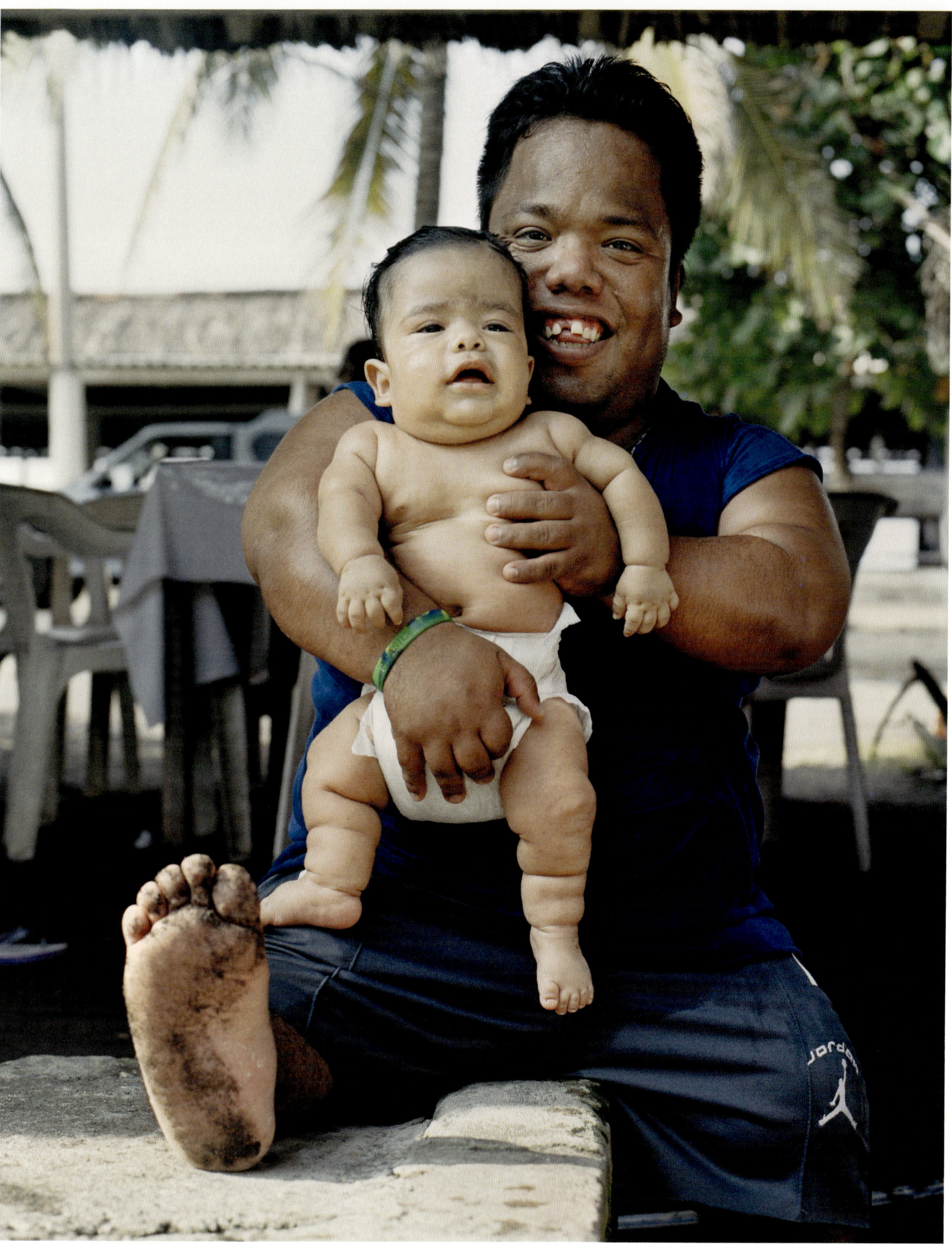

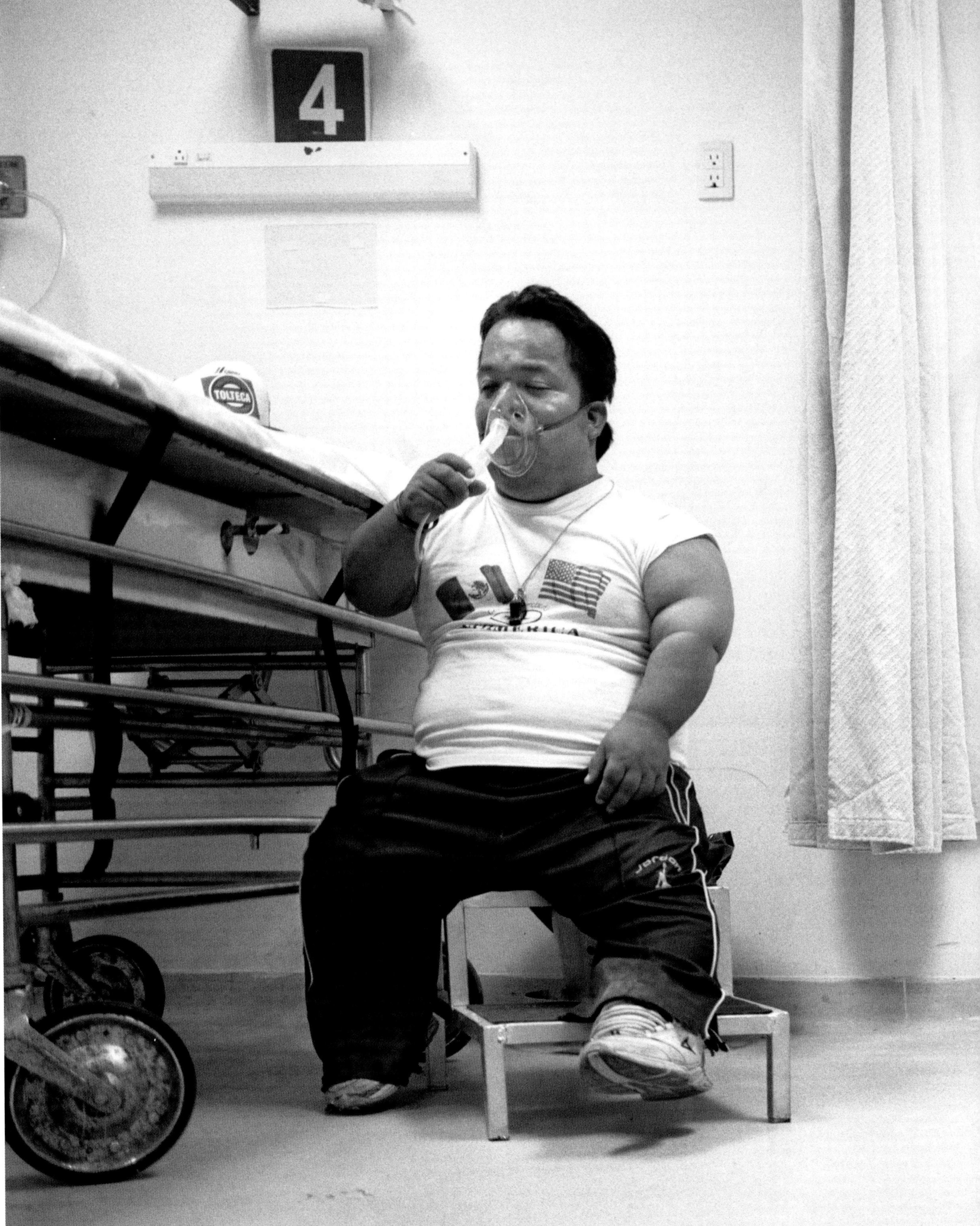
4
TOLTECA

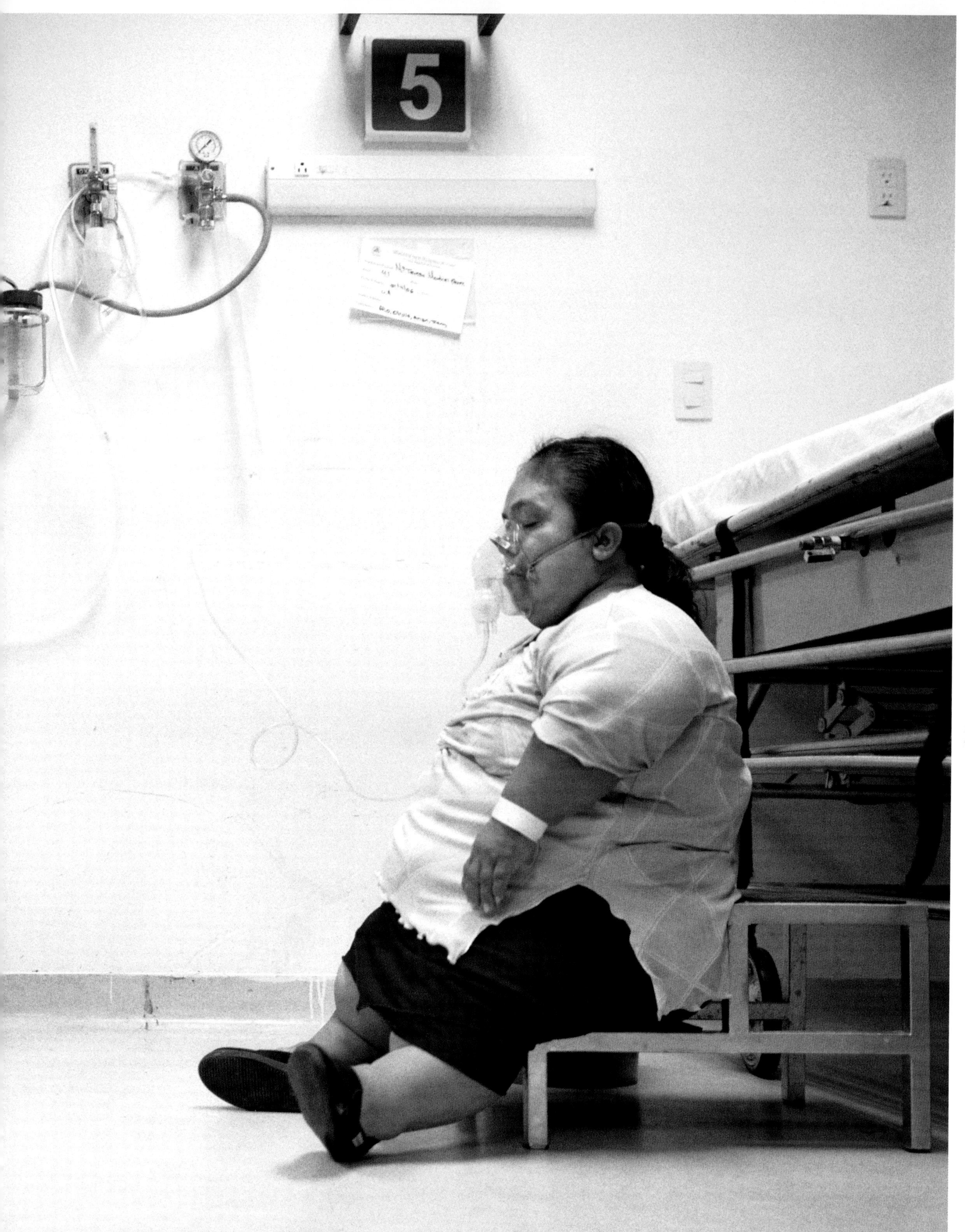

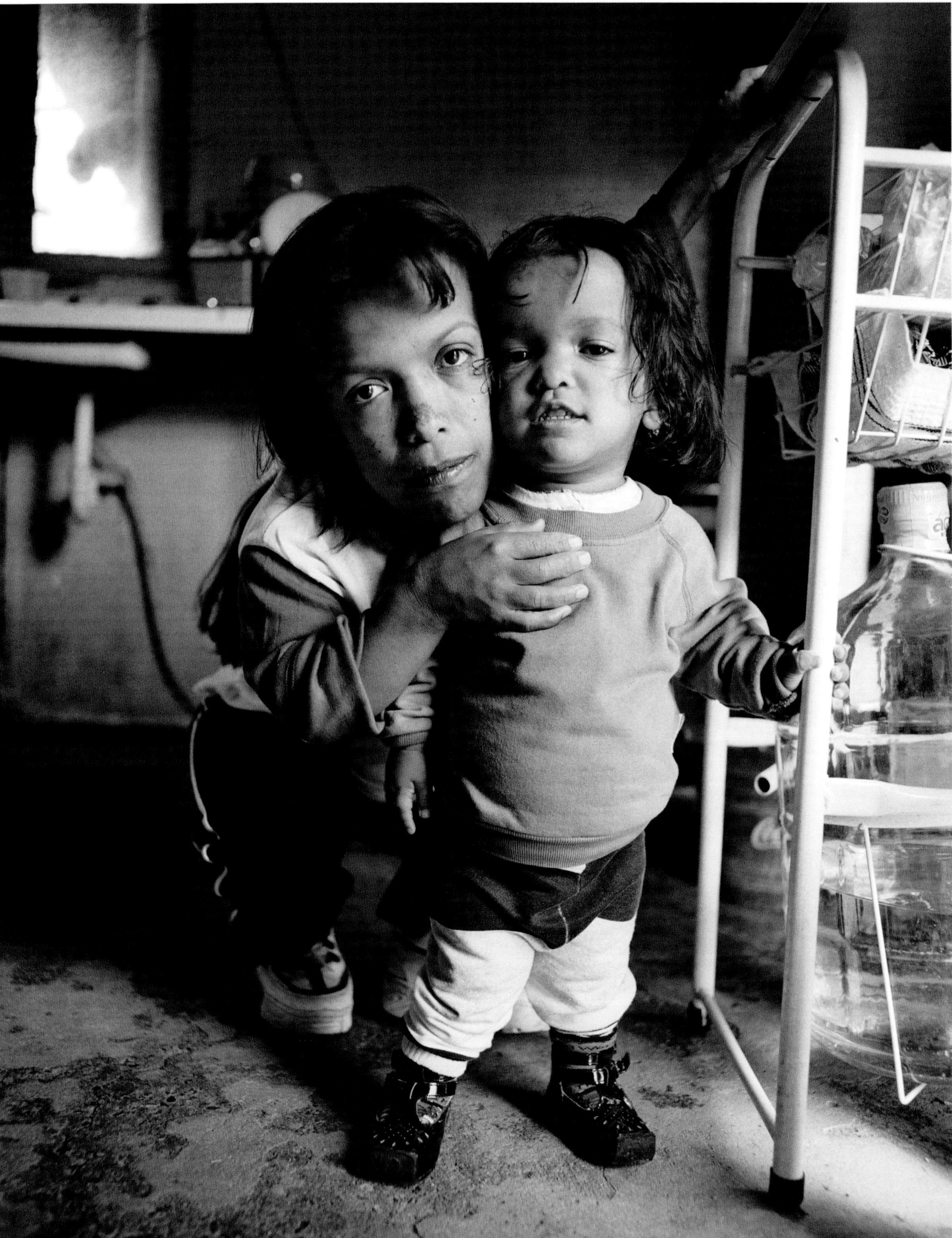

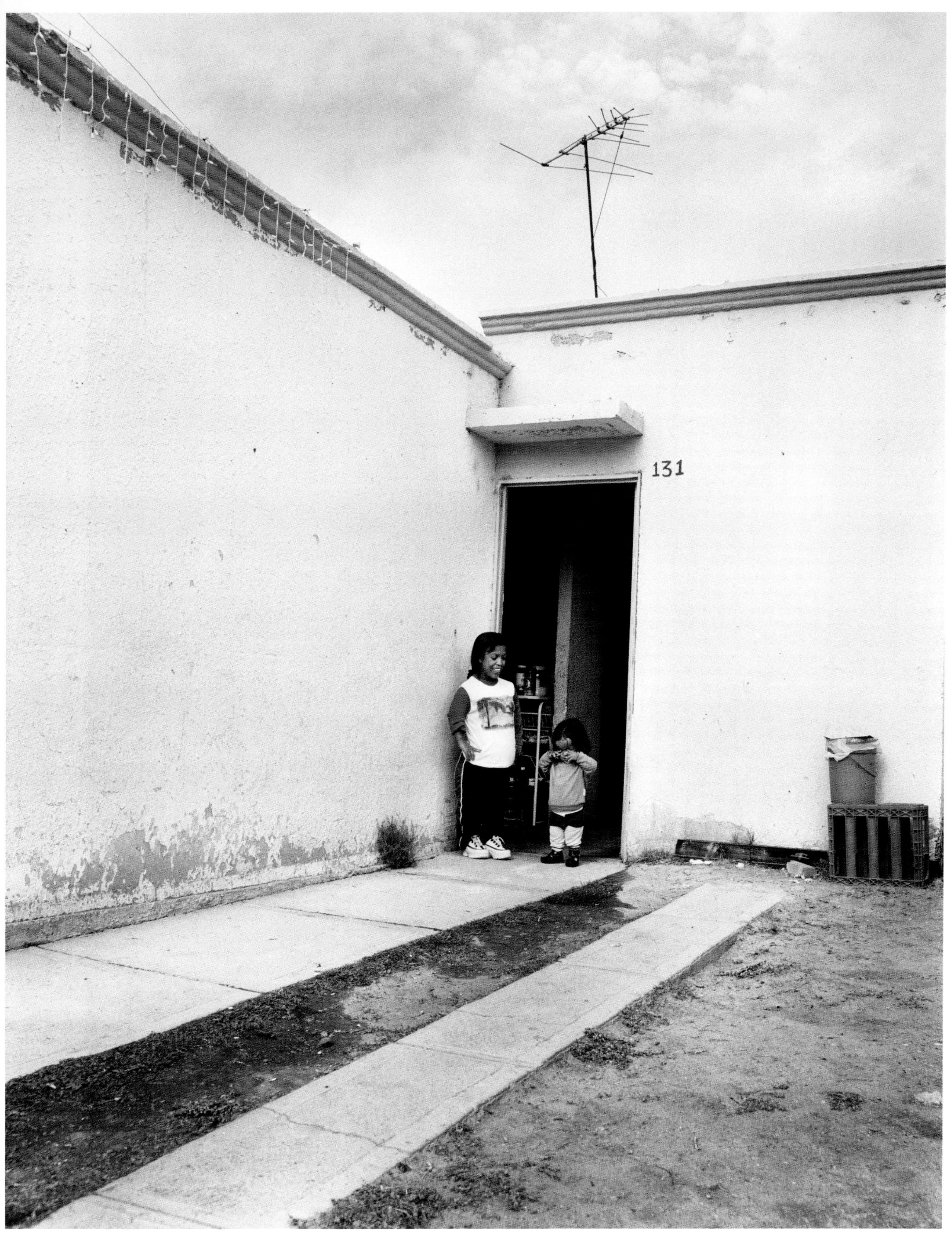
131

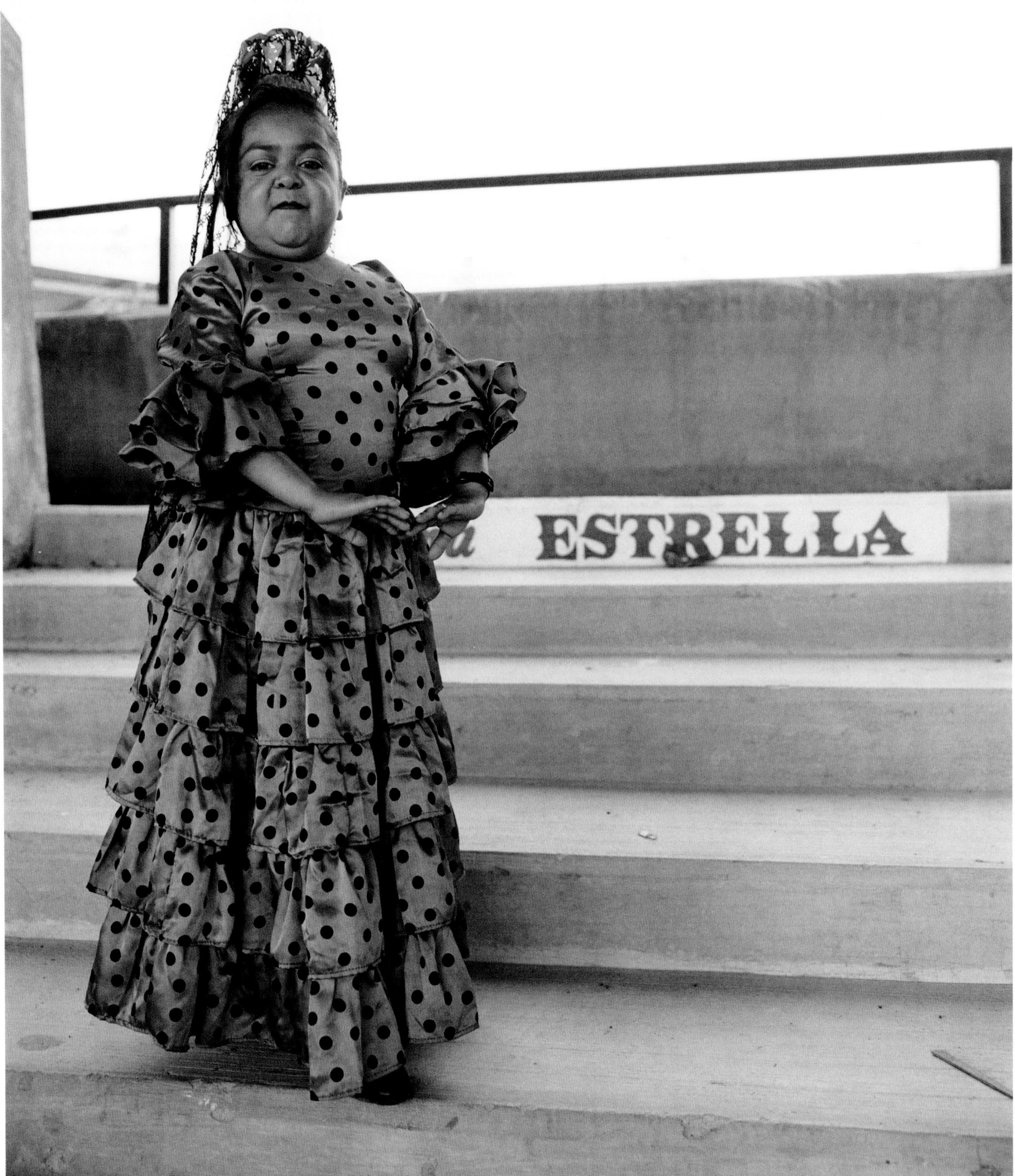

ESTRELLA

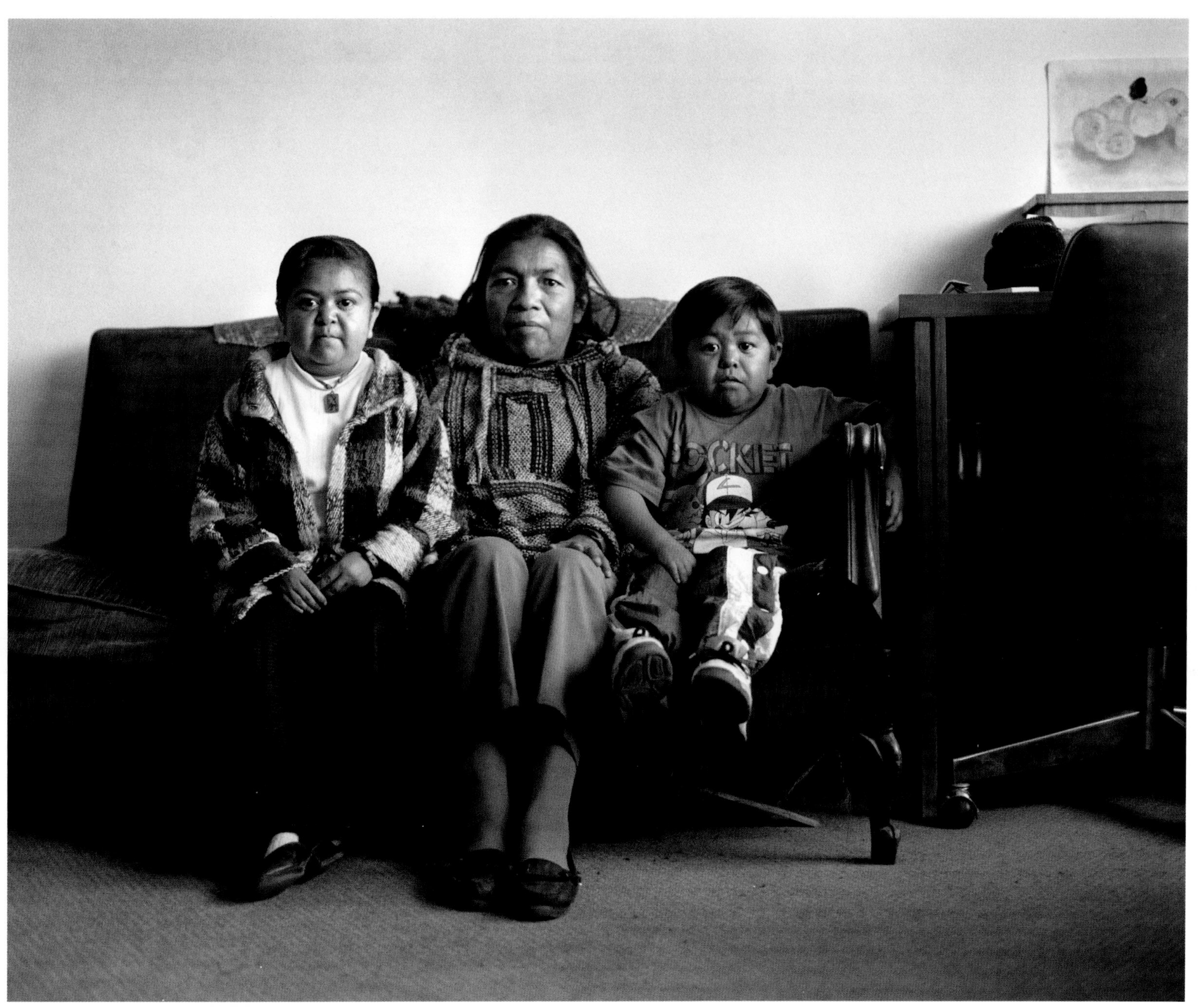

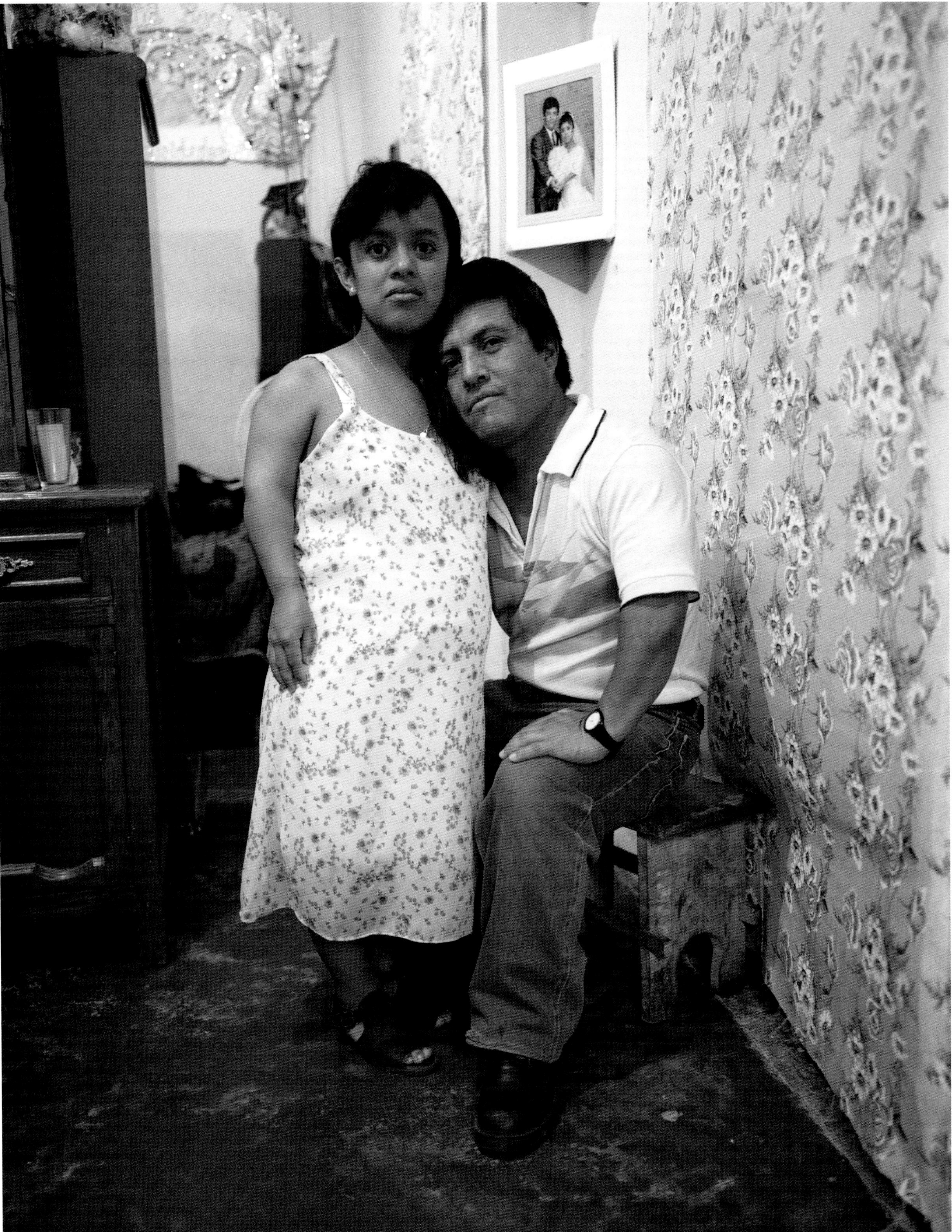

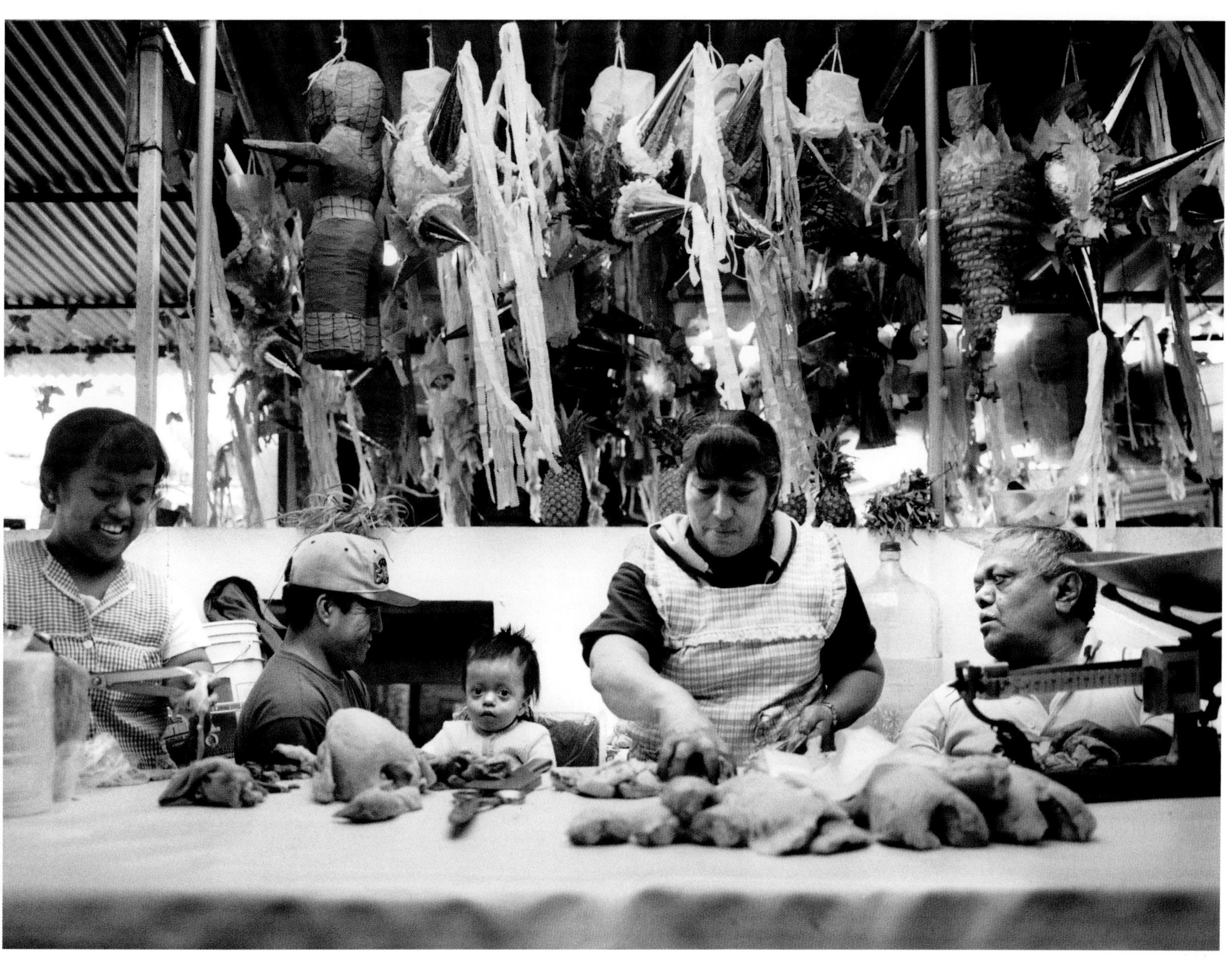

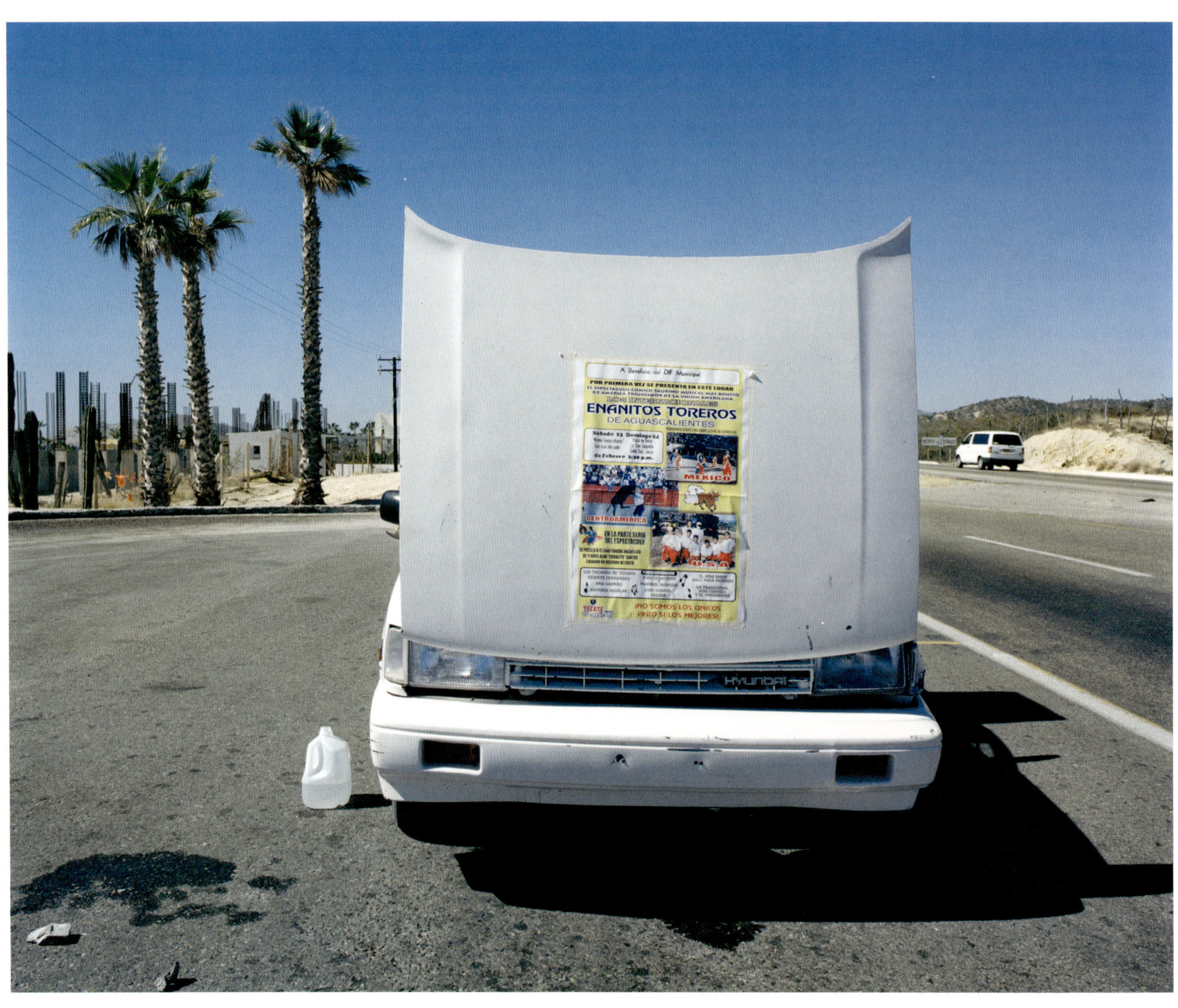

A Beneficio del DIF Municipal
POR PRIMERA VEZ SE PRESENTA EN ESTE LUGAR
EL ESPECTÁCULO CÓMICO TAURINO MUSICAL MÁS BONITO
DE AMÉRICA TRIUNFADOR DE LA UNIÓN AMERICANA
LOS INTERNACIONALES
ENANITOS TOREROS
DE AGUASCALIENTES
Sábado 23 Domingo 24
de Febrero 5:30 p.m.
MÉXICO
CENTROAMERICA
EN LA PARTE SERIA DEL ESPECTÁCULO
U.S.A.
¡NO SOMOS LOS ÚNICOS PERO SI LOS MEJORES!
TECATE

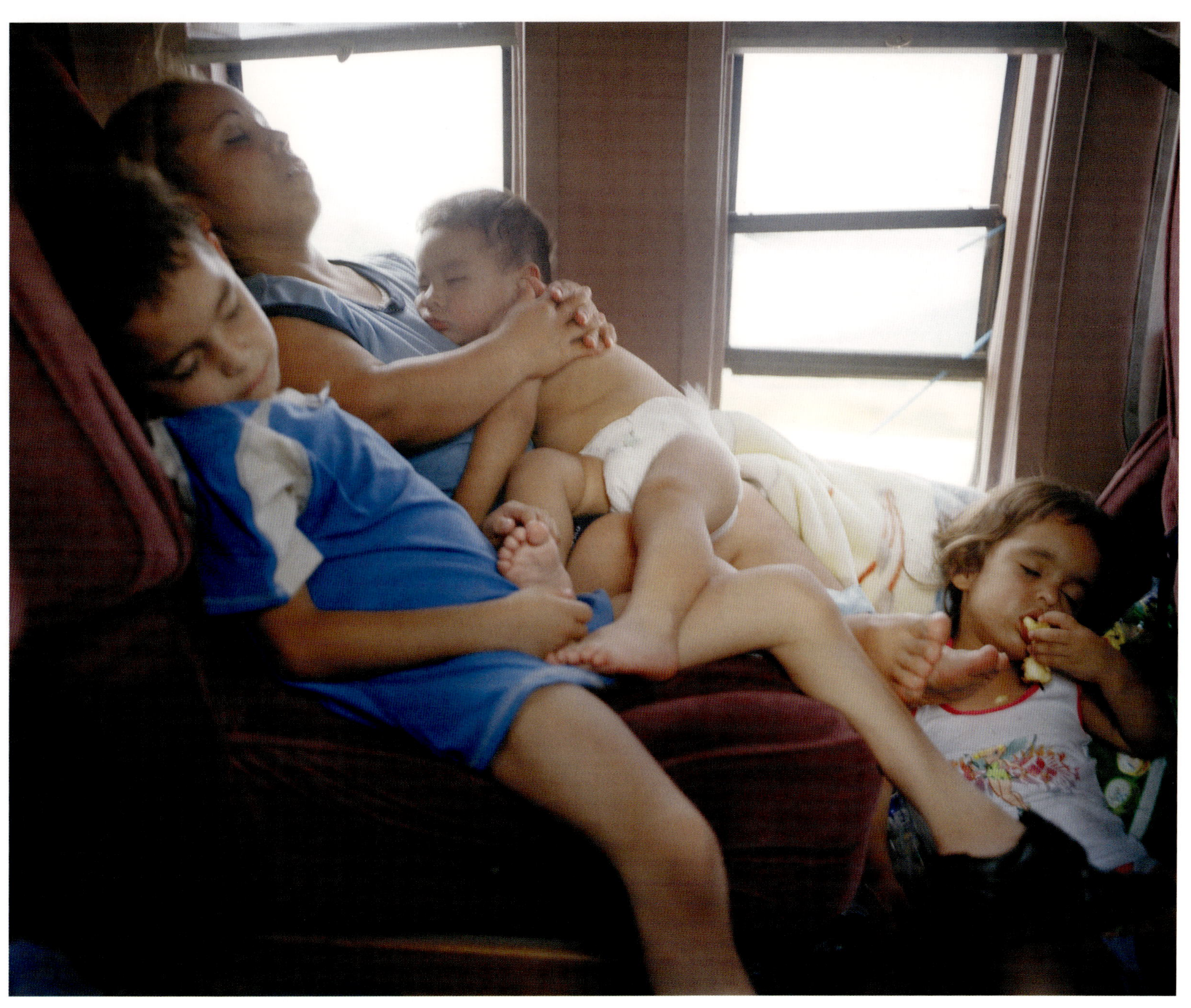

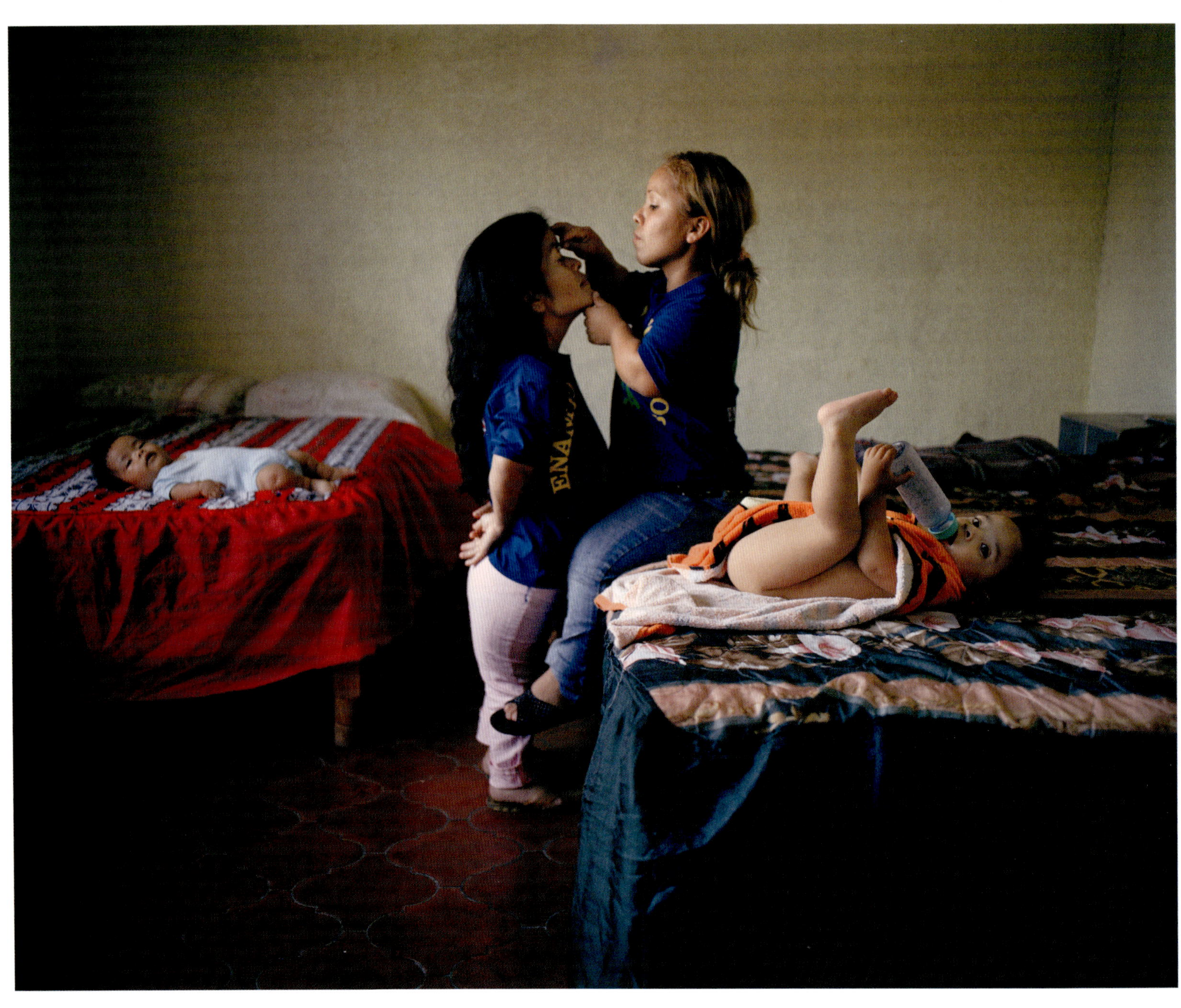

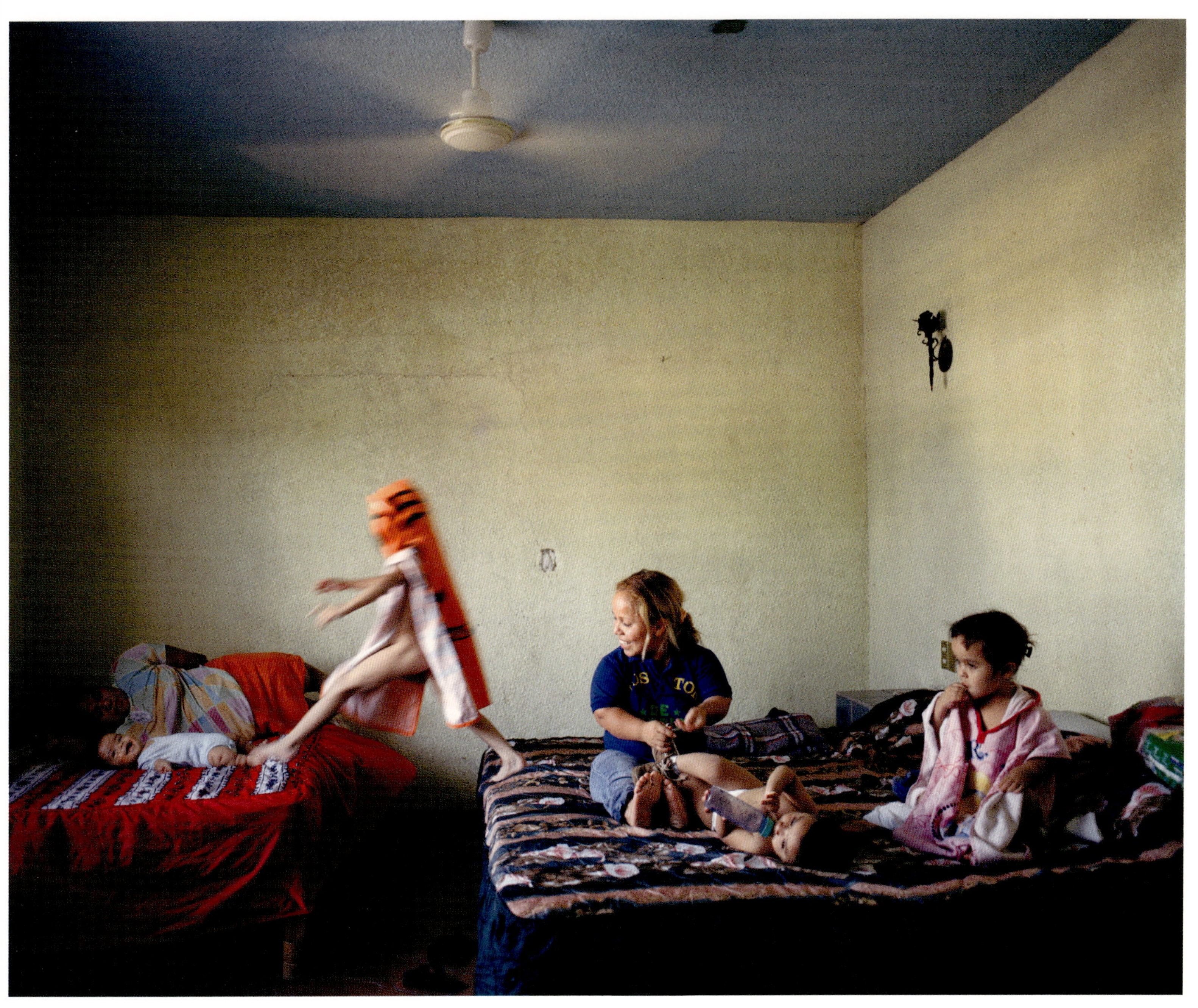

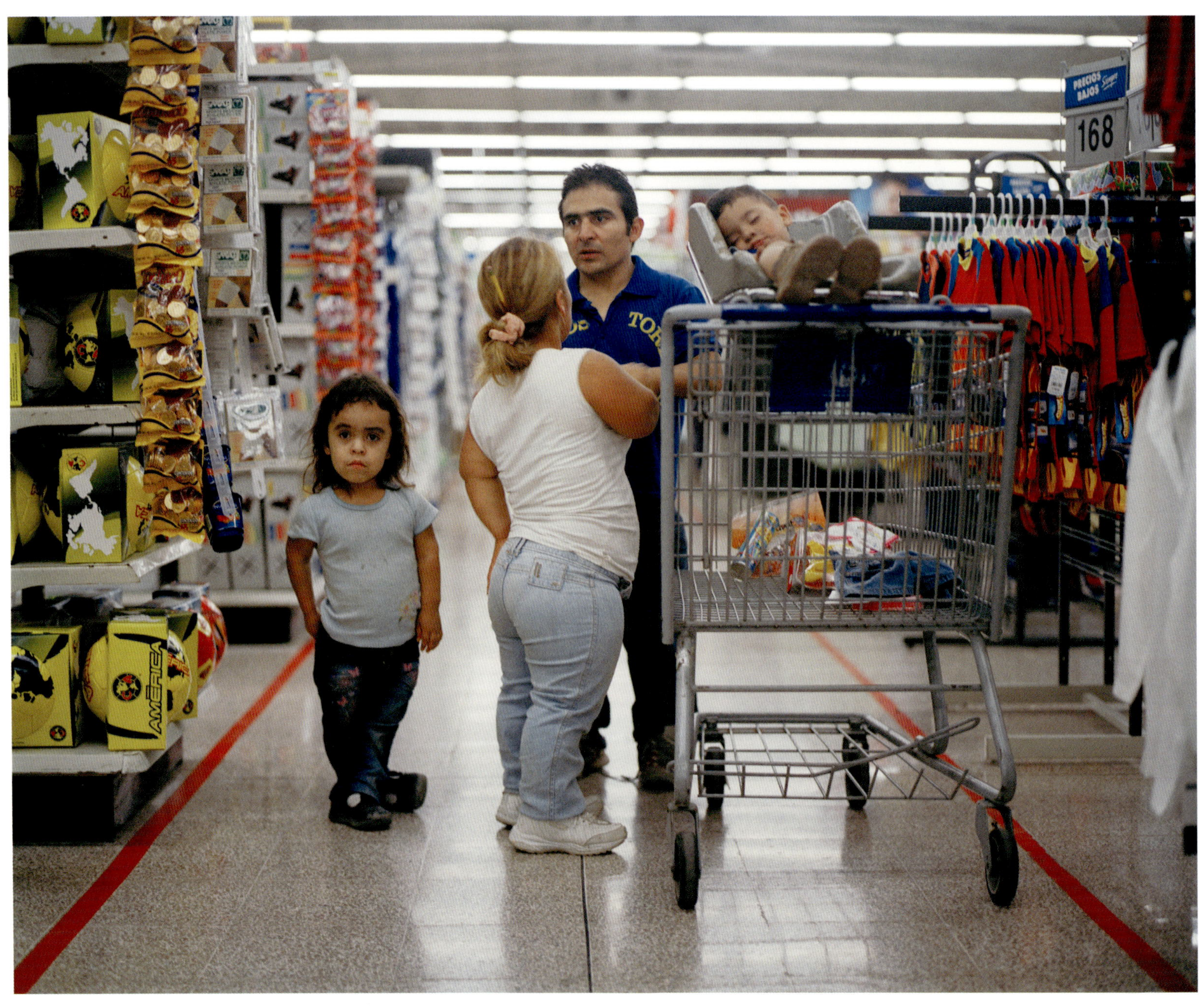

AMÉRICA
PRECIOS BAJOS
168

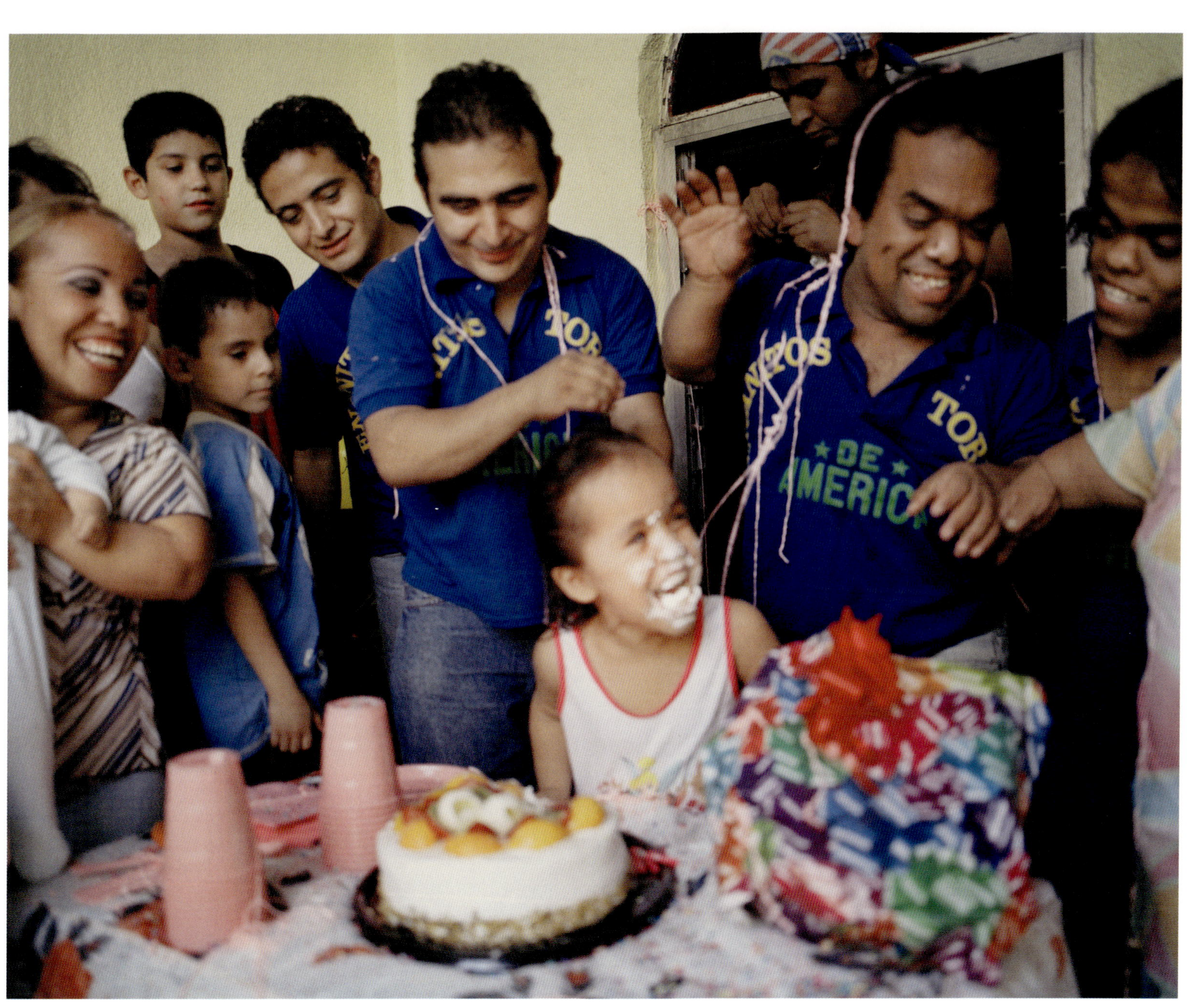

TOR
DE
AMERICA

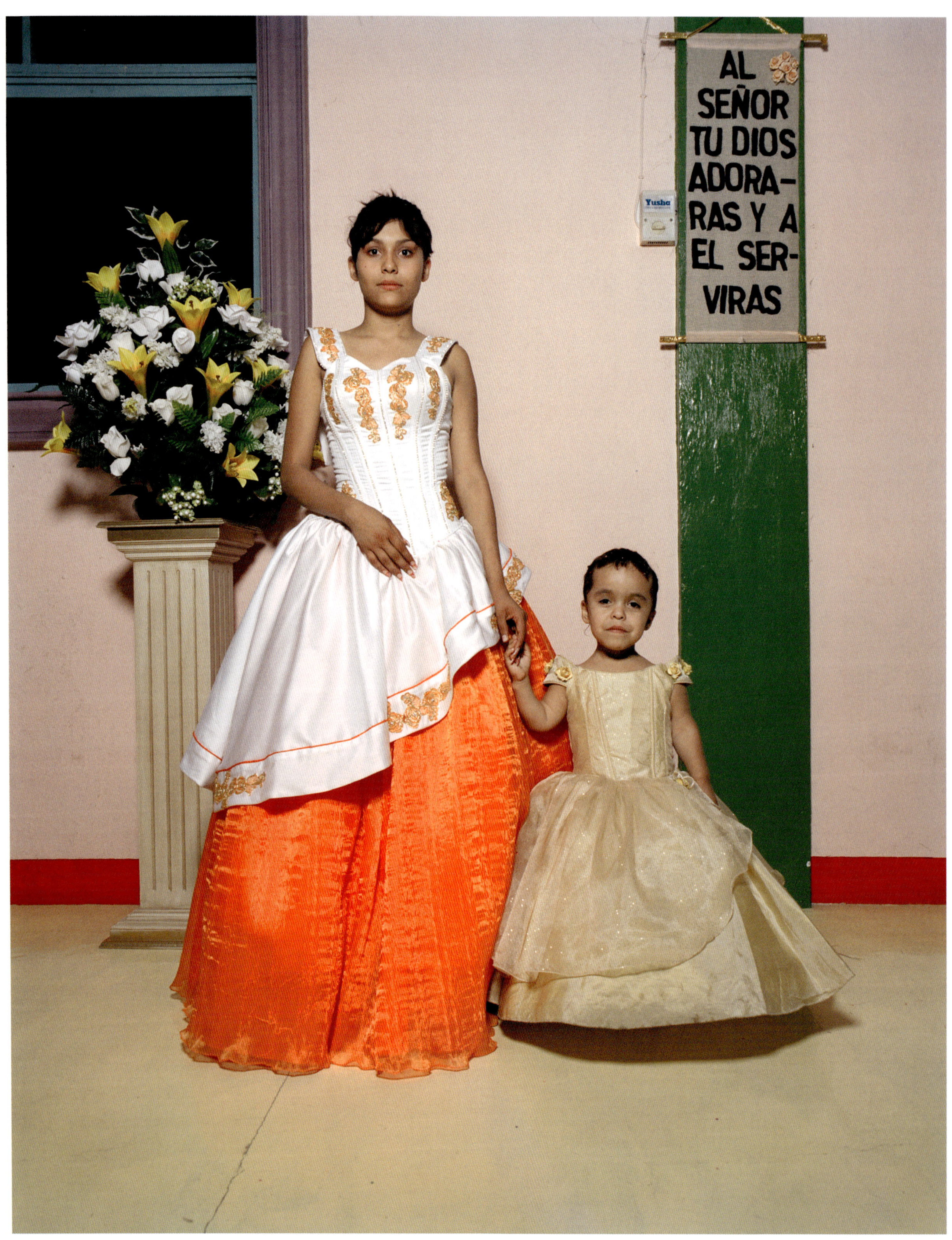
AL
SEÑOR
TU DIOS
ADORA-
RAS Y A
EL SER-
VIRAS

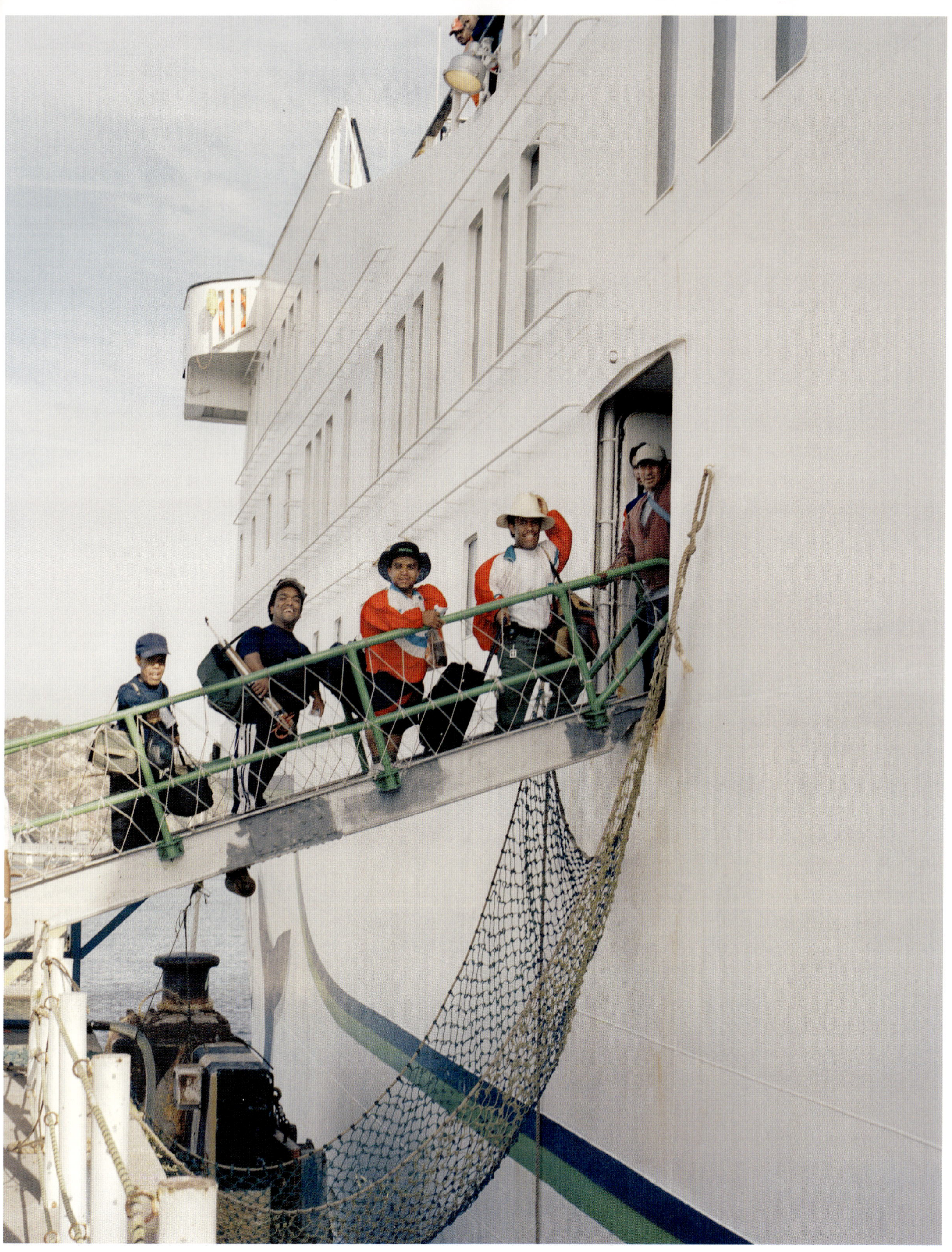

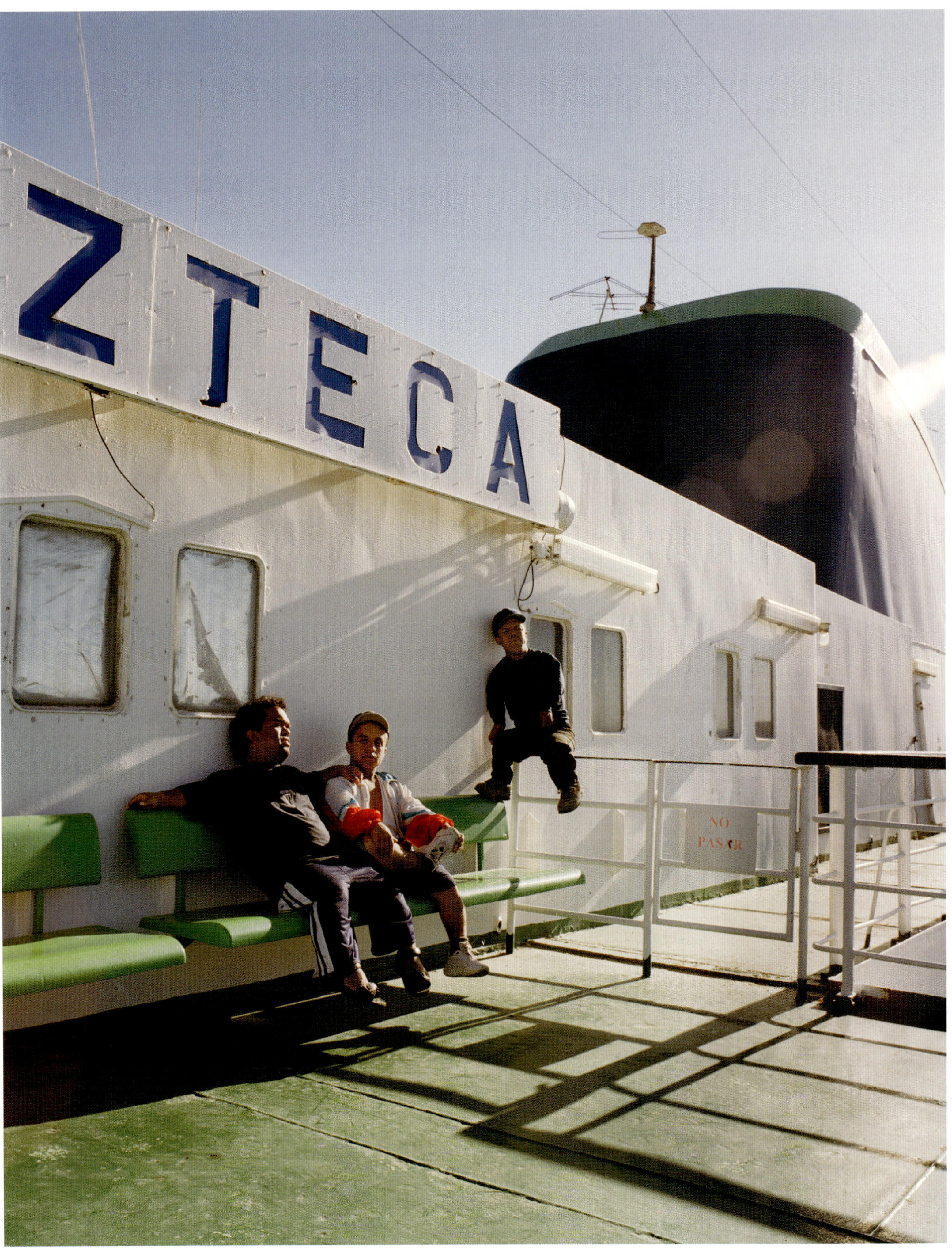
ZTECA
NO
PASAR

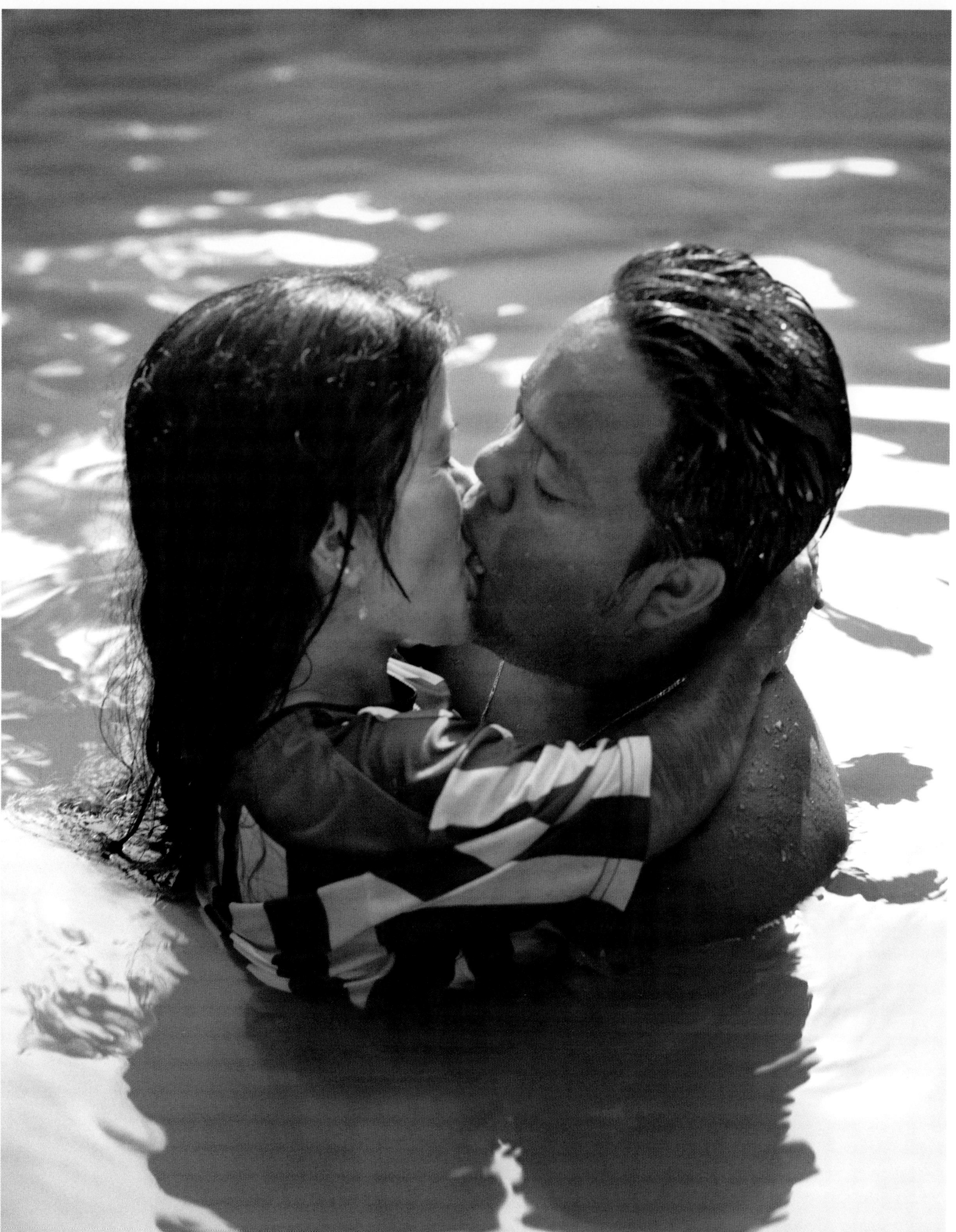

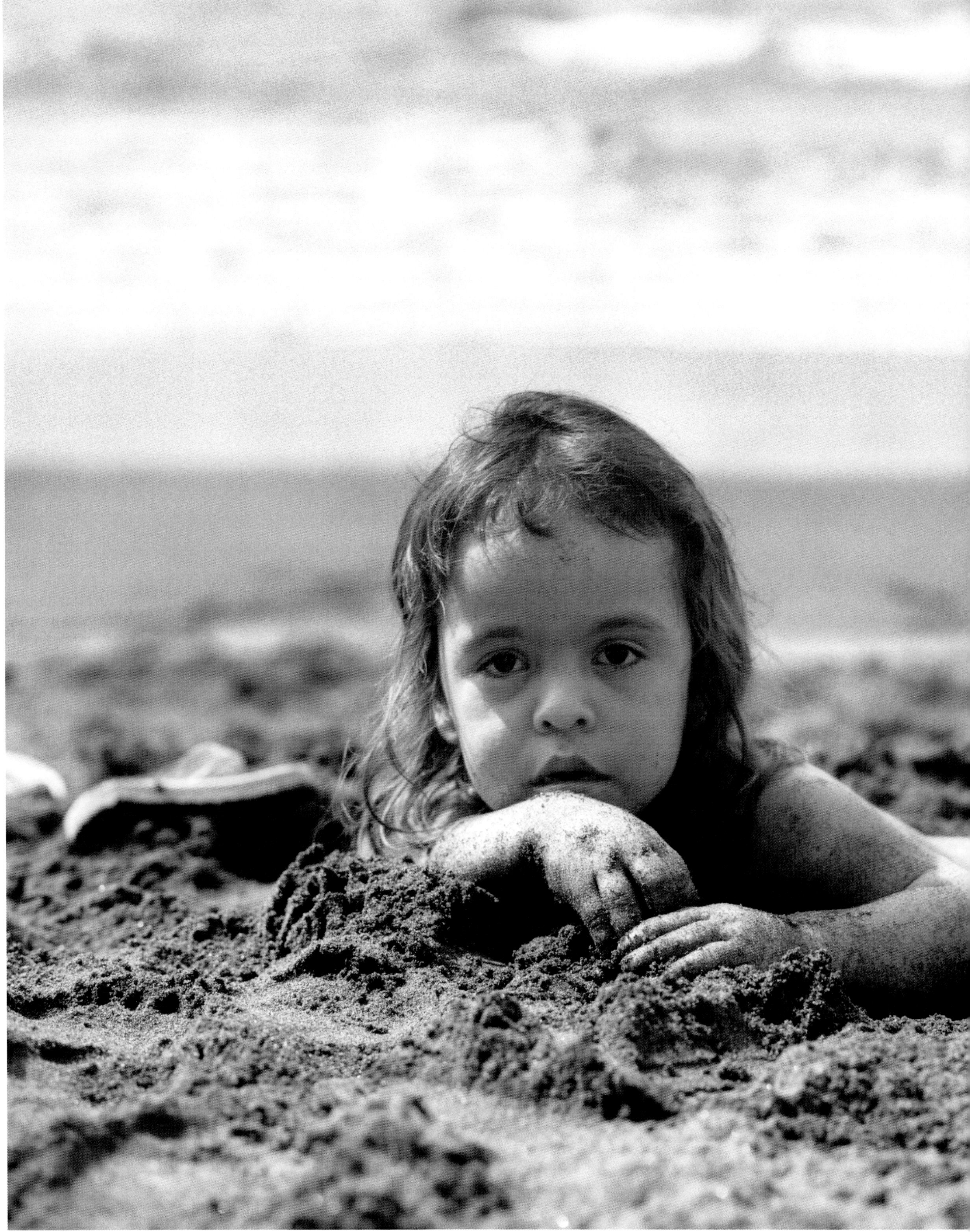

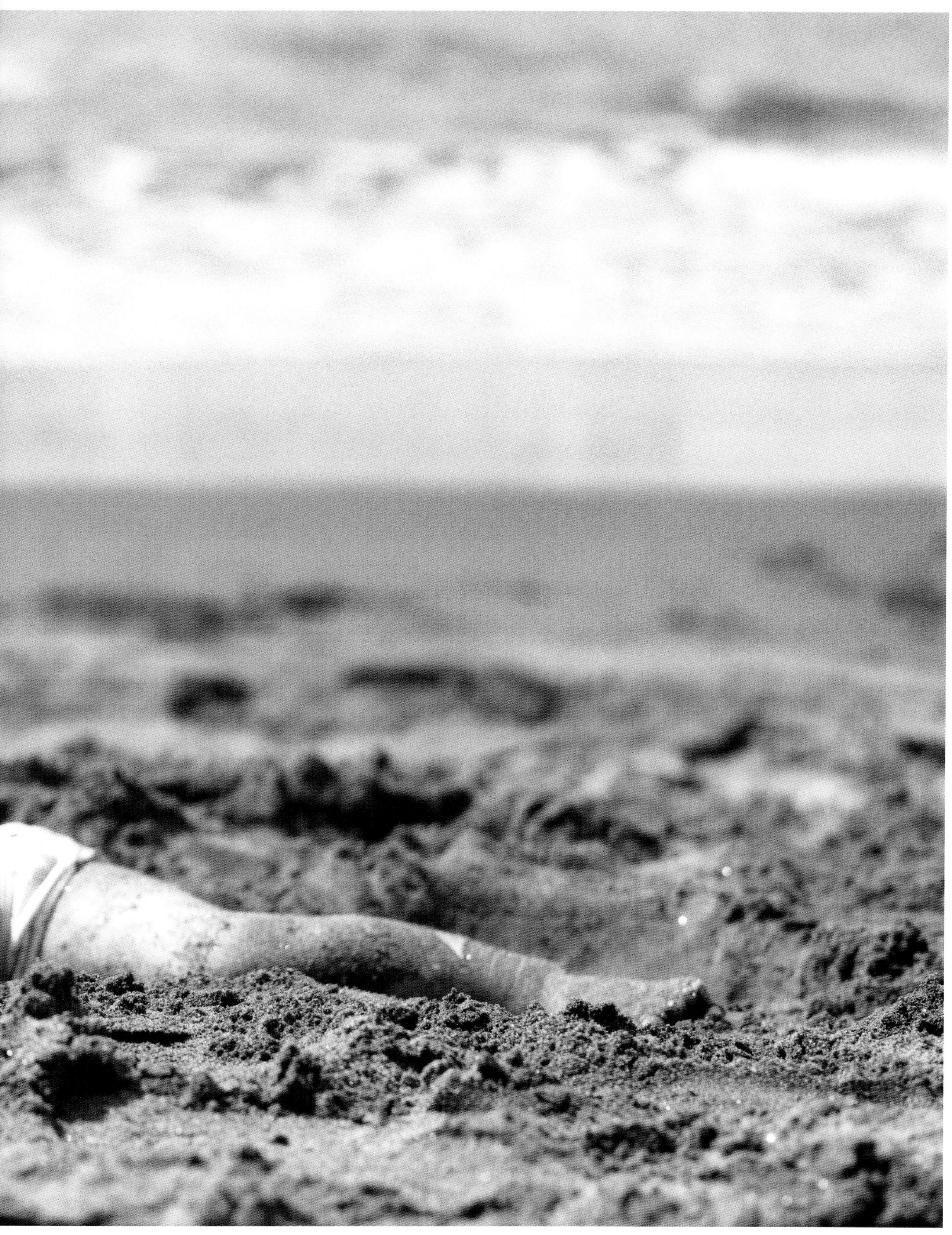

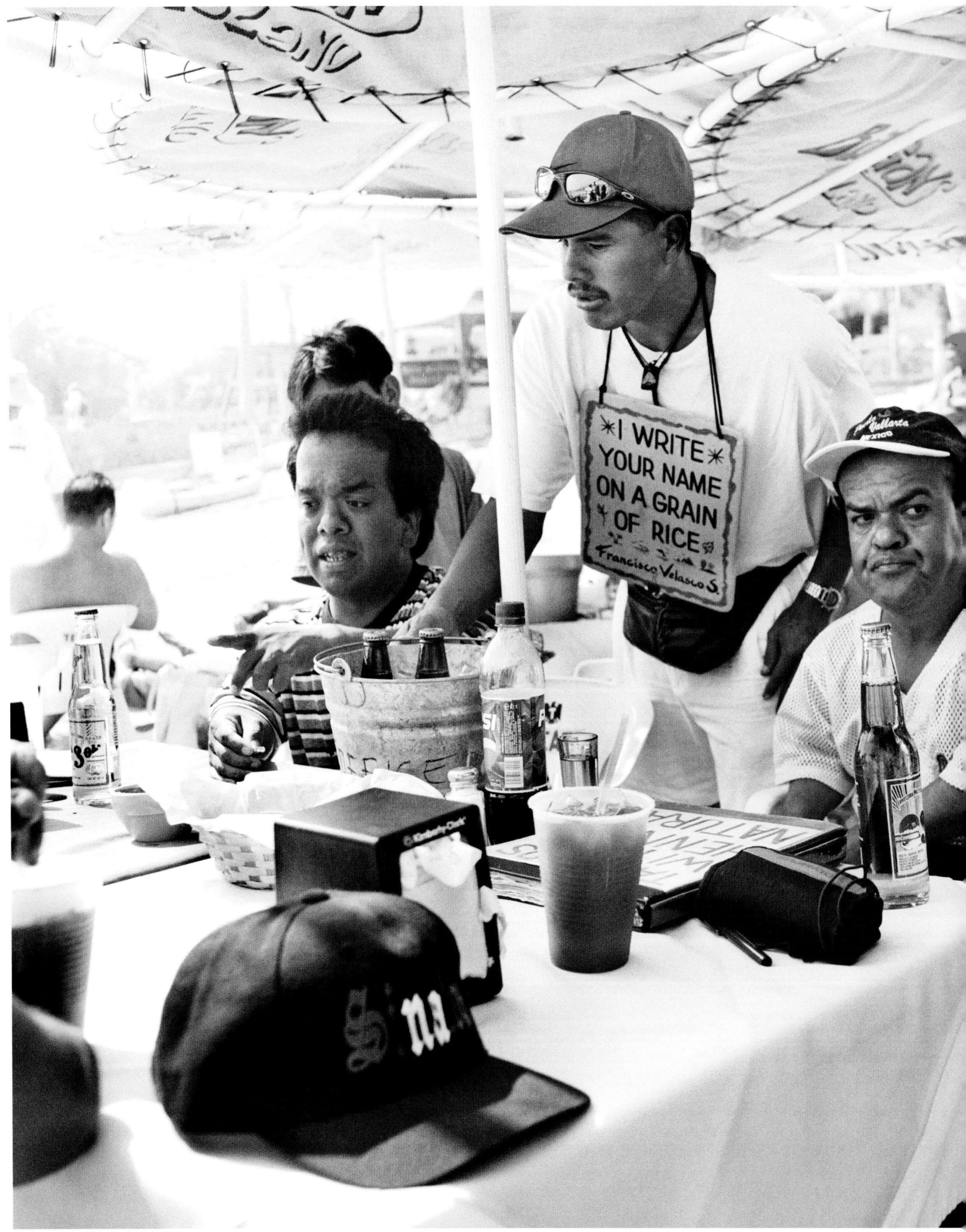

I WRITE
YOUR NAME
ON A GRAIN
OF RICE
Francisco Velasco S.

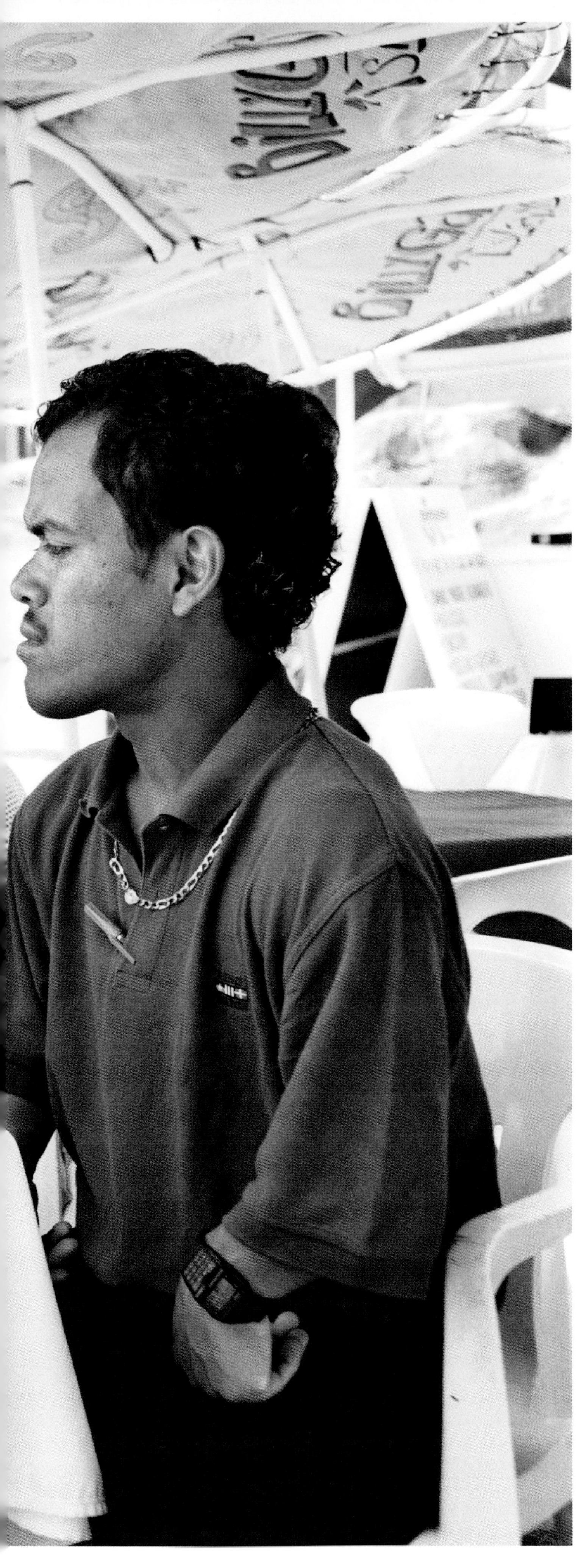

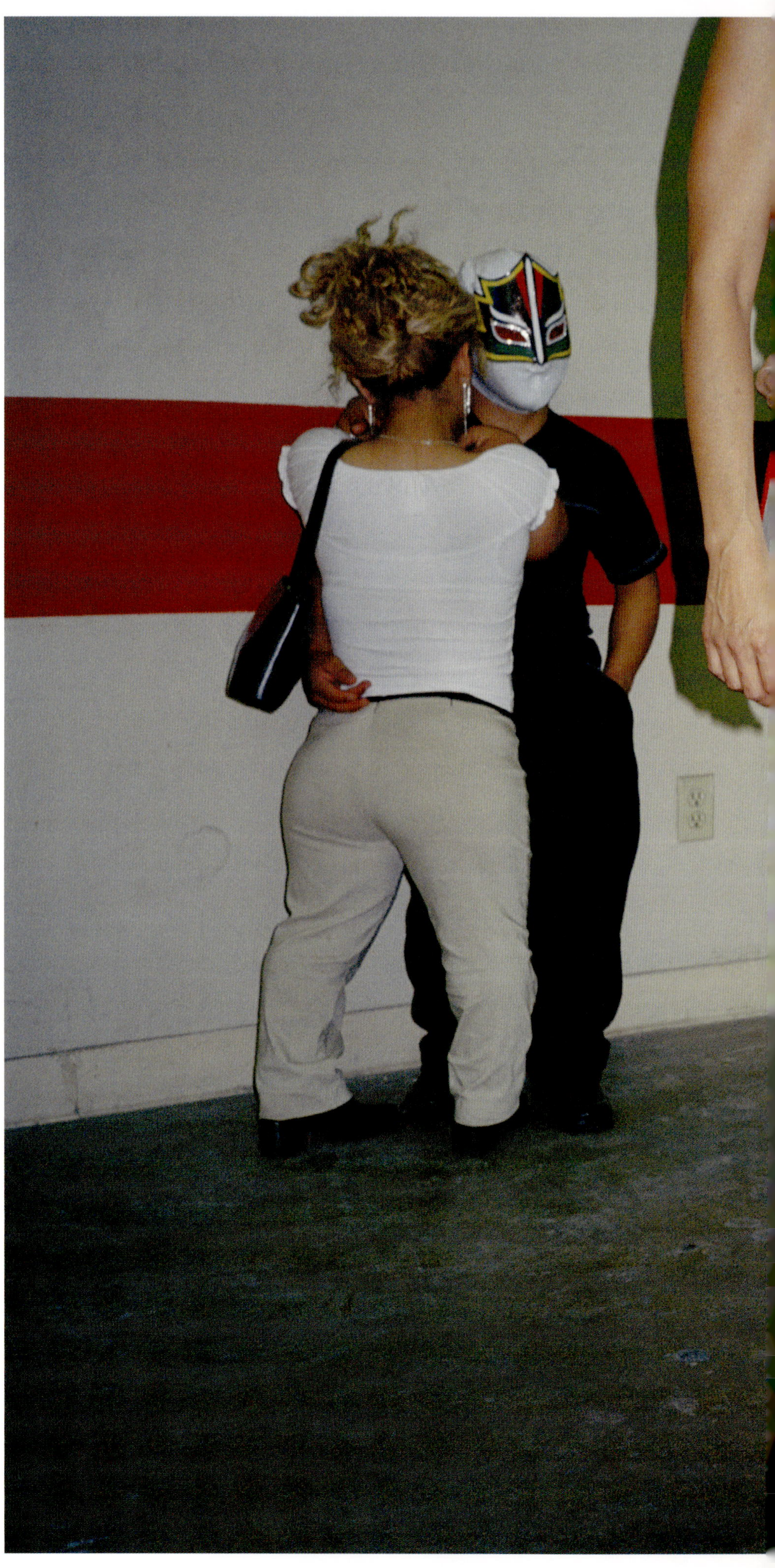

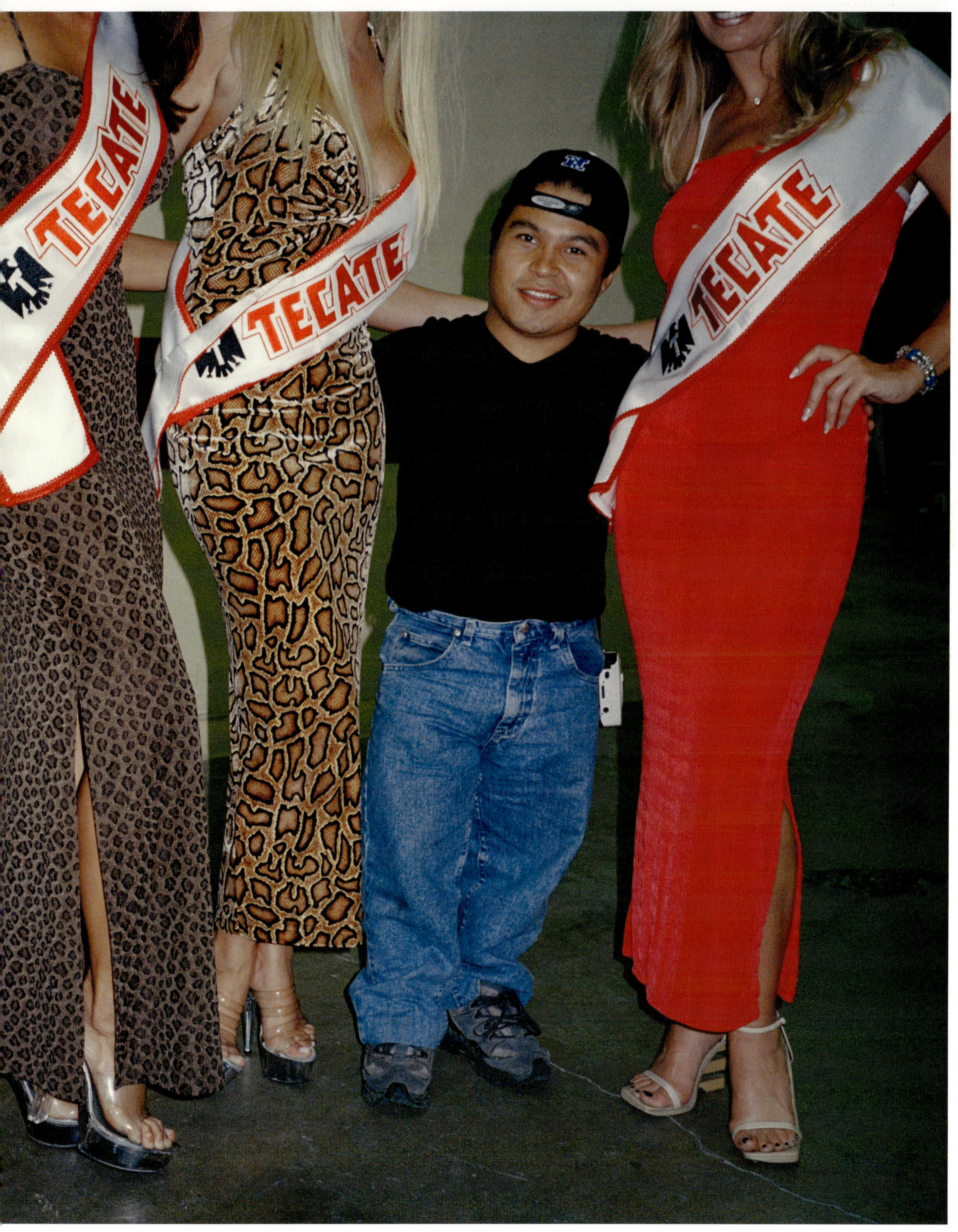

TECATE
TECATE
TECATE

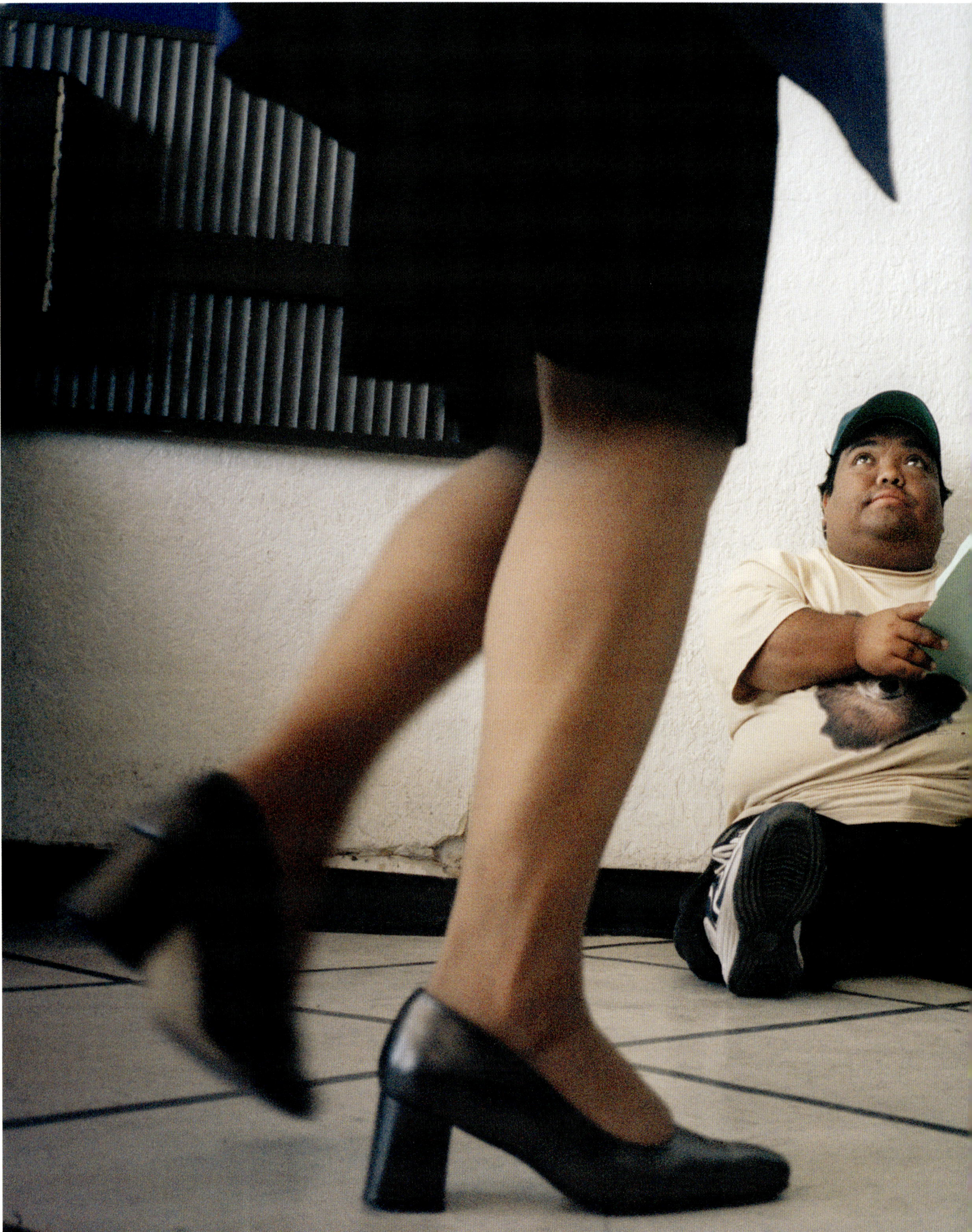

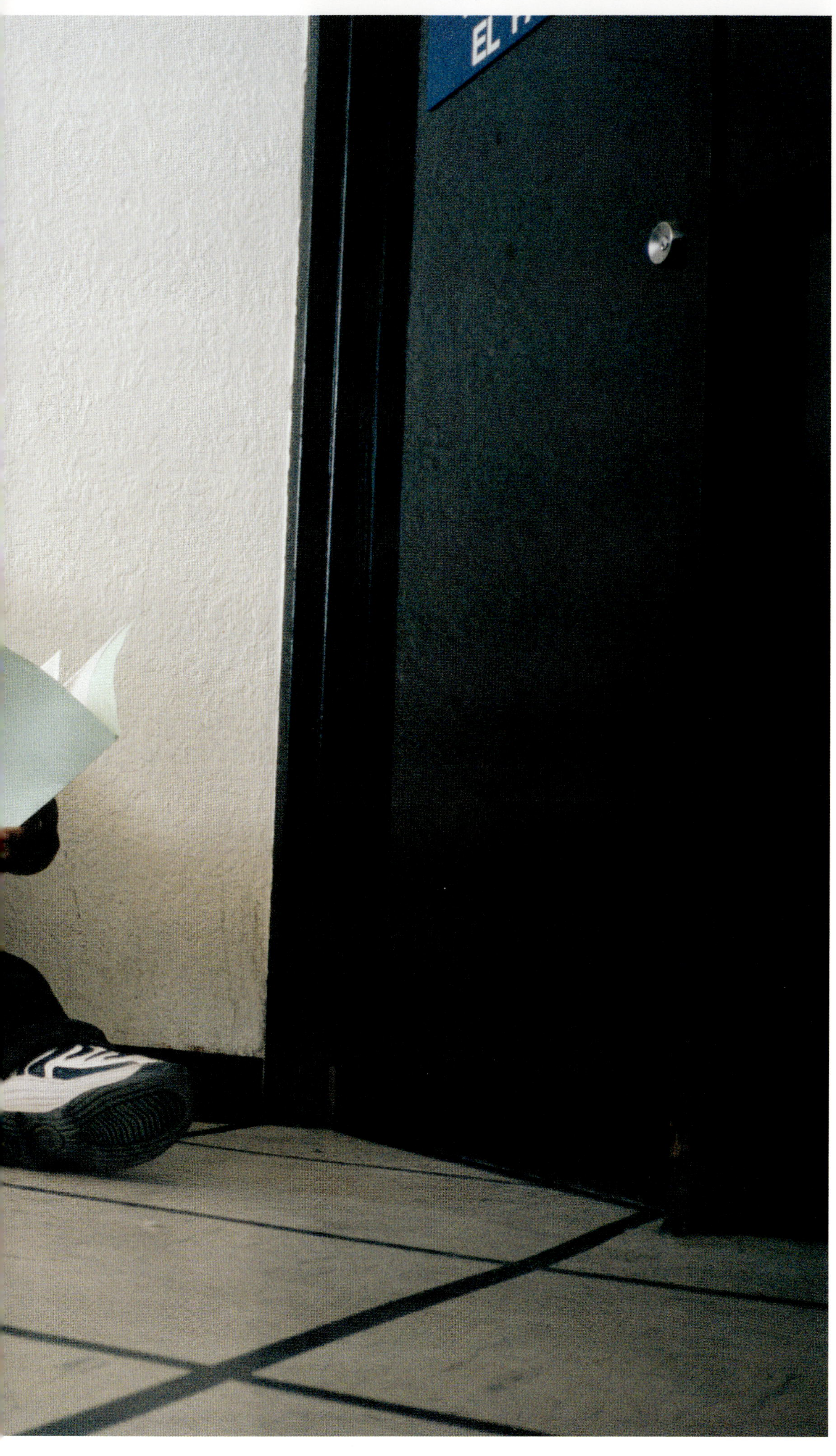
EL T

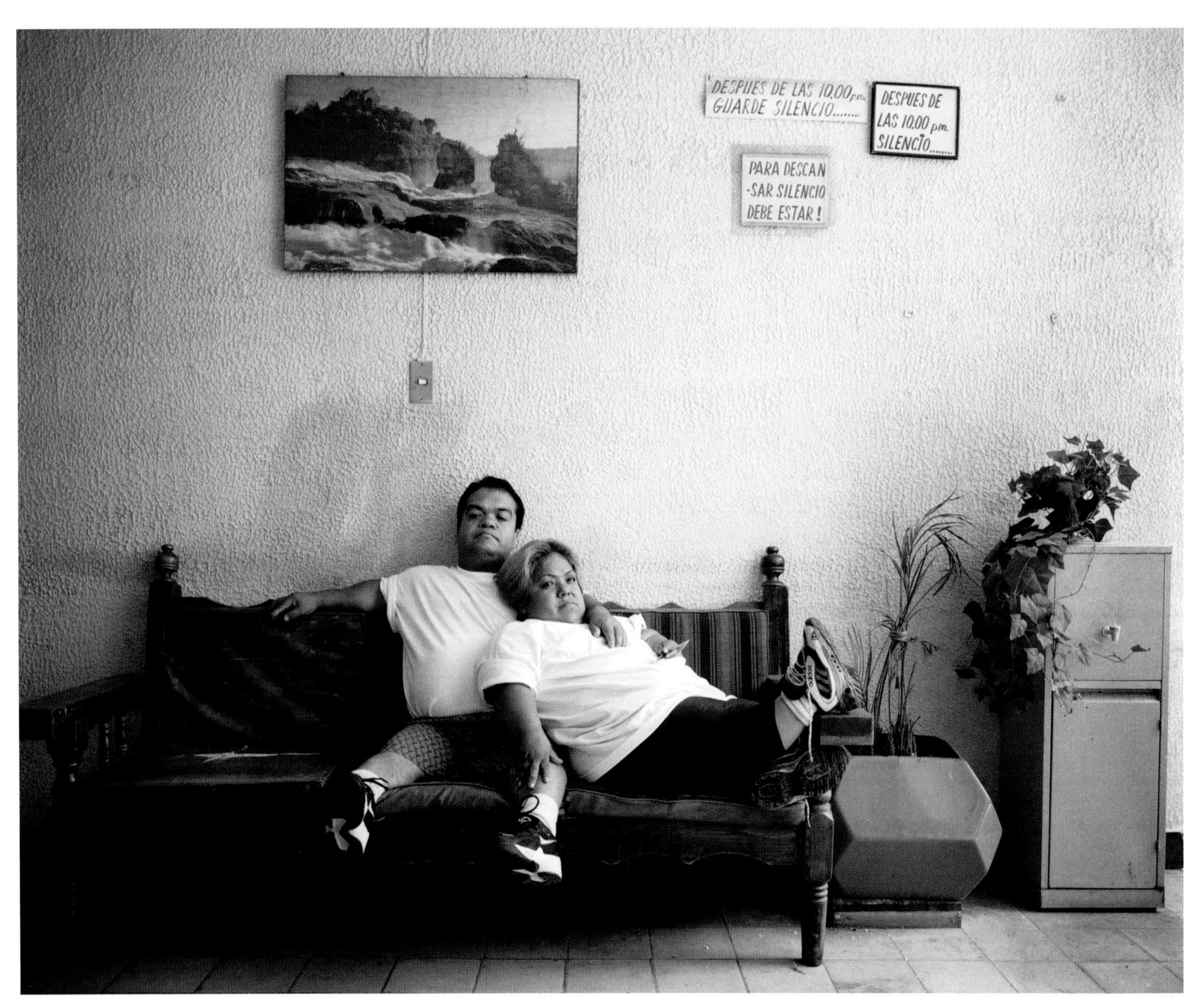
DESPUES DE LAS 10.00 p.m.
GUARDE SILENCIO........
DESPUES DE
LAS 10.00 p.m.
SILENCIO........
PARA DESCAN
-SAR SILENCIO
DEBE ESTAR !

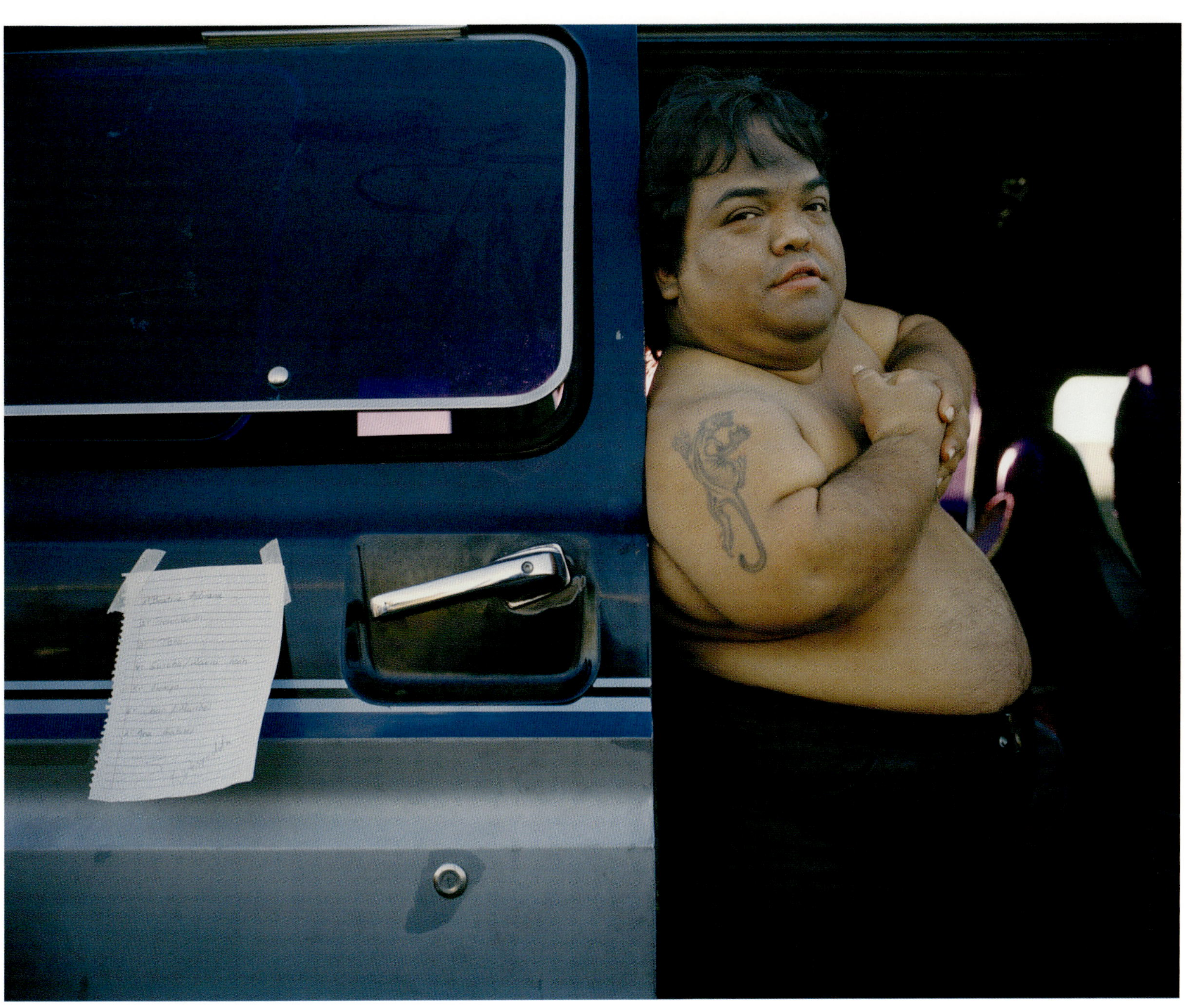

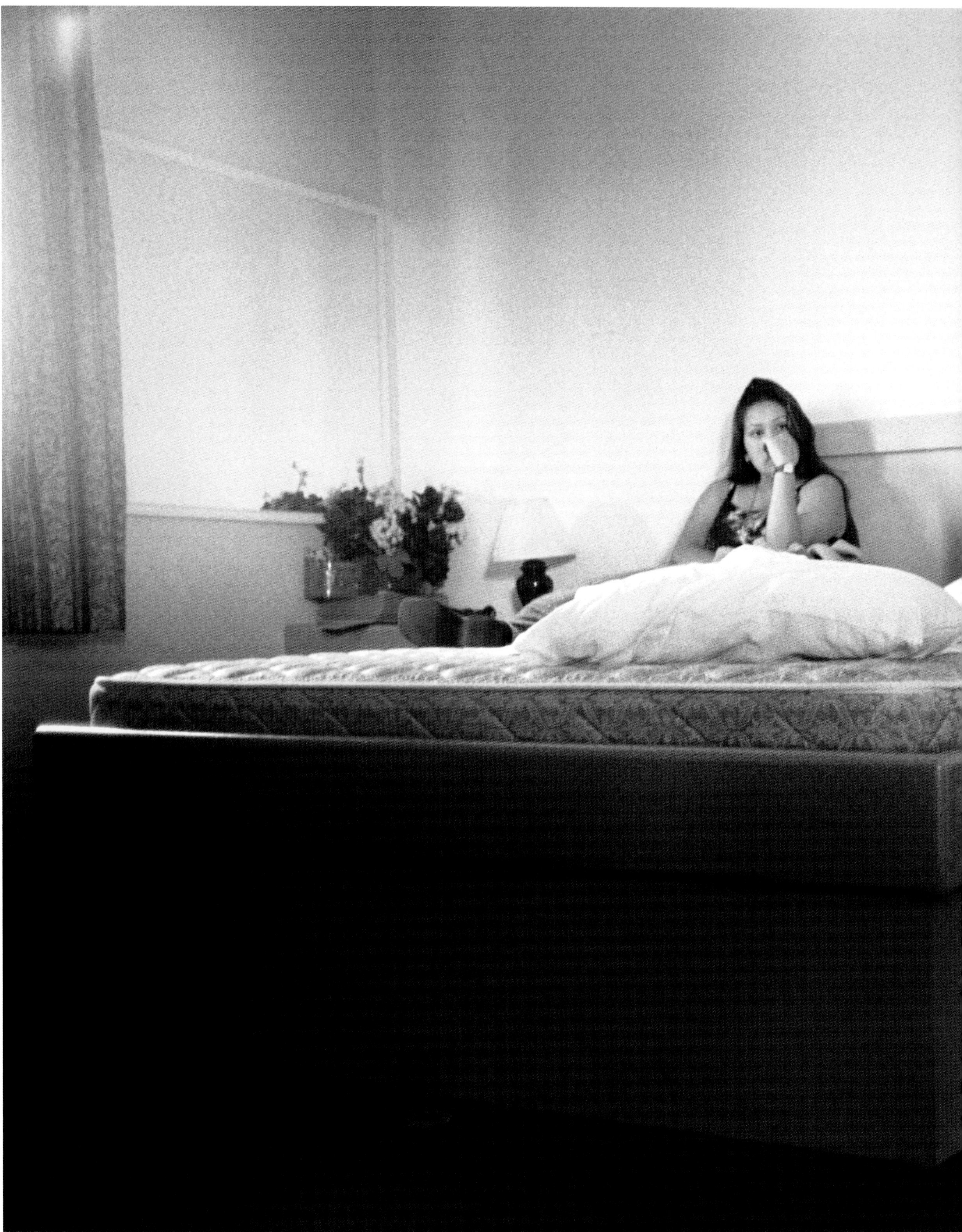

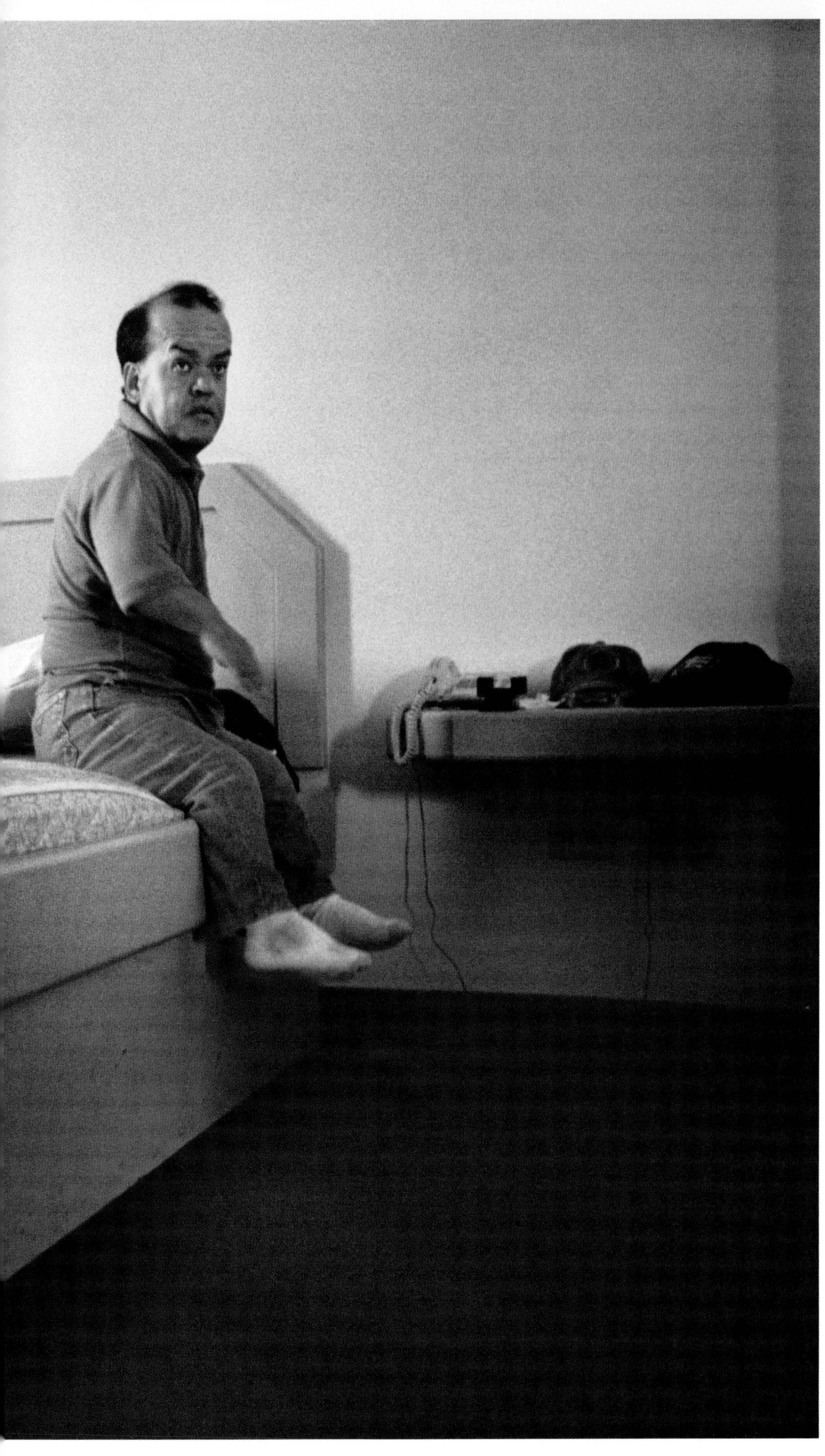

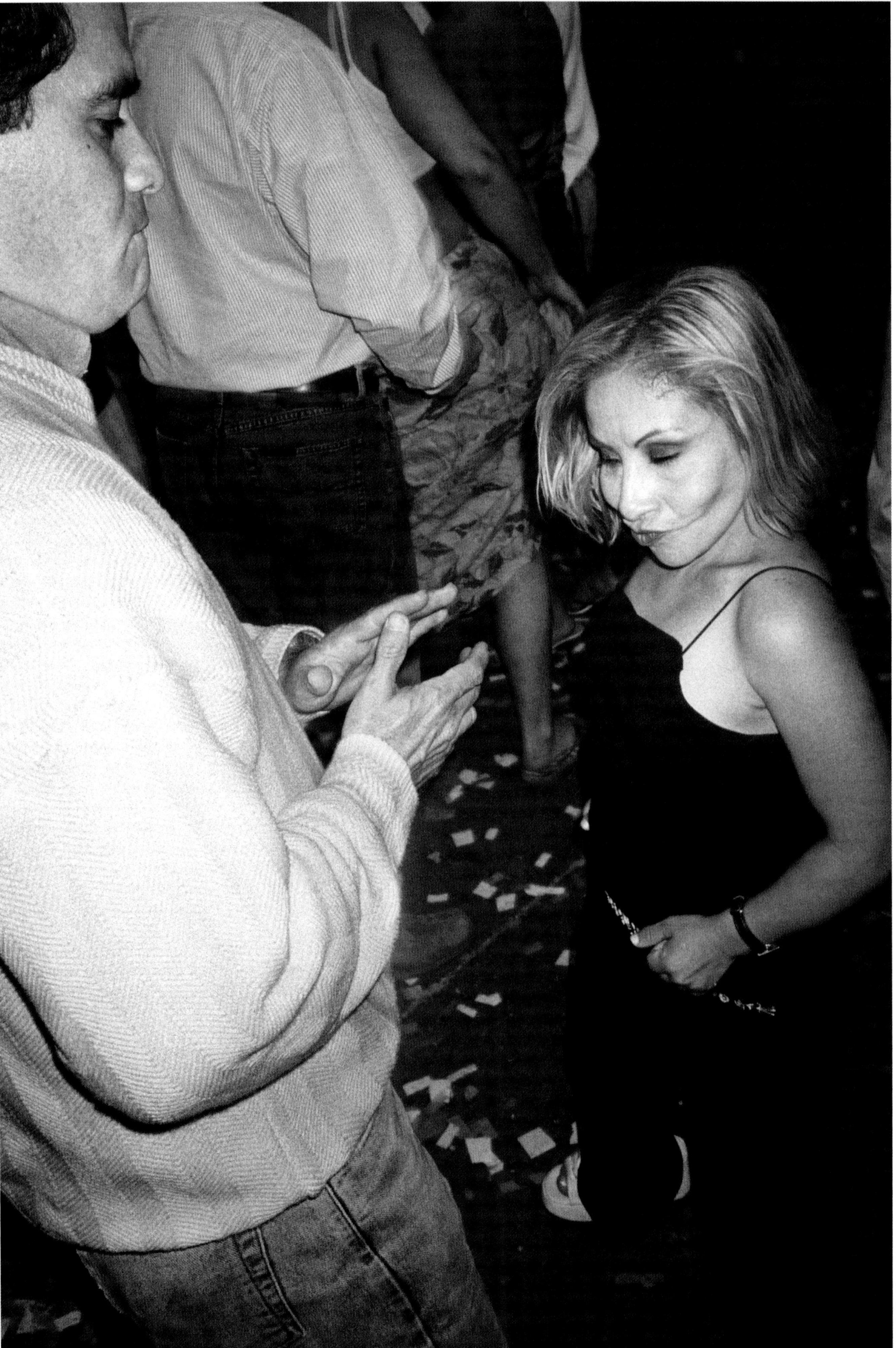

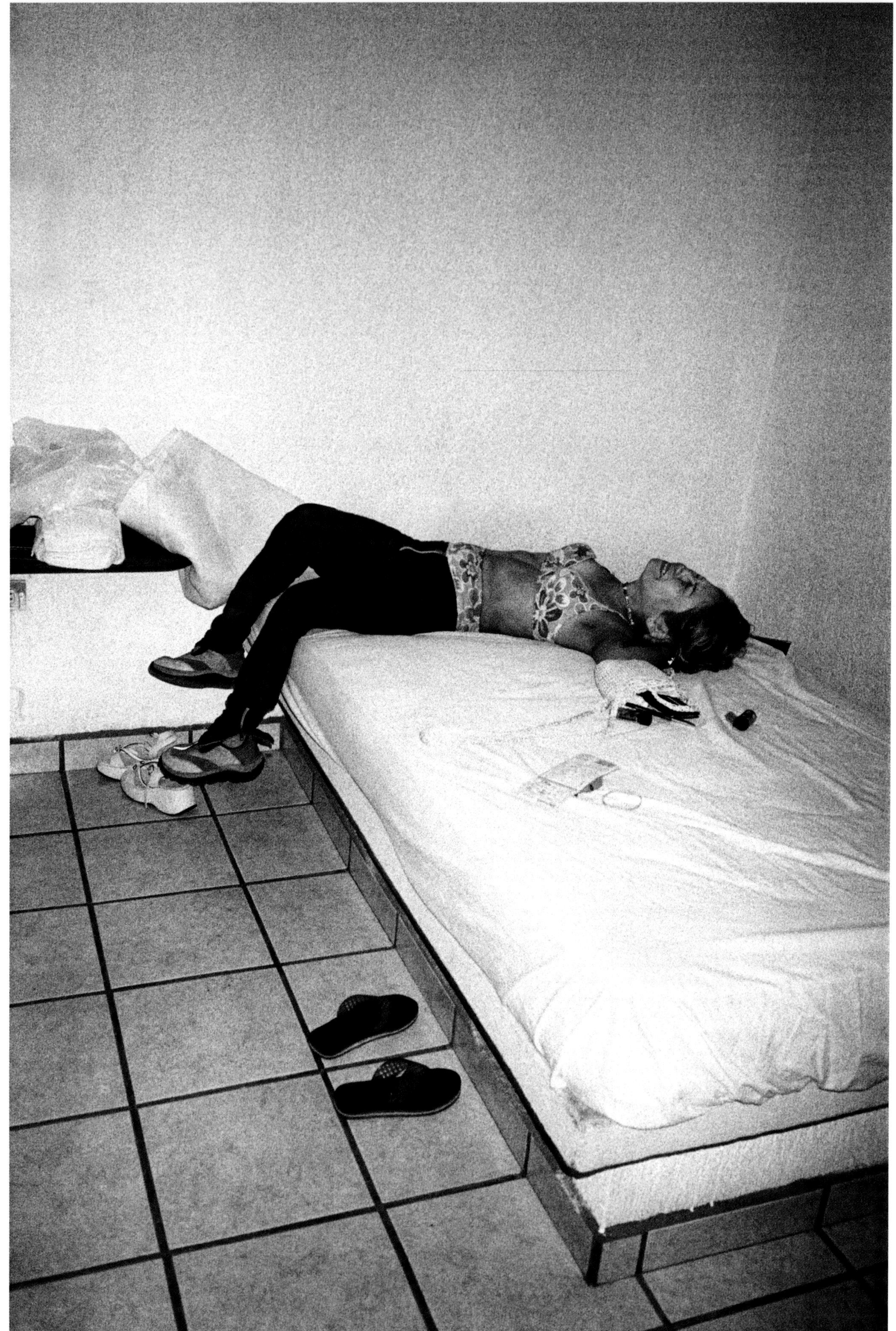

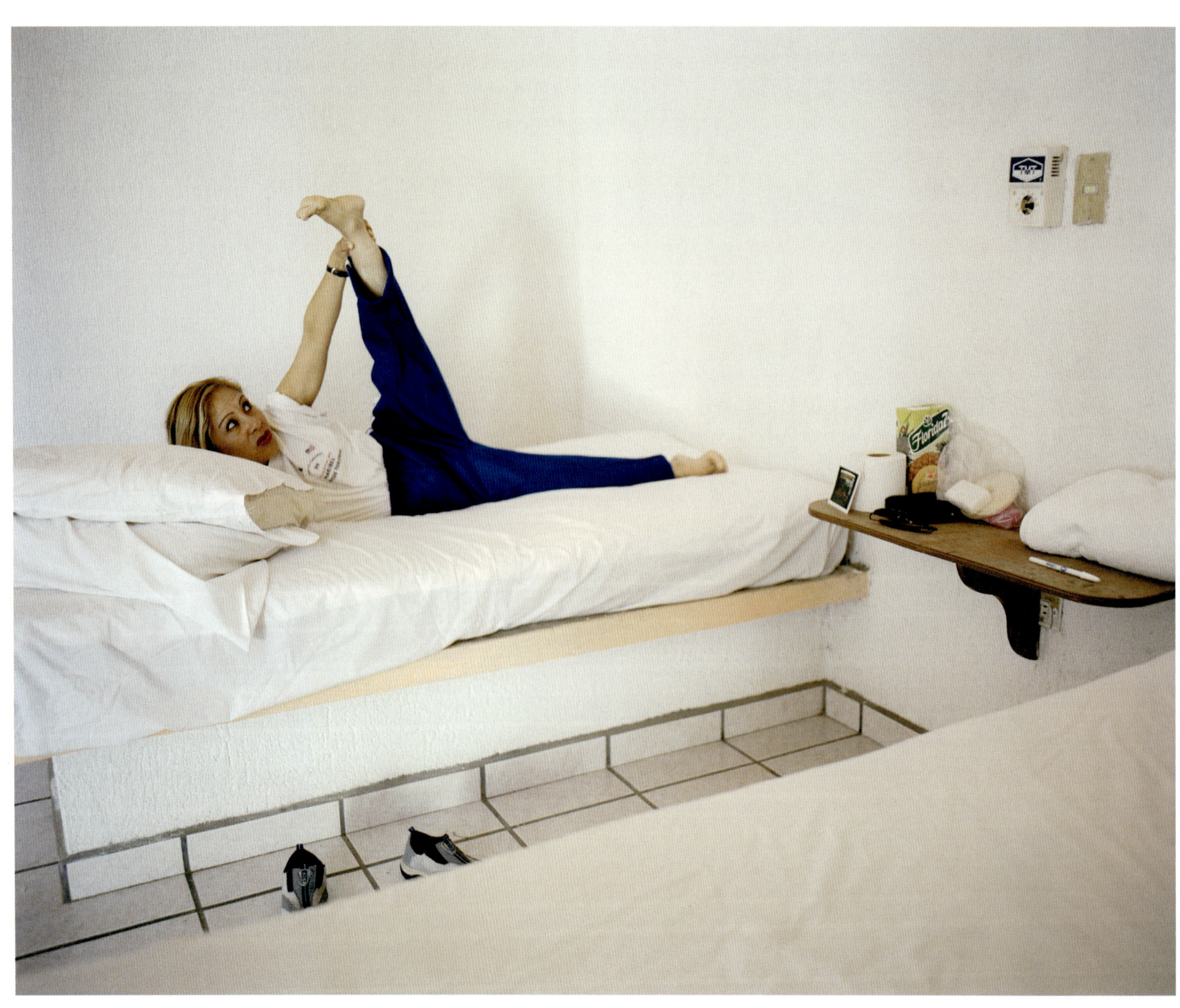

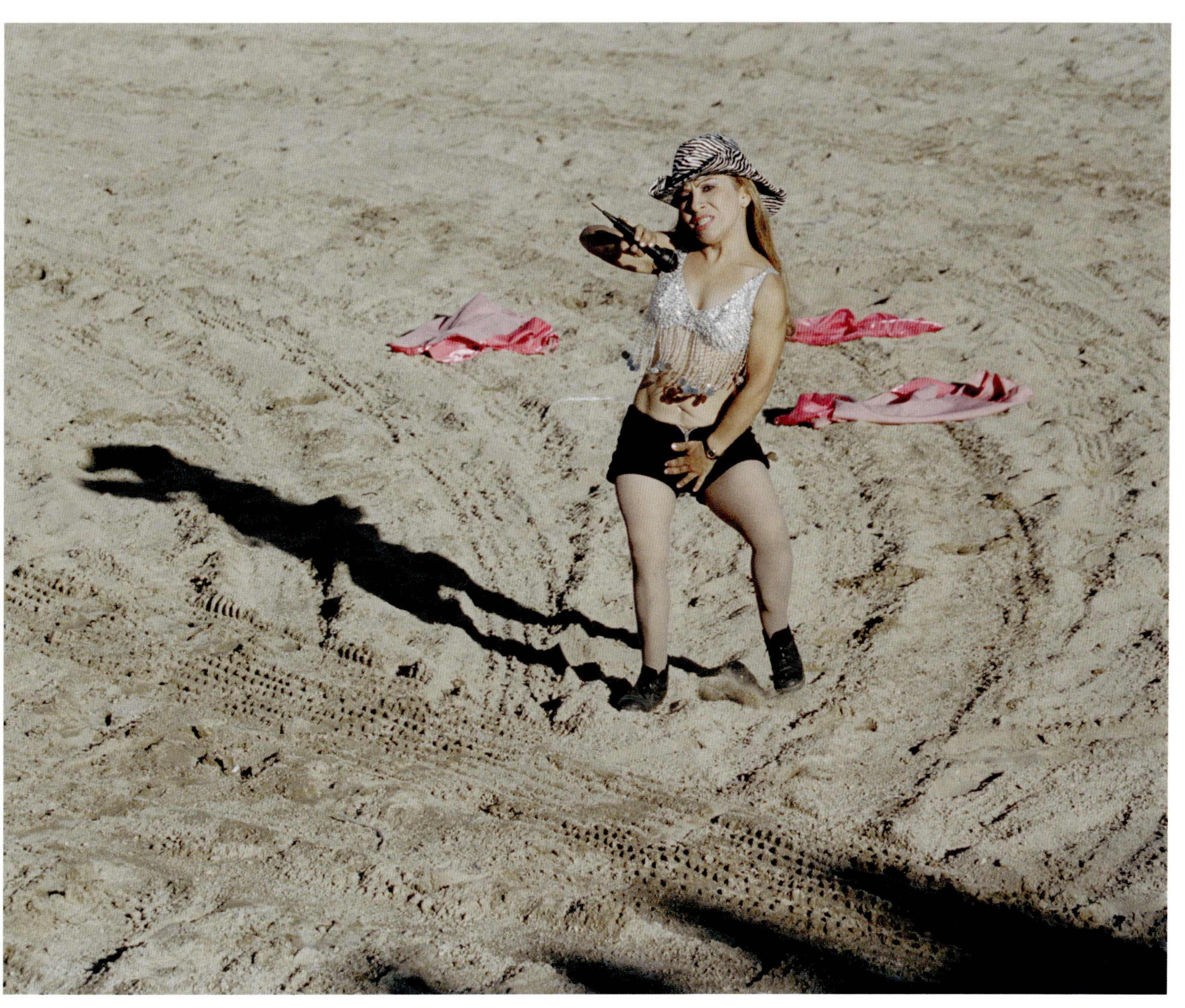

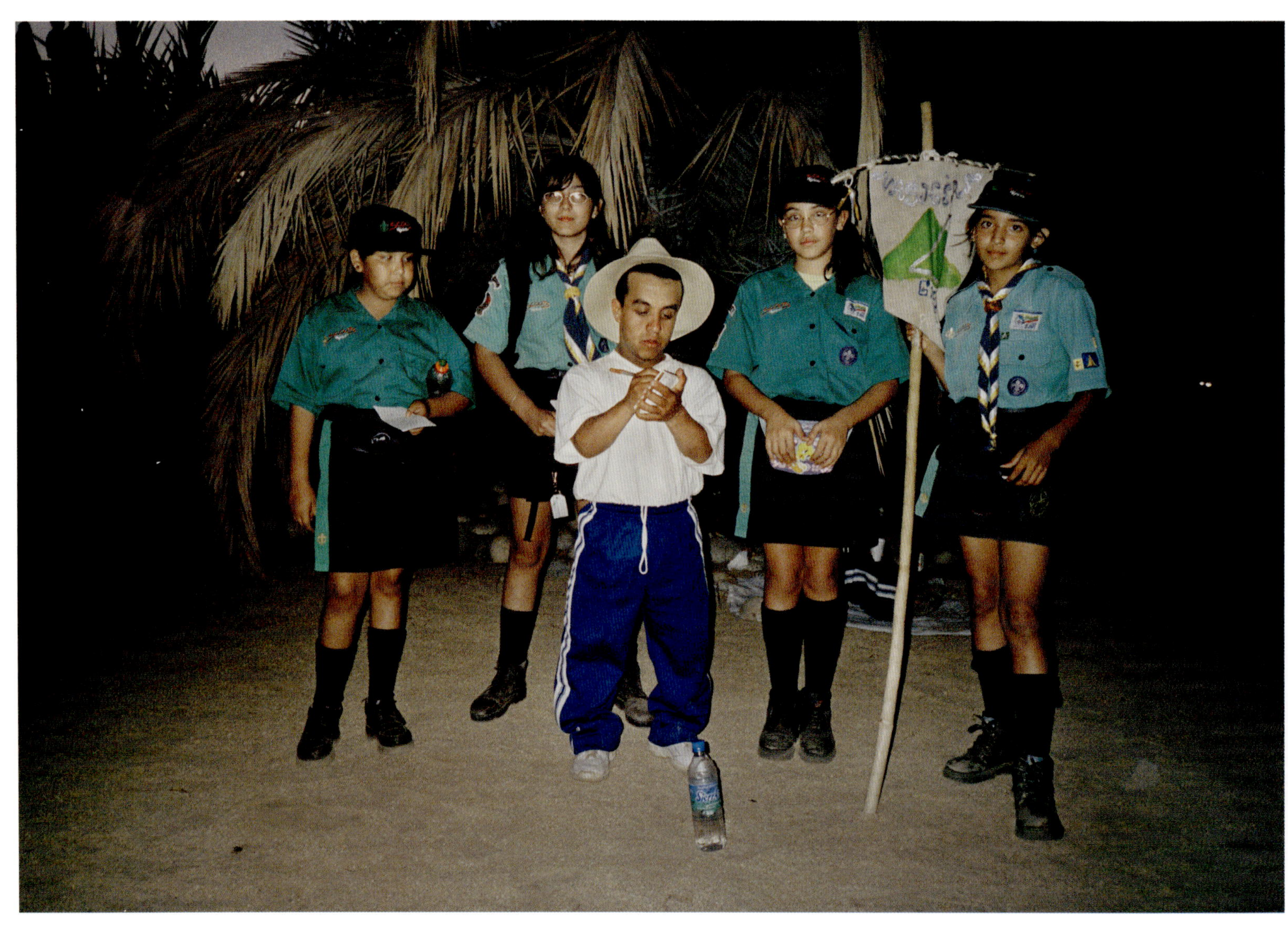

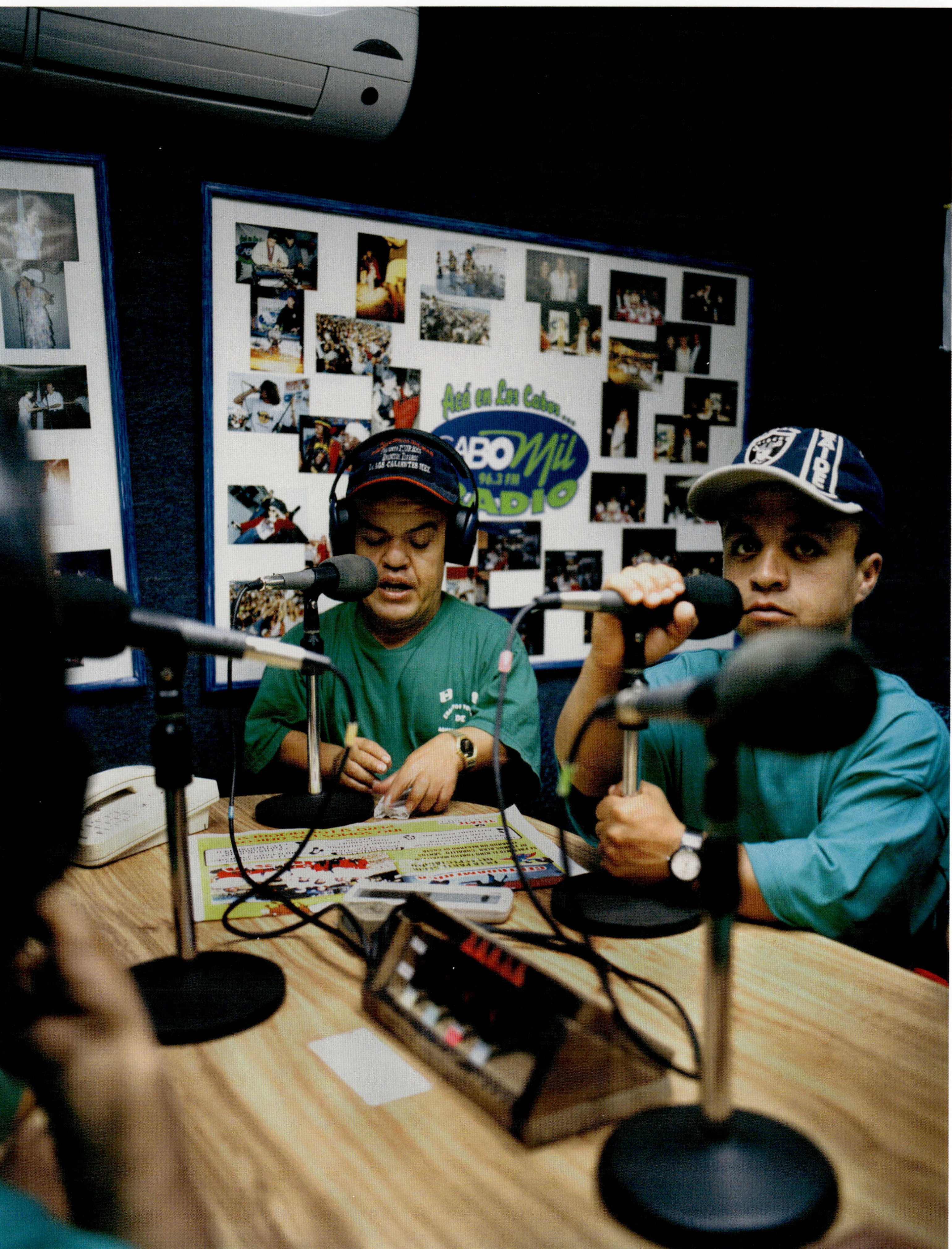

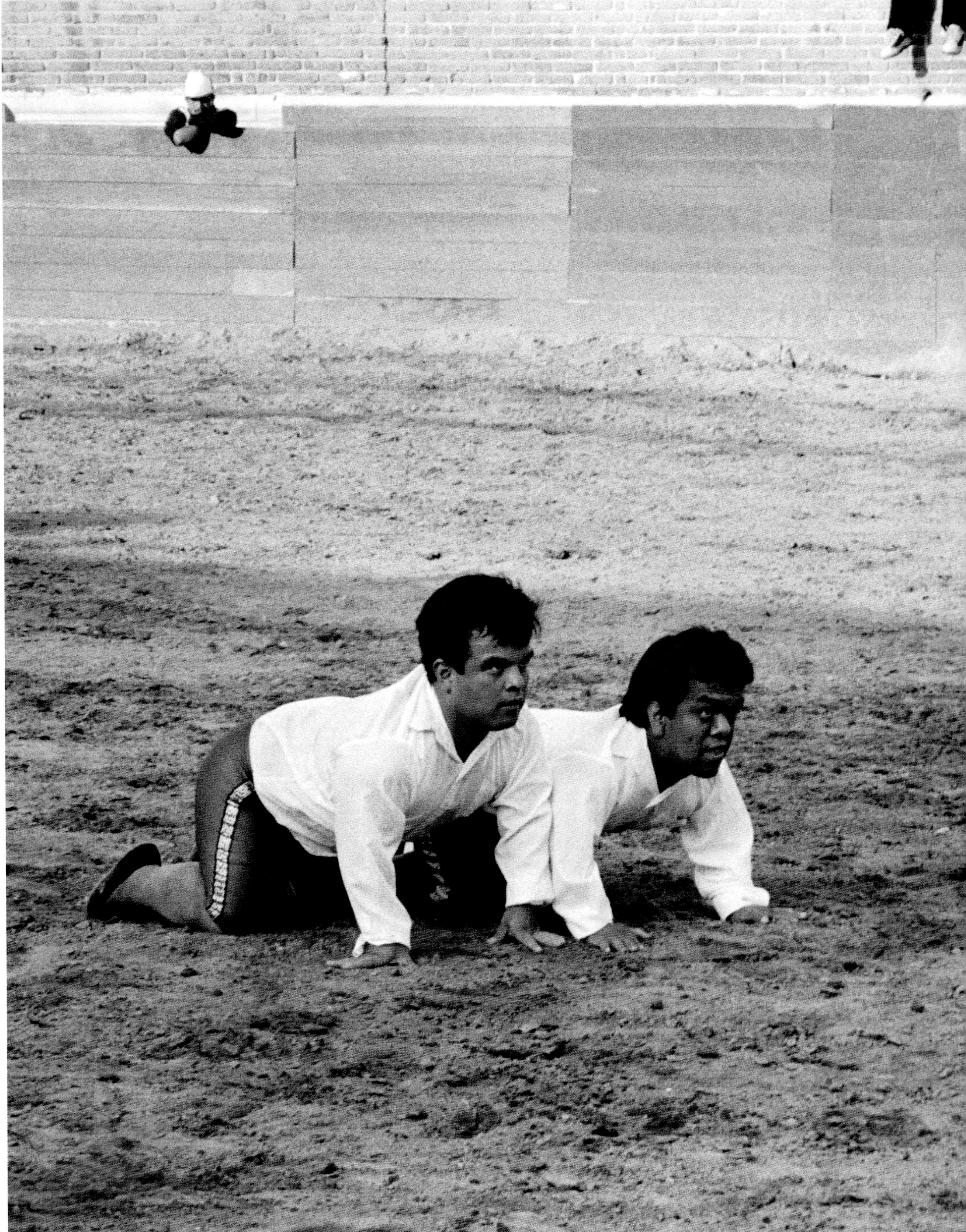

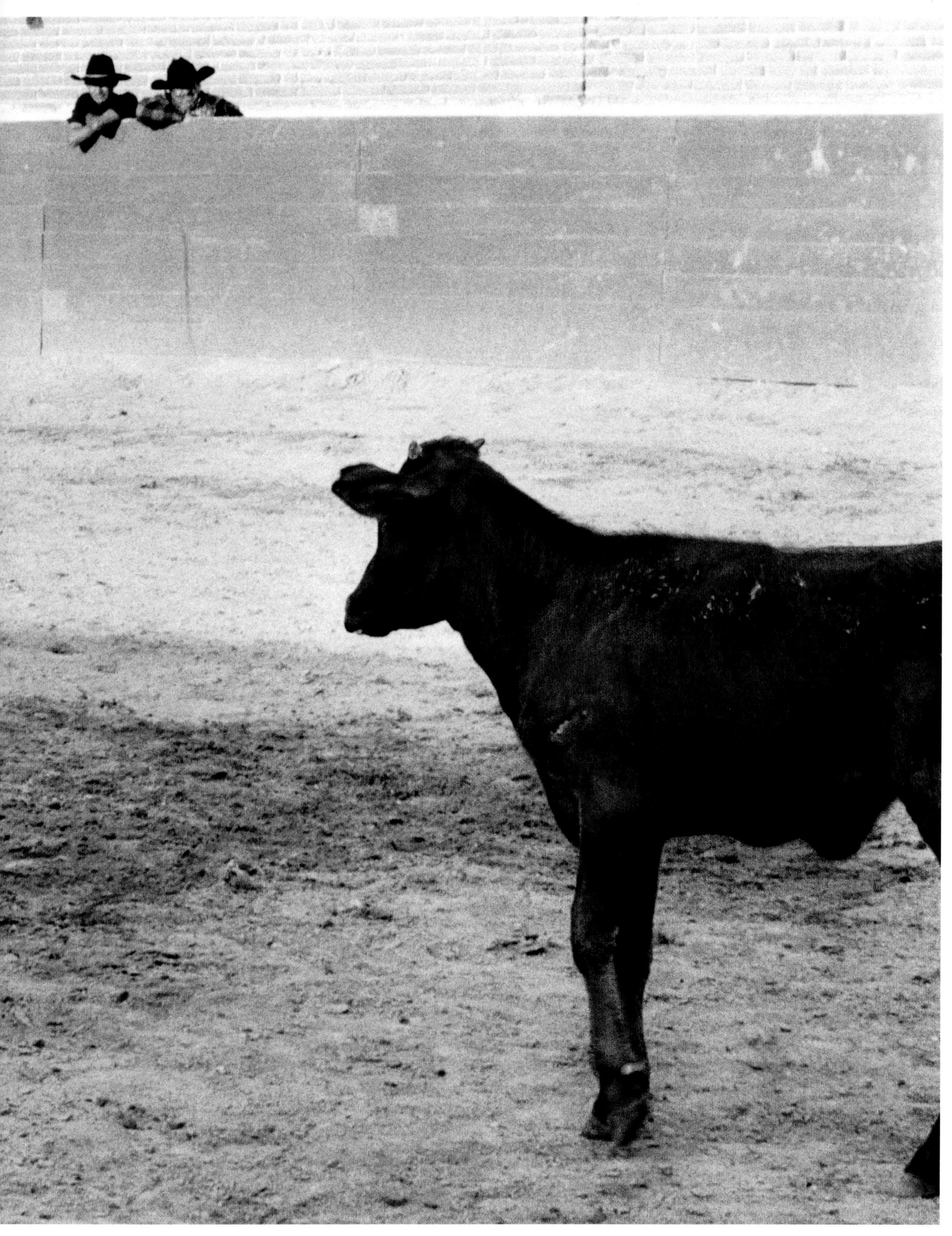

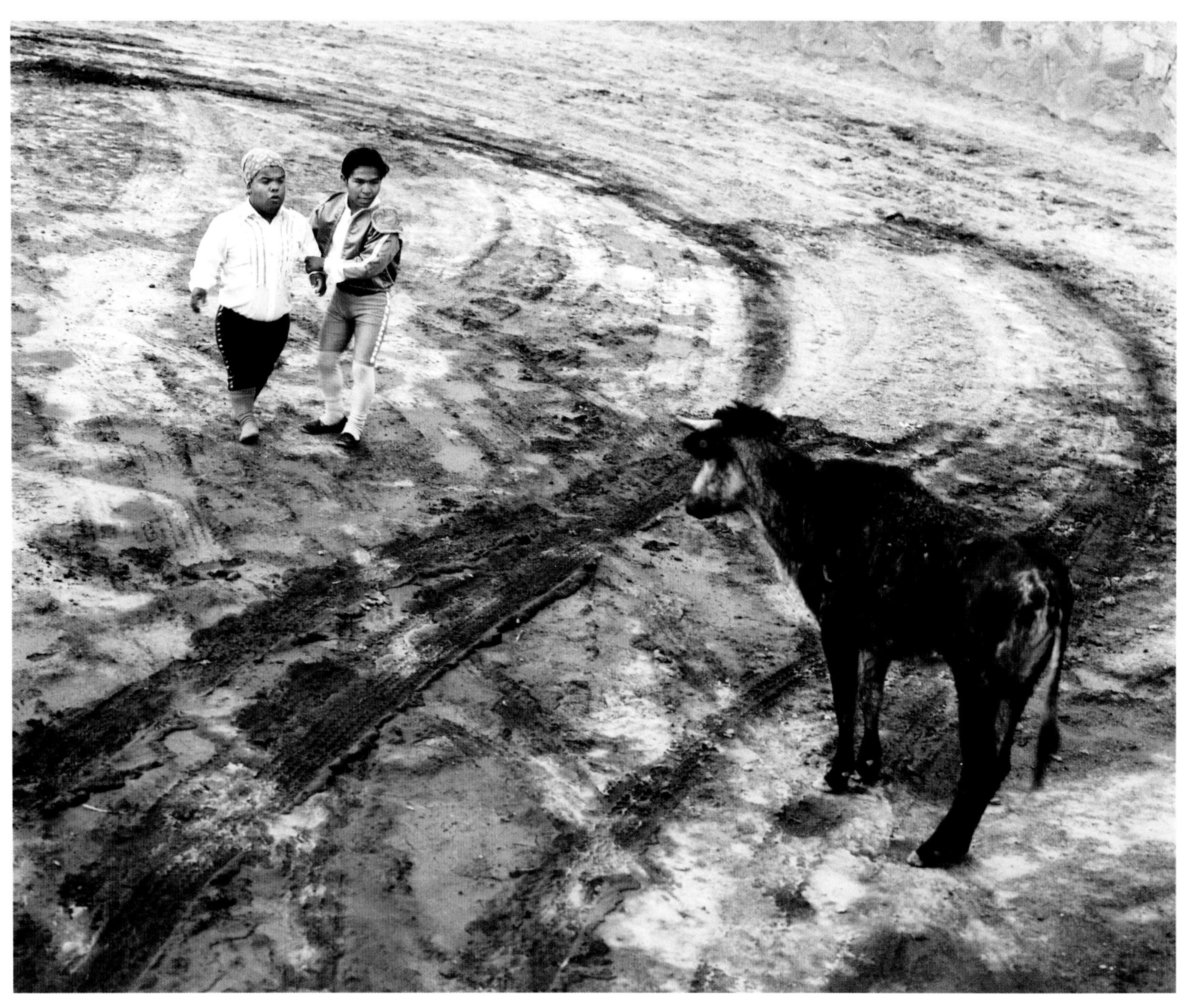

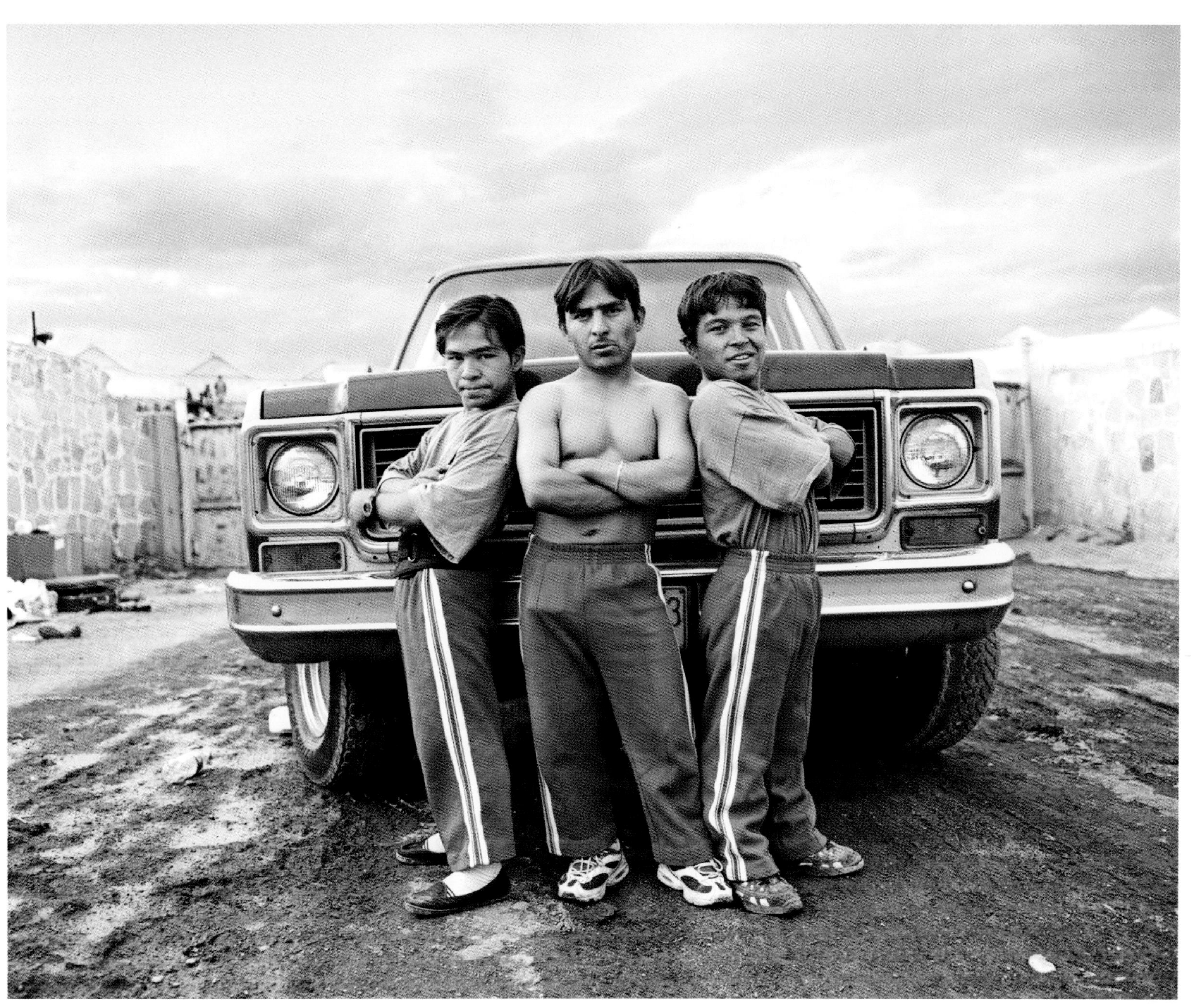

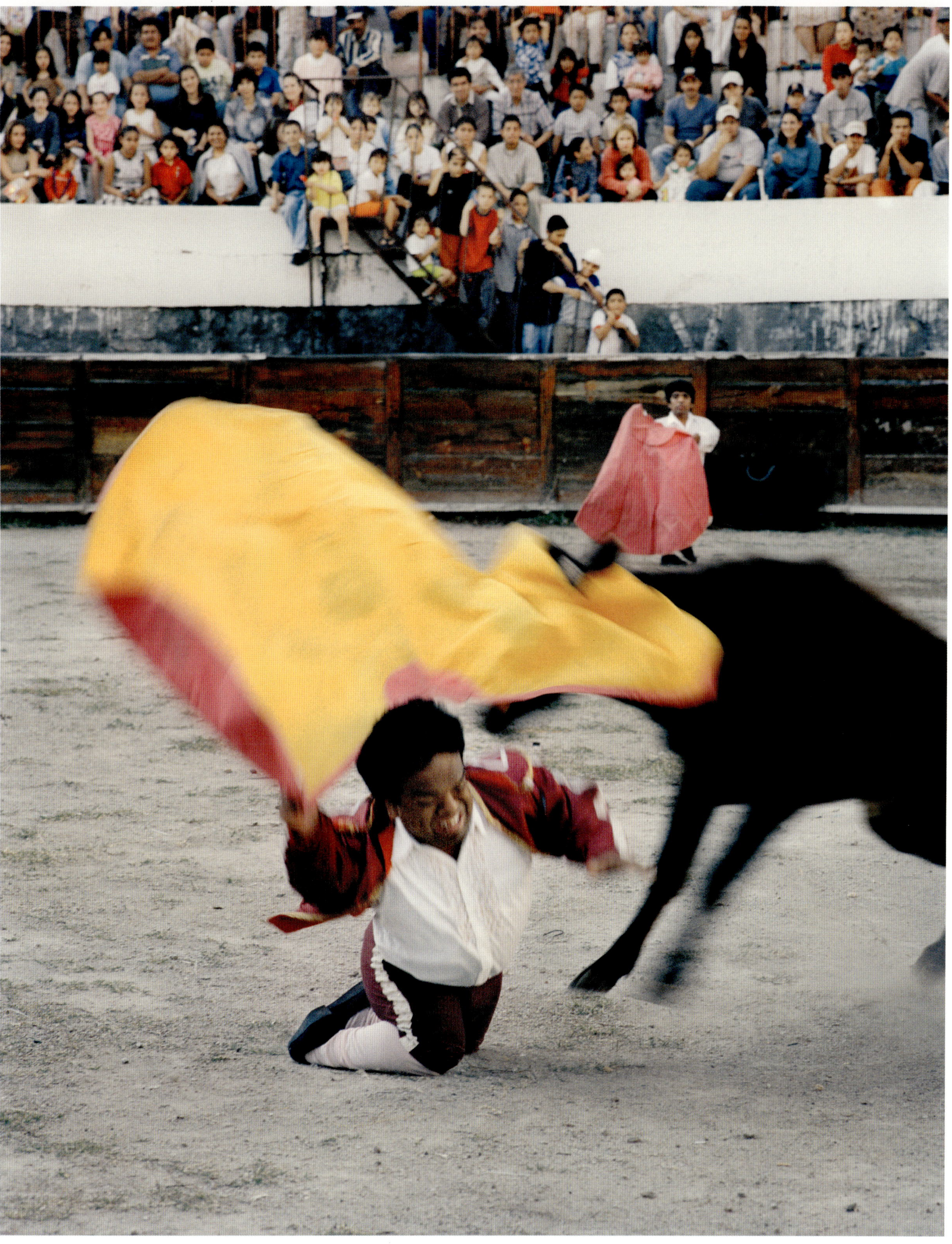

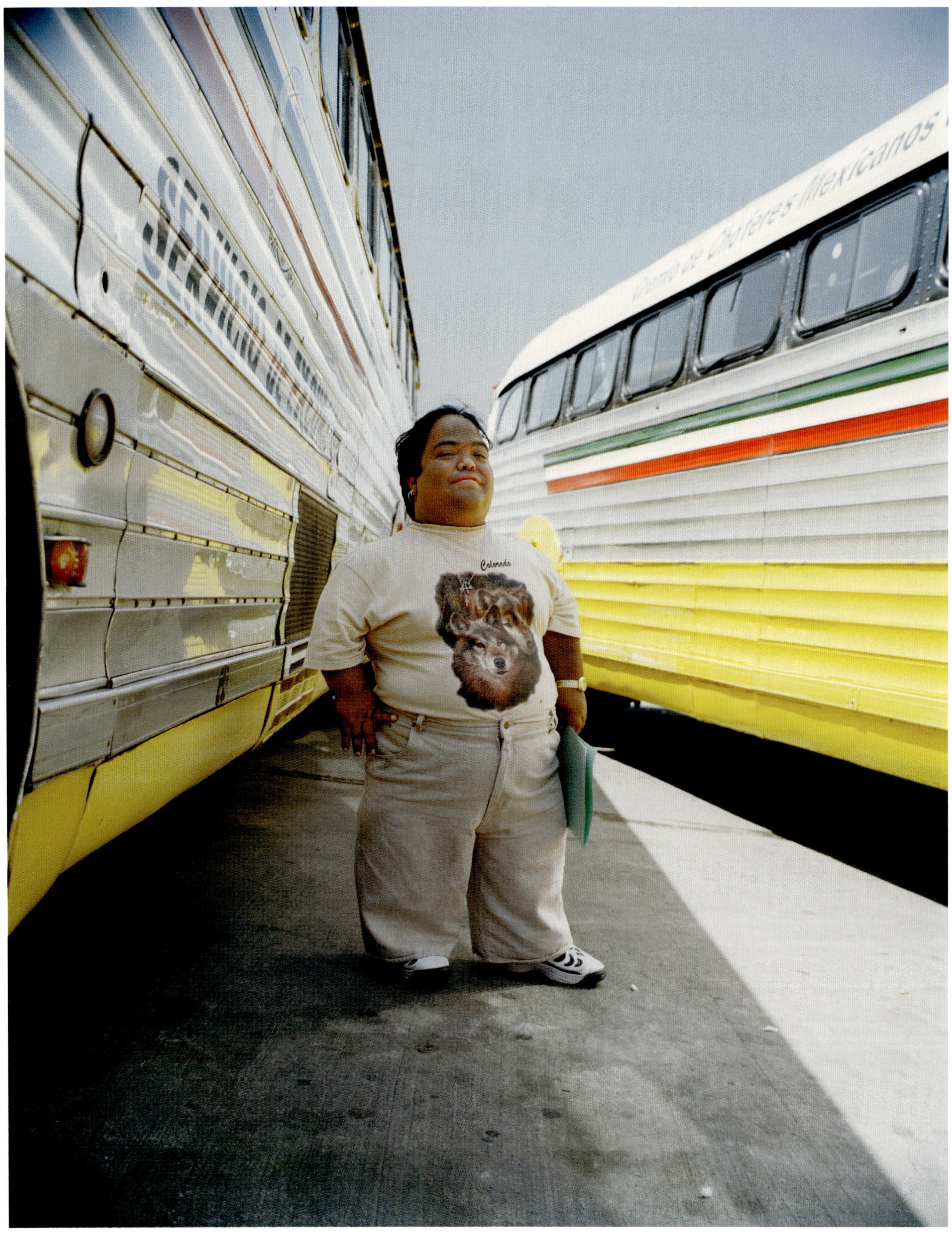
Colorado
Servicio de...
...de Choferes Mexicanos

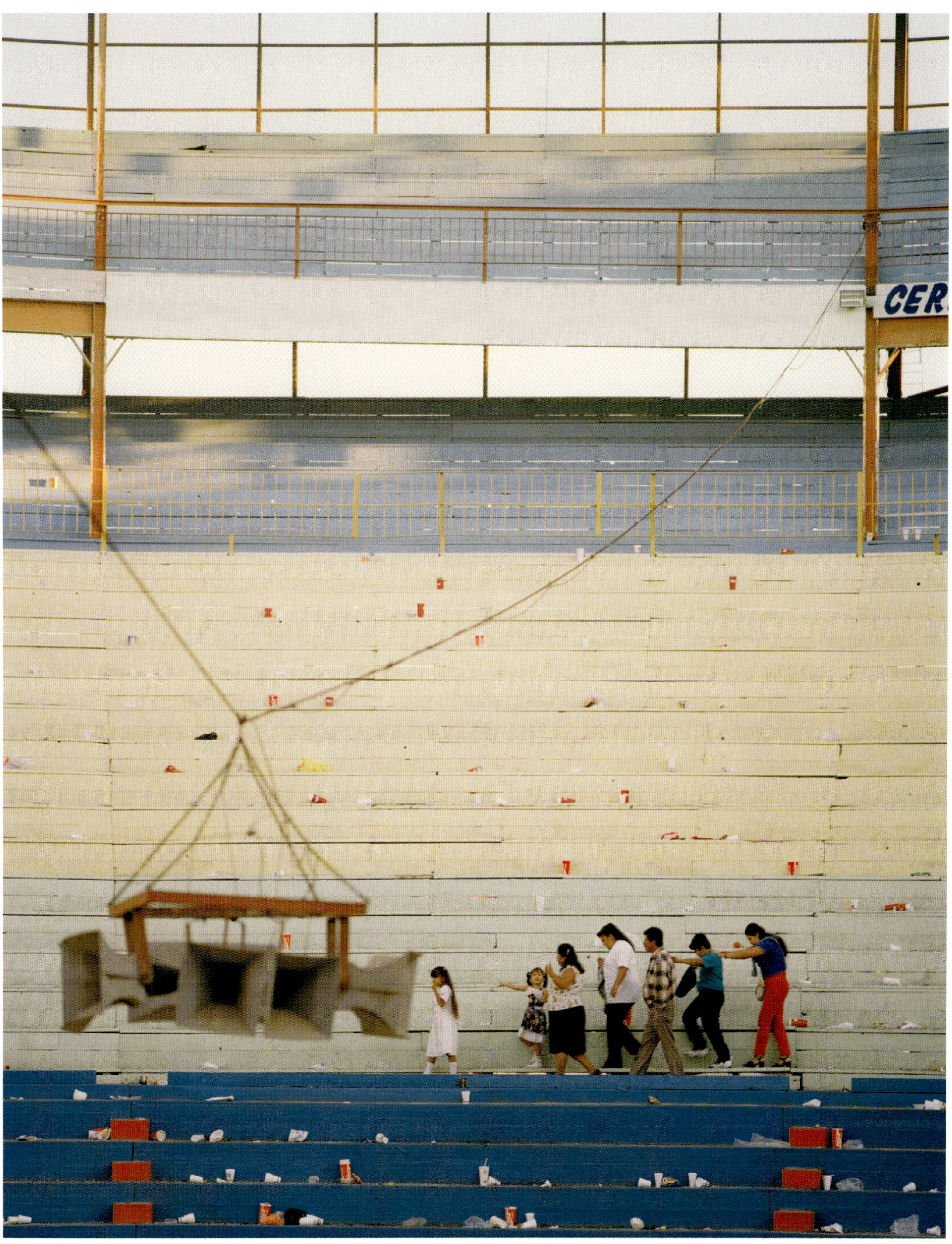

CER

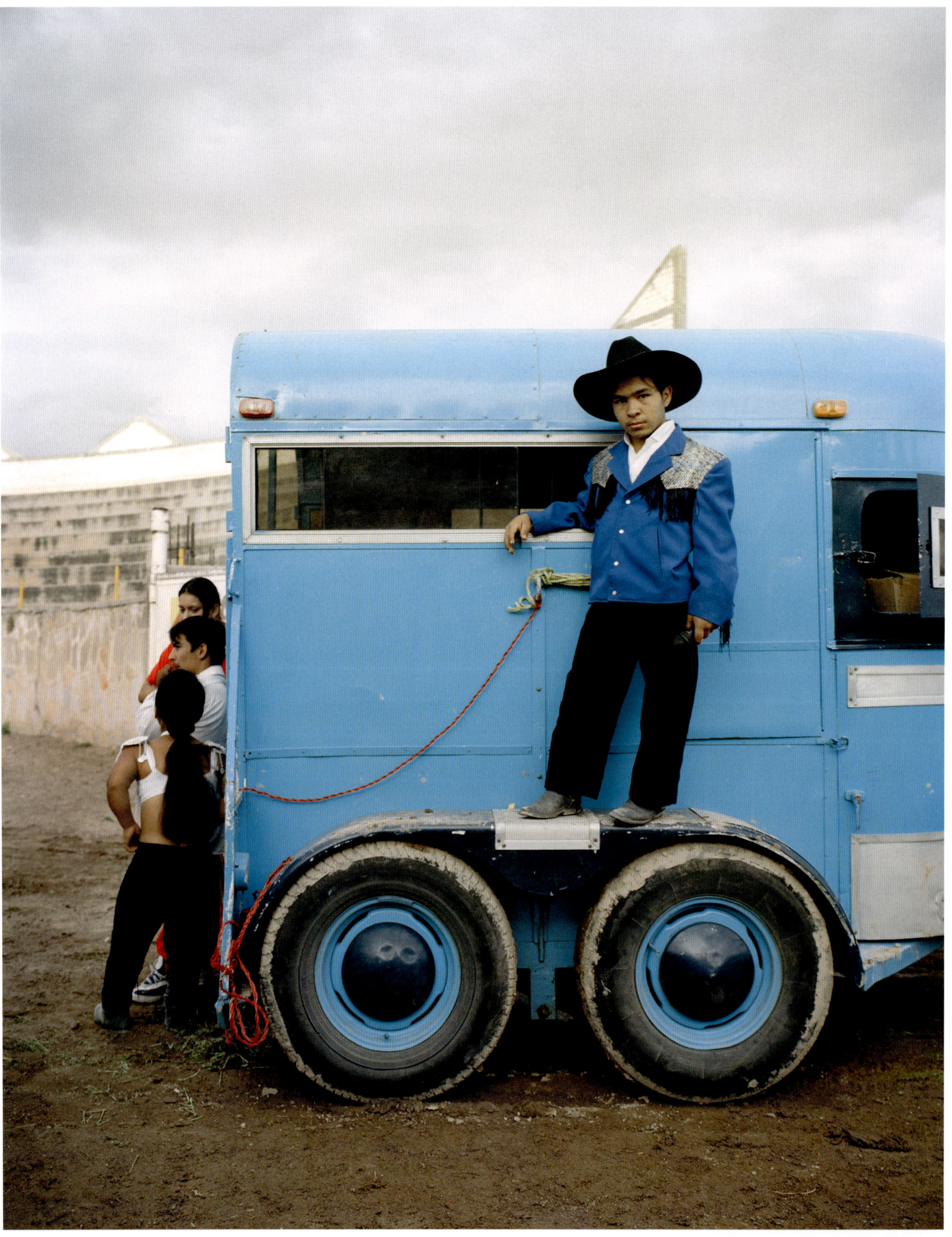

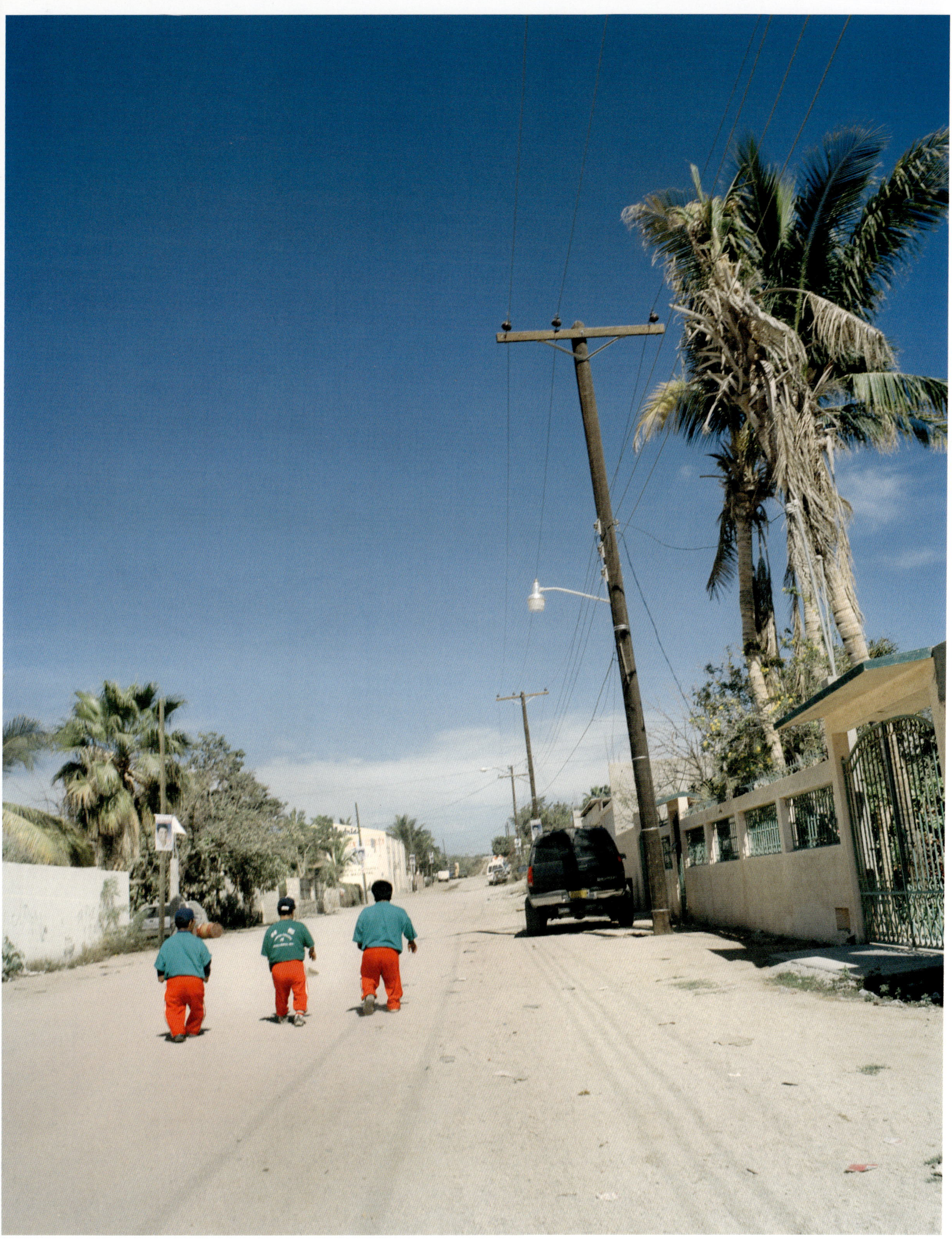

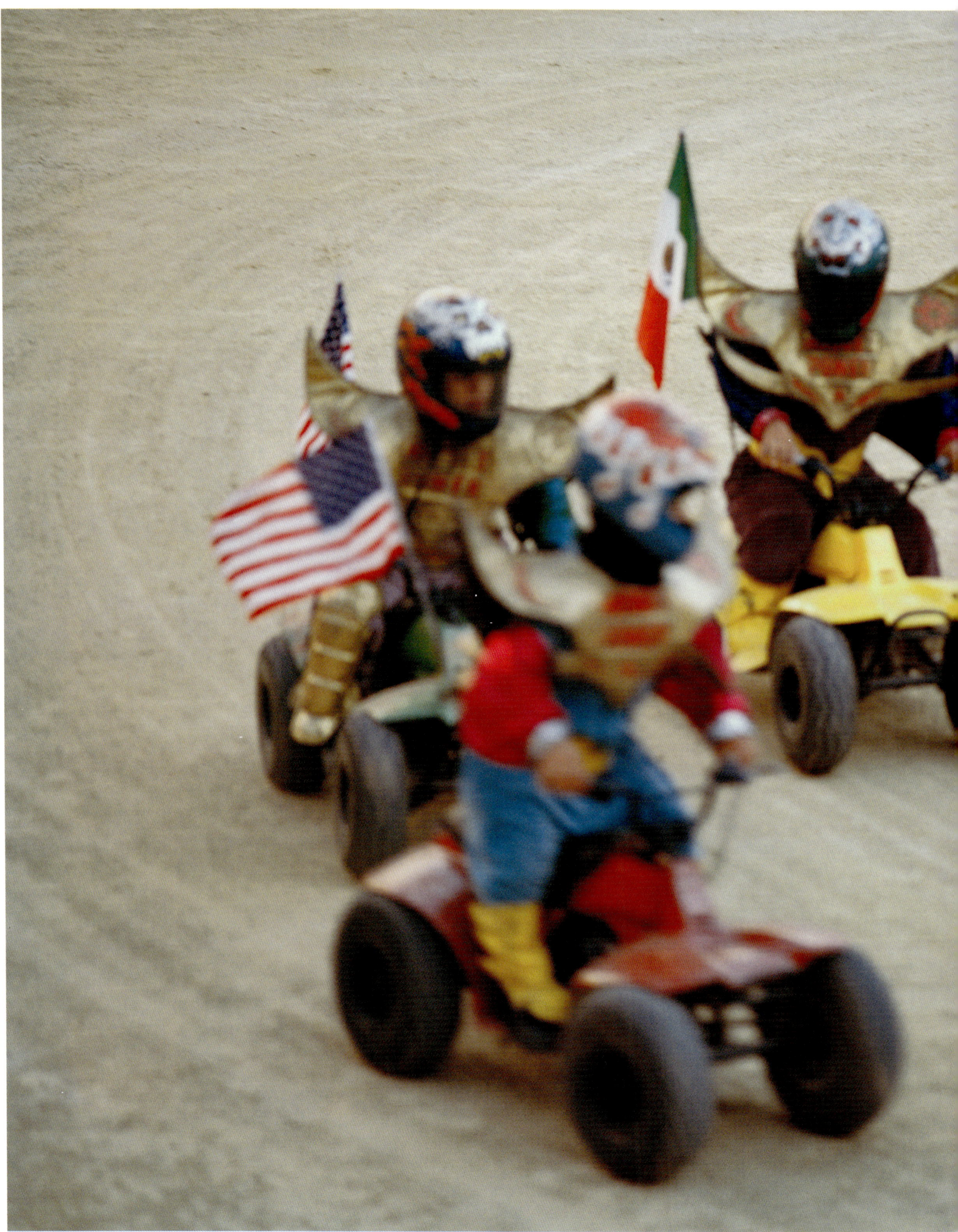

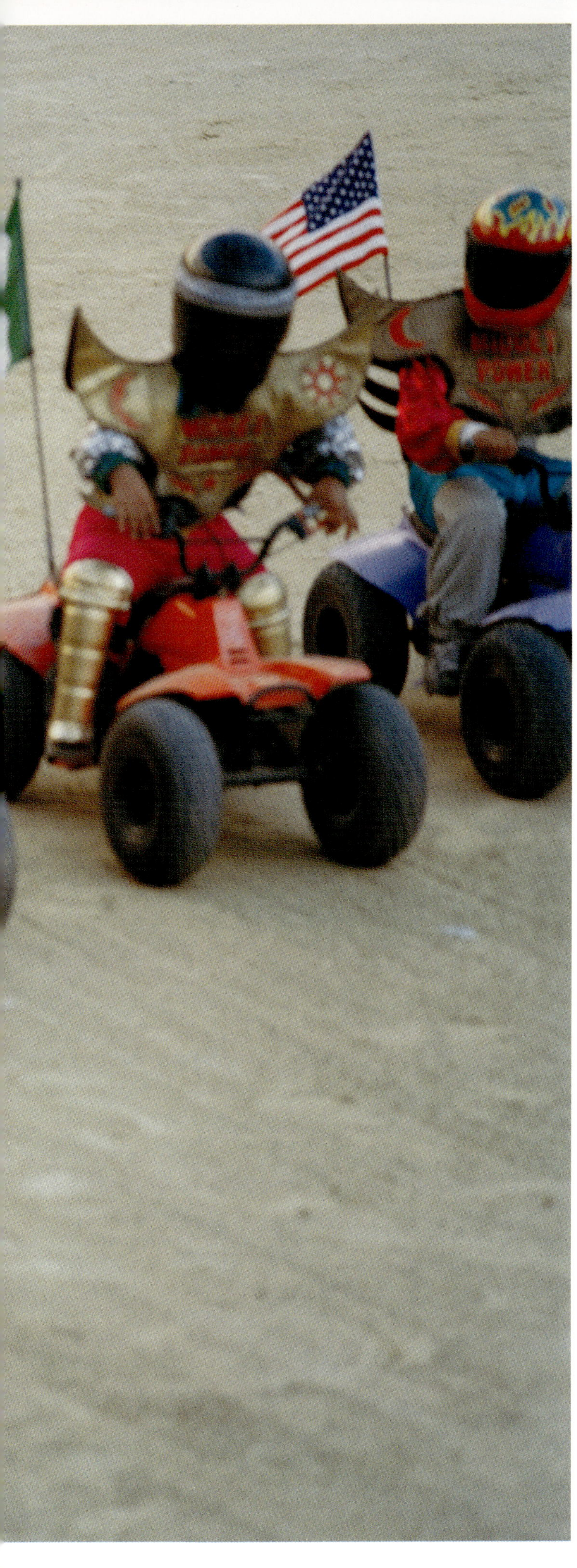

POWER

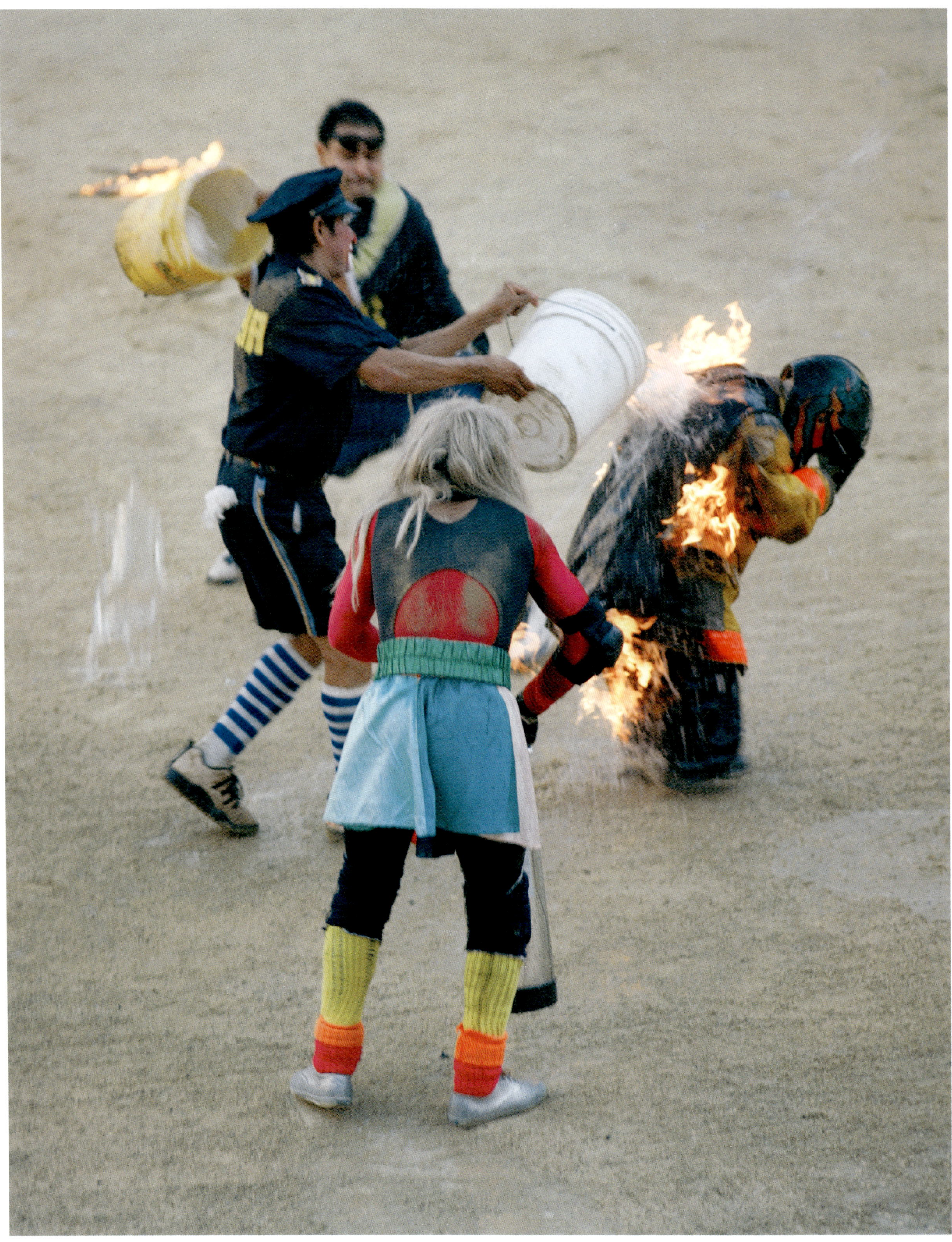

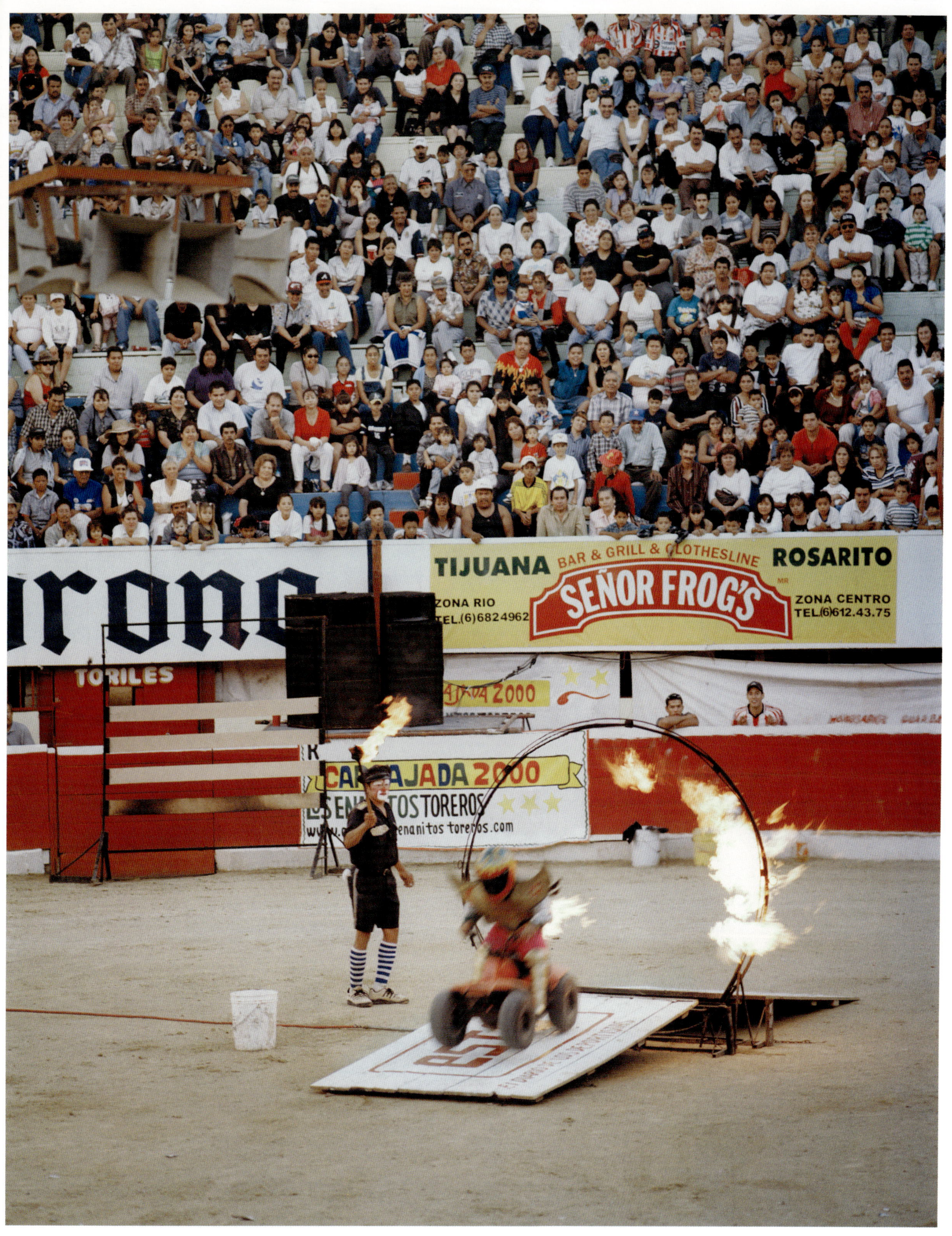
TIJUANA
ZONA RIO
TEL.(6)6824962
BAR & GRILL & CLOTHESLINE
SEÑOR FROG'S
MR
ROSARITO
ZONA CENTRO
TEL.(6)612.43.75
rong
TORILES
CARCAJADA 2000
LOS ENANITOS TOREROS
www.enanitostoreros.com

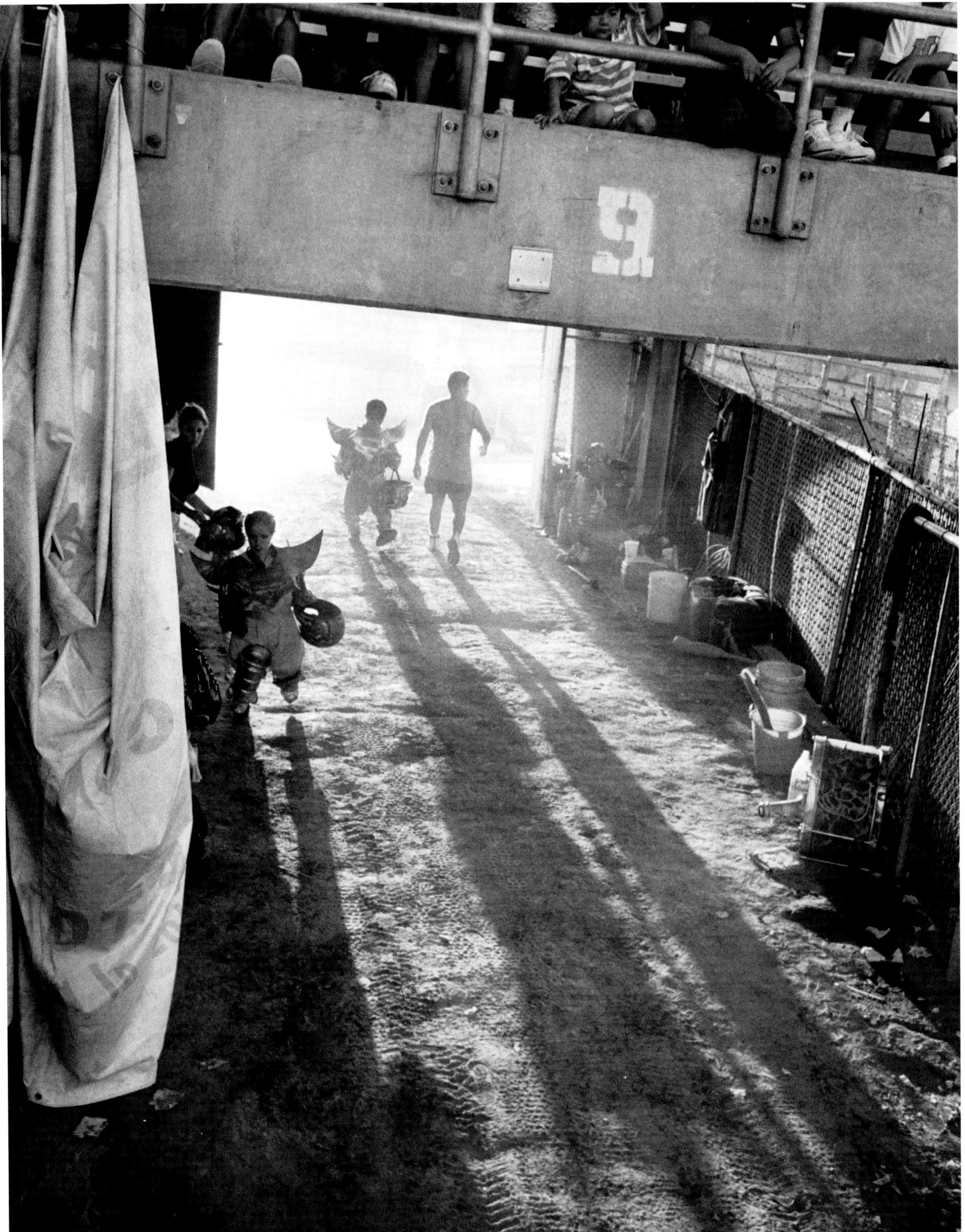

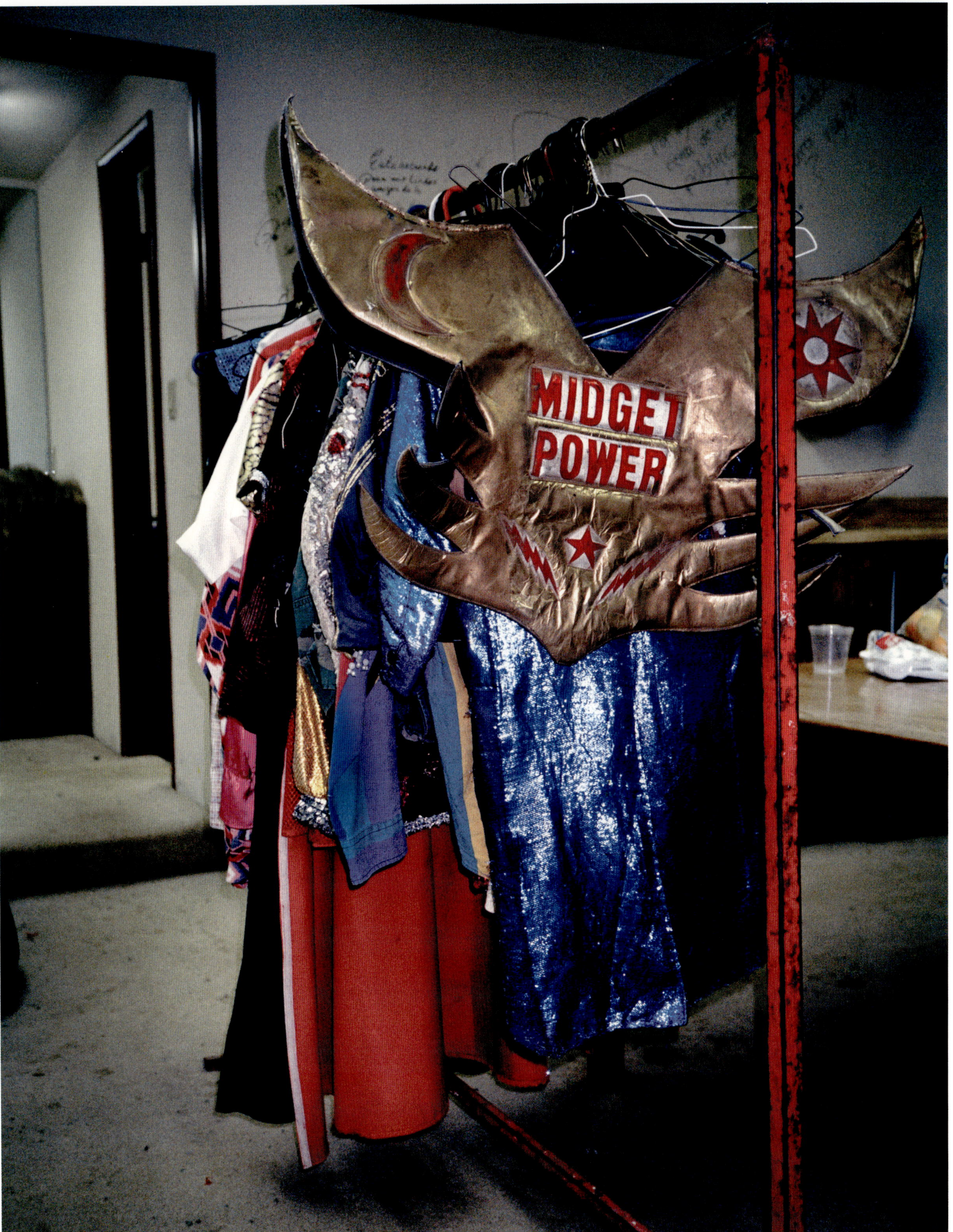
MIDGET
POWER

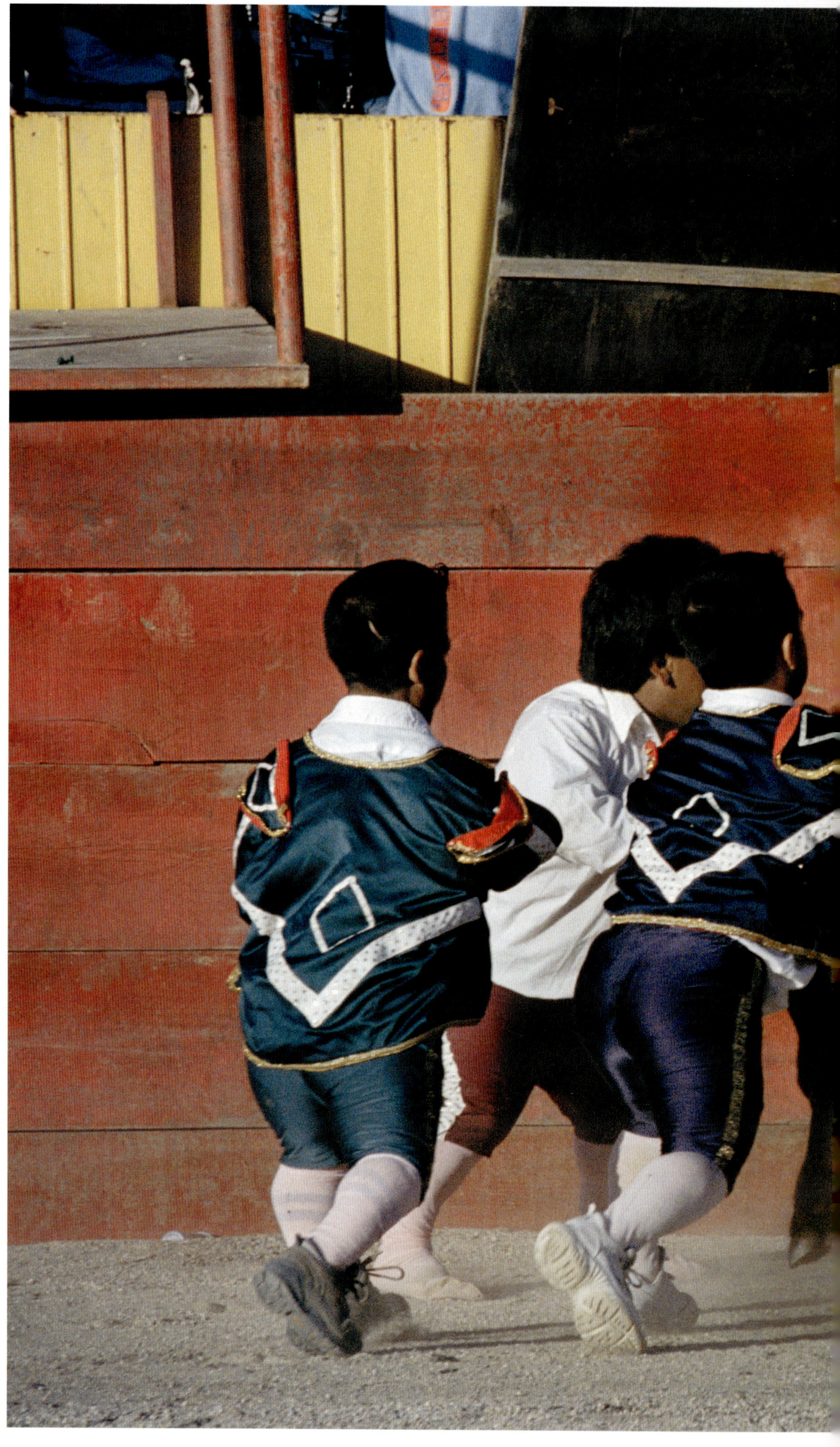

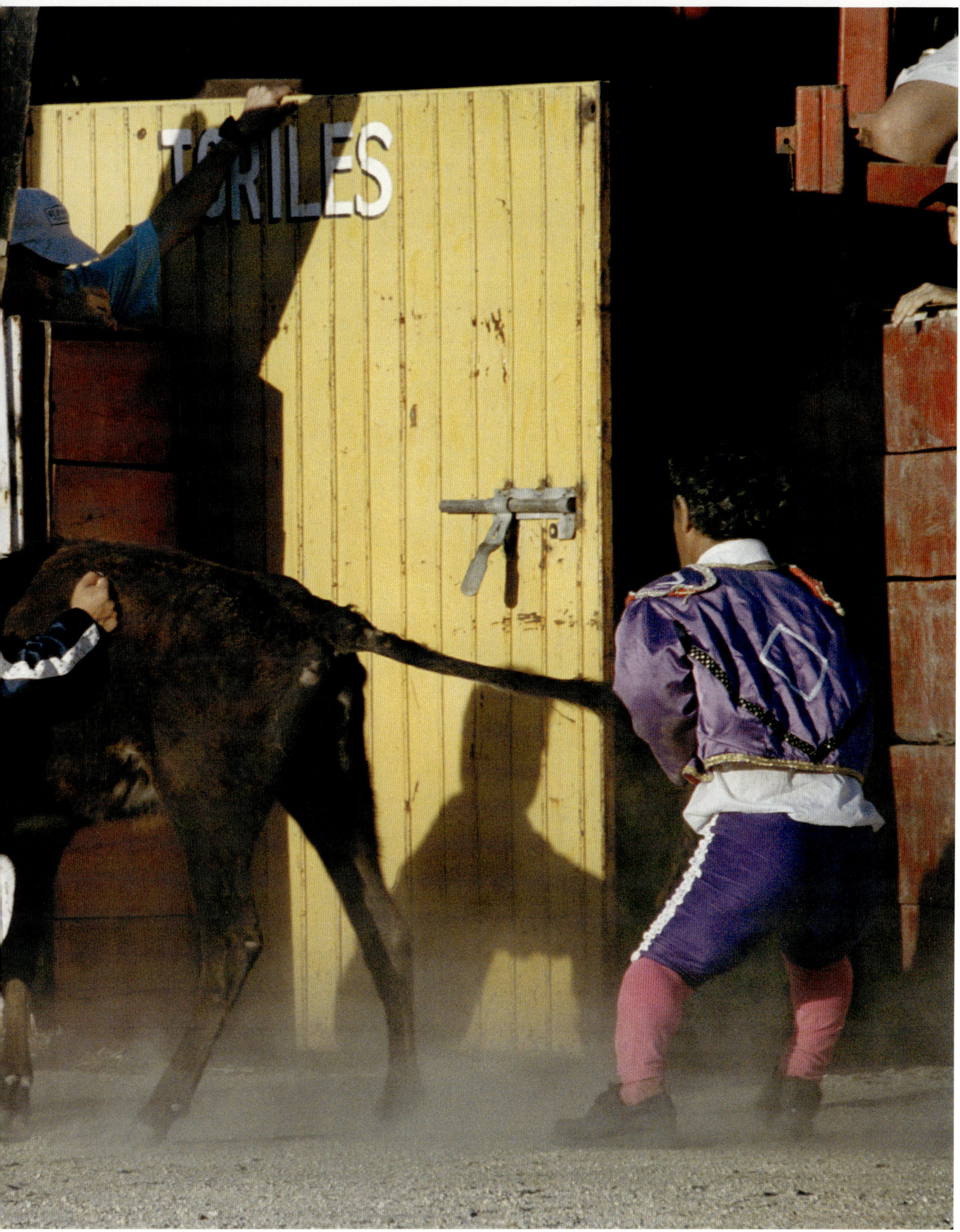
TORILES

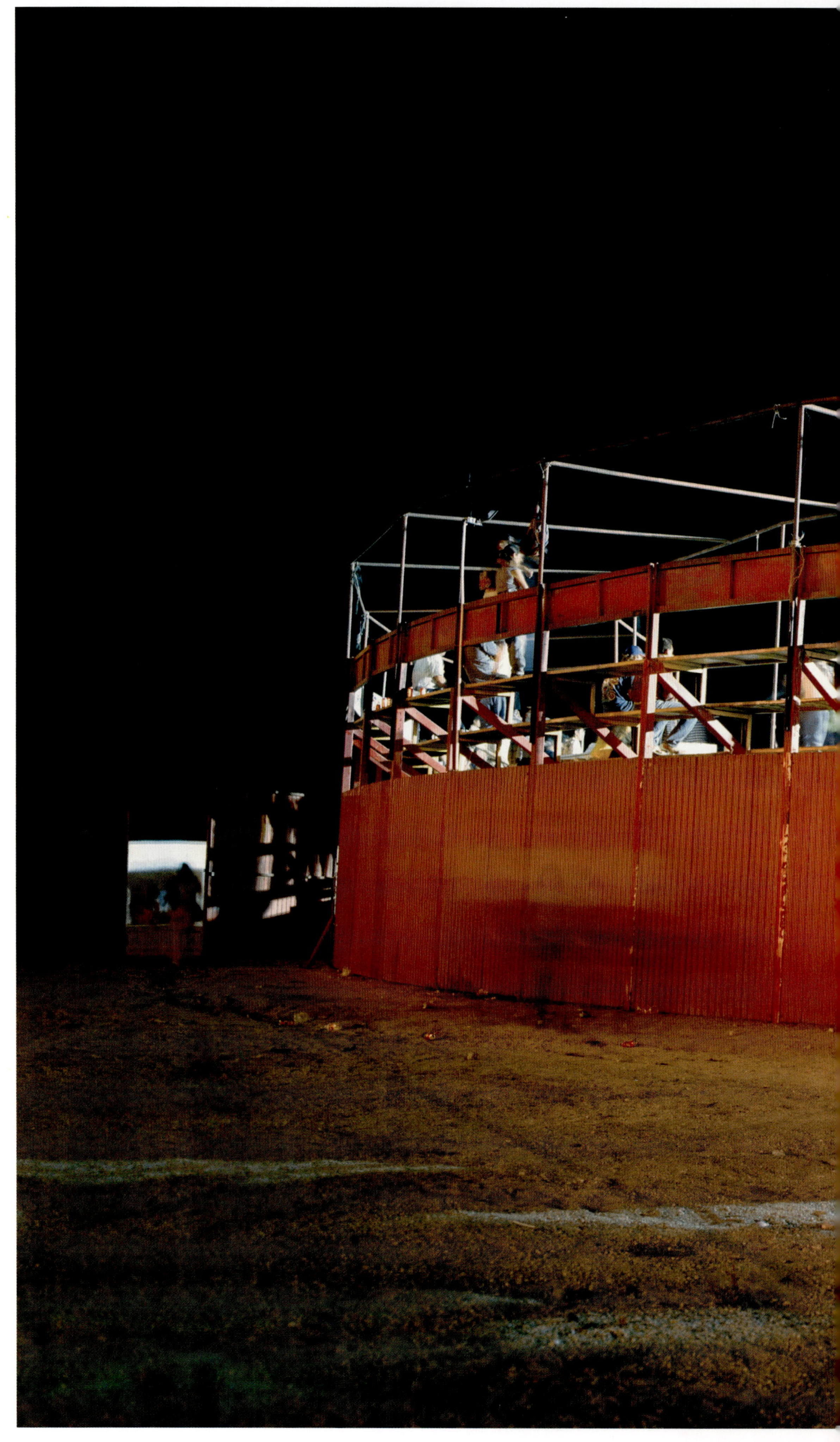

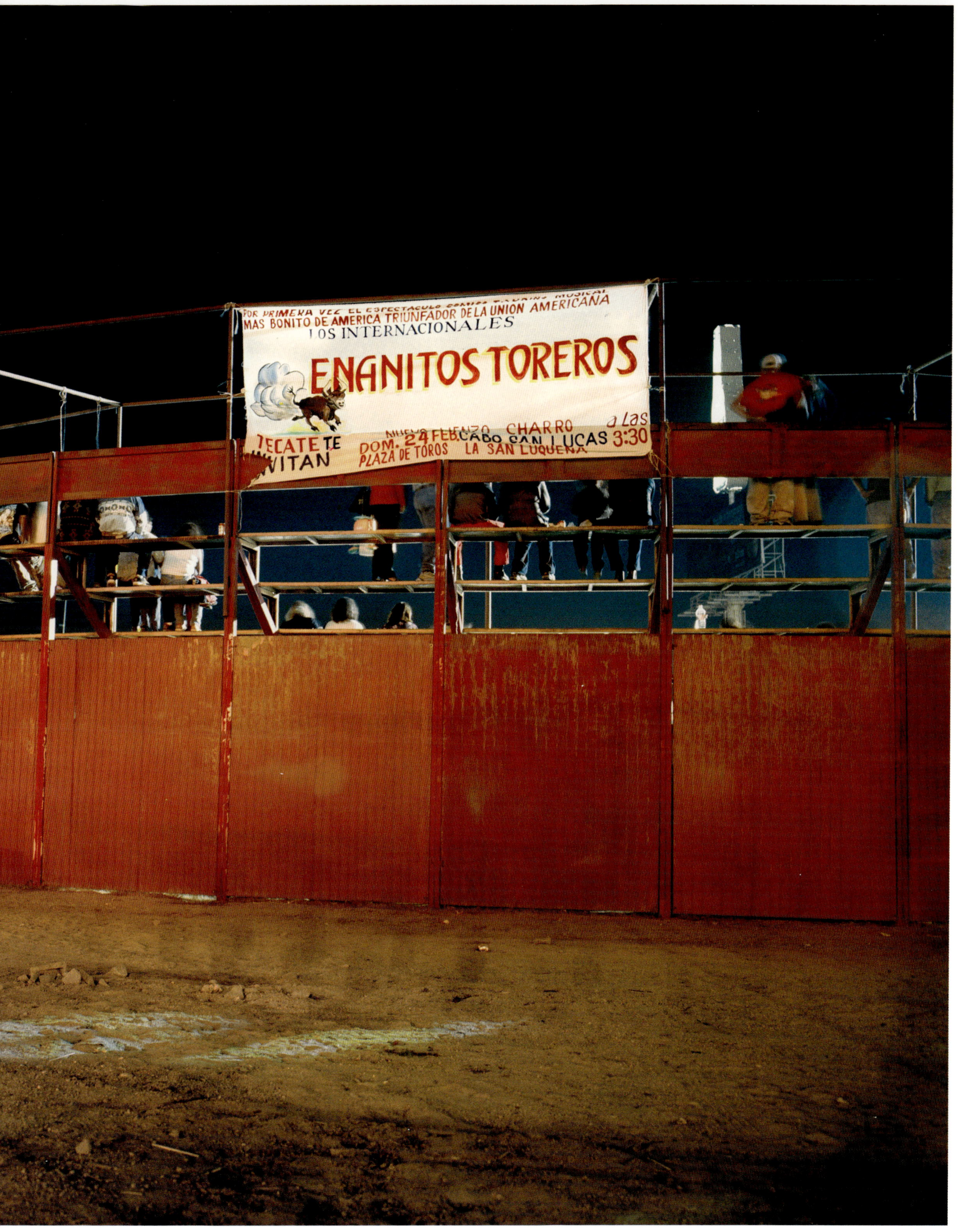

POR PRIMERA VEZ EL ESPECTACULO COMICO TAURINO MUSICAL
MAS BONITO DE AMERICA TRIUNFADOR DE LA UNION AMERICANA
LOS INTERNACIONALES
ENANITOS TOREROS
TECATE TE INVITAN
NUEVO LIENZO CHARRO
CABO SAN LUCAS
a LAS
DOM. 24 FEB.
PLAZA DE TOROS LA SAN LUQUENA
3:30

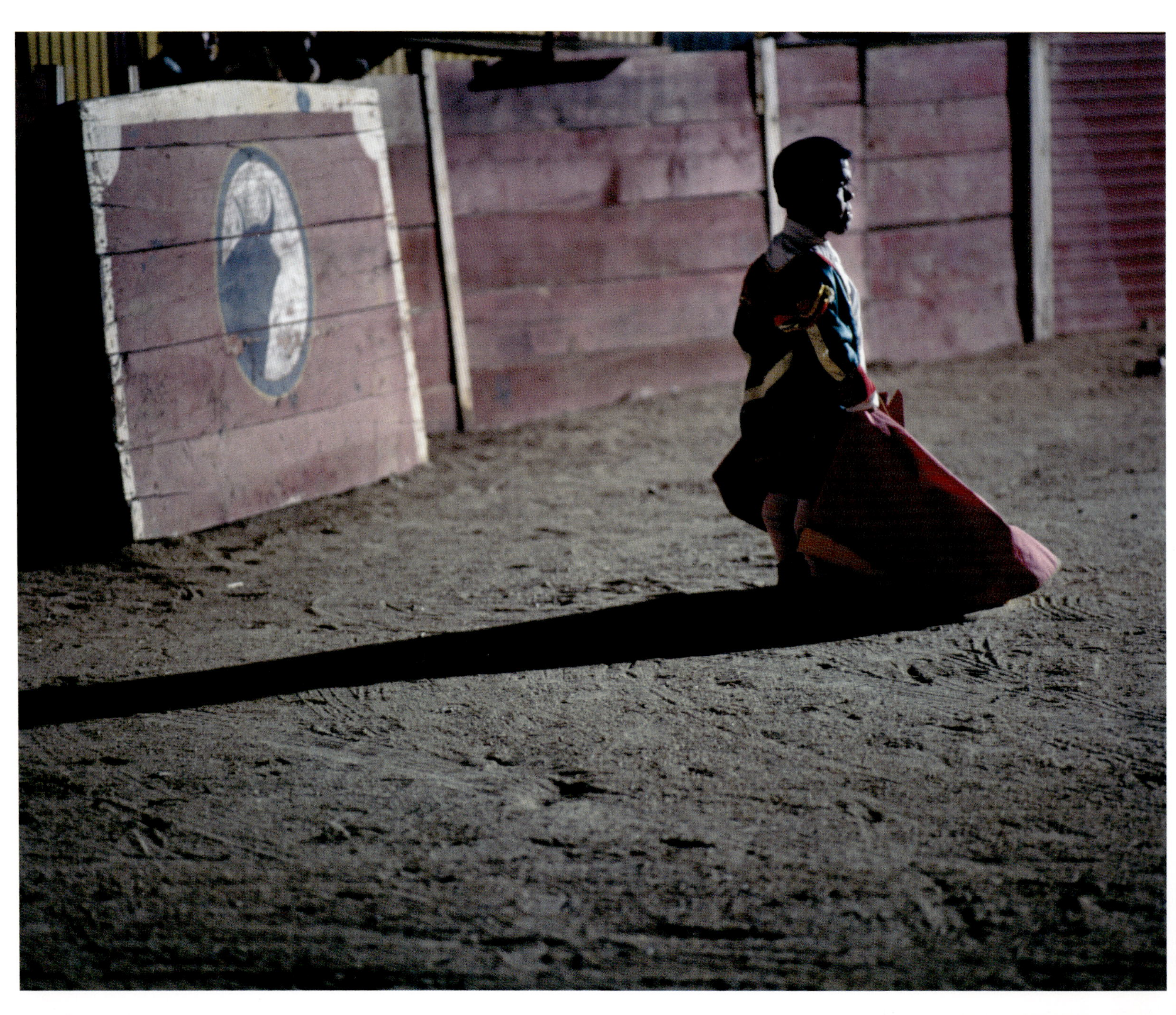

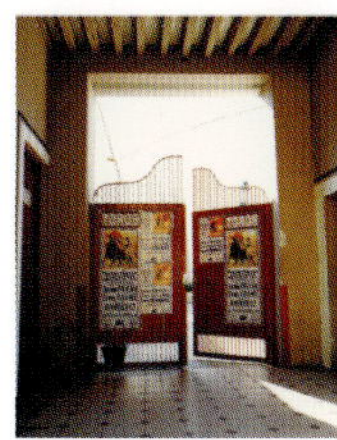

3   Swinging doors lead into Plaza de San Marcos, a nineteenth-century bullring in the city of Aguascalientes, where several cuadrillas of Enanitos Toreros live.

Puertas de entrada a la Plaza de San Marcos, construida en el siglo XIX en la ciudad de Aguascalientes, lugar de origen de varias cuadrillas de Enanitos Toreros.

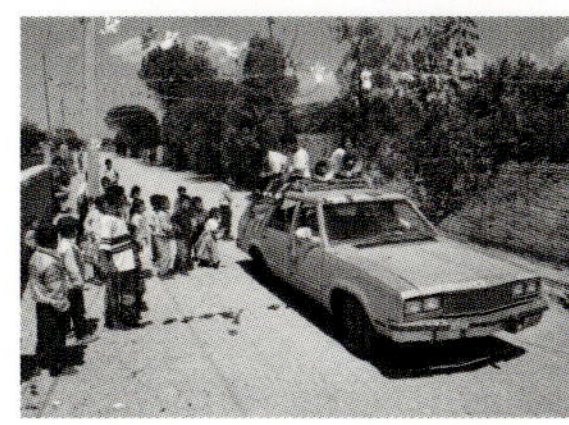

4   A promoter of Enanitos Toreros shows exhibits a cuadrilla through town to advertise the evening's performance. Tequisquiapan, Querétaro.

Los Enanitos Toreros son exhibidos por el promotor sobre el techo de un coche para anunciar la actuación de la tarde. Tequisquiapan, Querétaro.

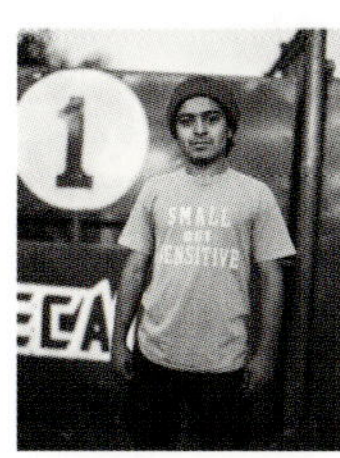

9   Josué Virgen. Totaltiche, Zacatecas.

Josué Virgen. Totaltiche, Zacatecas.

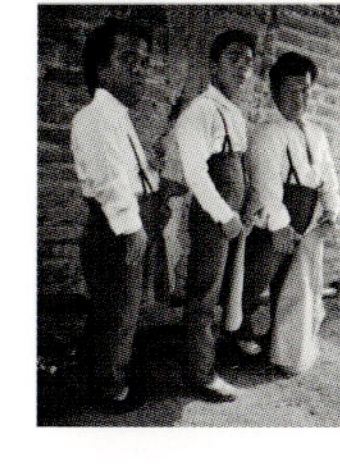

11   Lupillo, Josué, and Joaquín ready to perform as rejoneadores. El Limón, Jalisco.

Lupillo, Josué y Joaquín como rejoneadores. El Limón, Jalisco.

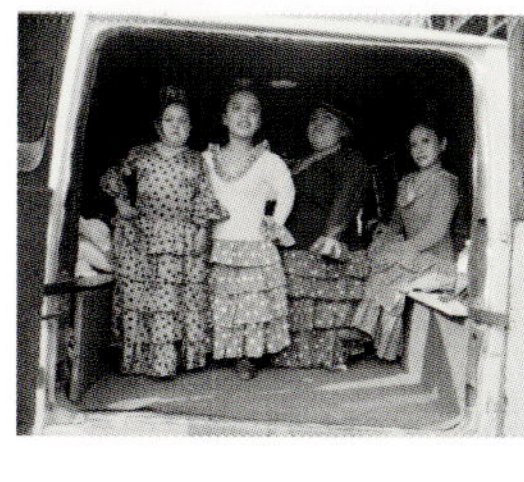

12   Yolanda Biviano, Claudia Rodriguez de Virgen, Teresa Montiel, and Veronica Alvarado in the tour van, used as a dressing room. Santa Maria de la Transportina, Jalisco.

Yolanda Biviano, Claudia Rodriguez de Virgen, Teresa Montiel y Veronica Alvarado en la camioneta de la gira la cual también usan como vestidor. Santa Maria de la Transportina, Jalisco.

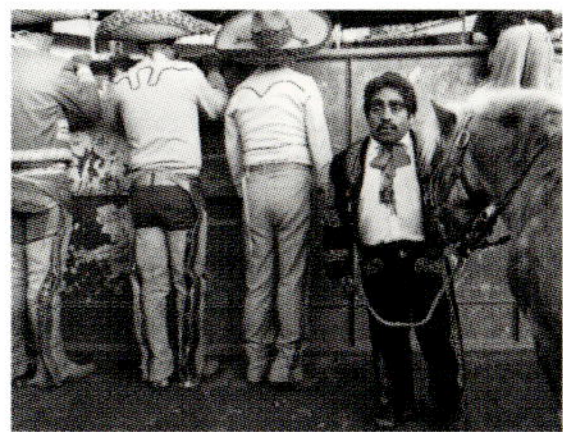

14   Jorge Ramos waits for his cue to lip-sync "Caballo Prieto Azabache," a classic ballad honoring a horse who died to save his owner. Tijuana, Baja California.

Jorge Ramos espera la indicación para entrar cantar en play back "Caballo Prieto Azabache, una balada compuesta en honor a un caballo que murió para salvar a su dueño. Tijuana, Baja California.

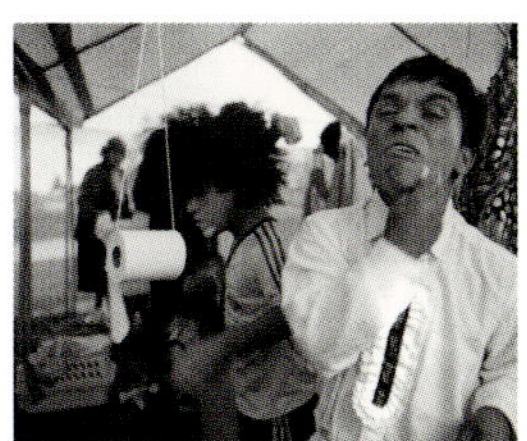

16   Ricardo "Cucuy" Reyes Acero prepares his costume as Maradona and José "Chepe" Tejada removes his makeup in preparation for his next act. Monterey Park, California.

Ricardo Reyes Acero, "Cucuy", se viste de Maradona mientras "Chepe" se quita el maquillaje preparandose para su siguiente acto. Monterey Park, California.

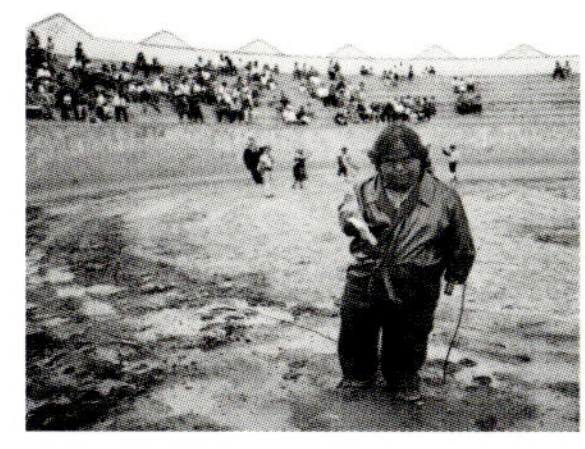

18   Tomás Emanuel, as master of ceremonies, introduces the Enanitos Toreros at a performance in Cosío, Aguascalientes.

Tomás Emanuel, como maestro de ceremonias, presenta a los Enanitos Toreros. Cosío, Aguascalientes.

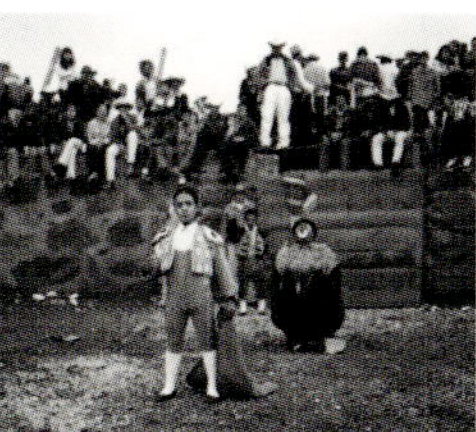

20   Josué Virgen enters the bullring followed by David Rodríguez Montiel and Joselito Hernández. El Volantín, Jalisco.

Josué Virgen abriendo plaza, seguido por David Rodríguez Montiel y Joselito Hernández. El Volantín, Jalisco.

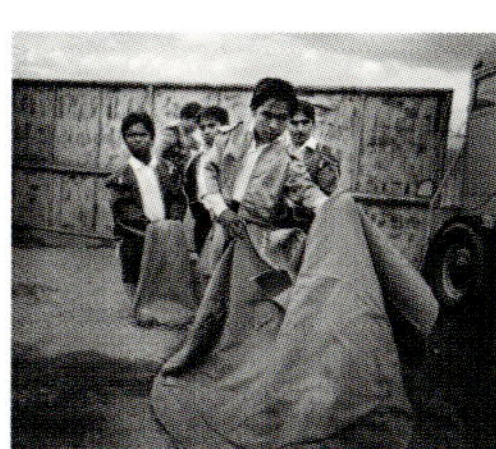

22   Arturo García, Gerson, Arnold, and Ezequiél Virgen. Cosío, Aguascalientes.

Arturo García, Gerson, Arnold y Ezequiél Virgen. Cosio, Aguascalientes.

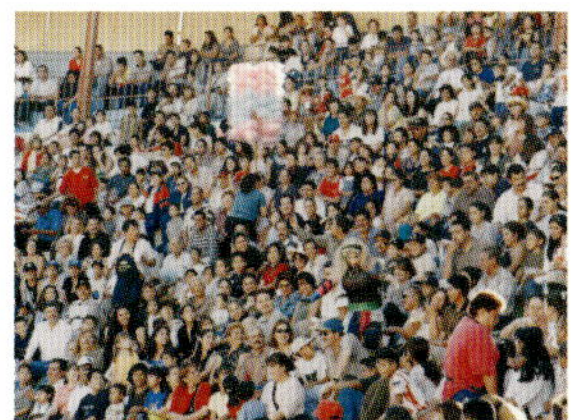

24   At a sold-out show for nearly 12,000 people, Joel Gudiño, dressed in costume as "La Güera Mitotes," riles up the audience before the bullfight begins. Tijuana, Baja California.

Ante una plaza abarrotada con casi 12,000 espectadores, Joel Gudiño, vestido como "La Güera Mitotoes," alborota a la audiencia antes de que empiece la corrida de toros. Tijuana, Baja California.

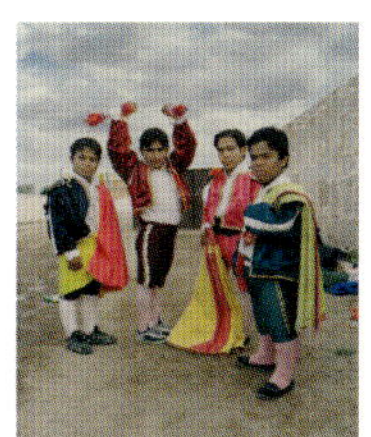

27   The Virgen brothers, Ezequías, Ezequiel, and Gerson, and Arturo García at the bullring in Cosío, Aguascalientes.

Los hermanos Virgen, Ezequías, Ezequiel y Gerson, y Arturo García en la plaza de toros de Cosío, Aguascalientes.

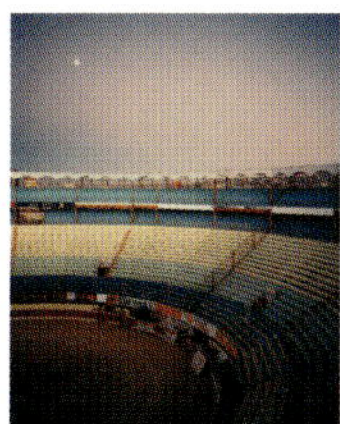

29   Dusk at the Toreo de Tijuana, following a sold-out show that afternoon.

Atardecer en el Toreo de Tijuana, después de una actuación donde se vendieron todos los boletos.

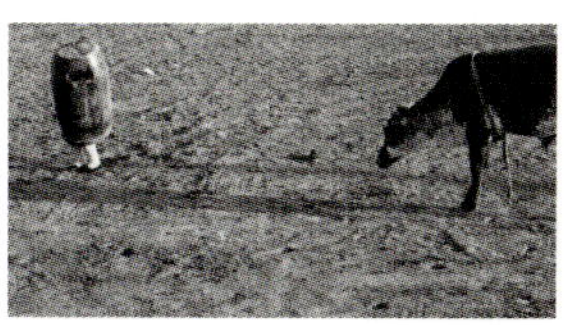

30   Donning a barrel for protection, Sergio retrieves a fellow bullfighter's shoe from the ring. La Mesa, Baja California.

Sergio, protegiéndose dentro de un barril, recupera el zapato de un colega torero. La Mesa, Baja California.

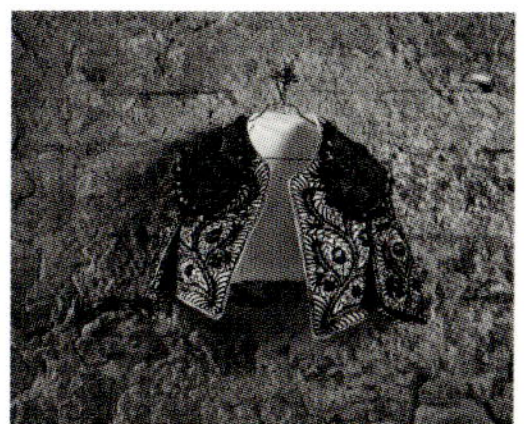

32   Enanito Torero costume. San Miguel de Allende, Guanajuato.

Casaca de enanito torero. San Miguel de Allende, Guanajuato.

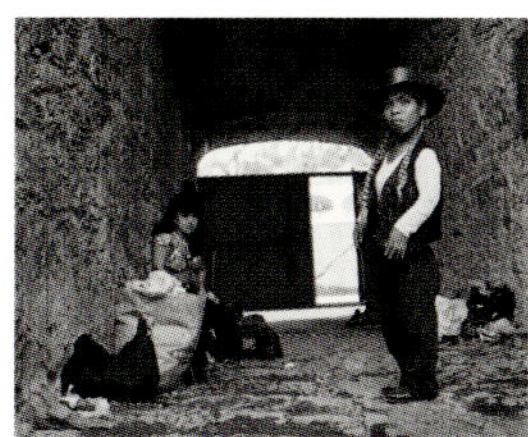

33   Cecilia Méndez and Isabel Cortés in the dressing area, which is also the tunnel through which the bulls are released into the ring. San Miguel de Allende, Guanajuato.

Cecilia Méndez e Isabel Cortés en la zona de vestidores, la cual también es el pasillo por el que salen los toros al ruedo. San Miguel de Allende, Guanajuato.

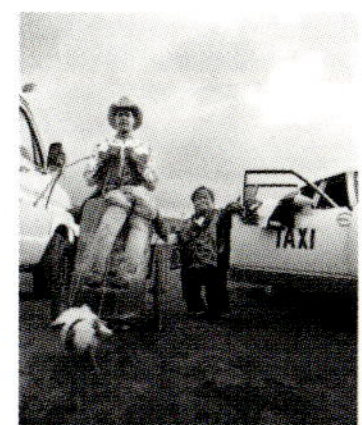

34   Tomás Emanuel and Juan Alfredo in the "chicken chariot." Ejido de Chilpancingo, Baja California.

Tomás Emanuel y Juan Alfredo en la "pollo carroza". Ejido de Chilpancingo, Baja California.

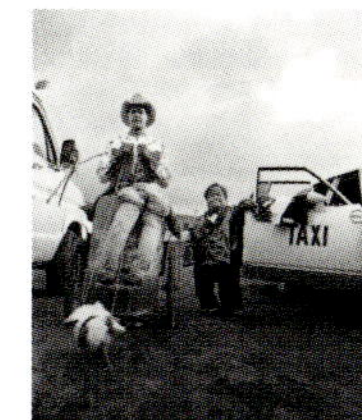

35   The Enanitos Toreros de Aguascalientes before their performance as Banda Limón. Cosío, Aguascalientes.

Los Enanitos Toreros de Aguascalientes antes de su actuación como la Banda Limón. Cosío, Aguascalientes.

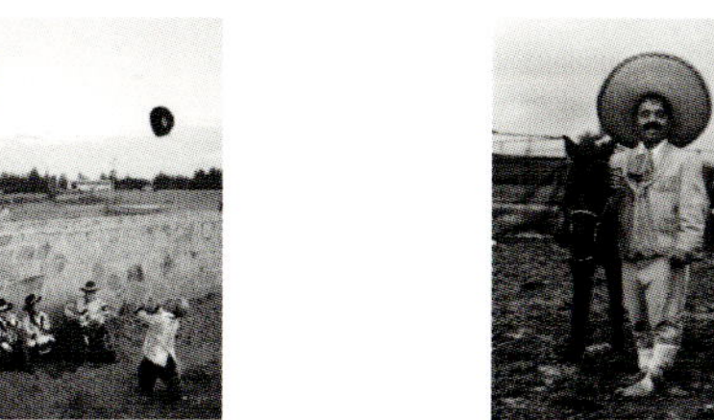

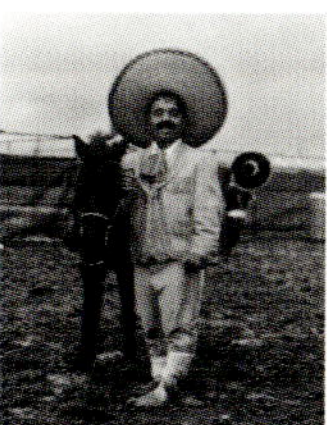

37   While performing in the rain, José "Chepe" Tejada sings a Vicente Fernández song about a loyal horse and an unfaithful woman. Monterey Park, California.

Después de perder sus zapatos en el lodo, José "Chepe" Tejada, interpreta una canción de Vicente Fernández acerca de un caballo y una mujer infiel. Monterey Park, California.

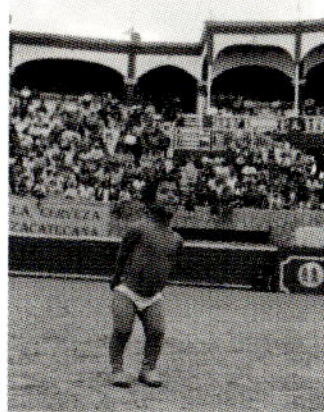

39   At the urging of his promoter, Alejandro moons the audience at a fund-raiser for DIF, a social welfare institution for Mexican families. Jerez, Zacatecas.

A sugerencia de su promotor, Alejandro se baja el calzón ante los espectadores en un evento a beneficio del DIF, una institución gubernamental de asistencia social. Jerez, Zacatecas.

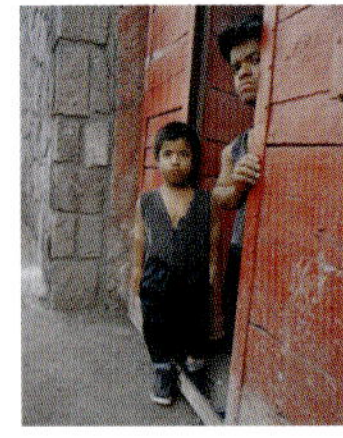

41   Cucuy with Alejandro, who, at ten years old, is the same age Cucuy was when he started performing. Aguascalientes.

Cucuy y Alejandro de diez años, quien tiene la misma edad que Cucuy cuando éste empezó actuar. Aguascalientes.

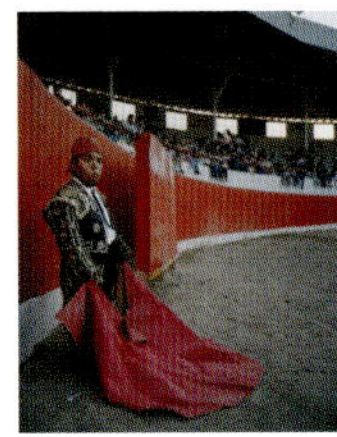

43   David Rodríguez Montiel at the edge of the bullring. El Canelo, Jalisco.

David Rodríguez Montiel a la orilla del ruedo. El Canelo, Jalisco.

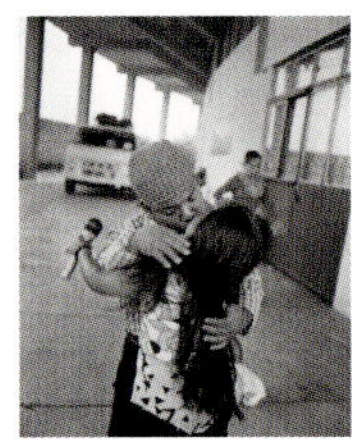

45   David and his girlfriend backstage. El Canelo, Jalisco.

David y su novia entre bastidores. El Canelo Jalisco.

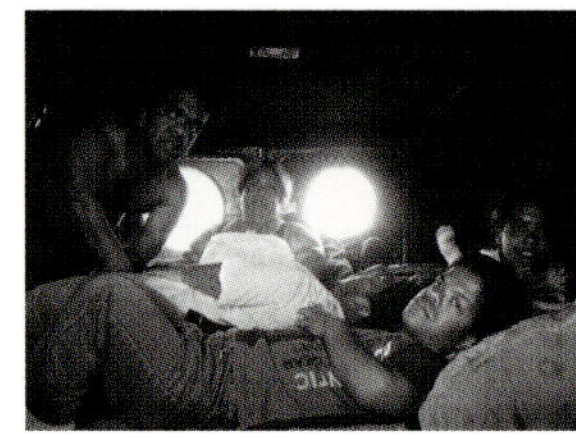

46   Lupillo, Teresa, David, Sergio, and Claudia ride in the back of the tour van.

Lupillo, Teresa, David, Sergio y Claudia en la camioneta durante una gira.

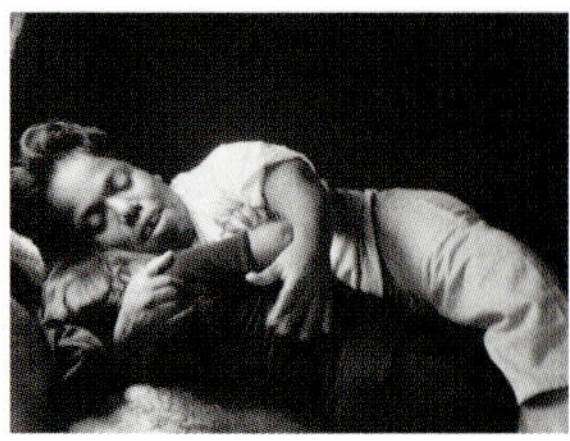

48   David Rodríguez Montiel and his girlfriend cuddle in the van while on tour through Zacatecas.

David Rodríguez Montiel y su novia, en la camioneta durante una gira en Zacatecas.

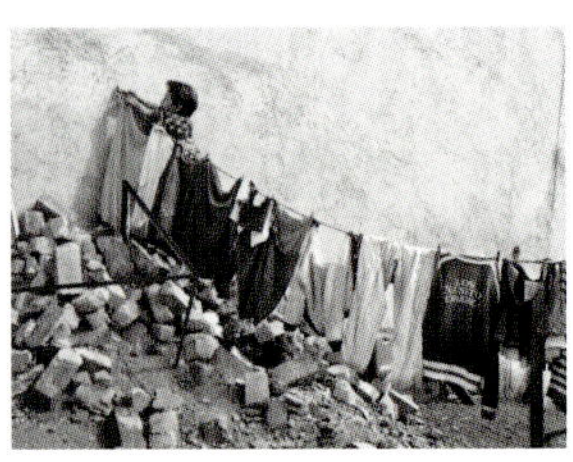

50   Isabel Cortez hangs the family laundry in the patio of their home in Ciudad Neza. Estado de Mexico.

Isabel Cortez cuelga la ropa en el patio de la casa, donde vive con su familia. Ciudad Neza, Estado de México.

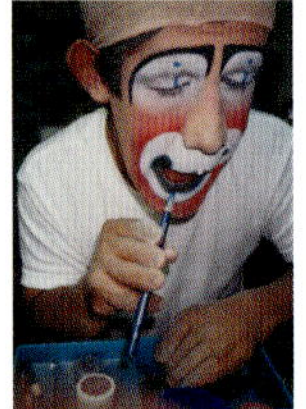

52   Gustavo Vázquez Buendía gets ready to perform at a neighbor's birthday party. Mexico City.

Gustavo Vázquez Buendía se prepara para amenizar la fiesta de cumpleaños de un vecino. Ciudad de México.

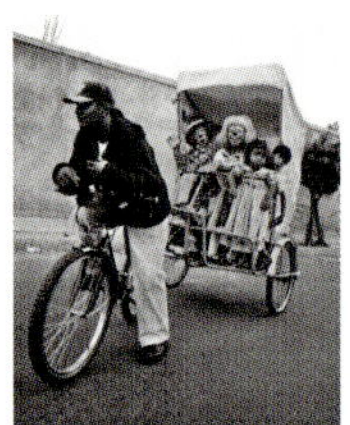

53   When not performing as Enanitos Toreros, Gustavo and Isabel perform at children's birthday parties in Ciudad Neza, acompanied by their children, Valeria and Azarel. Estado de México.

Cuando no trabajan como Enanitos Toreros, Gustavo e Isabel actuan en fiestas infantiles acompañados por sus hijos, Valeria y Azarel. Ciudad Neza, Estado de México.

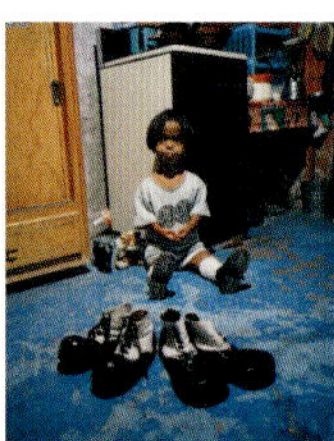

54   Valeria Parra Cortez with her father's clown shoes. Mexico City.

Valeria, hija de Gustavo e Isabel, con los zapatos de payaso de su padre. Ciudad de México.

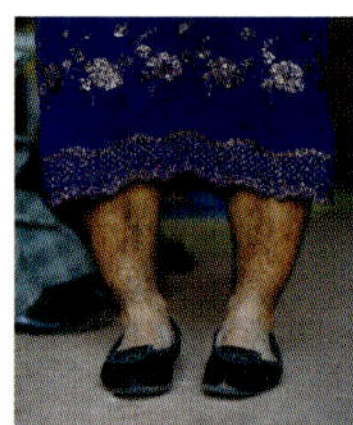

55   Chepe dressed as the female half of pop duo Pimpinela. Aguascalientes.

Chepe vestido del personaje femenino del dúo de pop Pimpinela. Aguascalientes.

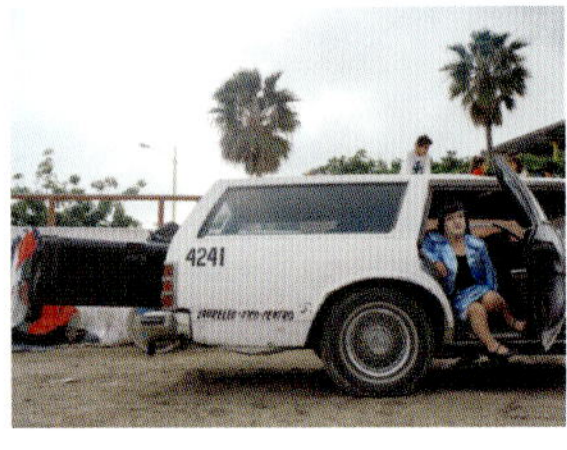

56   A hired taxi brings Juan López and his colleagues to a show in Tijuana.

Un taxi lleva a Juan López y a los demás miembros de la cuadrilla a su espectáculo en Tijuana.

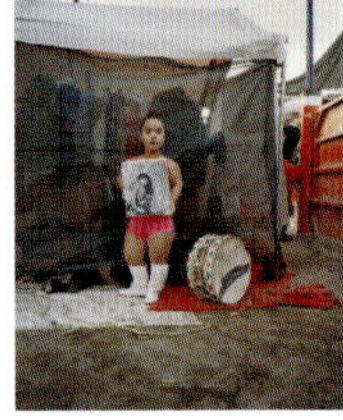

59   Claudia Rodríguez Montiel de Virgen holds a picture of Ceci Méndez. El Monte, California.

Claudia Rodríguez Montiel de Virgen sostiene una foto de Ceci Méndez. El Monte, California.

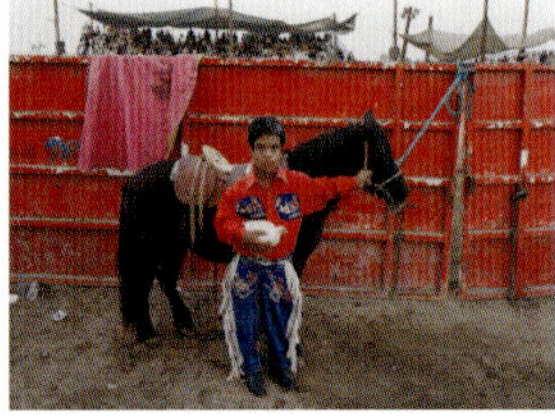

60   Ricardo "Cucuy" Reyes Acero, dressed as a cowboy during the United States tour. Pico Rivera, California.

Ricardo Reyes Acero "Cucuy", vestido de cowboy durante una gira por Estados Unidos. Pico Rivera, California.

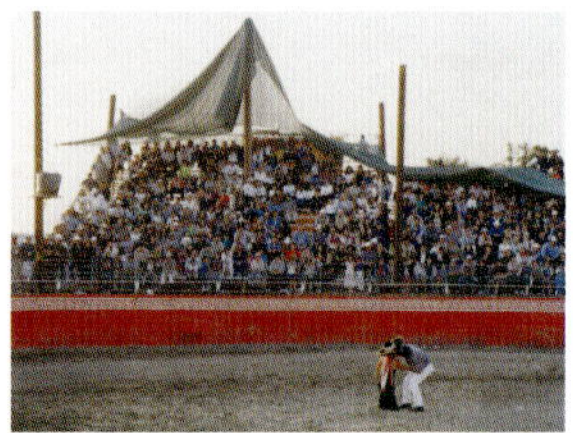

61   As part of the show, a spectator is brought down from the audience to give Claudia a kiss. Pico Rivera, California.

Como parte del espectáculo, bajan a un espectador del público para darle un beso a Claudia. Pico Rivera, California.

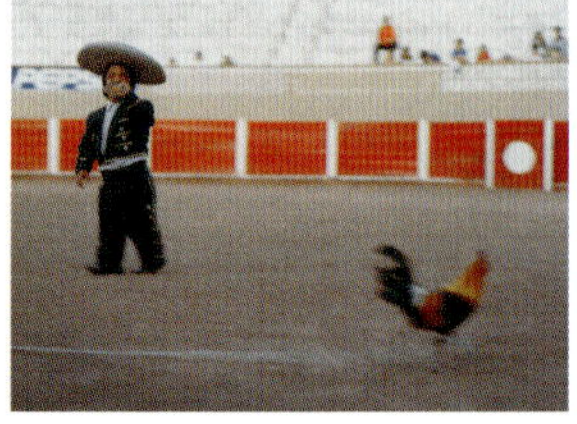

62   Dressed as ranchera singer Vicente Fernández, Lupillo sings a ballad about the bravery of a fighting cock. Plaza San Marcos, Aguascalientes.

Lupillo, vestido como el cantante de rancheras Vicente Fernández, canta una balada sobre la valentía de un gallo de pelea. Plaza San Marcos, Aguascalientes.

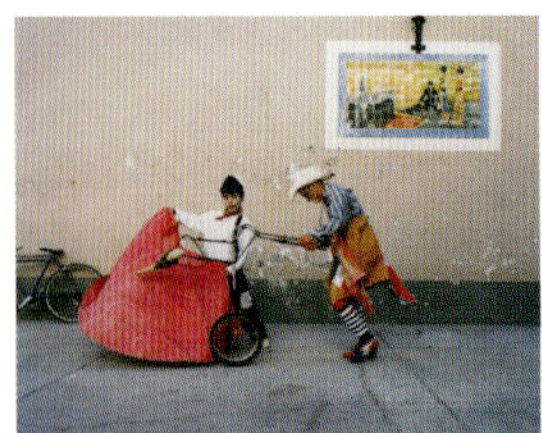

63   Joselito Hernández and Juan Alfredo practice at plaza San Marcos in Aguascalientes.

Joselito Hernández y Juan Alfredo practican en la plaza San Marcos de Aguascalientes.

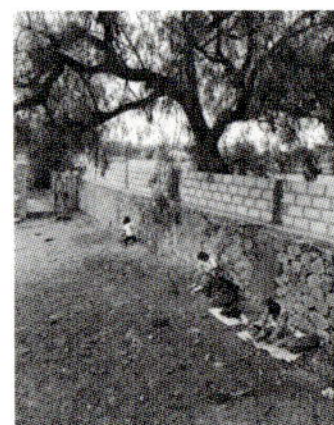

64   A vacant lot serves as a dressing room during a show in Cerritos, Querétaro.

Un lote baldío hace de camerino durante una presentación en Cerritos, Querétaro.

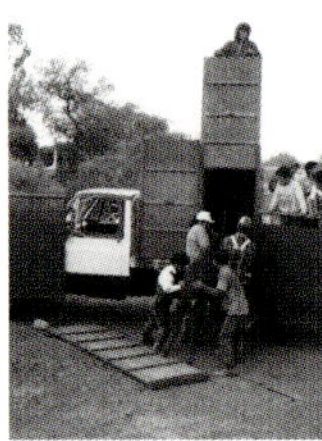

65   Putting the bull away after the show. Cerritos, Querétaro.

Guardando al toro después de la corrida. Cerritos, Querétaro.

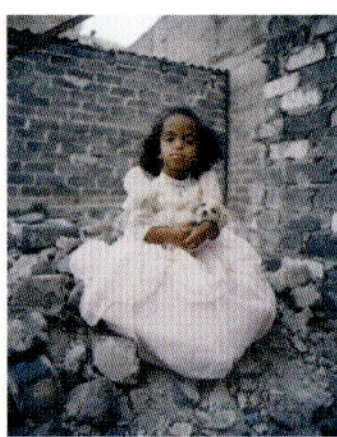

67   Valeria Parra Cortez poses in her kindergarten graduation dress. Mexico City.

Valeria Parra Cortez con el vestido de graduación de kinder. México DF.

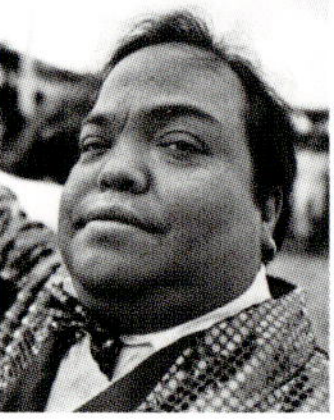

68   Tomás Emanuel as the master of ceremonies. Cosio, Aguascalientes.

Tomás Emanuel como maestro de ceremonias. Cosío, Aguascalientes.

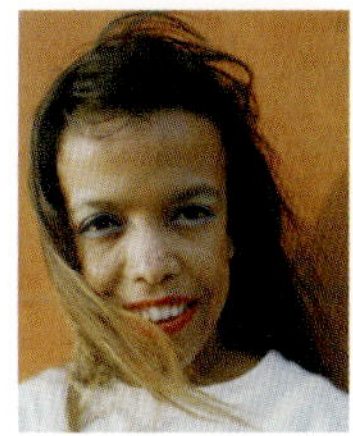

69   Verónica. Jerez, Zacatecas.

Verónica. Jerez, Zacatecas.

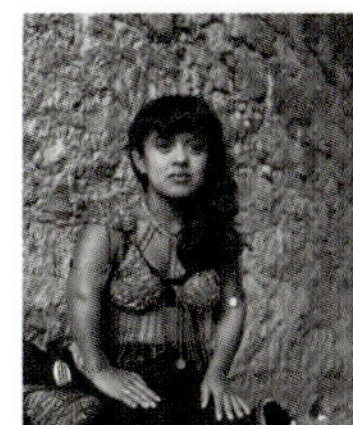

70   Ceci Méndez dressed as Selena. San Miguel de Allende, Guanajuato.

Ceci Méndez vestida como Selena. San Miguel de Allende, Guanajuato.

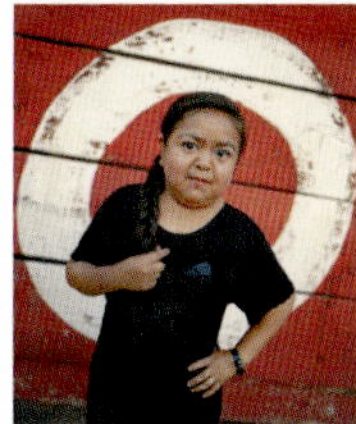

71   Yolanda Biviano. El Limón, Jalisco.

Yolanda Biviano. El Limón, Jalisco.

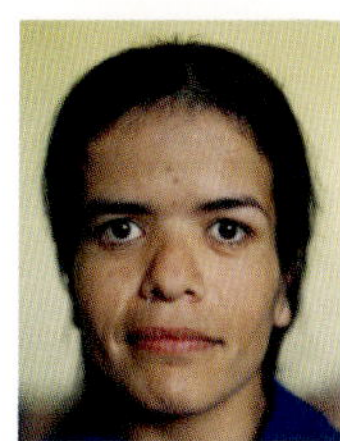

73   Imelda after her right eyebrow is plucked for the first time. El Trapiche, Colima.

Imelda con la ceja derecha depilada por primera vez. El Trapiche, Colima.

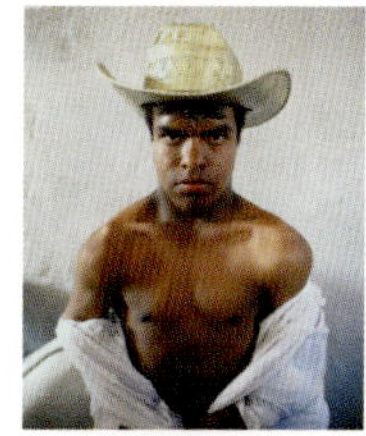

74   Ricardo Reyes Acero gets dressed to perform as Banda Machos. He got his nickname, "Cucuy" (boogeyman), as a child. Aguascalientes.

Ricardo Reyes Acero vestido con el atuendo del grupo Banda Machos. Desde niño le dicen "Cucuy" (espantaniños). Aguascalientes.

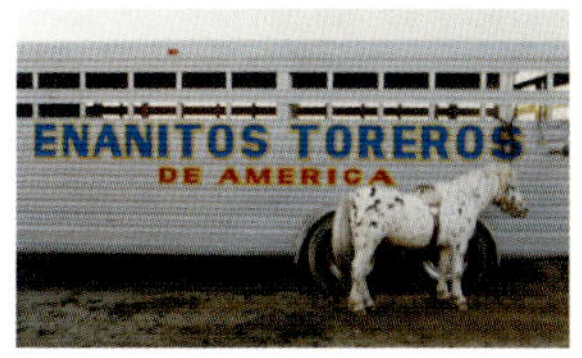

96   "Parches," a miniature horse, next to the transport trailers for the show animals. Monterey Park, California.

"Parches", un caballo miniatura, junto al equipo de transporte de los animales que forman parte del espectáculo. Monterey Park, California.

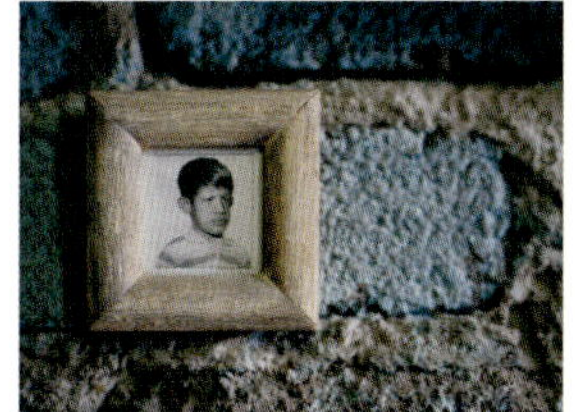

98   A boyhood portrait of Gustavo Vázquez Buendía hangs in his home in Mexico City.

Retrato de Gustavo Vázquez Buendía cuando era niño, en la pared de su casa en la Ciudad de México.

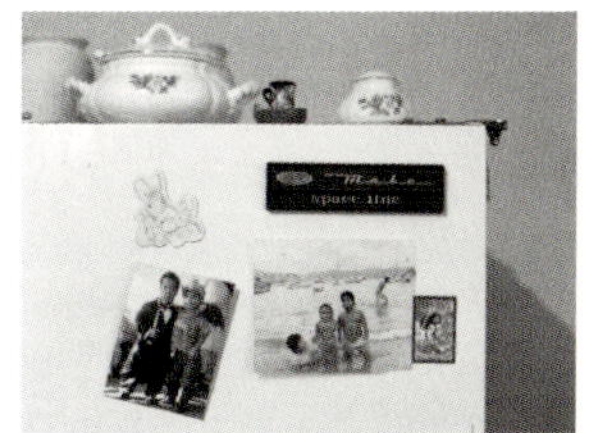

99   Photographs of David and Claudia Rodríguez Montiel, on their mother Teresa's refrigerator. One photograph is of the pair when they joined the Enanitos Toreros in their early teens.

Fotos de David y Claudia Rodríguez Montiel pegadas al refrigerador de su madre, Teresa Montiel. Una foto es de cuando eran adolescentes, recién se habían unido a los Enanitos Toreros.

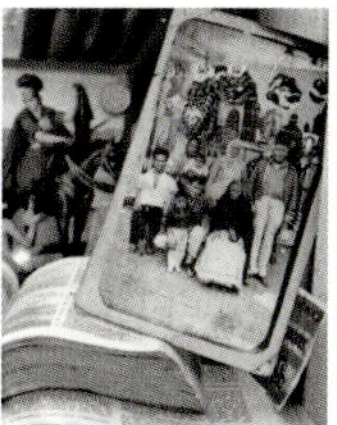

100   Teresa Montiel's father, David Montiel, in a family portrait taken in the 1950s in Acapulco.

El padre de Teresa Montiel, David Montiel, en un retrato familiar tomado en los años cincuenta en Acapulco.

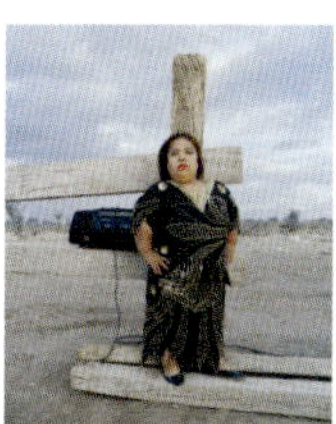

101   Teresa Montiel as popular feminist singer, Paquita la del Barrio, before a show in Jaltomate, Aguascalientes.

Teresa Montiel vestida de la popular cantante feminista, Paquita la del Barrio, antes de la función en Jaltomate, Aguascalientes.

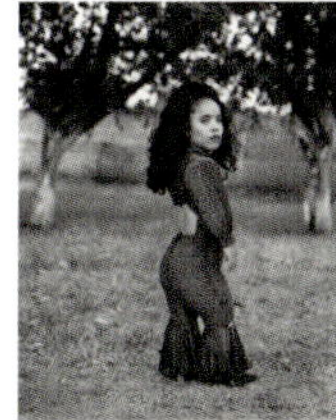

103   Claudia Montiel poses while dressed as Tejano singer Selena. Guadalajara, Jalisco.

Claudia Montiel posa vestida de la cantante tejana Selena. Guadalajara, Jalisco.

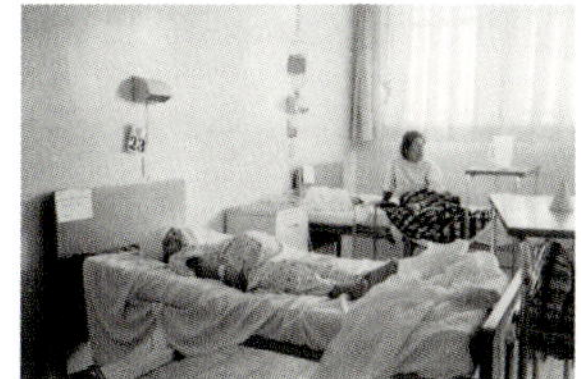

104   Claudia Montiel de Virgen, seven months pregnant, recovers from a high fever in a maternity ward. Guadalajara, Jalisco.

Claudia Montiel de Virgen, embarazada de siete meses, se recupera de una fiebre en una sala de maternidad. Guadalajara, Jalisco.

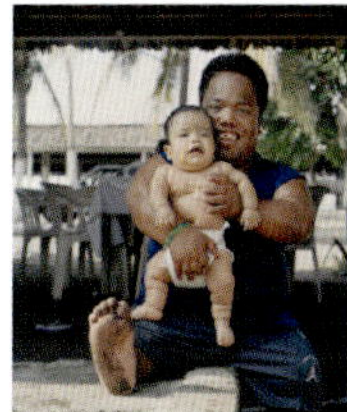

105   David Rodríguez Montiel and his son Emilio at the beach. Paraíso, Colima.

David Rodríguez Montiel y su hijo Emilio en la playa. Paraíso, Colima

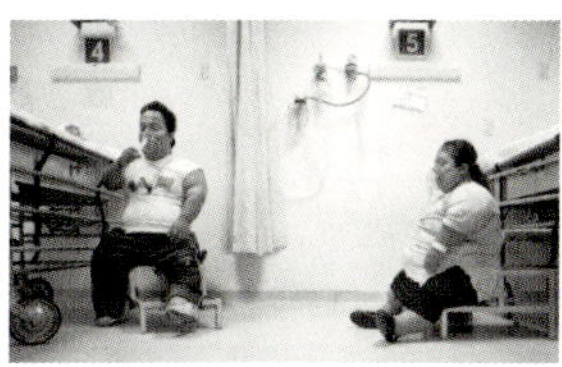

106   David and his mother, Teresa, visit an emergency room for treatment of chronic breathing problems, common to people with some forms of dwarfism. Paraíso, Colima.

David y su madre, Teresa, acuden a emergencias para tratar los problemas crónicos de respiración, comunes en personas con ciertas formas de enanismo. Paraíso Colima.

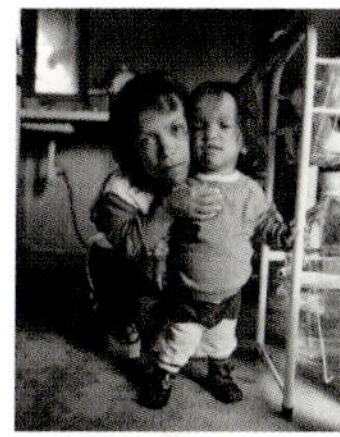

108   Verónica at home with her three-year-old daughter, Yesenia.

Verónica en casa, con su hija de tres años, Yesenia. Aguascalientes.

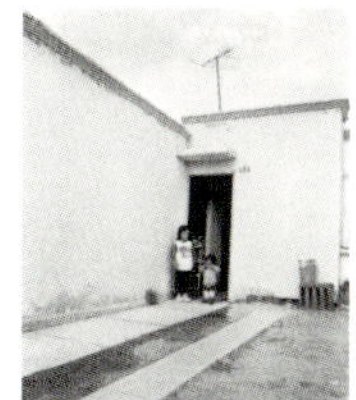

109   Verónica outside of her in-laws' home on the outskirts of Aguascalientes. She and her husband moved in just before their daughter, Yesenia, was born.

Verónica en la casa de sus suegros, a las afueras de Aguascalientes. Ella y su marido se mudaron ahí justo antes de que naciera su hija Yesenia.

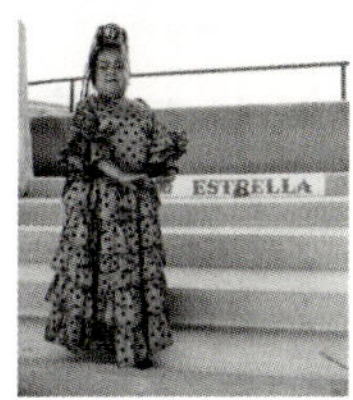

110   Yolanda Biviano as a sevillana. El Conde, Jalisco.

Yolanda Biviano vestida de sevillana. El Conde, Jalisco.

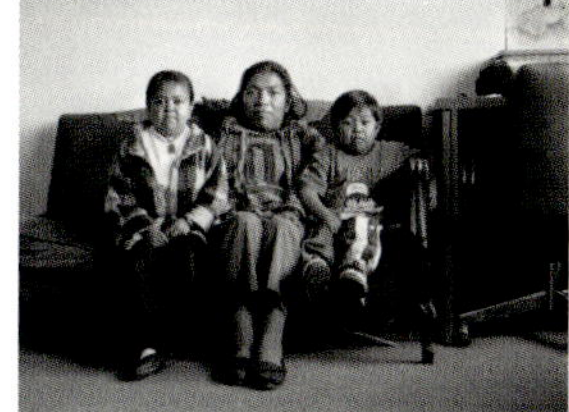

111   Yolanda, accompanied by her mother and brother, waiting her turn at a casting for a part as an elf in a Christmas parade. Mexico City.

Yolanda, acompañada por su madre y hermano, espera su turno en un casting para actuar de duende en un desfile navideño. México, DF.

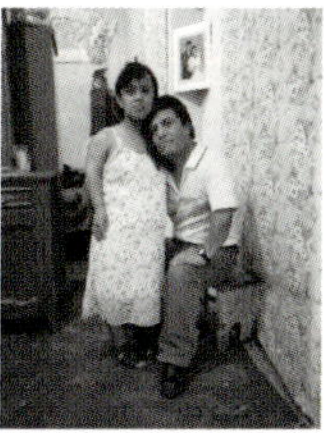

112   Ceci Méndez, five months pregnant, with her husband at home in Mexico City.

Ceci Méndez, embarazada de cinco meses, en casa con su esposo. México, DF.

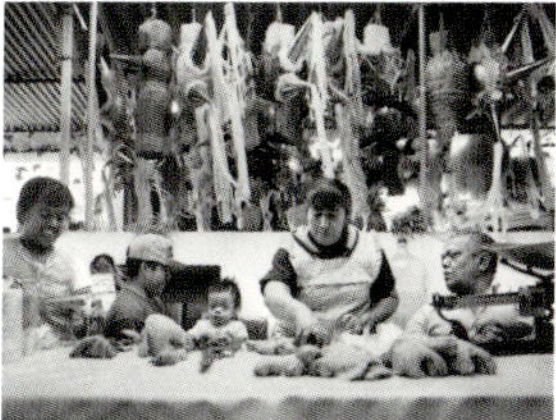

113   When Cecilia and José Luis Méndez aren't touring with the Enanitos Toreros, they work at her parents' poultry stand in Guadalajara, Jalisco.

Cuando Cecilia y José Luis Méndez no están de gira con los Enanitos Toreros, trabajan en el puesto de mercado que los padres de ella tienen en Guadalajara, Jalisco.

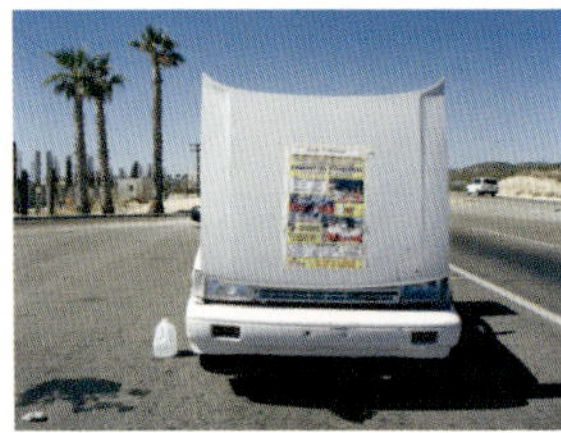

114 The tour car overheats in La Paz, Baja California Sur.

El coche de la gira se sobrecalienta en La Paz, Baja California Sur.

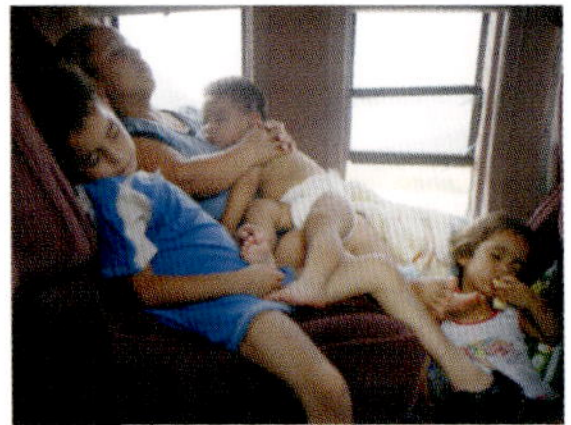

115 Claudia with her children, Isaac, Jonás, and Zuri, nap in the crowded tour van. This was the first tour that her husband Ezequiel led as a promoter. Colima, Mexico.

Claudia y sus hijos. Isaac, Jonás y Zuri toman una siesta en la camioneta repleta, durante la primera gira que su marido Ezequiel organizó como promotor. Colima, México. Colima, México.

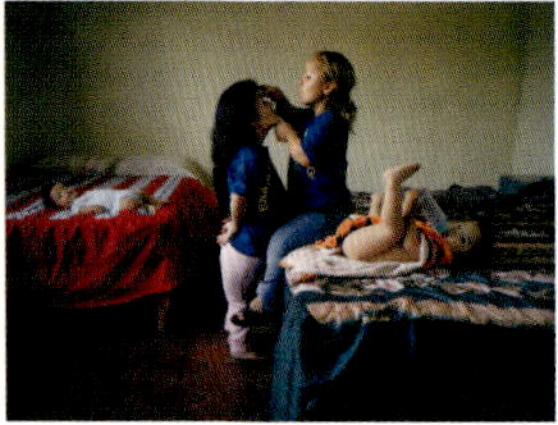

116 Imelda gets her eyebrows plucked by her sister-in-law, Claudia, with their children Emilio and Jonás beside them. El Trapiche, Colima.

Imelda y su cuñada Claudia depilándole las cejas en compañía de sus hijos, Emilio y Jonás. El Trapiche, Colima.

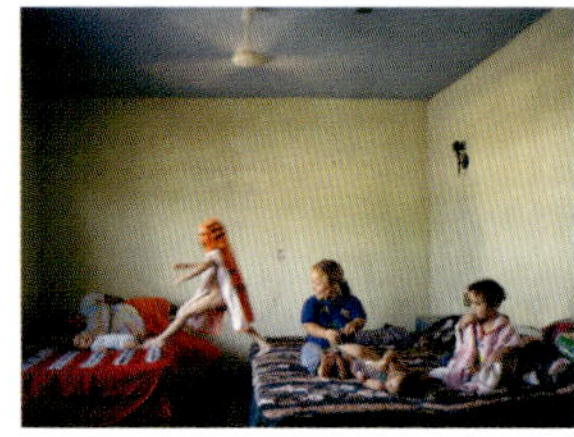

117 In the afternoon before a show, Teresa Montiel, her daughter, Claudia, and her grandchildren, Emilio, Elías, Jonás, and Zuri, hang out in a hotel room.

Por la tarde antes de la actuación en Colima, Teresa Montiel, su hija Claudia y su nietos Emilio, Elías, Jonás, y Zuri pasan el tiempo en la habitación del hotel.

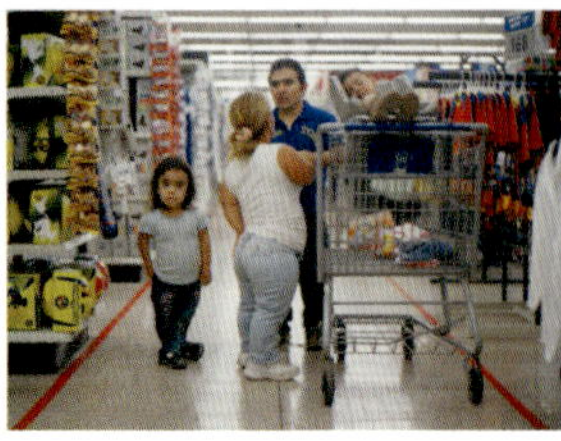

118 Claudia, Ezequiel, and Zuri Virgen shopping at Wal-Mart for Zuri's birthday party. Colima.

Claudia, Ezequiel, y Zuri Virgen de compras en Wal-Mart, para la fiesta de cumpleaños de Zuri. Colima.

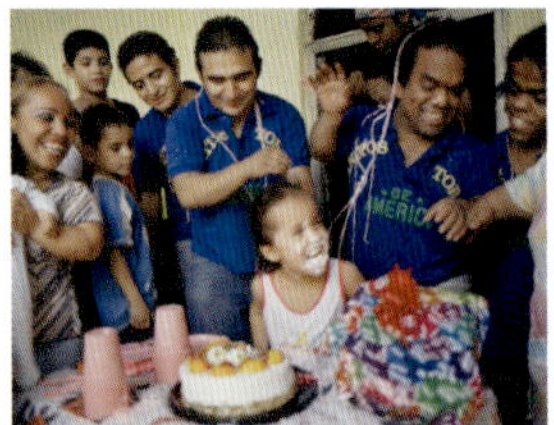

119 Lupillo pushes Zuri's face into a cake at her seventh birthday party. El Trapiche, Colima.

Lupillo mete la cara de Zuri en un pastel durante su séptimo cumpleaños. El Trapiche, Colima.

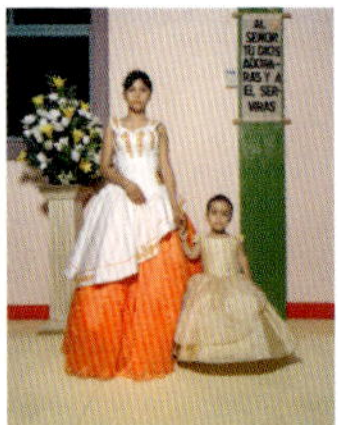

120 Zuri Virgen as a maid of honor at her aunt Gloria Virgen's quinceañera. Guadalajara, Jalisco.

Zuri Virgen vestida dama de honor en la misa de Quince Años de su tía, Gloria Virgen. Guadalajara, Jalisco.

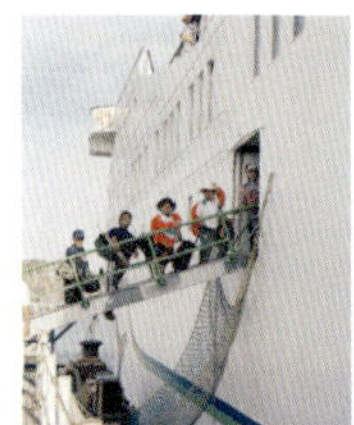

123 Baudelio, Lupillo, Ricardo, and Chuyito board a ferry to cross the Sea of Cortés for their tour through the Baja Peninsula. This was the first trip away from home for Ricardo and Baudelio.

Baudelio, Lupillo, Ricardo y Chuyito embarcando en un ferry en Mazatlán para cruzar el Mar de Cortés. Éste fue el primer viaje lejos de casa para Ricardo y Baudelio.

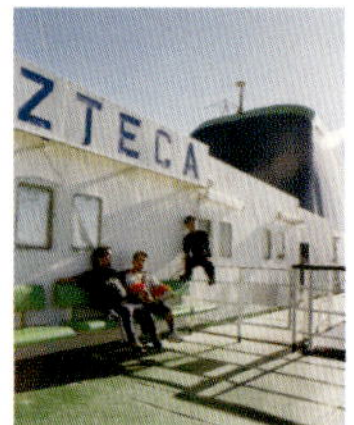

124 Lupillo, Ricardo, and Chuyito on board the S.S. Azteca, as they sail across the Sea of Cortés.

Lupillo, Ricardo, y Chuyito en la cubierta del S.S. Azteca, mientras cruzan el Mar de Cortés.

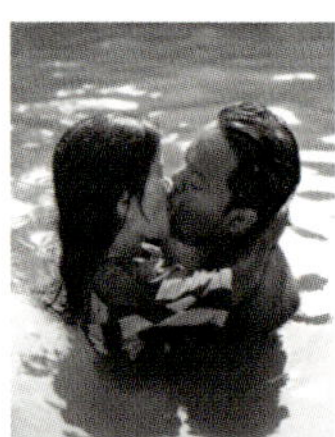

125 Imelda and David. Paraíso, Colima.

Imelda y David. Paraíso, Colima.

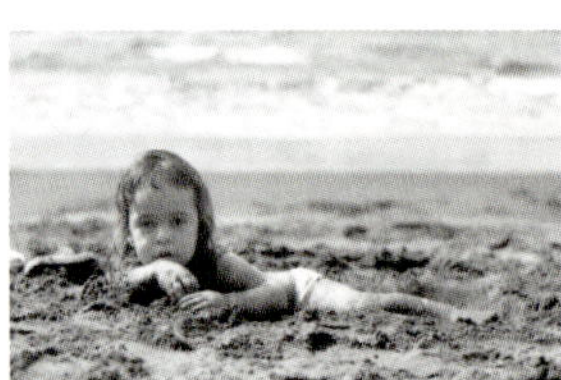

126 Zuri Virgen, the eldest of Ezequiel and Claudia Virgen's children. Paraíso, Colima.

Zuri Virgen, la hija mayor de Ezequiel y Claudia Virgen. Paraíso, Colima.

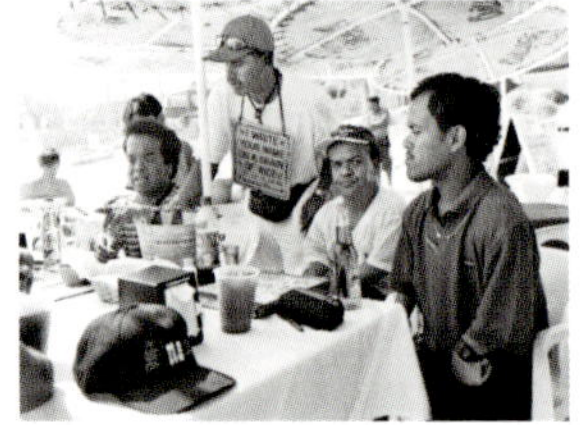

128 Lupillo, Juan, and Baudelio at the beach during a break after a show in Cabo San Lucas, Baja California Sur.

Lupillo, Juan, y Baudelio en la playa después de una actuación en Cabo San Lucas, Baja California Sur.

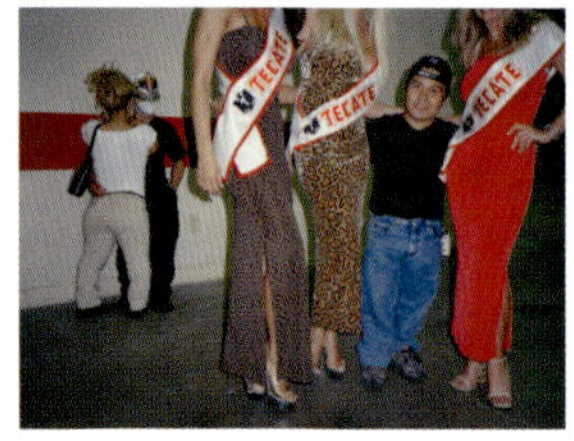

130 Ezequías Virgen with models for a beer brand hired to pose for photos with the audience at a wrestling match. Los Angeles, California.

Ezequías Virgen con unas modelos de una marca de cerveza, contratadas para posar con los espectadores en un evento de lucha libre. Los Ángeles, California.

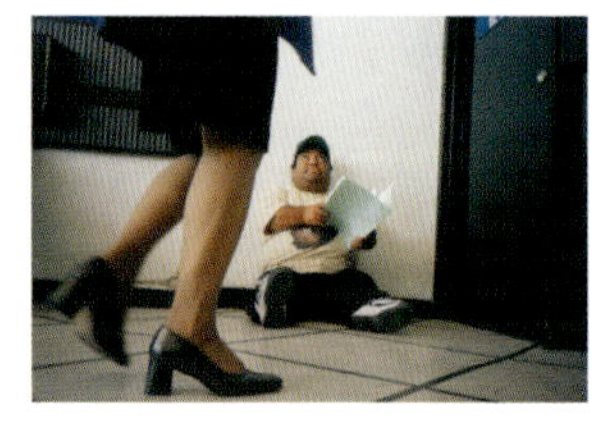

132 Tomás Emanuel waits at the United States consulate for an artist visa to join the Enanitos Toreros tour in the United States. Tijuana, Baja California.

Tomás Emanuel espera en el consulado de Estados Unidos para solicitar una visa de artista y así poder unirse a la gira de los Enanitos Toreros en ese país. Tijuana, Baja California.

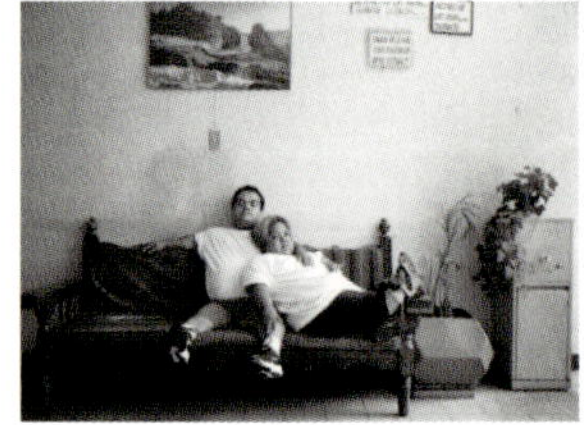

134 Teresa Montiel and Juan Chávez in a hotel in Guadalajara that serves as home during an extended tour in the state of Jalisco.

Teresa Montiel y Juan Chávez en un hotel de Guadalajara que hace de casa durante una larga gira por el estado de Jalisco.

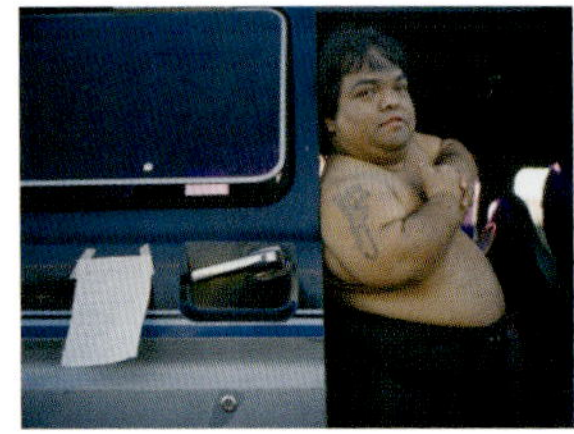

135 Tomás Emanuel, with a set list taped on the tour van. Riverside, California.

Tomás Emanuel con el programa pegado en la puerta de la camioneta. Riverside, California.

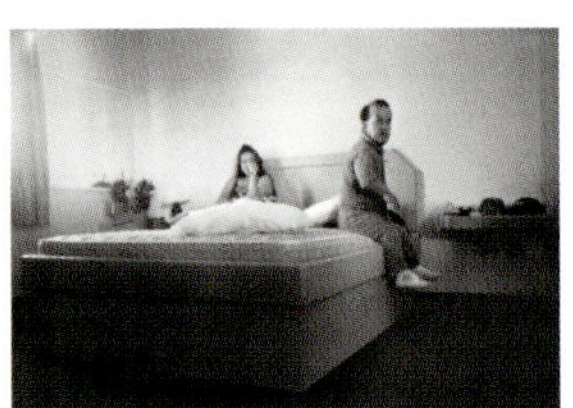

136 Juan López Mendoza and the promoter's daughter, Rocío Rocha, chatting in a hotel room while on tour in Tijuana.

Juan López Mendoza y Rocío Rocha, la hija de su promotor, conversando en un hotel durante su gira en Tijuana.

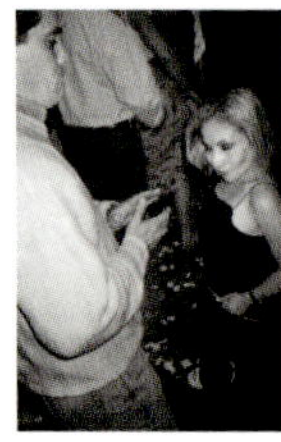

138 Verónica at a nightclub with an empresario. Cabo San Lucas, Baja California Sur.

Verónica en una discoteca con un empresario. Cabo San Lucas, Baja California Sur.

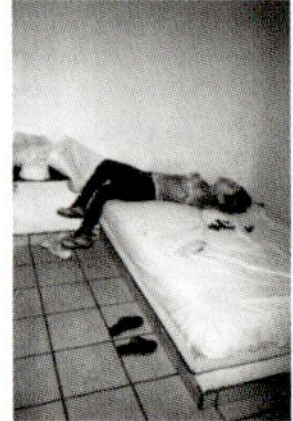

139 Verónica crying after a date. Cabo San Lucas, Baja California Sur.

Verónica llorando al regresar de una cita. Cabo San Lucas, Baja California Sur.

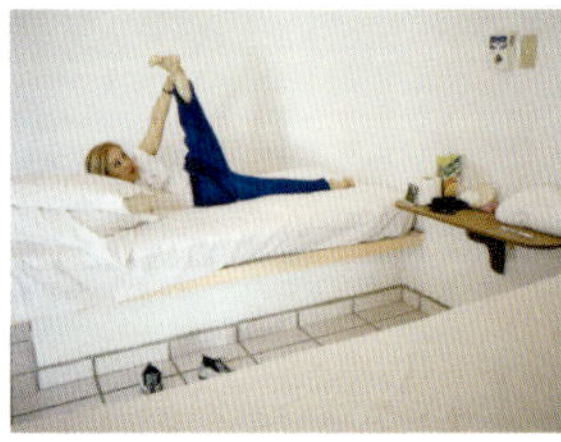

140 Verónica Alvarado González during her daily exercise routine while on tour. Cabo San Lucas, Baja California Sur.

Verónica Alvarado González mientras hace su rutina de ejercicios durante la gira. Cabo San Lucas, Baja California Sur.

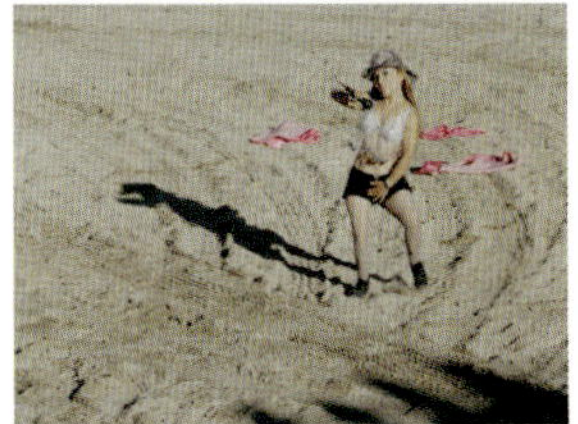

141 Verónica Alvarado González impersonating pop singer Paulina Rubio. San José del Cabo, Baja California Sur.

Verónica Alvarado González imita a la cantante de pop Paulina Rubio. San José del Cabo, Baja California Sur.

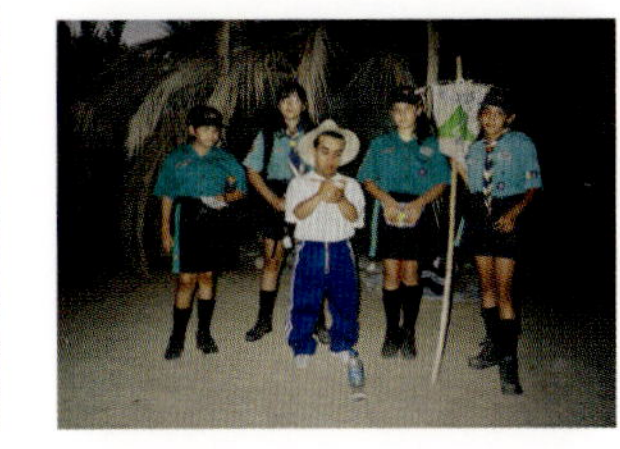

142 Ricardo León signs autographs for local Girl Scout fans. Cabo San Lucas, Baja California Sur.

Ricardo León firma autógrafos para unas admiradoras de un grupo de scouts. Cabo San Lucas, Baja California Sur.

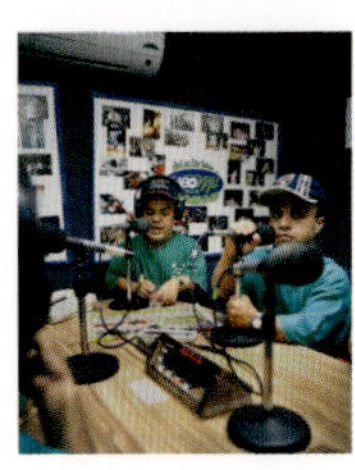

143 Ricardo León and Juan Morales on a radio interview to promote the Enanitos Toreros show. Cabo San Lucas, Baja California Sur.

Ricardo León y Juan Morales en la radio promocionando el espectáculo de los Enanitos Toreros. Cabo San Lucas, Baja California Sur.

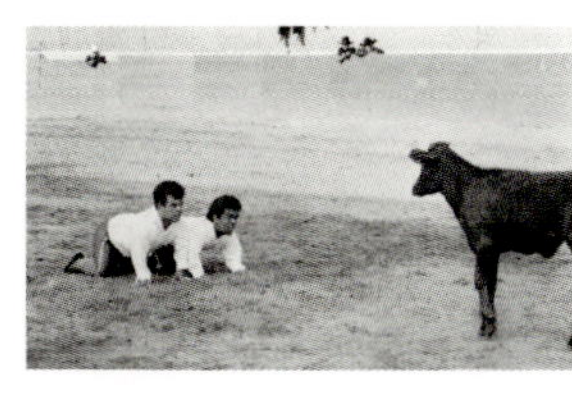

144 Joaquín and Lupillo team up to do the *paso de la muerte*. When the bull charges, they run in opposite directions to confuse the animal. El Limón, Jalisco.

Joaquín y Lupillo hacen el paso de la muerte: cuando el toro embiste, ellos corren en direcciones opuestas para confundir al animal. El Limón, Jalisco.

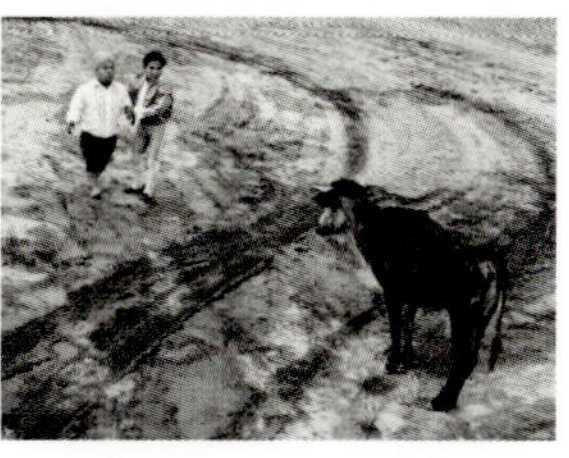

146 Juan Rezendis and Gerson Virgen prepare to do a paso de la muerte. Cosío, Aguascalientes.

Juan Rezendis y Gerson Virgen se preparan para hacer el paso de la muerte. Cosío, Aguascalientes.

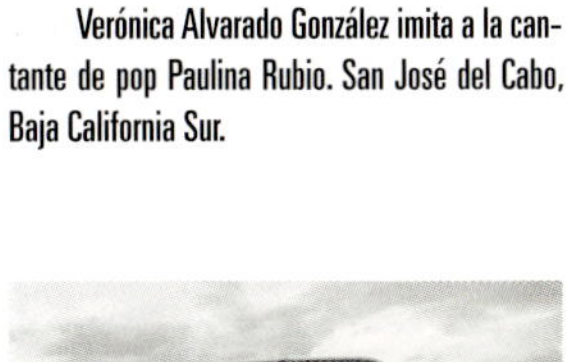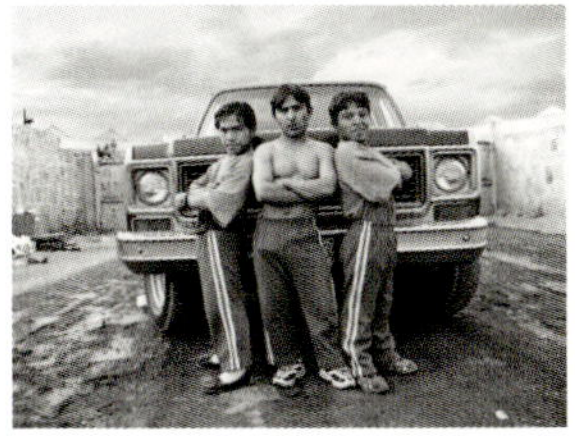

147 Brothers Ezequías, Ezequiel, and Gerson Virgen in front of their promoter's truck. Cosío, Aguascalientes.

Los hermanos Ezequías, Ezequiel, y Gerson Virgen, frente la camioneta del promotor de su cuadrilla. Cosío, Aguascalientes.

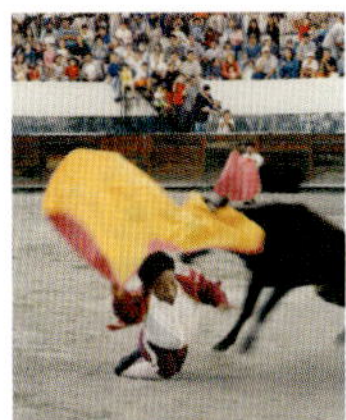

149 Lupillo executes a *farol de rodillas*, dropping to his knees and unfurling his cape above his head as the bull charges. Santa María de la Transportina, Jalisco.

Lupillo ejecuta un farol de rodillas, con el capote en alto mientras el toro embiste. Santa María de la Transportina, Jalisco.

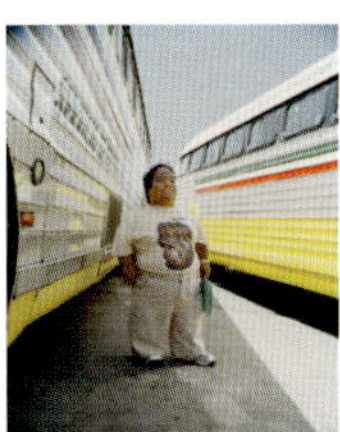

150 Tomás Emanuel waits to board a bus at the United States-Mexico border.

Tomás Emanuel espera para subirse al autobús en la frontera entre México y Estados Unidos.

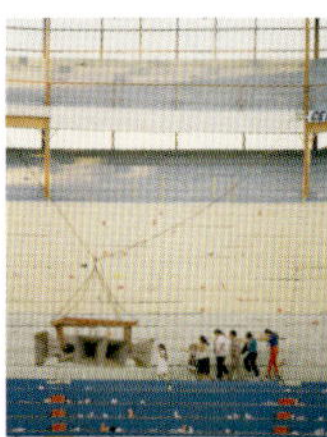

151 Audience members leaving the Toreo de Tijuana.

Miembros del público saliendo del Toreo de Tijuana.

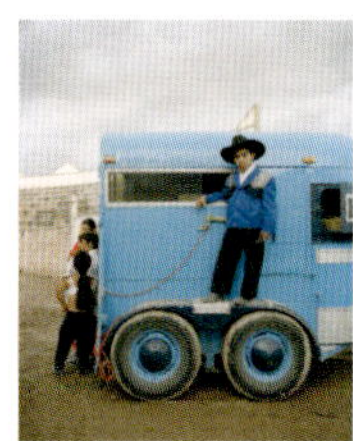

152 Gerson Virgen stands on the crew's horse trailer. Cosío, Aguascalientes.

Gerson Virgen de pie sobre el trailer de los caballos. Cosío, Aguascalientes.

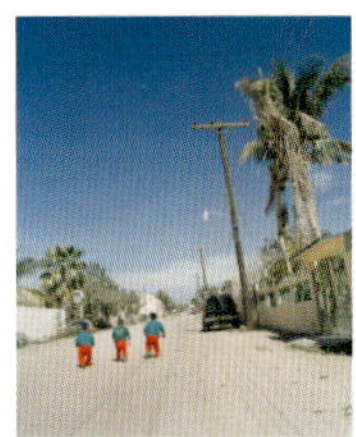

153 The bullfighters walk back to the construction site that serves as their hotel during a tour in Cabo San Lucas, Baja California Sur.

Los toreros caminan de regreso a un lugar en construcción que les sirve como hotel durante su gira en Cabo San Lucas, Baja California Sur.

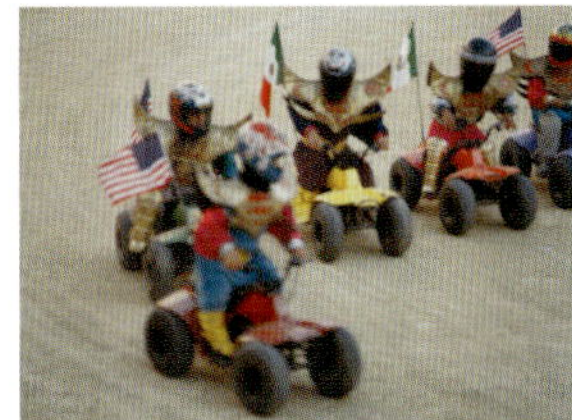

154 Enanitos Toreros perform "Mini Motos Midget Power" in Tijuana, the last stop before their United States tour.

Enanitos Toreros actuando en el show "Mini Motos Midget Power", en Tijuana, última parada antes de su gira en Estados Unidos.

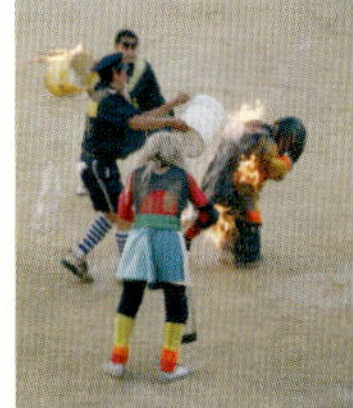

156 Handlers douse Fernando Solórzano after he has ridden a motorcycle through a ring of fire. Tijuana, Baja California.

Varios payasos de rodeo le echan agua a Fernando Solórzano después de atravesar con su motocicleta un aro de fuego. Tijuana, Baja California.

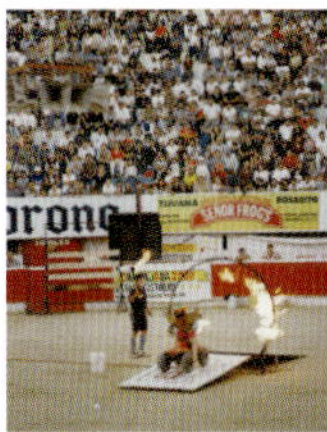

157 During the "Mini Motos Midget Power" show, Fernando Solorzano rides through a ring of fire. Tijuana, Baja California.

Durante el espectáculo de las "Mini Motos Midget Power", Fernando Solorzano atraviesa un aro de fuego. Tijuana, Baja California.

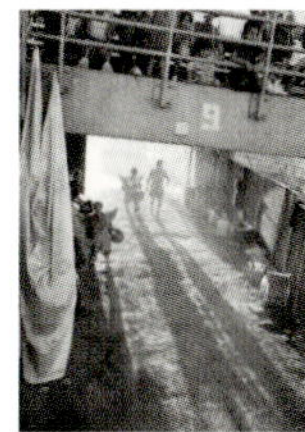

158 Enanitos Toreros enter the ring for a motorcycle show in Pico Rivera, California.

Enanitos Toreros entrando en la plaza para una actuación con motocicletas en Pico Rivera, California.

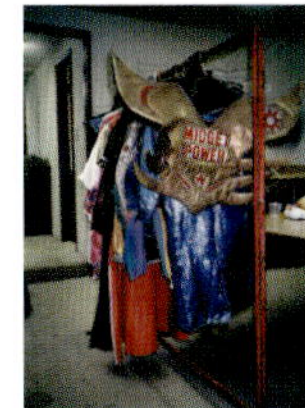

159 Costumes based on the TV show *Power Rangers*. Pico Rivera, California.

Disfraces basados en el programa de televisión *Power Rangers*. Pico Rivera, California.

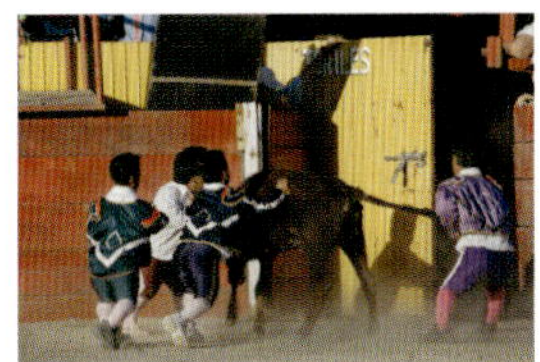

160 Putting the bull back in its pen after the performance. Cabo San Lucas, Baja California Sur.

Devolviendo el toro a su toril después de la actuación. Cabo San Lucas, Baja California Sur.

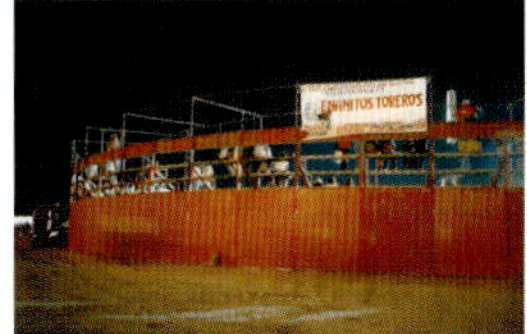

162 Collapsible bullring at night during an encore performance. San José del Cabo, Baja California Sur.

Plaza de toros desmontable durante una segunda función a petición del público. San José del Cabo, Baja California Sur.

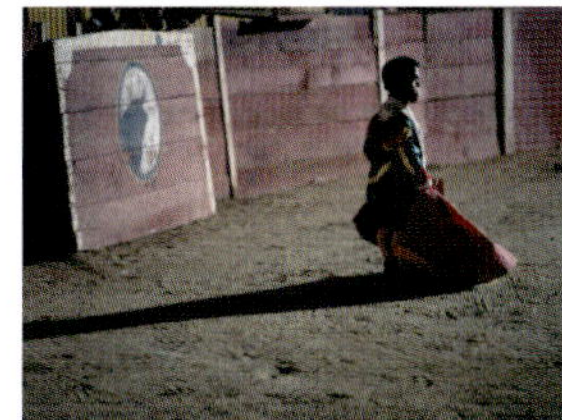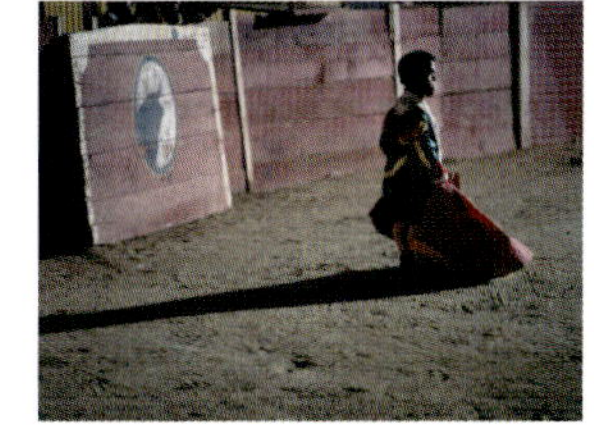

164 Jesús Castillo Lázaro in the bullring at a late-night encore performance, following a sold-out first show. San José del Cabo, Baja California Sur.

Jesús Castillo Lázaro durante una segunda función a petición del público. San José del Cabo, Baja California Sur.

GRACIAS

This book is dedicated to the people who appear in it. / Este libro está dedicado a la gente que aparece en él.

Alfonso Hernandez "El Algabeño", Alejandro, Andrés Márquez Ríos, Arturo García Olivares, Azarel Vázquez Cortéz, Baudelio "Mohamed" Cabrera, Cecilia Díaz de Méndez, Chava, Claudia Rodríguez de Virgen, David Rodríguez Montiel (Q.E.P.D.), Eladio "Yayo" Peralta, Emilio Rodriguez Lara (Q.E.P.D.), Eduardo Antonino "Yoyito" Vázquez Lopez, Ezequías "Arnold" Virgen, Edoardo Ferandel, Ezequiel Virgen, Felipe Morales, Félix Corona, Fernando Solórzano, Gerson Virgen, Gloria Virgen, Guadalupe "Lupillo" Avilez Garza, Gustavo Vázquez Buendia, Ileana Enriqueta Avila Valadez, Isaac Virgen Rodríguez, Isabel Cortéz Trujillo, Jesús "Chuyito" Castillo, Joaquín Gutierrez Perez, Joel Gudiño, Jonás Virgen Rodríguez, Jorge Arturo Cervantes, Jorge Ramos, Jorge Reyes Balbuena, José Guadalupe "Chepe" Tejada Rodríguez, José Luis Méndez, Josué Virgen, Juan Chávez, Juan López Mendoza, Juan Morales, Juan Resendiz, Karlita Andrade, Sergio "Marcelo" Torres, Maria Gloria Lopez de Virgen, Ricardo "Cucuy" Reyes Acero, Ricardo Leon, Roberto Marcelino Virgen Mederos, Rocio Rocha, Rogelio Amador, Samuel Lopez "El Patorro", Samuel Virgen, Saúl Grimaldo (Q.E.P.D.), Sebastian Alva, Sotero Lugo, Susana Edith Hernández García, Tomás Emanuel Loaiza Gonzaga, Valeria Parra Cortéz, Verónica, Verónica Alvarado González, Veronica Alvarez Castro, Yesenia, Yolanda Biviano, Zuri Virgen Rodríguez.

Cuadrillas: Los Enanitos Toreros de San Román, Los Siete Enanitos—Originales del Toreo, Los Enanitos Toreros de América, Los Enanitos Toreros de Torreón, Los Enanitos Toreros de Aguascalientes, Los Enanitos Toreros de Guadalajara, Patorro y sus Siete Enanitos, Los Enanitos Toreros—Gigantes Del Toreo.

Thank you to all the people whose contribution and support made this book possible. / Gracias a todos aquellos cuyo apoyo y contribución hicieron posible este libro.

Adriana Lara, Agustina Ferreyra, Alexandra Brez, Alfredo Hubard, Alfredo Rocha, Alicia Tokle, Andres Rodríguez, Anthony LaSala, Aurora Morfín, Bárbara Matas, Betriz Merry, Betty M. Adelson, Brett Rattner, Brian Paumier, Carl Saytor, Catherine Harris, Cecilia Jurado, Charlie Castañeda, Craig Cohen, Daniel Corona Gidwani, Danette Newcomb, Daniel Power, Darren Ching, David Fahey, Diego Berruecos, Dilian Mintchev, Dona Abuaf, Daoud Tyler-Ameen, Doug Mark, Dulce Pinzón, Edoardo Chavarin, Ellen Segal, Estela Corona Velázquez, Fernando Mesta, Fernando Paz, Fredrik Janka, Gabriela Galván, George Pitts, Gerardo Corona Velázquez, Guadalupe Bitterlin, Gus Van Sant, James Fee, Jason Constanzo, Jenny Burgos, Joaquín Trujillo, Joe Loya, Jonnie Ross, José Luis Corona Diazinfante, Judith Rocha, Lidiya Kan, Lorena Bojórquez, Mara Mahía, Malika Cosme, Marta Elena Virgen, Marta Rocha, Maureen Drennan, Maya Choi, Michelle Roberts, Michelle Suderman, Miguel Calderón, Mireya Rocha, Mónica Ruzansky, Olivier Debroise, Patricia Careaga, Paul Gagner, Paul Moakley, Phillip Nardulli, Priscilla Ptacnik Corona, Rafael Ptacnik Corona, Rebecca Silvers, Renee Hersey, Rhinnen Kith, Richard Mozska, Rocio Rocha, Ronald Hudson, Rubén Gallo, Sabrina Bajaj, Sally Cave, Sara Rosen, Steven Berkman, Svetlana Duboin, Tan-Ya Garrodette, Travis Ruse, Vanessa Rendón Bitterlin, Víctor Manuel Muñoz, Zora O'Neill, *Magenta Magazine*, Perros Negros, *Photo District News*, *Truce*, Print Space New York, and all the photo editors who have supported my work through the years.

With special thanks to / Un agradecimiento especial a Isabel Cortéz, Teresa Montiel (Q.E.P.D.), Estela Velázquez DeAvila, Danny Elfman y David Benjamin.

LIVIA CORONA

Livia Corona grew up in Mexico and is a graduate of Art Center College of Design in Pasadena, California. She is the recipient of numerous awards and recognitions, including the American Photography Award and the BMW Inszenierte Kraft Prize. She was nominated for the Agfa International Prize for Young Photojournalism and the ING Real Photography Award. Corona was selected by *Photo District News* for PDN's 30 New and Emerging Photographers to Watch. Her photographs have been featured in publications including *Domus, Life, The New York Times Magazine*, and the book *Open House: Intelligent Living by Design* (Vitra Design Museum, 2006). Her work has been exhibited in the United States, Mexico, France, Germany, and the Netherlands. She lives in New York and Mexico City. www.liviacorona.com

Livia Corona creció en México y se graduó en el Art Center College of Design en Pasadena, California. Ha recibido numerosos premios y reconocimientos, incluyendo el American Photography Award y el premio BMW Inszenierte Kraft. Fue nominada para el Agfa International Prize for Young Photojournalism, el ING Real Photography Award. Corona fue seleccionada por la revista *Photo District News* para PDN's 30 New and Emerging Photographers to Watch. Sus fotografías han aparecido en diversas publicaciones como *Domus, Life, The New York Times Magazine*, y en el libro *Open House: Intelligent Living by Design* (Vitra Design Museum, 2006). Su trabajo fotográfico ha sido expuesto en Estados Unidos, México, Francia, Alemania y Países Bajos. Livia Corona vive en Nueva York y la Ciudad de México. www.liviacorona.com

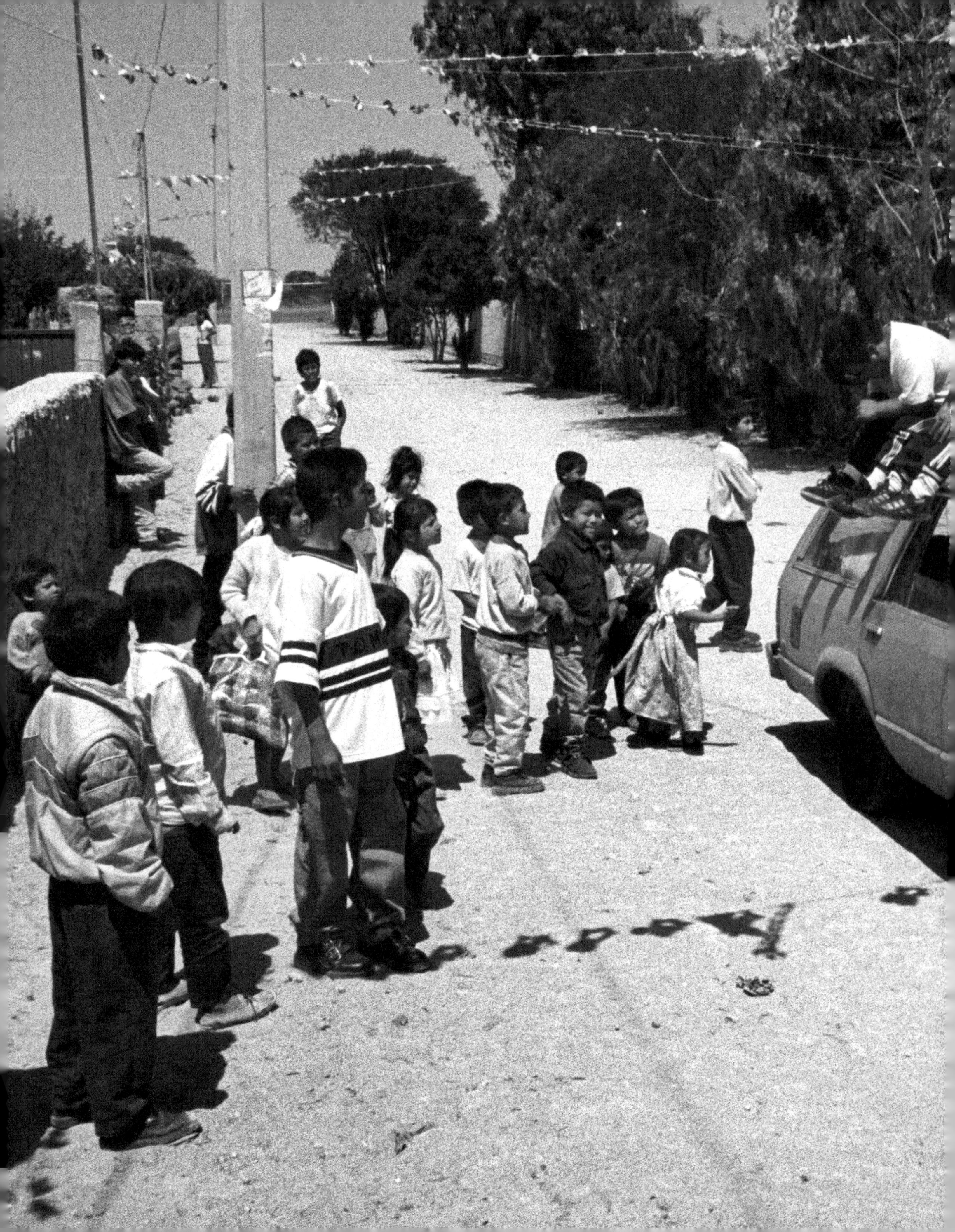